*Conventional
Forces and American
Defense Policy*

Conventional Forces and American Defense Policy

AN *International* *Security* READER

EDITED BY

Steven E. Miller

PRINCETON UNIVERSITY PRESS

PRINCETON, NEW JERSEY

Published by Princeton University Press, 41 William Street, Princeton, New Jersey 08540
In the United Kingdom: Princeton University Press, Guildford, Surrey

Library of Congress Cataloging in Publication Data will be found on the last printed page of this book

First Princeton Paperback printing, 1986
First Hardcover printing, 1986

LCC 85-20992   ISBN 0-691-07700-2   ISBN 0-691-02246-1 (pbk.)

Printed in the United States of America by Princeton University Press, Princeton, New Jersey

Contents

The Contributors

STEVEN E. MILLER teaches defense studies in the Department of Political Science at the Massachusetts Institute of Technology and is Co-Editor of *International Security*.

LAWRENCE J. KORB, former Assistant Secretary of Defense (Manpower, Installations, and Logistics), is now vice-president of the Raytheon Corporation, Washington Operations.

LINDA P. BRADY is program analyst in the Directorate of International Logistics in the Office of the Assistant Secretary of Defense.

BARRY R. POSEN is Assistant Professor in the Department of Politics and the Woodrow Wilson School at Princeton University.

STEPHEN VAN EVERA is Managing Editor of *International Security*.

JEFFREY RECORD is a Senior Fellow at the Institute for Foreign Policy Analysis, Washington, D.C.

JOHN J. MEARSHEIMER is Associate Professor in the Political Science Department at the University of Chicago.

BENJAMIN S. LAMBETH is a Senior Staff Member of the Rand Corporation.

RICHARD K. BETTS is a Senior Fellow at the Brookings Institution.

EDWARD N. LUTTWAK is a co-founder and executive officer of C & L Associates, a consulting firm specializing in defense analysis.

SAMUEL P. HUNTINGTON is the Eaton Professor of the Science of Government and Director of the Center for International Affairs, Harvard University.

ELIOT A. COHEN is Assistant Professor of Government at Harvard University.

JOSHUA M. EPSTEIN is a Research Fellow at the Brookings Institution.

Nuclear weapons dominate the American defense debate. They grab headlines, capture public concern, and preoccupy scholars and experts. Issues relating to conventional forces and strategy, on the other hand, are far less familiar and attract far less attention. It is understandable that this is so. For one thing, conventional forces lack the apocalyptic implications associated with nuclear weapons. In addition, conventional strategy is more complicated and more difficult to master than is nuclear strategy. The number of factors relevant to issues of conventional warfare is larger and they are harder to assess. Familiarity with a substantial body of military history is often required. And the operational matters that are central to the analysis of conventional forces are generally viewed as the province of the uniformed military. As a consequence, while the nuclear debate is far-flung, the public debate on the non-nuclear dimensions of American defense policy is limited to a small number of specialized experts.

The relative neglect of conventional forces is a deficiency that should be remedied. There are at least four reasons why they deserve more public scrutiny than they receive. First, nuclear weapons, while enormously destructive, are actually quite cheap. In recent years, for example, spending on strategic nuclear forces has averaged under 10% of the U.S. defense budget. Even costly major nuclear weapons programs such as the MX ICBM have only a very minor impact on the overall magnitude of defense spending. Thus, while nuclear weapons may be the most dramatic defense issue in the public eye, they are far from being the largest spending issue. Rather, most of the American defense budget is spent acquiring and supporting conventional capabilities. In a typical year, the United States invests a few *tens* of billions in nuclear weapons programs, but a few *hundreds* of billions in conventional forces. Those concerned that America's defense dollars are spent wisely, as well as those interested in reducing the federal budget deficit, the defense budget, or both, would be well advised to devote some careful attention to by far the largest defense spending issue, U.S. conventional forces.

Second, not only are conventional forces much more costly than nuclear forces, but they are much more likely to be used. Nuclear weapons have not been fired in anger since 1945. American conventional forces have fought two substantial, albeit limited, wars in Korea and Vietnam. They have also been involved in a series of lesser operations, including interventions in Lebanon (1958), the Dominican Republic (1965), and Grenada (1983). And there have been a variety of incidents involving the small-scale use of U.S. conventional forces, including the Mayaguez incident in 1975, the Iranian hostage rescue operation in 1980, and the Gulf of Sidra confrontation with Libya in 1981. The United States has been at war roughly ten years out of the four decades since the end of World War II. Hence, while the use of nuclear weapons seems quite remote and is recognized by virtually all political persuasions as something to be avoided, use of conventional military power is really quite likely, and is viewed by some as necessary to sustain the credibility of American power. The decisions made about what conventional forces to buy and how they ought to be employed determine the military options available to the United States and the likelihood of success in the event of conflict. Few issues of foreign and military policy could be more important.

Third, conventional forces are commonly used for diplomatic purposes. In literally dozens of instances, American naval forces have steamed, troops have been moved, or exercises have been conducted for the purpose of influencing a crisis, coercing a troublesome government, or communicating U.S. commitment or resolve. Nuclear weapons, in contrast, are so dangerous that they are almost never put on alert or otherwise explicitly manipulated for diplomatic ends. Thus, in the diplomatic context, also, conventional weapons provide American policy makers with usable options. Judgments about the deployment of U.S. conventional forces and about the efficacy of conventional threats of force can greatly influence the conduct of American diplomacy.

Fourth, the conventional balance can influence the likelihood of nuclear war. It has long been widely believed that escalation from a large-scale NATO-Warsaw Pact conventional conflict is one of the more plausible paths to nuclear war. Hence, preventing such a conflict is a significant factor in reducing the risk of nuclear war. There is, of course, a nuclear dimension to the deterrence of conventional war in Europe, since the threat (or the possibility) of nuclear escalation is thought to help stay the hand of a potential conventional attacker; indeed, NATO doctrine relies explicitly on the threat of nuclear escalation to help deter Soviet conventional aggression in Europe.

But in an age of nuclear plenty and nuclear parity, many have come to believe that the nuclear forces of the two superpowers are effective primarily for negating the nuclear forces of the other and have little credibility as a deterrent of other, non-nuclear forms of conflict. This possibility raises the importance of conventional deterrence, that is, of ensuring that NATO's conventional force posture is adequate to deter conventional attack. In the context of nuclear stalemate, possession of inadequate conventional forces may allow, or even invite, an adversary to contemplate or to undertake conventional aggression, which in turn could result in the nuclear escalation that everyone hopes to avoid. Consequently, judgments about the requirements of conventional deterrence and the adequacy of NATO's conventional forces are directly related to the question of nuclear war. Concern with the nuclear danger ought to provoke serious consideration of conventional force issues.

For these several reasons, then, it is both worthwhile and important that those interested in American national security policy and in broader issues of war and peace devote more attention to the questions and issues associated with the choice of conventional strategies, the acquisition of conventional forces, and the employment of conventional military power. The essays collected in this volume are intended to serve this end by offering analyses of and perspectives on several major conventional problems in American defense policy.

The first section addresses the broad question of overall military strategy as it influences the magnitude and character of the American defense effort. In "Rearming America," Defense Department officials Lawrence Korb and Linda Brady outline the underlying premises of the case for the Reagan Administration's substantial defense buildup and answer some of the criticisms that have been levelled at that program. They suggest that the past two decades witnessed an adverse shift in the Soviet-American military balance and an erosion of U.S. military capabilities that made the Administration's rearmament program imperative. They further argue that President Reagan's defense policy is the result of sensible, feasible, and necessary strategic, economic, and military choices, regardless of what critics may say.

In the succeeding two essays, the critics have their say. Barry Posen and Stephen Van Evera note that how much needs to be spent on defense and how it should be spent depends to a considerable extent on decisions about what is to be defended and how it is to be defended. They argue that the Reagan Administration has chosen an unrealistic, extremely demanding, strategy—one that seems to imply a requirement to fight multiple wars on a large scale simultaneously—that makes U.S. military power seem inadequate and the Reagan buildup seem necessary. Measured against a more reasonable strategy, they suggest, U.S. military capability is sufficient. Jeffrey Record, in "Jousting With Unreality," sounds a similar theme in arguing that there is an enormous lack of congruence between the Administration's ambitious "strategy" of worldwide war and the inevitably limited military capabilities at its command. Record suggests that the Reagan Administration's defense policy has neglected the essential foundations of sound strategy: appreciation of the link between military means and ends; the establishment of priorities among commitments; recognition of the reality of finite resources; and differentiating between the desirable and the feasible. Consequently, while Posen and Van Evera argue that the Reagan Administration has chosen the wrong strategy, Record ends up concluding that, in effect, it has no strategy at all.

The single most important non-nuclear issue in American defense policy is the commitment to defend NATO Europe. It is in central Europe that the United States, along with its allies, most directly confronts the threat of Soviet power. It is here that the Soviet Union most directly threatens vital American interests. And, not surprisingly, it is this contingency which consumes the lion's share of American defense spending. Sections II and III focus on two of the crucial considerations in assessing U.S. participation in the defense of Europe: the state of the NATO-Warsaw Pact conventional balance and the effectiveness of NATO's conventional strategy.

Perceptions of the conventional balance in Europe have pervasive implications for U.S. defense policy. Concerns about NATO inferiority have been a major factor driving the American defense buildup. Fear that the Soviet Union might well prevail quickly in a conventional war has led NATO to embrace doctrines of nuclear first-use in order to deter such an attack or to thwart it should war come. Furthermore, these issues are at the center of diplomacy *within* the Atlantic Alliance, as the U.S. has steadily pressed its allies to bolster their defense efforts as part of an overall effort to enhance NATO's conventional (and nuclear) force postures. In short, America's conventional force posture, its nuclear doctrine and requirements, and its relations with its allies are deeply, if not always directly, influenced by judgments about the relative capabilities of the two large and heavily armed military forces that face one another in the center of Europe.

Thus, assessing the conventional balance in Europe is a vitally important exercise. But evaluating conventional capabilities is notoriously difficult to do because effectiveness on the battlefield often turns on intangible factors such as leadership and morale, or on unpredictable and uncontrollable factors such as weather, and because military forces may be procured, organized, deployed and employed according to different strategies and doctrines in response to different security situations. As a consequence, crude comparisons of numbers of men and equipment are very close to meaningless, although unfortunately commonplace. All this guarantees that the process of evaluating the conventional balance in Europe is not merely important, but complex, and fraught with possibilities for dispute and subjective judgment.

The three essays in Section II discuss the factors and the complexities that are inevitably involved in serious assessments of the conventional balance. In "Measuring the Conventional Balance," Barry Posen provides an inventory of the key variables—buildup rates, exchange rates, attrition rates, movement rates, and so on—in thorough balance assessment and discusses how one goes about assigning values to these variables on the basis of historical experience. Posen shows how these variables can be combined in a model that captures some of the complexities missed in simplistic force comparisons. He argues that NATO and the Warsaw Pact procure military capability according to very different doctrines (with NATO investing much more heavily in command and control, logistics, and training) and shows that conclusions about the state of the military balance are directly related to assumptions about which doctrine is correct. If NATO forces are measured against Soviet doctrine, they appear to be inadequate. If, however, NATO is given credit for the different sorts of military investments it makes, then its military capability appears sufficient to hold its own against the Warsaw Pact in central Europe.

Soviet doctrine for conventional conflict in Europe calls for a blitzkrieg attack in the hope of achieving a quick and decisive victory. An important measure of the adequacy of NATO's forces, therefore, is whether they are capable of thwarting such a Soviet blitzkrieg. This question is analyzed by John Mearsheimer in "Why the Soviets Can't Win Quickly in Central Europe." He argues that, although it is commonly believed that the Red Army could rapidly overrun NATO's conventional forces in central Europe, in fact NATO's chances of stopping a Soviet blitzkrieg are really quite good. He arrives at this conclusion by carefully examining the forces, the geography, the terrain, and the operational difficulties that would obtain in any large armored battle in central Europe. He argues that the Soviets would find it extremely difficult to achieve in the key sectors the huge ratios of superiority necessary to successfully effect armored breakthroughs and further suggests that the Soviet military is not well prepared to conduct such a campaign.

Benjamin Lambeth, in "Uncertainties for the Soviet War Planner," discusses factors that would influence *Soviet* perceptions of the liklihood of success in war. He focuses on potential vulnerabilities that would likely cause Soviet leaders to hesitate when contemplating the initiation of conflict. The Soviets, he notes, are keenly aware of the shortcomings of their own forces, and are as prone to exaggerate U.S. military strength as the U.S. is prone to exaggerate Soviet strength. Further, the Soviets have to worry about irrational American behavior, untrustworthy allies, and the frightful possibility of having to fight a two-front war against both NATO and the Chinese. These, and other, tempering factors, Lambeth concludes, limit Soviet military options and put the Soviet threat in a more realistic perspective.

In Section III, we shift our attention from the adequacy of American and NATO forces to the adequacy of their strategy. Because a flawed strategy can negate huge investments in military capability by causing forces to be maldeployed or misused, disputes over strategy tend to be both important and intense. In recent years, a swelling chorus of voices has questioned the wisdom and appropriateness of Western strategy. Richard Betts provides a critical overview of several major criticisms of American strategy in "Conventional Strategy: New Critics, Old Choices." Betts is responding to a loose coalition of defense critics in the United States who have come to be known as the military reform movement. One strand of reformist criticism dismisses U.S. defense policy as strategically sterile and excessively preoccupied with managerial concerns aimed at efficient procurement and logistics; the reformers, in contrast, counsel bold strategic innovations as the best approach to solving America's security problems. A second strand of reformist criticism finds fault with NATO conventional doctrine in Europe, judging it guilty of a commitment to attrition and firepower at the expense of maneuver and agility. Third, the reformers accuse the U.S. military of an addiction to costly, high technology military equipment, even at the expense of military effectiveness (since on the battlefield, simpler is sometimes better), with the result that U.S. forces grow ever smaller and ever more expensive. Betts examines each of these issues in turn, and finds much to criticize in the arguments of the critics.

The remaining three essays in Section III focus on NATO conventional strategy. There has emerged in recent years a controversy over the efficacy of NATO's traditional strategy of forward defense, which calls for NATO forces to be deployed along the inner-German border in order to stop a Soviet invasion as far forward as possible. Skeptics believe that adherence to forward defense causes NATO forces to be poorly deployed (because stretched in a line across the front), requires more ready forces than NATO is able to muster, and results in a defensive line in central Europe that is vulnerable to catastrophic rupture. Consequently, there has been much consideration of alternative strategies, despite the political constraints that seem to make inviolate NATO's commitment to forward defense.

Edward Luttwak describes one such alternative in his essay, "The Operational Level of War." He contrasts the attrition style of warfare that characterizes the approach of the U.S. Army (and that undergirds NATO's forward defense strategy) with a strategy based on relational maneuver. Much of

Luttwak's essay is given over to defining and describing the maneuver-oriented approach, which calls for side-stepping the brunt of an enemy's assault rather than meeting it head on, for being deceptive and elusive on the battlefield rather than fighting grinding battles of attrition, and for seeking to exploit the enemy's vulnerabilities (exposed flanks, for example) rather than colliding with his concentrations of strength. Only by the adoption of such an approach, Luttwak concludes, can NATO hope to prevail over the formidable Soviet capabilities that could be brought to bear in central Europe.

In contrast, in "Maneuver, Mobile Defense, and the NATO Central Front," John Mearsheimer springs to the defense of NATO's forward defense strategy. A maneuver-oriented defense, he argues, is a risky strategy even in the best of circumstances, and furthermore is particularly ill-suited for NATO. He suggests, for example, that the geography and terrain of West Germany is inappropriate for maneuver defense, since the lack of geographical depth means that uncontested Soviet assaults would soon be pushing into the western frontier regions of West Germany and since the combination of mountains, rivers, bogs, and urban sprawl inhibits the free-wheeling employment of armored forces called for by a strategy of maneuver. Moreover, Mearsheimer believes that NATO's coalition forces, comprised of contingents from half a dozen different countries, do not have the necessary command and control capabilities to successfully execute a strategy that, in its nature, places great demands on command and control. Mearshiemer concludes that for NATO maneuver warfare is an invitation to disaster and that the strategy of forward defense holds more promise of effectively stopping Soviet attack.

In "Conventional Deterrence and Conventional Retaliation in Europe," Samuel Huntington proposes a second alternative to the forward defense strategy: he makes the case for a strategy based on a conventional retaliatory offensive, whereby NATO would respond to a Soviet conventional attack in Central Europe by itself striking into Eastern Europe. Doing so, he suggests, would threaten the Soviet Union's highly valued control of Eastern Europe, would disrupt the Soviet Union's own offensive plans, requiring of the Soviet military the kind of wartime innovation unsuited to its rigid approach to war, would force the Soviets to divert some of their offensive forces to defensive tasks, and would increase the likelihood that the war would be protracted, thus producing the outcome the Soviets hope to avoid. Huntington argues, therefore, that such a conventional retaliatory threat would shore up NATO's ability to deter conventional attack and thereby help to compensate for the dwindling credibility of NATO's nuclear threats.

While the European contingency is the most important on the agenda of conventional defense issues, defending American interests in the Third World also raises many troublesome (and very different) defense problems. Indeed, some of the gravest difficulties the United States has faced since World War II have resulted from involvement in conflict in the Third World, as manifested particularly in the brutal and frustrating war in Korea and in the nightmarish experience in Vietnam. Third World contingencies raise a host of potential troubles: American interests are often not well-defined, frequently making decisions about where to fight tough ones; public support may be shaky (to say the least), which can undermine a war effort, as it did in Vietnam; American forces may not be well-prepared for the kind of war they have to fight; distances are often great and bases not ample, posing challenging logistical problems; host governments may be frail; enemies may be elusive and unwilling to fight the kind of war the American military would prefer. Despite these potential difficulties, the United States has a long legacy in this century of fighting such wars (including a number of commonly overlooked interventions in Mexico and Central America in the early years of this century), it continues to have significant interests to protect in the Third World, and, moreover, such wars seem more likely to occur than the more important but more remote specter of large-scale war between NATO and the Warsaw Pact. Hence, preparing to fight "small" or "limited" wars in the Third World, or to protect Third World interests against the projection of Soviet military power, will remain a highly salient issue in U.S. defense policy.

It is to this set of issues that we turn in Section IV. In "Constraints on America's Conduct of Small Wars," Eliot Cohen argues that the most serious impediment to successful American participation in small wars is the unsuitability of U.S. military power to the conditions and requirements of such conflicts. To be sure, Cohen notes, there are political considerations—the state of public opinion, the role of allies, the power of Congress—that must be taken into account in the conduct of small wars. But the larger problem, he believes, is that small wars have particular characteristics all their own, and American military power, shaped as it is primarily to meet the contingency of a large war in Europe, is inappropriate, not at all tailored to meet the special challenges of these conflicts. Cohen outlines the distinct nature of small wars and suggests that in almost every way—manpower, doctrine, equipment, and organization—the U.S. military is unprepared for such conflict.

Since the oil crises of the 1970s, the Persian Gulf has assumed special importance in American consideration of projecting military power in the Third

World. The disruption, destruction, or capture of the oil-bearing regions of the Gulf by hostile forces has been feared as a potential disaster for the United States and its import-dependent industrial allies. While there are many potential threats to the oil fields of the Persian Gulf that might require a military response, the largest military threat is the possibility of Soviet intervention in the region. It is this scenario that Joshua Epstein analyzes in "Soviet Vulnerabilities in Iran and the RDF Deterrent." He carefully examines the likely nature of a Soviet invasion aimed at the oil fields in the southwestern region of Iran and the capability of the United States to deter or to defeat such an attack. This is, without doubt, one of the most difficult parts of the world in which to operate American military forces because its distance from the United States is so great, the number of useful American bases is so few, the climate is so severe, the logistics requirements are so substantial, and the government of Iran is so hostile. Nevertheless, Epstein notes that military operations in this area pose many daunting difficulties for the Soviet Union as well, and he argues that if the United States makes effective use of the warning time that would be available and if it devises a strategy that exploits Soviet vulnerabilities, then it is capable of mounting a quite formidable military capability in southern Iran—one that should serve as an effective deterrent to Soviet aggression.

The dozen essays collected in this volume do not, of course, exhaust the menu of non-nuclear issues in American defense policy, nor do they even cover every aspect of the several major issues that are addressed. They do, however, provide a good indication of the kinds of issues, problems, and debates that arise in connection with three of the most important, and enduring, components of American defense policy: its overall military strategy; its commitment to defend West Europe; and its need to project military power in the Third World. For the foreseeable future, these issues will not go away, and American security will depend to a considerable extent on the ways in which the dilemmas and disputes that attend them are addressed and resolved. Many controversies remain. Much work is left to do. It is hoped that this volume will inspire greater attention to these subjects and will provoke efforts to enlarge and enrich the debate over America's conventional military power.

*Conventional
Forces and American
Defense Policy*

Rearming America

The Reagan Administration
Defense Program

*Lawrence J. Korb and
Linda P. Brady*

$\mathbf{I}$n January 1981, President Reagan assumed office with a mandate from the American people to rebuild U.S. military capabilities, which had been neglected for nearly two decades. The 1980 election had ratified the growing concern of Americans that the United States must strengthen its armed forces and restore the military balance that is a prerequisite for successful deterrence. At the same time, the American public has expressed the belief that the United States must pursue genuine arms control as a complement to its defense improvement program. A consensus has apparently emerged that the preservation of peace requires that the United States reassume its leadership role—a role that does not cast the United States as a world policeman, but rather as a peacemaker committed to the preservation of peace with freedom and the protection of U.S. interests in a changing world.

Twenty years ago, the Soviet Union was distinctly inferior to the United States according to most meaningful indicators of military power. U.S. nuclear capabilities, in particular, were clearly superior to those of the Soviet Union. In 1964, for example, the United States had deployed more intercontinental ballistic missile (ICBM) and submarine-launched ballistic missile (SLBM) launchers and re-entry vehicles (RVs) than had the Soviet Union. The U.S. also had larger numbers of intercontinental-capable bombers in its inventory. Although the Warsaw Pact has consistently maintained sizeable ground forces, in the early 1960s these forces possessed qualitatively inferior weapons. And the Soviet navy then had only a limited potential for interdicting the West's vital sea lanes.[1]

By the early 1980s, however, the strategic situation of the U.S. *vis à vis* the Soviet Union had changed dramatically, and for the worse. During the 1960s

---

Lawrence J. Korb is Assistant Secretary of Defense (Manpower, Installations, and Logistics). Linda P. Brady is an international program analyst in the Office of the Assistant Secretary of Defense (Manpower, Installations, and Logistics).

---

1. Caspar W. Weinberger, *Soviet Military Power 1984* (Washington, D.C.: U.S. Government Printing Office, April 1984), pp. 22–30. This is the fourth edition of a report that documents the modernization of Soviet forces. The 1984 edition includes NATO–Warsaw Pact comparisons and data on U.S. and Allied forces to place Soviet modernization efforts in the proper context. The discussion that follows draws from this report.

International Security, Winter 1984/85 (Vol. 9, No. 3) 0162-2889/84/030003-16 $02.50/0

and 1970s, the military power of the Warsaw Pact increased steadily relative to that of the West. The Soviet Union, through its extensive modernization program, has deprived the United States of its advantage in nuclear arms. Between 1968 and 1984, for example, the Soviet Union increased by six-fold its deployment of RVs on ICBMs; during the same period, the number of U.S. RVs deployed on ICBMs doubled. The net result has been a situation in which overall Soviet capabilities now exceed the American by a ratio of six to one. With respect to intercontinental-capable bombers (a category that includes Soviet Backfire bombers), the U.S. inventory has declined while the Soviet inventory has increased; by 1983, the Soviet inventory in fact had exceeded the U.S. inventory. Although the U.S. has retained its superiority in the deployment of RVs on SLBM launchers, Soviet capabilities in this area have increased dramatically since the late 1960s, and this trend continues.

Soviet and non-Soviet Warsaw Pact ground forces also have been modernized, and the readiness and sustainability of these forces have improved substantially. The Soviet tank force has been upgraded since the mid-1960s, and the Soviet Union has begun to field its latest tank—the T-80—which accords nuclear, biological, and chemical protection to its crew and possesses enhanced firepower and survivability. Moreover, artillery fire support available to ground forces has been expanded and upgraded substantially with the introduction of some nuclear-capable artillery pieces and multiple rocket launchers. With respect to readiness and sustainability, the Soviet Union has reorganized its ground and air force elements to ensure that peacetime organization more closely approximates wartime needs. In addition, the Soviet Union has prestocked large quantities of supplies forward and created large strategic reserves.

The Soviet navy has developed a clear "blue water" capability, with all this implies for its ability to threaten U.S. sea lanes and project Soviet power. The years 1967–1968 were critical ones for the Soviet navy, for during this period second generation missile-equipped submarines and surface ships were introduced, and the Soviet Union began to deploy its combat forces some distance away from home waters. The Soviet navy has continued to incorporate increasing levels of advanced technology into all its ships.

During this same period the United States neglected its force modernization program, due in part to its involvement in the Vietnam War and the expectations of its policy of détente. With respect to strategic forces, the United States did not introduce any new ICBM or SLBM types, SSBN classes, or heavy strategic bombers during the period 1972–1978. The resulting asymmetry in U.S. and Soviet modernization programs has eroded the perception of U.S. strategic superiority and brought into question the U.S. ability to maintain the peace. In contrast to the Soviet buildup and rapid modernization of its forces in Europe, the U.S. and its allies have engaged in a restrained program to modernize their conventional and theater nuclear forces.

For their part, America's NATO allies have assumed a larger share of the European conventional defense burden during this period. On the basis of historical trends in a variety of major burden-sharing indicators, the Allies have gradually taken on more of the common burden. For example, between 1971 and 1981, real U.S. defense spending declined by around 7 percent, whereas defense spending of the Allies increased by 27 percent. For the same period, U.S. civilian defense manpower declined by almost 20 percent, while that of the Allies declined by around 3.5 percent.[2]

In response to these unfavorable trends, the Reagan Administration embarked on an ambitious program to rearm America and encourage similar efforts by its allies. This program recognizes the need to modernize U.S. strategic forces, to modernize and increase the readiness and sustainability of U.S. conventional forces, to develop a critically needed capability to execute new missions in regions such as Southwest Asia, and to pursue all of these initiatives while striving for greater Allied burden-sharing in a time of worldwide economic recession.

Public consensus on the necessity of the President's program seemed to hold through 1981.[3] But late in 1981 and throughout 1982 and 1983, serious objections were raised concerning President Reagan's defense program.[4] Some critics agree that the U.S. needs to rearm, but argue that now is not the right time. These critics believe we should postpone major efforts to improve U.S. military capabilities until the domestic economy recovers. Others have charged that, even if the economy were better, the Administration does not have a clear, coherent security policy, and the result is a defense "program" that simply throws money at problems, but does not solve them.

---

2. U.S. Department of Defense, *Report on Allied Contributions to the Common Defense—A Report to the United States Congress*, June 1983, p. 1. At the time of this writing, the unclassified version of the 1984 report had not been published.

3. A forum on the Reagan Administration's foreign and defense policies published in 1981 suggests the strength of this early support. See "Forum: Reagan's Foreign and Defense Policies," *Orbis*, Vol. 25, No. 3 (Fall 1981), pp. 487–510.

4. Fluctuating support for the Reagan Administration's program to rearm America is demonstrated in John E. Rielly, "American Opinion: Continuity, Not Reaganism," *Foreign Policy*, No. 50 (Spring 1983), pp. 86–104.

A third group agrees that the U.S. needs to rearm, and to rearm now, but argues that the Administration is not spending enough money on the critical areas of force readiness and sustainability. Finally, some critics have asked, since war is not imminent, why is the Administration in such a hurry to rearm?[5]

This essay addresses each of these criticisms in turn, and indicates why we believe they are fundamentally unfounded. None of these criticisms should be dismissed lightly: each one has some basis in fact, and each has been put forward by knowledgeable observers of U.S. national security affairs. But each also, in our view, is premised on a misunderstanding of the objectives and dynamics of the current U.S. effort to improve its defense capabilities.

Now Is Not the Right Time

Most critics of the Reagan Administration's program do not disagree with the premise that major improvements in U.S. defense capabilities are required. Some believe, however, that now is not the right time to make the enormous financial investments that such improvements entail. The country has experienced an extended period of economic crisis, characterized by unacceptable levels of inflation and unemployment. The situation has only begun to turn around; economic recovery will demand the full attention, efforts, and resources of the American people. Under these circumstances, so the argument goes, now is not the right time to make the financial sacrifices required by the Administration's defense program.[6]

There has never been any doubt that the Reagan Administration's program to revitalize America's defense posture would require substantial increases in the level of resources allocated to defense. The Administration's first five-

---

5. General criticisms of the Reagan Administration approach to foreign and defense policy include: Charles W. Kegley, Jr. and Eugene R. Wittkopf, "The Reagan Administration's World View," *Orbis*, Vol. 26, No. 1 (Spring 1982), pp. 223–244; Joseph S. Nye, Jr., "U.S. Power and Reagan Policy," *Orbis*, Vol. 26, No. 2 (Summer 1982), pp. 391–411; and Kenneth A. Oye, Robert J. Lieber, and Donald Rothchild, eds., *Eagle Defiant: United States Foreign Policy in the 1980s* (Boston: Little, Brown and Company, 1983). An important critique of the Reagan Administration defense policy is Barry R. Posen and Stephen Van Evera, "Defense Policy and the Reagan Administration: Departure from Containment," *International Security*, Vol. 8, No. 1 (Summer 1983), pp. 3–45.
6. For an excellent analysis of the new "guns versus butter" debate in Washington, see Jacques S. Gansler, "We Can Afford Security," *Foreign Policy*, No. 51 (Summer 1983), pp. 64–83.

year defense program, drafted in 1981, called for an average real budget increase of 8.1 percent per year from 1981 to 1987, for a net real increase of 59 percent.[7] Substantial progress has been made since 1981 towards restoring U.S. military capabilities. But that progress must be sustained. The Administration's current five-year defense program (for the FY 1985–1986 period) calls for an average real budget increase of 5.1 percent per year from 1985 to 1989, for a net real increase of 22 percent. Under the current five-year plan, the defense share of the gross national product (GNP) will average about 7 percent.[8]

There has been considerable debate about whether the U.S. economy can afford this defense program without increasing inflationary pressures and supply shortages. Clearly the U.S. has come through a very difficult economic period. And we cannot deny that the defense budget affects the economy; nor can we deny that the state of the economy should be taken into account when the defense budget is designed. But if we postpone the hard decisions about modernizing U.S. defense capabilities until the economy recovers fully, we will never begin the program of rearming America.

Historically, every President from Truman through Carter has been pressed by advisors to wait until the economy improves before pursuing major defense initiatives. In 1949, for example, Secretary of Defense James Forrestal became alarmed at the fact that, while the United States was demobilizing, the Soviet Union was not only increasing its military capability but also extending its worldwide presence. Although President Truman was persuaded that the situation demanded greater resources for defense, Truman's budget director, Frank Pace Jr., argued convincingly that increased defense spending should await the country's recovery from a slight recession. Wait they did, until the Korean War caused them to increase the defense budget from $11 billion to some $60 billion while avoiding the economic collapse that some had predicted.[9] In 1957, following the launch of Sputnik, President Eisenhower was urged to increase defense spending. The country was in the

---

7. Caspar W. Weinberger, *Annual Report to the Congress: Fiscal Year 1983* (Washington, D.C.: U.S. Government Printing Office, 1982), p. B-3.
8. Caspar W. Weinberger, *Annual Report to the Congress: Fiscal Year 1985* (Washington, D.C.: U.S. Government Printing Office, 1984), pp. 71, 68; hereinafter *Annual Report 1985*. This report is available free on request from the Defense Department Public Affairs Office.
9. Two significant pieces on the Truman budget process are: Warner Schilling, "The Politics of National Defense: Fiscal 1950," in Warner Schilling, ed., *Strategy, Politics, and Defense Budgets* (New York: Columbia University Press, 1962), pp. 5–266; and Douglas Kinnard, *The Secretary of Defense* (Lexington, Ky.: The University Press of Kentucky, 1980), pp. 8–43.

midst of a mild recession and, once again, the President chose not only to not increase defense spending but to decrease it.[10]

We cannot afford to wait until the economy recovers fully to do what must be done to improve U.S. defense capabilities. We have waited too long already. Many current defense problems are a consequence of decisions made while the U.S. was involved in Vietnam. That war was fought, essentially, out of America's defense hide. For example, rather than modernizing U.S. bases in Western Europe, the U.S. government used the money that should have been invested in these improvements to build Cam Ranh Bay. And rather than building additional ships, it used those funds to cover the operating costs of U.S. ships in the Gulf of Tonkin. Decisions to cut defense spending during the 1970s were made, paradoxically, during the period when the government should have been allocating more for defense to counter the effects of Vietnam on America's military capabilities.[11]

Although total federal spending has increased substantially since 1960, there has been a dramatic change in its composition. In the 1950s, the defense share of federal outlays averaged 48 percent. By the 1980s, the defense share had dropped to about 30 percent. The non-defense share of federal outlays increased from about 50 percent to more than 70 percent of the budget during this period.[12]

It is important to recognize that defense spending is not the cause of America's economic problems. Arbitrary cuts in defense spending will not solve these problems, but will harm U.S. national security interests. The economic effects of the Reagan defense program have just begun to be felt. Because of the delay between the submission of the President's budget to Congress and the appropriation and actual expenditure of funds, the amount of money that has been spent on defense in 1981, 1982, and even into 1983 is the product of decisions that were made in 1978, 1979, and 1980—before President Reagan assumed office.

Rather than having negative effects on the American economy, the need

---

10. For the Eisenhower period, see Glenn Snyder, "The New Look of 1953," in Warner Schilling and Edward Kolodziej, *The Uncommon Defense and Congress* (Columbus: Ohio State University Press, 1966); and Samuel P. Huntington, *The Common Defense* (New York: Columbia University Press, 1961). On the impact of Sputnik, in particular, see Kinnard, *The Secretary of Defense*, pp. 59–61.

11. The impact of the U.S. involvement in Vietnam on U.S. military posture has been amply documented. See, for example, Lawrence J. Korb, *The Fall and Rise of the Pentagon: American Defense Policies in the 1970s* (Westport, Conn.: Greenwood Press, 1979), especially pp. 10–11.

12. *Annual Report 1985*, p. 68.

to deal with the defense challenge facing the United States may, in fact, have some positive consequences. The production requirements generated by future procurement, for example, can help fuel expansion of industrial capacity in the private sector. The current defense buildup also will encourage advance planning and increased manpower training, with positive although indirect effects on the health of the economy.[13]

Large cuts in defense spending, contrary to beliefs in some circles, should not be viewed as the primary means of lowering future deficits. Large cuts in procurement accounts produce only relatively small reductions in annual outlays. This is because expenditures for major weapons systems are spread over many years, with the largest expenditures relegated to out-years. Cuts in major programs in the near term tend to come at the expense of increased costs in future years. The procurement of fewer units each year raises unit costs and, consequently, total costs of these programs.[14]

The first priority of any government is to provide for the common defense. Of course there are other priorities, such as fostering social and economic environments in which citizens can support their families and achieve their personal objectives. But without an adequate defense posture, these other priorities are unachievable. In one sense, it is never the "right" time to make enormous financial investments in defense programs—America's domestic economy and the welfare of its citizens can always stand further improvement. But the alternative to making critically needed improvements now in the U.S. defense posture is, we submit, unacceptable.

Throwing Money at Problems Does Not Solve Them

The second criticism leveled at the Administration is that we do not have a policy to support our defense program. The result, according to these critics, is that we are simply throwing money at defense problems, not solving them. Even if the domestic economy were better, so these critics contend, the absence of a clear, coherent, well-thought-out defense policy means our efforts are bound to be unsuccessful.

Let's examine these criticisms in greater detail. Barry Posen and Stephen Van Evera have charged that the Reagan Administration has failed to explain the grand strategy it pursues and, furthermore, that we have neglected to

---

13. *Annual Report 1985*, p. 69.
14. *Annual Report 1985*, pp. 69–70.

detail the capabilities and weaknesses of U.S. forces.[15] This means, in their view, that analysts and the American public are left without a yardstick by which to measure whether the proposed military buildup is either necessary or appropriate. Secondly, Posen and Van Evera suggest that, based upon what can be inferred from Reagan Administration defense programs, our defense strategy is both extravagant and dangerous.

Other critics have taken a different tack. Jeffrey Record, for example, has argued not that the Administration lacks a strategy in support of its defense buildup, but that the military strategy adopted by the Administration is unsound because its goals far exceed the resources available to implement them.[16] And Joshua Epstein believes that "horizontal escalation"—which he dubs the United States' most recent experiment with asymmetrical doctrines—fails to meet the basic requirements of credibility.[17]

We would agree with an implicit assumption in most of these criticisms. Seldom has there been a greater need for the reexamination of America's defense strategy. The United States and its European allies have been notably successful during the last thirty years in preserving the peace in Europe. However, changes in the nature and magnitude of the worldwide threat demand the reexamination and possible modification of America's defense strategy. A strategy that has worked for Europe—flexible response—may be inappropriate or inadequate when pitted against newly emerging challenges in the less-developed world. Similarly, the configuration of military forces that has served to deter a Soviet attack against America's European allies may be of little military value when measured against the special demands of a Southwest Asia contingency.

These concerns prompted the Reagan Administration to formulate U.S. defense policy with an honest look at the threats the country faces, a critical analysis of the strategy of previous Administrations, and a realistic appraisal of available resources. We recognized the need to respond to short-term problems and concerns (particularly the importance of quickly improving the readiness and sustainability of America's current forces), while anticipating

---

15. Posen and Van Evera, "Defense Policy and the Reagan Administration," p. 4.
16. Jeffrey Record, "Jousting with Unreality: Reagan's Military Strategy," *International Security*, Vol. 8, No. 3 (Winter 1983/84), pp. 3–18.
17. Joshua M. Epstein, "Horizontal Escalation: Sour Notes of a Recurrent Theme," *International Security*, Vol. 8, No. 3 (Winter 1983/84), pp. 19–31.

longer-term requirements (such as undertaking the research and development and force modernization efforts needed to meet emerging threats).

For the past thirty years, the Soviet Union has presented the most serious challenges to U.S. security objectives throughout the world. Despite widely recognized domestic economic problems, the Soviets currently allocate an estimated 15 percent of their gross national product to defense. During the last twenty years, Soviet military forces have increased in numbers and have undergone extensive modernization. Another useful indicator of trends in the balance of military forces is the resources devoted to military investment and production. Since the early 1960s, U.S. investment (measured in terms of outlays for procurement, military construction, and research, development, testing, and evaluation) has declined while Soviet investment has increased. By the early 1980s, Soviet military investment was nearly double that of the United States.[18]

The increased size and quality of the Soviet Union's armed forces have changed the nature and extent of the threat facing the United States in the 1980s. Modernization of the Soviet strategic nuclear arsenal has turned its previously primarily defensive force posture into forces increasingly structured for offensive use. With respect to conventional forces, modernization has been accompanied by changes in doctrine and concepts for employment that suggest a more offensive posture. These trends have been exacerbated by the geographic expansion of Soviet influence and access to bases in strategic locations.[19]

In addition, the United States is now faced with threats to its security objectives apart from the serious challenges posed by the Soviet Union. As recent events in Central America and Southwest Asia have demonstrated, the decade of the 1980s will be fraught with instability and conflicts in the Third World that could have serious consequences for U.S. interests. Moreover, the emergence of new military technologies, such as man-portable surface-to-air missiles, and their growing availability have created additional tensions. Perhaps most serious in terms of its potential consequences is the continuing proliferation of nuclear weapons.[20]

It is the Reagan Administration's view that if we permit these trends to

---

18. *Annual Report 1985*, pp. 19–20.
19. *Annual Report 1985*, pp. 21–26.
20. *Annual Report 1985*, pp. 18–19.

continue, the United States will become increasingly vulnerable to both Soviet expansionism and other military confrontations and dangers we may face in the future. The strategy for coping with these trends is based on three major principles:[21]

1. OUR STRATEGY IS TO DETER WAR. Deterrence remains the key objective of United States defense policy. To ensure deterrence, U.S. forces must demonstrate that they could survive a first strike and threaten losses that would offset any gains an adversary might expect from an attack. In order to maintain deterrence, the United States is modernizing all three legs of its strategic triad and improving its strategic command and control systems. In joint efforts with its allies, the U.S. is modernizing the NATO triad. And in response to threats to U.S. interests in other areas, the Administration is improving America's ability to rapidly deploy its general purpose forces.

2. OUR STRATEGY IS DEFENSIVE. The United States will use its military forces only in response to aggression. This defensive orientation means America's forces must be maintained in a high state of readiness, its C^3I capabilities must be sufficient to provide adequate warning and to execute the appropriate response, and its reserve forces must be capable of rapid mobilization.

3. SHOULD DETERRENCE FAIL, OUR STRATEGY IS TO RESTORE PEACE ON FAVORABLE TERMS. If attacked, the United States must be able to restore the peace on favorable terms while seeking to limit the scope, duration, and intensity of the conflict. In our efforts to limit the scope of a conflict, we must recognize that, because the Soviet Union has the capability to conduct simultaneous operations in multiple theaters, the United States should develop sufficient capabilities to assure success in single or multitheater conflicts. With respect to limiting the duration of a conflict, the Soviet Union's ability to engage in a prolonged war means preparing for a short war could weaken the credibility of our deterrent. The President's defense strategy is based on a very straightforward assumption—U.S. forces should be able to fight as long as the other side can fight. In order to limit the intensity of a conflict, this Administration has placed increased emphasis on new technologies and techniques to improve conventional defense.

Supporting this strategy are three critical policies. First, the United States places great reliance on its allies and the contributions they make to the common defense. The Administration is pursuing programs to modernize

---

21. These principles and the supporting policies are presented in greater detail in *Annual Report 1985*, pp. 27–38.

U.S. conventional and theater nuclear forces and to improve the readiness, sustainability, and mobility of U.S. forces committed in support of its allies. Second, the forward deployment of U.S. forces is critical to maintaining the credibility of the U.S. conventional deterrent. It would be a serious mistake for the United States to adopt a "fortress America" posture and withdraw from its responsibilities as a global power. And, third, the United States must be prepared to respond to threats across the entire spectrum of conflict— from coercive threats designed to intimidate America's allies to deterrence of a nuclear attack. The Reagan Administration's defense program includes initiatives designed to provide the U.S. with a variety of options with which to respond to threats to its interests in the last part of the twentieth century.

In short, the Reagan Administration does have both a policy and a strategy to support its defense program. Our approach is based on a candid assessment of the threats we face and is grounded in the principles of a deterrent strategy, a defensive orientation, and the ability to restore peace on favorable terms should deterrence fail. Moreover, the Administration has taken into account the state of the economy in the design of its defense program and has, in fact, made adjustments in that program while pursuing the sustained force improvements necessary to rebuild U.S. defense capabilities. It seems to us that some critics of the Administration's defense program who argue that we have *no* strategy simply disagree with the strategy we have pursued. We believe the burden lies with these critics to propose a viable alternative.

Modernization at the Expense of Readiness and Sustainability

A third group of critics agree that the U.S. needs to rearm, and to rearm now, but argue that the Administration is neglecting the critical areas of force readiness and sustainability. Excessive emphasis on force modernization means the U.S. may end up ten to fifteen years from now with more forces but with less capability to deploy those forces in a timely manner or to sustain them in combat. And in the near term, so these critics argue, the United States is not taking critically needed steps to improve the readiness and sustainability of existing forces—those forces that would be called upon to defend U.S. interests should conflict occur in the immediate future.[22]

This tension between the near term and the long term, between force

---

22. Posen and Van Evera, "Defense Policy and the Reagan Administration," pp. 39–40.

readiness and sustainability, on the one hand, and force modernization, on the other hand, is not new. Every administration is confronted with difficult choices in allocating defense resources between these two equally important areas.

The Reagan Administration assumed office following a period in which both areas had been inadequately funded. This situation had led to serious deficiencies in America's conventional force posture in both readiness and sustainability as well as equipment. Many active combat units were not ready for combat. Training had been cut back. Other indicators of readiness, such as flying hours for Air Force tactical fighter pilots, were extremely low. Not only were U.S. forces unprepared to respond quickly in a crisis; they also were not capable of sustaining operations adequately. Our stockpiles of munitions and secondary items were insufficient for combat operations. And, with respect to equipment, many elements of the armed forces were operating with shortfalls of major items of equipment, such as armored personnel carriers, or aging and obsolete equipment compared with new Soviet hardware.[23]

Thus, there existed a near-term requirement to improve readiness and sustainability in order to be prepared to deter aggression in the immediate future. Should deterrence fail, U.S. forces must be prepared to respond immediately, at appropriate levels, and to sustain conflict as long as the adversary is prepared to fight. This requirement puts a premium on those areas that contribute to improved readiness and sustainability, such as adequate manning and training of the force, proper maintenance, and sufficient spare parts and ammunition.

At the same time, the Administration recognized that the extended period of inadequate defense spending also had led to shortfalls in defense "capital stock," that is, the quantity and quality of equipment provided to the troops. This situation prompted comments by some military and defense officials that the United States Army had become a "hollow" Army. There also was a near-term requirement to invest in force modernization in order to ensure the longer-term improvement of the nation's military posture. This requirement puts a premium on those areas that are essential to force modernization, such as procurement and research, development, testing, and evaluation.

This Administration has attempted to make balanced decisions in both

---

23. *Annual Report 1985*, pp. 43–49.

areas, while recognizing the resource constraints under which defense judgments must be made. While the U.S. should not neglect readiness and sustainability improvements because of near-term requirements, it also needs to make decisions now to guarantee a modernized force for the late 1980s and 1990s.

With respect to readiness and sustainability, the Reagan Administration has launched a concerted effort to attract and retain higher-caliber men and women in the armed forces. America's most valuable defense resource is well-trained and highly motivated people in its armed forces. When the Administration took office, recruit quality (as measured by educational level and test scores) was at an all-time low, and large numbers of experienced career personnel were leaving the services. President Reagan committed his Administration to revitalizing the armed forces; we have made great progress in this regard. Today, educational levels and test scores of recruits exceed those of the civilian population and are higher than the levels achieved under conscription. Reenlistments are up significantly, and the career force is growing in size and quality.[24]

Moreover, readiness and sustainability funding has increased substantially. Funding for the operations and maintenance accounts—which significantly affect readiness and sustainability—increased by nearly 30 percent between FY 1982 and FY 1985.[25]

With respect to force modernization, the Administration has initiated programs to build greater numbers of increasingly capable weapons. We have taken advantage of newly emerging technologies to improve the quality of weapons and other equipment provided to the troops. Funding for research, development, testing, and evaluation—which are essential for the long-term improvement of U.S. military posture—increased by approximately 69 percent between FY 1982 and FY 1985. And funding for procurement increased by approximately 67 percent during the same period.[26]

When the Reagan Administration assumed office, we were confronted with dual defense problems. First, we had to act quickly to improve the readiness and sustainability of U.S. forces in order to be prepared to deter aggression in the near term. Second, we also had to act to modernize U.S. conventional and nuclear forces and to increase efforts in research, development, testing,

---

24. Ibid., pp. 78–86.
25. Ibid., p. 279.
26. Ibid.

and evaluation. After several years of sustained effort, we have made progress in both areas. Critics who argue that we have sacrificed readiness and sustainability on the altar of force modernization imply that we were confronted with a choice. Such was not the case. Instead, we faced a situation that demanded quick action both to improve force readiness and sustainability and to modernize the force. We continue to move forward in both areas.[27]

War Is Not Imminent

If war is not imminent, some critics have asked, why is the Administration in such a hurry to rearm? Since the Warsaw Pact stands to benefit little from an attack against NATO, so the argument goes, a U.S.–Soviet military confrontation is exceedingly remote. Why, then, particularly given the serious economic problems facing the United States, should we attempt to rearm as quickly as the Reagan Administration has proposed?[28]

First, it is important to recall that the primary objective of U.S. defense policy is deterrence. If the U.S. continues to neglect its military establishment, after the unfavorable trends of the last twenty years, it will weaken deterrence and risk increasing the possibility of war. Honorable intentions are not enough to keep the peace. The United States must be prepared to use force and to use it successfully. Only then will it be in a position to pursue genuine, significant, and verifiable arms reductions.

Second, the United States cannot afford to wait until war occurs to make critically needed improvements in its military posture. It takes time to increase the readiness and sustainability of military forces, and even more time to field the modern, highly capable weapons systems essential for successful defense. If the U.S. does not begin now to remedy the existing deficiencies in its military posture, it may be caught unprepared should deterrence fail.

Finally, the U.S. needs to be prepared to handle contingencies short of a direct U.S.–Soviet military confrontation. The capability to deploy forces

---

27. Interestingly enough, Congressman Les Aspin (D-WIS), Chairman of the Military Personnel Subcommittee of the House Armed Services Committee, argues that the Administration may be over-funding readiness. See Aspin's "The Mayaguez Stumper, or How to Figure What's Enough for Military Readiness," Unpublished paper, April 1984. This view is shared by the Congressional Budget Office.
28. This assumption underlies much of the discussion in Oye, Lieber, and Rothchild, eds., *Eagle Defiant*.

rapidly to areas of the world where the United States maintains little or no presence is essential. Potential contingencies in Southwest Asia, the Pacific, and elsewhere pose unique demands for U.S. defense strategy and military forces. The low probability of a direct U.S.–Soviet military confrontation does not relieve the burden of being prepared for other contingencies that may, in fact, be more likely to confront the United States in the immediate future.

In short, the United States cannot and should not wait until its leaders believe war is imminent to begin a program of critically needed improvements in its defense capabilities. The long lead times required for the design, testing, development, and deployment of new systems demand that we begin now to take steps to ensure adequate capabilities in the latter part of this century. Such a strategy is not only consistent with a strategy of deterrence, but necessary for the credibility of that strategy.

Conclusion

When President Reagan assumed office, he was confronted with two critical defense challenges—the realities of an increasingly dangerous world and a serious deterioration of U.S. military capabilities. Moreover, he was also confronted with the paradox of peace, namely, that to preserve peace the peacemaker must be prepared to use force and use it successfully. The Administration had little choice but to embark on a serious program to address across the board the many problems we faced—erosion of the readiness and sustainability of U.S. forces, declining morale in the armed forces, aging and obsolete equipment, and an outdated defense procurement system that contained few incentives to reduce costs.

President Reagan's program to rearm America in the face of growing challenges to U.S. national interests has become the focus of heated debate. Serious objections have been raised about whether we need to rearm now, and to the extent the President has proposed. Some critics have charged that the Administration does not have a clear, coherent policy. Others have suggested that we are not spending enough money on force readiness and sustainability. And a final group insists that we should not be in such a hurry to rearm, given that war is not imminent.

Let us address these objections again, in conclusion:

First, the U.S. cannot afford to wait until the economy recovers fully to do what must be done to improve its defense capabilities. It has waited too long already to make the hard decisions and to accept the financial sacrifices required for an adequate defense posture.

Second, the Administration has a strong policy to support its defense program. Our policy is based on a realistic assessment of the threats the U.S. faces and a candid appraisal of the economic constraints within which we must operate. Our strategy emphasizes deterrence and defense and seeks to limit the scope, duration, and intensity of conflict, should deterrence fail.

Third, the Administration has attempted to make balanced decisions in allocating scarce defense resources to force modernization and improved readiness and sustainability. After an extended period of neglect in both areas, the U.S. cannot afford to support one at the expense of the other. Moreover, we are not.

And, *fourth*, U.S. leaders cannot afford to wait until they believe war is imminent to make critically needed improvements in America's defense posture. We must begin now to remedy the existing deficiencies in U.S. military posture in order to strengthen deterrence.

The defense improvement program on which we have embarked will require a sustained effort. The effects of the Reagan defense program are only beginning to be reflected in the improved readiness and sustainability of U.S. military forces. And it will be several years before decisions taken now to modernize U.S. forces are translated into better-equipped troops in the field. We have taken the first steps towards reversing the unfavorable trends of the last twenty years. Our continued success will depend in large part on whether we can maintain the public consensus on the necessity of the President's program.

Defense Policy and the Reagan Administration

Barry R. Posen and Stephen Van Evera

Departure from Containment

The Reagan Administration has proposed the biggest military buildup since the Korean War. The first Administration five-year defense program, drawn up in 1981, would have required an average real budget increase of 8.1 percent per year from 1981 to 1987, for a net real increase of 59 percent. Under this five-year plan, United States defense spending would have risen from 5.6 percent of gross national product (GNP) in 1981 to 7.4 percent of GNP in 1987.[1] Later the Administration cut these proposed increases slightly, and Congress is bound to impose further reductions, especially if sizable budget deficits continue. Nevertheless, the Administration has made clear that it favors a major transfer of resources into defense, and the general direction of the Administration budget will continue to be sharply upward.

The budget has become the focus of a growing debate over whether the buildup is necessary and whether the new money is well spent. So far this debate has dwelled chiefly on the specifics of Administration proposals. By contrast, we believe that to assess the value of Reagan's defense policy we must first clarify the United States' grand strategy: What are America's basic aims? What missions must the United States military perform to achieve these aims? Can current U.S. forces already perform these missions, or do they fall short?

Defense policy cannot be properly evaluated unless national strategy and national military capabilities are specified first. Otherwise—as is generally

---

This article is a revised version of a chapter which will appear in Kenneth A. Oye, Robert J. Lieber, and Donald Rothchild, eds., *Eagle Defiant: U.S. Foreign Policy in the 1980s* (Boston: Little, Brown, 1983).

Barry R. Posen is a Council on Foreign Relations International Affairs Fellow; this essay was written while he was a fellow at the Center for International Affairs, Harvard University. Stephen Van Evera is a Lecturer in Politics at Princeton University. The views expressed here are the authors' own.

---

1. William W. Kaufmann, "The Defense Budget," in Joseph A. Pechman, ed., *Setting National Priorities: The 1983 Budget* (Washington, D.C.: Brookings, 1982); hereafter Kaufmann, SNP 1983. Also, William W. Kaufmann, "The Defense Budget," in Joseph A. Pechman, ed., *Setting National Priorities: The 1982 Budget* (Washington, D.C.: Brookings, 1981), p. 135; hereafter Kaufmann, SNP 1982. The earlier essay is also published as a booklet: William W. Kaufmann, *Defense in the 1980's* (Washington, D.C.: Brookings, 1981).

International Security, Summer 1983 (Vol. 8, No. 1) 0162-2889/83/010003-43 $02.50/1

the case—planners lack goals and guidelines to measure national defense requirements, foreign and defense policies are bound to be mismatched, and policymakers risk wasting money on areas in which their forces are already strong, while failing to correct weaknesses. Defense budget cuts make sense only if a leaner force can still carry out national strategy. Increases make sense only if current forces cannot carry out assigned missions and military reforms cannot make up the shortfall. In short, defense planners should ideally ask the big questions first—they should clarify basic aims and strategy before choosing forces and tactics; if they do not, their programs and policies run the risk of being incoherent and uneconomical. In practice, defense policy is seldom properly matched to strategy, and clear strategy itself is rare. But American defense planners will produce a better defense policy if they approximate this ideal as closely as possible.

Disputes about American defense needs often spring from hidden disputes about strategy. Analysts may differ on how much to spend on defense because they differ on whether the United States should adopt a more or less demanding strategy; it costs more to perform many missions than to perform fewer, so deciding how much is enough depends on first deciding "enough to do what?" Analysts also differ on the merits of specific weapons systems because they differ on what missions the military must perform. Different missions require different forces, so debates about hardware often grow from unacknowledged disputes about which strategy is best. Likewise, disputes about the East–West military balance often spring from hidden disagreements about how many missions the military is expected to perform. The U.S. and its allies appear strong if the requirements are few and weak if they are many. Pessimists and optimists often differ less on what American forces *can* do than on what they should be *asked* to do. In short, although the issues one hears debated most often are about specific weapons, force deployment, and resource allocations, the hidden agenda of the defense debate is a dispute about strategy.

The Reagan Administration, however, has failed to fully explain what grand strategy it pursues and has neglected to detail the capabilities and weaknesses of current American forces, leaving defense analysts and the public without yardsticks by which to measure whether the proposed buildup is necessary or appropriate. Administration statements merely suggest the outline of a strategy, while leaving important questions unanswered. Secretary of Defense Caspar Weinberger's two annual reports to Congress, for example, the main public documents explaining the buildup, failed either to define roles and missions or to specify shortfalls between current capabilities and required missions. In fact, the secretary rejects "arbitrary and facile" estimates of the number of contingencies for which American forces must prepare.[2] He believes that the United States should "discard artificial definitions and contrived categories," and avoid "the mistaken argument as to whether we should prepare to fight 'two wars,' 'one and a half wars,' or some other such tally of war."[3] He demands a "necessary recasting of our strategy"[4] without explaining what the old strategy was, or what the new one will be. He points to "serious deficiencies in our military forces"[5] without explaining which missions cannot be met. The Administration, in short, does not publicly explain its proposed military buildup in terms concrete enough to allow us to measure its benefits against its costs. Thus, the first fault with President Reagan's defense program lies with its lack of a clearly articulated strategy.

Second, based on what the Administration suggests about its programs, its strategy seems to be extravagant and dangerous. Policy statements and procurement programs indicate that this Administration has adopted a more demanding strategy than any since Eisenhower's. Granted, all postwar administrations have adopted defense strategies that included more missions than the original Cold War containment strategy would require; but the implicit Reagan strategy defines containment even more broadly than did its predecessors by adding more and harder missions and putting more emphasis on offensive missions and tactics.

This demanding new strategy helps drive the Reagan defense budget upward, but the extra missions it requires have not been explained or debated, and the prima facie case that they protect vital American interests seems weak. On the whole, then, when we do catch a glimpse of the Administration's grand strategy, it appears to depart from original Cold War strategic ideas and toward a more ambitious and more dangerous grand strategy.

The following describes the original Cold War strategy of containment and the four essential military missions that follow from it. Then NATO forces are measured against these missions to assess current NATO military strength. The second section outlines which additional missions are implicit

---

2. Caspar W. Weinberger, *Annual Report to the Congress: Fiscal Year 1983* (Washington, D.C.: U.S. Government Printing Office, 1982; also available free on request from the Defense Department Public Affairs Office), p. I-15; hereafter *Annual Report 1983*.
3. *Annual Report 1983*, p. I-15.
4. *Annual Report 1983*, p. I-11.
5. *Annual Report 1983*, p. I-3.

in Reagan Administration statements and programs, while the third and fourth sections discuss the causes of current public alarm about Western military strength, and suggest reforms which could strengthen NATO forces without a major defense budget increase.

U.S. Strategy and Capabilities

CONTAINMENT AND U.S. STRATEGY

To evaluate the current defense debate, we begin by assessing current American military strength. To do that, we need a set of missions against which to measure American forces. Past consensus held that American forces had four main missions. First, American strategic nuclear forces must be able to deter a Soviet nuclear attack on the United States by being able to inflict unacceptable damage on the Soviet Union even after a Soviet nuclear first strike against U.S. forces. Second, American forces must be strong enough to halt a Soviet invasion of Western Europe for several weeks, against whatever weapons Soviet invaders chose to use—conventional, chemical, or tactical nuclear.[6] A third mission was added once the West became dependent on Middle East oil: to defeat a Soviet seizure of the Persian Gulf oil fields. Finally, most strategists agree that the United States requires the capacity to fight an extra "half war" against another country, even while fighting a major war against the Soviet Union, thus creating a total "one-and-a-half-war" requirement. For planning purposes an attack by North Korea on South Korea was taken as the "half-war," but the half-war mission had no defined adversary, and might be fought anywhere against anyone.

These four missions reflect the basic aim of containment, as framed by George F. Kennan, Walter Lippmann, and other strategists in the 1940s: to prevent the industrial power of Eurasia from falling under the control of any single state.[7] They warned that any state controlling all Eurasia could threaten

---

6. "Strategic nuclear" forces are those that would strike the enemy homeland, while "tactical nuclear" or "theater nuclear" forces are those that would be used in a regional battle, in neither homeland.

7. An excellent summary of early containment thinking is John Lewis Gaddis, *Strategies of Containment* (New York: Oxford University Press, 1982), pp. 25–88. See also Gaddis, "Containment: A Reassessment," *Foreign Affairs*, Vol. 55, No. 4 (July 1977), pp. 873–887; George F. Kennan, *Realities of American Foreign Policy* (New York: W.W. Norton, 1966); and Walter Lippmann, *The Cold War: A Study in U.S. Foreign Policy* (New York: Harper & Brothers, 1947). For an earlier discussion of American grand strategy from the Kennan/Lippmann perspective, see Nicholas John Spykman, *America's Strategy in World Politics: The United States and the Balance of Power* (1942; reprint ed., Hamden, Conn.: Archon, 1970), pp. 3–199.

the security of the United States, since the total industrial power of Europe and Asia (64 percent of gross world product [GWP] in 1978) far exceeds that of the United States (24 percent of GWP in 1978).[8] A hegemonic Eurasian superstate could convert this superior economy into a stronger war machine: hence the United States must prevent such a superstate from arising. In short, containment was a geopolitical security strategy; its purpose was to maintain the political division of industrial Eurasia, to thereby protect the United States from a hostile Eurasian power concentration.

After World War II, containment was directed against the Soviet Union because the Soviets became the principal threat for dominating Europe once Nazi German power had been destroyed. According to George Kennan, the stakes in this Soviet–American competition were the centers of military-industrial production—places where military power could be created. The purpose of containment was to keep the Soviets from seizing these industrial regions and mobilizing them against the United States. This would be achieved by cooperative effort among the states threatened by Soviet expansion, not by solitary action on the part of the United States. The final goal was to limit Soviet power but not to destroy it, both because this would be too difficult to achieve and because, even if it succeeded, it might create a new potential hegemony, just as the destruction of German power created the Soviet threat to Europe in 1945. Containment did not seek the destruction of the Soviet Union: it succeeded if Soviet hegemony over Eurasia was prevented.

As it was originally conceived, containment thus was more a geopolitical than an ideological strategy. It opposed the expansion of the Soviet state, not of communism per se—although American leaders often confused the issue by explaining containment with simplistic anti-communist rhetoric. The original logic of containment would have defined the Soviet Union as the American adversary even if it had abandoned communism for democracy, as long as it remained strong and aggressive.

Containment also was fundamentally defensive: Eurasia was to be divided, not dominated or policed. Containment was directed toward the industrial world, not the Third World, since industrial war-making power was the prize. And it assumed that the defense of the West was a joint effort, not an exclusive American operation. The basic purpose of containment was the

---

8. Ruth Leger Sivard, *World Military and Social Expenditures 1981* (Leesburg, Va.: World Priorities, 1981), pp. 25–26.

same basic purpose that led the United States to ally with the Soviets against Hitler: namely, to keep the rest of Europe free from being overrun by the strongest European state. Kennan summarized the logic of containment in these terms:

It [is] essential to us, as it was to Britain, that no single Continental land power should come to dominate the entire Eurasian land mass. Our interest has lain rather in the maintenance of some sort of stable balance among the powers of the interior, in order that none of them should effect the subjugation of the others, conquer the seafaring fringes of the land mass, become a great sea power as well as land power, shatter the position of England, and enter—as in these circumstances it certainly would—on an overseas expansion hostile to ourselves and supported by the immense resources of the interior of Europe and Asia.[9]

Kennan identified five important military-industrial regions: the Soviet Union, the Rhine valley, the British isles, Japan, and the United States.[10] Today the Persian Gulf is a sixth important region, since Europe and Japan depend on Persian Gulf oil. In Kennan's terms, the task of the United States is to contain the Soviets within their military-industrial region, which in practical terms means defending Western Europe, Japan, and now the Persian Gulf. The direct Soviet military threat to Japan is minimal, so the defense of Europe and the Gulf are the main military missions.

Besides containing the Soviets, the United States, in traditional postwar thinking, has a second basic aim: to keep America out of a nuclear war. This aim involves two objectives: to keep any war conventional, avoiding the use of nuclear weapons as long as possible; and to keep any nuclear war off American territory if possible, confining it to the theater where it breaks out. Because a theater nuclear war could escalate to a strategic exchange, the U.S. has a further interest in ending any theater nuclear war as quickly as possible. These goals are not required by containment per se, but rather by the invention of nuclear weapons, which demand more careful tactics of containment.

These general aims—containing the Soviet Union and keeping the United States out of a nuclear war—engender the specific requirements for American conventional and tactical nuclear forces. Hypothetically, the United States could defend Europe and the Gulf simply by threatening to attack Soviet

---

9. George F. Kennan, *American Diplomacy 1900–1950* (New York: New American Library, 1951), p. 10.
10. Kennan, *Realities*, pp. 63–64; and Kennan, *Memoirs 1925–1950* (Boston: Little, Brown, 1967), p. 359.

cities with strategic nuclear weapons if the Soviets invaded. But the Soviets could retaliate against American cities, and American strategists do not want to "trade Boston to defend Bonn." Moreover, the Soviets might not be convinced that American leaders would carry out such a threat. This fear led to the requirement that American theater forces in Europe and the Gulf should be strong enough to halt Soviet invaders. The hope is to keep the war away from American soil, confining it to the theater of action.

The United States would try to defend Europe and Japan conventionally, if the Soviets attacked conventionally, to lower the risk of nuclear escalation. American conventional forces are intended to form a buffer between peace and nuclear war—to give us a choice, in other words, between all or nothing. In official thinking, such a buffer lowers the risk of a holocaust by widening Western options: the United States can defend conventionally if the Soviets attack conventionally.[11] Before 1967 the United States had planned to defend Europe chiefly with tactical and strategic nuclear weapons, but then NATO endorsed a new plan to fight conventionally for at least several weeks, to give statesmen time to seek peace through negotiation. This plan, of course, does not guarantee a nuclear war would not happen anyway. Any major East–West conventional war may escalate even against the wishes of both sides.[12] Moreover, Soviet military writing indicates that the Soviets might use nuclear weapons from the outset of the war.[13] But conventional forces are intended to reduce this risk.

Past administrations have often added a fifth or a sixth mission to these four—most notably, an anti-China mission, a "counterforce" mission,[14] or a Third World intervention mission. Before 1969, American strategists planned for a simultaneous war against Russia, China, and a third enemy, creating a total "two-and-a-half-war" requirement, in contrast with the "one-and-a-half-war" strategy adopted by the Nixon, Ford, and Carter administrations. In addition, before 1964, and again after 1974, official policy included an ambiguous counterforce requirement, and during the 1960s, planners assumed

---

11. For a critique of this thinking, see Bernard Brodie, *Escalation and the Nuclear Option* (Princeton: Princeton University Press, 1966).

12. For escalation scenarios see Barry R. Posen, "Inadvertent Nuclear War? Escalation and NATO's Northern Flank," *International Security*, Vol. 7, No. 2 (Fall 1982), pp. 28–54.

13. A useful short summary of Soviet military thought is Benjamin S. Lambeth, "How To Think About Soviet Military Doctrine," in John Baylis and Gerald Segal, eds., *Soviet Strategy* (Montclair, N.J.: Allenheld, Osmun, 1981), pp. 105–123. A typical Soviet military view on European war is Col. A.A. Sidorenko, *The Offensive* (Washington, D.C.: U.S. Government Printing Office, 1970).

14. On "counterforce," see below, pp. 24–28.

that the U.S. must be capable of intervening against Third World insurgencies. Kennan, Lippmann, and others often pointed out that American foreign policy goals were expanding beyond the original aims of containment; likewise, American defense policy incorporated more missions than pure containment would seem to require. But the four missions outlined above have been the only missions to receive continuous consensus support. They are also the only four that follow unambiguously from a containment grand strategy,[15] so these are the missions against which we should measure American forces.

One other factor is relevant to an assessment of U.S. ability to carry out a policy of containment: America's strategists have traditionally assumed that its allies would help carry out these missions and the United States would not shoulder the burden alone. Eurasian states on the Soviet periphery have at least as much at stake in containment as does the United States, since Soviet expansion threatens their freedom more directly. American strategists have therefore assumed that these states will contribute a major share of NATO defenses. A chief purpose of the Marshall Plan and postwar military assistance programs was to strengthen Western Europe so it could defend itself against the Soviets. The notion was always that the United States would stand with those who were attacked and with others whose interests were threatened by Soviet expansion; but the United States would not perform solo, since containment served a general Western interest. The proper comparison, then, should be between NATO and Warsaw Pact forces, not between the United States and the Soviet Union.

Depending on whether we add or subtract missions from this list of four, American defense costs will vary sharply. A strictly bare-bones containment strategy might require only the three anti-Soviet missions—a nuclear retaliatory capability and denial capabilities in Europe and the Persian Gulf, with no extra "half-war" mission—because, as a containment purist might argue, only Soviet expansion poses a threat, and the Soviets can threaten only Europe and the Gulf. On the other hand, Reagan Administration defense requirements are exceptionally high because, as we shall see below, this Administration even more than past ones assumes a longer list of missions than a pure containment strategy would require.

---

15. The "half-war" mission is a possible exception, since some might argue that it doesn't protect important interests from the Soviets, as we note below.

UNITED STATES MILITARY CAPABILITIES

Administration statements and press accounts paint a picture of serious American military weakness. President Reagan declares that, "in virtually every measure of military power the Soviet Union enjoys a decided advantage."[16] Defense Secretary Weinberger, for example, points to "serious deficiencies" and "major weaknesses" in American defenses and warns of "our collective failure to pursue an adequate balance of military strength" while the Soviets have pursued "the greatest buildup of military power seen in modern times."[17] *The Wall Street Journal* declares that the Soviet Union "now is superior to the U.S. in almost every category of strategic and conventional forces."[18]

A close examination of the evidence, however, suggests that such claims are exaggerated. American forces do suffer from some deficiencies, and a higher level of confidence in their capabilities would be prudent; but these problems can be alleviated by reforms and/or a modest spending increase. Indeed a convincing case can be made for the argument that American forces are actually capable of carrying out their four basic missions today. More pessimistic views of American capabilities generally rest on hidden assumptions that more missions are demanded or that American allies do not help.

NATO forces *should* be capable of achieving their basic missions, given the total size of the NATO defense effort. NATO states have more men under arms than the Warsaw Pact (5.0 versus 4.8 million men)[19] and spend more money on defense than do the Pact states. Latest United States government figures show NATO narrowly outspending the Pact ($215 to $211 billion in 1979, a 2 percent difference),[20] while figures from the London-based International Institute for Strategic Studies (IISS) give NATO a wider margin ($180 billion to $160 billion in 1978, a difference of 12½ percent).[21] Moreover, about 15 percent of the Soviet defense effort is directed toward China. If we deduct these Soviet forces, United States government figures show a NATO spend-

---

16. "Transcript of President's Address on Nuclear Strategy Toward Soviet Union," *The New York Times*, November 23, 1982, p. A12.
17. *Annual Report 1983*, pp. I-3, I-4.
18. "The Wrong Defense" (editorial), *The Wall Street Journal*, March 25, 1982.
19. International Institute for Strategic Studies, *The Military Balance 1982–1983* (London: IISS, 1982), p. 132.
20. U.S. Arms Control and Disarmament Agency, *World Military Expenditures and Arms Transfers 1970–1979* (Washington, D.C.: ACDA, 1982); Spain is included.
21. International Institute for Strategic Studies, *The Military Balance 1979–1980* (London: IISS, 1979), p. 94.

ing lead of 17 percent, and IISS figures show NATO leading by 30 percent. These numbers are based on rough estimates rather than precise calculations, but they suggest the approximate balance of total assets invested on both sides.

Moreover, some analysts claim that official American figures exaggerate Soviet defense spending and understate allied spending. One expert suggests that government figures underestimate Western European NATO spending by perhaps 22 percent.[22] If so, NATO outspends the Pact by 12 percent using official figures, or by 29 percent if Soviet forces facing China are deducted. Another expert recently guessed that the C.I.A. may exaggerate Soviet spending by as much as 25–30 percent.[23] If we adjust United States government figures accordingly, NATO actually outspends the Pact by 25 percent. If Soviet forces facing China are then deducted, NATO outspends the Pact by 42 percent.

In short, NATO has the men and the resources needed to defend successfully. If NATO forces are weak, this reflects mistaken force posture, doctrine, and choice of weapons, not inadequate defense spending. Moreover, a detailed look reveals that NATO forces probably can perform their basic missions.

U.S. STRATEGIC NUCLEAR CAPABILITIES. U.S. strategic nuclear forces consist of a triad of 1,052 intercontinental ballistic missiles (ICBMs) based in the U.S.; 576 submarine-launched ballistic missiles (SLBMs) carried in 36 nuclear-powered submarines; and 316 strategic bombers, which carry nuclear gravity bombs and nuclear-tipped short-range missiles. These strategic forces consume only 15 percent of the U.S. defense budget, with the rest going to conventional forces,[24] but they are the most important and powerful U.S. military forces.

The Soviets also have a triad, theirs consisting of 1,398 ICBMs, 989 SLBMs, and 150 bombers. Because more U.S. missiles have multiple independently targetable reentry vehicles (MIRVs)—more than one warhead—U.S. strategic

---

22. Sivard, *World Military and Social Expenditures 1981*, p. 37, col. 3.
23. Franklyn D. Holzman, "Is There a Military Spending Gap?" (mimeo, March 16, 1982), p. 6. See also Holzman, "Are the Soviets Really Outspending the U.S. on Defense?" *International Security*, Vol. 4, No. 4 (Spring 1980), pp. 86–105. For shorter summaries, see Holzman, "Is There A Soviet–U.S. Military Spending Gap?" *Challenge*, September–October 1980, pp. 3–9; and Holzman, "Dollars or Rubles: The CIA's Military Estimates," *Bulletin of the Atomic Scientists*, June 1980, pp. 23–27.
24. *Annual Report 1983*, p. I-17.

forces carry more warheads (9,268 to the Soviets' 7,300); however, Soviet warheads are bigger, so the Soviet force carries more total explosive power.[25]

The Administration warns that these U.S. strategic forces are dangerously weak. President Reagan declares that Soviet strategic forces have a "definite margin of superiority" over American forces,[26] while Defense Secretary Weinberger warns that the Soviets hold a "degree of superiority and strategic edge" in strategic nuclear capability which "will last for some years through the decade even if we pursue all the programs the President has sought."[27]

In fact U.S. strategic nuclear capability depends on the missions against which U.S. forces are measured. U.S. strategic forces have much more than a "second-strike capability" (the capacity to inflict "unacceptable damage"[28] on Soviet population and industry even after absorbing a Soviet nuclear first strike), and far less than a "first-strike capability" (the capacity to render Soviet forces incapable of inflicting "unacceptable damage" on U.S. population and industry). Nor do U.S. forces have a "second-strike counterforce" capability (the capacity to absorb a Soviet first strike, and then render remaining Soviet nuclear forces incapable of inflicting unacceptable damage on remaining U.S. population and industry). In short, U.S. forces *could not* prevent the Soviets from devastating U.S. population and industry after a U.S. first strike, or after a U.S. mid-war strike against Soviet reserve nuclear forces; but they *could* destroy most of the Soviet Union in retaliation after a Soviet first strike.

Thus, overall, American counterforce capability—the ability to destroy Soviet retaliatory capability—is minimal, while American retaliatory capability is enormous. Neither side can disarm the other, and both sides can retaliate. An estimated 3,500 American strategic nuclear warheads could survive a Soviet surprise attack,[29] enough to destroy Soviet society several times over. Just 73 U.S. warheads could destroy over 70 percent of Soviet petroleum production capacity.[30] Just 631 small (50 kiloton) American warheads or 141

25. IISS, *The Military Balance 1982–1983*, pp. 140–141.
26. "President's News Conference on Foreign and Domestic Matters," *The New York Times*, April 1, 1982, p. A22.
27. Theodore Draper, "How Not To Think About Nuclear War," *The New York Review of Books*, Vol. 29, No. 12 (July 15, 1982), p. 38.
28. What damage is "unacceptable" to either side depends on the intentions of the parties and the nature of the dispute: what damage is each side willing to suffer to achieve its aims?
29. Kaufmann, SNP 1982, p. 63.
30. Office of Technology Assessment, *The Effects of Nuclear War* (Washington, D.C.: U.S. Government Printing Office, 1979), p. 76.

large (1 megaton) American warheads could destroy over 50 percent of total Soviet industrial capacity.[31] Some doubts surround the survivability of the American strategic command, control, communications, and intelligence apparatus (C^3I), but public information on strategic C^3I is not adequate to judge the extent of the deficiency, or what is needed to correct it.[32] Assuming sufficient C^3I survives, the United States now has many more than enough survivable warheads to retaliate effectively.

This does not mean the United States can stand still. The Soviets invest heavily in counterforce nuclear forces, and American strategic forces must be continuously modernized to cope with these Soviet threats to U.S. second-strike capabilities as they emerge. Improved high-accuracy Soviet ICBMs are now threatening American ICBMs, and improving Soviet air defense capabilities may eventually threaten the penetration capability of American strategic bombers; hence, some improvement or replacement of current ICBMs and bombers will be required to keep U.S. second-strike capability at current levels.[33] But certainly current American forces can retaliate effectively today.

In short, American strategic forces are strong or weak depending on the missions required: the United States is a long way from a meaningful counterforce capability, but American second-strike capability is robust. This reflects the basic attributes of nuclear weapons: they are very powerful, cheap, small, light, easily hidden, easily protected, and easily delivered. As a result, a second-strike capability is very cheap and easy to maintain, while a first-strike capability is virtually impossible under any known technology. It is much harder to find new ways to destroy enemy warheads than it is for the enemy to find new ways to protect them. The "cost-exchange ratio"—the ratio of the cost of producing a capability to the cost of neutralizing it—lies very heavily in favor of the second-strike capability. As a result *neither* superpower can deny the other a second-strike capability, because technology simply will not allow it. The notion that either superpower could gain a militarily meaningful "margin of superiority" is an illusion.

---

31. Arthur M. Katz, *Life After Nuclear War: The Economic and Social Impacts of Nuclear Attacks on the United States* (Cambridge, Mass.: Ballinger, 1982), p. 316.
32. On U.S. strategic C^3I, see John D. Steinbruner, "Nuclear Decapitation," *Foreign Policy*, No. 45 (Winter 1981–1982), pp. 16–29; Desmond Ball, *Can Nuclear War Be Controlled?*, Adelphi Paper No. 169 (London: International Institute for Strategic Studies, 1981); and Congressional Budget Office, *Strategic Command, Control and Communications: Alternative Approaches for Modernization* (Washington, D.C.: CBO, 1981).
33. A good analysis of current options to enhance the survivability of American ICBMs is Albert Carnesale and Charles Glaser, "ICBM Vulnerability: The Cures Are Worse Than the Disease," *International Security*, Vol. 7, No. 1 (Summer 1982), pp. 70–85.

WESTERN EUROPE. The common assumption holds that Warsaw Pact conventional forces could quickly overrun Western Europe in a conventional war. Former Secretary of State Alexander Haig warned in 1982 that the United States must "triple the size of its armed forces and put its economy on a war footing" before NATO could defend Europe successfully.[34] The Committee on the Present Danger notes "a near consensus on the inadequacy of present NATO forces to defend Western Europe successfully with conventional arms."[35]

In fact, NATO conventional forces in Europe are substantially stronger than these gloomy views suggest, although they remain weaker than prudence requires.[36] If Warsaw Pact forces perform a little better than best evidence suggests they will, or if NATO forces perform worse than expected, or if NATO leaders fail to mobilize NATO forces promptly after they receive warning of a Pact mobilization, then Pact forces *can* win the battle. But overall the odds favor NATO, if NATO leaders mobilize their forces quickly once they receive warning[37] and if Pact forces demonstrate no surprising margin of strength over NATO forces. Although NATO forces could not crush Pact attackers decisively, they probably could deny the Soviets a quick victory and thereby turn the conflict into a long war of attrition.

In short, NATO forces cannot promise victory with the level of confidence that NATO leaders should demand, but they seem more likely to win than to lose. Moreover, NATO could be substantially strengthened without a major military buildup, if NATO forces are reformed along the lines outlined below. NATO forces are now close to speed, and could be brought up to

---

34. *The New York Times*, April 7, 1982, p. A8.
35. Committee on the Present Danger, *Is America Becoming Number 2? Current Trends in the U.S.–Soviet Military Balance* (Washington, D.C.: CPD, 1978), p. 31.
36. An excellent essay on the NATO conventional balance is John J. Mearsheimer, "Why the Soviets Can't Win Quickly in Central Europe," *International Security*, Vol. 7, No. 1 (Summer 1982), pp. 3–39; also reprinted in Mearsheimer, *Conventional Deterrence* (Ithaca, N.Y.: Cornell University Press, 1983). Also useful are Robert Lucas Fischer, *Defending the Central Front: The Balance of Forces*, Adelphi Paper No. 127 (London: IISS, 1976); and Congressional Budget Office, *Assessing the NATO/Warsaw Pact Military Balance* (Washington, D.C.: CBO and U.S. Government Printing Office, December 1977). In addition to these and other sources, we base our discussion of U.S. conventional capabilities on interviews with Defense Department officials and other members of the American defense community.
37. A substantial percentage of both NATO and Warsaw Pact military capability becomes battle-ready only after several days of preparation, so it is critically important that NATO not allow the Pact a large head start in mobilization. NATO leaders must respond quickly when they receive warning of Pact mobilization measures. Failure to keep up with Pact mobilization would soon allow the Pact to muster sufficiently favorable force ratios to achieve a breakthrough against NATO.

speed, without a large spending increase, by improving NATO force structure and procurement practices.

A Warsaw Pact attack would be likely to fail because Pact forces probably lack the superiority in firepower and manpower they would need to overcome the natural advantage held by the defender, and to compensate for the obstacles that West German geography could pose to an aggressor. The Pact has only a slender manpower and material advantage in Central Europe—between 15 and 20 percent in total manpower, and 20 percent in total ground firepower (i.e., firepower in all NATO and Pact army formations available in Central Europe).[38] Moreover, this firepower ratio may undercount NATO firepower because it omits some NATO weapons held as replacements for combat losses, leaves out some German reserve units, and ignores NATO's greater investment in divisional command, control, and intelligence hardware and staff, which increase the effectiveness of NATO firepower. If these factors were included, the Pact advantage might disappear.

Furthermore, the Pact trails NATO in tactical airpower. Total NATO tactical aircraft in Europe have triple the aggregate payload of Pact aircraft at distances of 100 miles, and seven times the payload of Pact aircraft at distances of 200 miles, according to the latest available data.[39] This reflects the much greater carrying power of NATO aircraft. A NATO F-4 Phantom carries 16,000 pounds, while a Soviet MiG-27 carries only 6,600 pounds.

NATO planes should also be superior in air-to-air combat. NATO fighters are more sophisticated, NATO has better "battle-management" systems (the AWACS aircraft), and NATO pilots are better than Pact pilots. American pilots have more combat experience, they fly more hours, and their training is more realistic.[40] Overall, as Air Force Director of Plans General James Ahmann has testified, NATO fighter forces are "superior to the Warsaw Pact" and could achieve "very favorable aircraft exchange ratios" against Pact fighters.[41]

---

38. Mearsheimer, "Why the Soviets Can't Win Quickly," pp. 7–8. This "firepower" score is a composite index that includes the killing power of all tanks, anti-tank weapons, artillery, and so on—all the killing instruments in the division.
39. Carnegie Endowment for International Peace, *Challenges for U.S. National Security: Assessing the Balance: Defense Spending and Conventional Forces*, Part II (Washington, D.C.: Carnegie Endowment, 1981), p. 71. A similar qualitative advantage for NATO tactical air forces may be construed from figures offered by Alain C. Enthoven and K. Wayne Smith, *How Much Is Enough?* (New York: Harper Colophon, 1971), p. 145, and *Annual Report 1983*, p. II-18.
40. Joshua M. Epstein, "Soviet Vulnerabilities in Iran and the RDF Deterrent," *International Security*, Vol. 6, No. 2 (Fall 1981), pp. 149–150.
41. U.S., Congress, House of Representatives, *Hearings Before a Subcommittee of the Committee on*

These facts are often overlooked because press accounts stress Pact advantages in unrepresentative subcategories, such as numbers of tanks or artillery or planes, where the Pact does have an advantage (150, 180, and 15 percent respectively).[42] Such comparisons ignore NATO quality advantages (NATO planes, artillery, and antitank weapons and ordnance are better than those of the Pact) and categories in which NATO leads (major warships, helicopters). In general, NATO forces in Europe are not significantly outnumbered and may even hold the advantage in overall military capability.

The advantage of the defender also favors NATO. As a rule, attackers require substantial material superiority for success—between three- and six-to-one at the point of attack, and between one-and-one-half-to-one and two-to-one in the theater of war.[43] But the Pact probably cannot gain enough superiority unless NATO mobilizes late. In fact, NATO can maintain force ratios close to the premobilization ratio if NATO mobilizes simultaneously with the Pact. If NATO waits several days and then mobilizes, the balance in favor of the Pact would briefly exceed one-and-one-half-to-one but still would not reach two-to-one in favor of the Pact. Then it would fall back to a level close to the pre-mobilization ratio. The odds clearly favor the Pact only if NATO delays mobilization more than a week after receiving warning.[44]

German terrain further complicates a Pact attack. German forests, mountains, and other obstacles limit the Pact to four possible attack routes: the North German plain, the Hof Corridor (toward Stuttgart), the Fulda Gap (toward Frankfurt), and the Göttingen Corridor (toward the Ruhr). Because the Pact attack is canalized by this geography, NATO can focus its defensive efforts, and Pact forces are compressed to the point where they cannot fight efficiently. NATO troops can "cross the T"—chew up forward Pact units

---

Appropriations, Subcommittee on the Department of Defense, Part 4, 95th Congress, 2nd session (Washington, D.C.: U.S. Government Printing Office, 1978), p. 347. On deficiencies in Soviet pilot training, see also Joshua M. Epstein, "On Conventional Deterrence in Europe: Questions of Soviet Confidence," *Orbis*, Vol. 26, No. 1 (Spring 1982), pp. 71–88.
42. Mearsheimer, "Why the Soviets Can't Win Quickly," p. 4; Carnegie Endowment, *Challenges for U.S. National Security*, p. 71.
43. These ratios represent a best estimate for average situations. There are, however, some historical cases of successful armored assaults by attackers who enjoyed less than a three-to-one force ratio. It is possible, though not likely, that the Pact could achieve local successes against some NATO forces with less than a three-to-one advantage at the point of attack. If so, NATO might find itself without enough ground forces. This possibility is one of the uncertainties against which the reforms suggested below are designed to buffer.
44. Mearsheimer, "Why the Soviets Can't Win Quickly," p. 9.

serially—while other Pact units sit idly in the rear, since the Pact will not have room in these narrow channels to bring all its units forward at once. Moreover, three of these channels run the width of Germany, so attacking Soviet forces cannot spread out even if they break through NATO front-line defenses. The war would not unfold like the German attack on France in 1940, when the Germans burst into open plains, ideal tank country, after crossing the Meuse. Instead, Pact forces would be confined by geography to a narrow area until they penetrated deep in Germany.[45]

NATO suffers some unique weaknesses, but these are roughly counter-balanced by unique Pact handicaps. NATO's seven European armies have not standardized their weapons, so ammunition, spare parts, and communications gear are not fully interchangeable. As a result NATO armies cannot easily feed on one another's supplies, a limitation that undercuts their wartime flexibility. In contrast, the Soviets have imposed Soviet arms on all their Pact armies. But this advantage is offset by the fact that Pact forces are less reliable than NATO forces; in wartime the Soviets cannot be sure whether the Poles and Czechs will fight with them, sit the war out, or even fight against them. Some 45 percent of Pact standing ground forces in Europe are East European, a circumstance that greatly complicates Soviet planning.

Most published estimates of the European balance are admittedly more pessimistic than ours,[46] but they fail to fully utilize available information. Key data required for a thorough assessment are missing from their analyses: aggregate firepower estimates for the forces on both sides,[47] terrain factors, and estimates of troop movement and interdiction rates. Instead, their judgment of NATO's weakness is supported by unrepresentative statistics and by conclusions based on unduly pessimistic political and factual assumptions. An overwhelming Pact firepower advantage, for example, is suggested by focusing on subcategories of weapons in which the Pact has the lead. Sometimes the number of Soviet divisions promptly available is exaggerated. Other

45. Ibid.
46. Pessimistic estimates include those of John M. Collins, *U.S.–Soviet Military Balance: Concepts and Capabilities 1960–1980* (New York: McGraw-Hill, 1980), pp. 291–330, 539–549; Jeffrey Record, *Force Reductions in Europe: Starting Over* (Cambridge, Mass.: Institute for Foreign Policy Analysis, 1980), pp. 5–33; Joseph M.A.H. Luns, *NATO and the Warsaw Pact: Force Comparisons* (n.p.: NATO, 1980); Phillip A. Karber, "The Growing Armor/Anti-Armor Imbalance in Central Europe," *Armed Forces Journal International*, July 1981, pp. 37–48; and Congressional Budget Office, *U.S. Ground Forces: Design and Cost Alternatives for NATO and Non-NATO Contingencies* (Washington, D.C.: CBO, 1980).
47. The Congressional Budget Office's *U.S. Ground Forces* is an exception.

estimates overlook Soviet weaknesses, such as the unreliability of East European armies. Still others neglect the advantage of fighting on the defense. In short, pessimistic estimates are more common, but they are based on sketchier information and less comprehensive analysis.[48]

THE PERSIAN GULF. Conventional wisdom holds that American forces could not block a Soviet seizure of the Iranian oil fields, or even the Saudi Arabian oil fields, without using nuclear weapons. One columnist suggested that American forces "could never be a match for the Soviet juggernaut across the Iranian border."[49] Defense Secretary Weinberger warned that American

---

48. See, for instance, the 1980 Congressional Budget Office study *U.S. Ground Forces,* which is perhaps the most thorough pessimistic assessment, but which exaggerates the number of Soviet divisions available to attack Western Europe, undercounts forces available to NATO, and plays down terrain factors favoring NATO.

The CBO assumes that Soviet Category III cadre divisions can be readied and moved from the Soviet Union to Germany in 35 days, although another analyst estimates this would require three to four months. (See Jeffrey Record, *Sizing Up the Soviet Army* [Washington, D.C.: Brookings, 1975], pp. 21–22, estimating that Soviet Category III divisions cannot be ready before 90 to 120 days. See also William W. Kaufmann, "The Defense Budget," in Joseph A. Pechman, ed., *Setting National Priorities: Agenda for the 1980s* [Washington, D.C.: Brookings, 1980]; Kaufmann notes that the Afghanistan invasion indicates that "it takes the Soviet establishment a substantial amount of time—months rather than weeks—to organize a small operation against a weak and relatively disorganized country" [p. 30]. For an assessment of the readiness of Soviet Category III divisions which suggests that they mobilize slowly, see testimony by the Defense Intelligence Agency to the Joint Economic Committee, published in "Allocation of Resources to the Soviet Union and China–1981," *Hearings before the Subcommittee on International Trade, Finance, and Security Economics of the Joint Economic Committee,* Congress of the United States, 97th Congress, 1st session, Part 7 [Washington, D.C.: U.S. Government Printing Office, 1982], p. 199.)

As a result the CBO credits the Pact with a 120-division force 30 days after mobilization, instead of the 90-division force that most NATO plans assume the Pact can field, or the 71-division force the Pact could field if the Soviets chose not to employ any Category III divisions early in the war, relying exclusively on Category I and Category II divisions (Robert Shishko, *The European Conventional Balance: A Primer,* P-67-7 [Santa Monica, Calif.: Rand Corporation, 1981], p. 8). The CBO's pessimistic conclusions depend on this unexplained assumption, since the CBO grants that NATO could halt a 90-division Pact assault (p. xiii).

Second, the CBO understates the capability of the German territorial forces. The German territorials are trained reserves that can be mobilized at least as fast as Soviet Category III divisions, to a total 750,000 men. By simply mobilizing the German territorials, NATO almost doubles the size of total NATO European forces, which would grow from 780,000 to 1,530,000 men. Yet the CBO credits the territorials with only six mechanized brigades—roughly two divisions, or at most 70,000 men, a fraction of the total German territorial forces actually available to NATO.

Third, the CBO understates the advantage conferred on the defender by terrain in the North German Plain, instead repeating the conventional wisdom that the plain is an easy invasion route for Soviet forces. In fact, this area is crossed by rivers, bogs, and urban sprawl, which make defense easier.

49. Jack Anderson, "Frightening Facts on the Persian Gulf," *The Washington Post,* February 3, 1981, p. 18, quoting "top military hands."

forces were "incapable of stopping an assault on Western oil supplies,"[50] while one prominent defense analyst proclaimed that Iran "may be inherently indefensible."[51] But these predictions, like those pessimistic predictions concerning Europe, do not make full use of available information. In fact, American forces could probably halt the Soviets short of the oilfields, chiefly because a Soviet attack would require an enormous transportation and logistics effort, which probably lies beyond Soviet capabilities.

The United States stands a good chance in the Gulf because Soviet forces could not gain decisive materiel superiority in the battle area. Even though the Soviets are much nearer, the United States can probably bring as much firepower to bear in the Persian Gulf theater as can the Soviets.[52]

Proximity would seem to give the Soviets the upper hand; but appearances are misleading, for three reasons. First, the United States has invested more money in mobility equipment (transport aircraft and amphibious assault ships, aircraft carriers, airmobile and seamobile forces), which partially offsets greater Soviet proximity.

Second, the Soviets have not tailored their military to invade the Persian Gulf, so their forces are not ready to attack on short notice. As a result NATO would gain valuable advance warning if the Soviets chose to invade. Before the Soviets attack, they must assemble and test a command and control apparatus in Transcaucasia, which would make telltale radio noises. They must amass tens of thousands of trucks in the Caucasus, to supply Soviet divisions advancing into Iran, because Soviet forces near Iran do not have enough trucks. Soviet army divisions are structured for war in Europe, with its many railroads. As a result, these divisions are designed to operate no farther than 100 miles from a railhead, so they normally include relatively few trucks. Soviet forces invading the Gulf would be fighting hundreds of miles from any functioning railroad, requiring an enormous additional complement of trucks to ferry supplies on Iranian roads. By one estimate all the trucks from more than 55 Soviet army divisions (one-third of the *mobilized* Soviet army) would be required to support a Soviet invasion force of seven

---

50. Robert S. Dudney, "The Defense Gap That Worries the President," *U.S. News and World Report*, February 16, 1981.
51. Jeffrey Record, "Disneyland Planning for Persian Gulf Oil Defense," *The Washington Star*, March 20, 1981, p. 17.
52. The best assessment of the East–West balance in the Gulf is Epstein, "Soviet Vulnerabilities." For brief assessments see Kaufmann, SNP 1981, pp. 304–305, and SNP 1982, p. 160. Also useful is Keith A. Dunn, "Constraints on the USSR in Southwest Asia: A Military Analysis," *Orbis*, Vol. 25, No. 3 (Fall 1981), pp. 607–631.

divisions in Iran, assuming no trucks break down or are destroyed in fighting.[53] By another estimate almost all the trucks in the Soviet army might be required.[54] This armada could not be assembled quickly or discreetly.

These preparations would give NATO at least one month's warning.[55] In the meantime, the United States could move substantial forces into the Gulf to greet Soviet attackers—perhaps 500 land- and sea-based tactical fighters, the 82nd Airborne Division, and two Marine brigades within two or three weeks. Later the United States could bring in much bigger forces by sea.

Third, although the Soviets are much closer to the Gulf oilfields than is the United States, each mile the Soviets must travel is much harder to traverse. Soviet invasion forces must move 850 miles overland to reach the Iranian oil fields in Khuzestan province in southwest Iran. If they attack from the Soviet Union, they must cross two formidable mountain ranges: those along the Iranian northern tier, and the Zagros Mountains, which separate Khuzestan from central Iran. If they attack from Afghanistan they must pass over the fierce, desolate Khorassan desert and the Zagros. Only a handful of roads cross the northern mountains, and only four roads and one railroad span the Zagros.[56] In the mountains these roads cross bridges, run through tunnels, cling to the sides of countless gorges, and wind beneath overhanging cliffs. As a result Soviet supply arteries would be dotted with scores of choke points—places where the artery could be destroyed or blocked. The blockage could not be bypassed or easily repaired.

With all the geographical barriers, Soviet movements in Iran would be exceptionally vulnerable to delaying action by American airstrikes, commando raids, or attacks by Iranian guerrillas on the scores of choke points between Khuzestan and Russia. This distance is too great for the Soviets to erect solid air defenses along their entire groundline of communication, so American airpower could probably continue striking these choke points even if they were overrun by advancing Soviet forces. These air strikes could be flown from aircraft carriers, by land-based aircraft that could be moved to the Mideast after warning is received, or by B-52s based on Diego Garcia in the Indian Ocean, on Guam in the Pacific, or even in the U.S.[57] Iranian forces

---

53. Epstein, "Soviet Vulnerabilities," p. 144.
54. Andrew Krepinevich, "The U.S. Rapid Deployment Force and Protection of Persian Gulf Oil Supplies" (unpublished paper, Kennedy School of Government, Harvard University, 1980).
55. Epstein, "Soviet Vulnerabilities," pp. 139–140; and Kaufmann, SNP 1981, p. 305.
56. Epstein, "Soviet Vulnerabilities," p. 139.
57. Ibid., p. 136.

could also slow down Soviet forces and disrupt Soviet supply lines, especially if they organized in advance for guerrilla war.

By one estimate, American air strikes and helicopter infantry teams working in the Zagros Mountains could slow the Soviet advance toward Khuzestan by sixty days. If we assume the United States receives and uses thirty days of warning, then American forces have ninety days to prepare the defense of Khuzestan. In this time the United States can move enough ground forces to Khuzestan to equal the firepower of Soviet divisions coming through the Zagros. Moreover, the United States can probably bring more airpower to bear in Khuzestan than can the Soviets, giving the United States a net firepower advantage.[58] If so, American forces have more than enough firepower to win.

Some Westerners suggest that the Soviets might mount a surprise airborne attack on Iran, seizing key airfields and other facilities with airborne units and holding them until Soviet ground forces could follow up, instead of mounting a prepared ground assault. But such an airborne strike seems even more likely to fail than a ground assault, because the Soviets could not assemble the trucks their ground forces require without giving away the surprise which an "airborne grab" would require. As a result, any airborne divisions dropped into southern Iran would have to hold off American and Iranian counterattacks for weeks while the Soviets readied their ground invasion force in the southern Soviet Union. Morever, these airborne units could not be easily resupplied by air in the meantime, because Soviet fighter aircraft probably lack the range to provide adequate air cover over southern Iran from bases in the Soviet Union or Afghanistan, and the Soviets probably could not quickly seize, secure, and prepare enough air bases in Iran suitable for modern fighter aircraft. As a result, the Soviets probably could not defend their transport aircraft over southern Iran against American fighters, leaving their airborne units stranded. In sum, a Soviet "airborne grab" against southern Iran seems even harder than a Soviet ground attack.

Lord Robert Salisbury once remarked, concerning British fears that Russia would sweep through Afghanistan into India: "A great deal of misapprehension arises from the popular use of maps on a small scale."[59] Likewise, American fears that the Soviets could sweep through Iran spring from dismissal of geographic and military realities. Overall, as one analyst notes,

---

58. Ibid., pp. 140, 145–148.
59. Quoted in Bernard Brodie, *War and Politics* (New York: Macmillan, 1973), p. 356.

"the invasion of Iran would be an exceedingly low confidence affair for the Soviets."[60]

As with the European balance, pessimistic estimates of the Gulf conventional balances do not fully utilize available data, or they rest on dubious factual or political assumptions.[61] Again, aggregate firepower estimates, geographic factors, movement tables, interdiction rates, and warning estimates are usually missing. Instead, misleading statistics are combined with unduly pessimistic political assumptions: e.g., that the Gulf states refuse American help or cooperate with Soviet invaders, or that the United States loses simply because it lacks the will to fight, or that the American mission is to defend only *northern* Iran, which would be much harder than defending the southern oilfields, or that American leaders would simply fail to heed the warning they receive.[62]

In short, public alarm about American capabilities to achieve basic missions seems exaggerated. Publicly available information is spotty, so estimates of our current capabilities must be tentative—partly because the government has not published much useful information about military balances. Nevertheless, the best evidence indicates that these missions are not beyond the capacity of current U.S.–NATO forces.

The Implicit Reagan Military Strategy

We believe that the Reagan defense buildup is driven by the tacit assumption that, in addition to the four traditional containment missions, American forces must perform five extra missions, which in most cases were not publicly accepted elements of American strategy a decade ago.[63] Moreover,

---

60. Epstein, "Soviet Vulnerabilities," p. 157.
61. Pessimistic estimates include Jeffrey Record, *The Rapid Deployment Force and U.S. Military Intervention in the Persian Gulf* (Cambridge, Mass.: Institute for Foreign Policy Analysis, 1981), pp. 8–42, 61–68; Collins, *U.S.–Soviet Military Balance*, pp. 367–394; Albert Wohlstetter, "Meeting the Threat in the Persian Gulf," *Survey*, Vol. 25, No. 2 (Spring 1980), pp. 128–188; and W. Scott Thompson, "The Persian Gulf and the Correlation of Forces," *International Security*, Vol. 7, No. 1 (Summer 1982), pp. 157–180.
62. Regarding the "half-war" balance, published information on U.S. capacity to fight a Korean "half-war" is so scanty we cannot supply a detailed analysis of American capabilities. However, most public sources indicate American forces can perform the Korean "half-war" mission they are sized against. See Kaufmann, SNP 1983, pp. 89–90; and Congressional Budget Office, *U.S. Ground Forces*, p. 67.
63. For Reagan strategy ideas, see: Thomas C. Reed, "Details of National Security Strategy," Speech delivered to the Armed Forces Communications and Electronics Association, June 16, 1982 (mimeo, available from the White House, Office of the National Security Adviser); "Revised

the case made against these missions in the past—that they do not serve traditional containment aims—still seems sound. In short, the Reagan defense buildup is predicated largely on an unacknowledged and undebated shift from a cheaper to a more expensive strategy. In this section we enumerate these five missions and the arguments about them.

COUNTERFORCE

The counterforce debate has continued nonstop since the 1940s. Policy analysts agree that the United States requires a second-strike capability, but America's need for a counterforce capability (either a first-strike or a second-strike counterforce capability) has always been controversial. The size and shape of American strategic forces depend on how this argument is resolved, since a meaningful counterforce capability requires much bigger and rather different nuclear forces from those deployed today.

A successful disarming counterforce attack against the Soviet Union would require two operations: a strike against Soviet nuclear forces and a battle to limit the damage done to American cities by surviving Soviet nuclear warheads launched in retaliation. Accordingly, counterforce weapons include those that can preemptively destroy Soviet nuclear warheads before they are launched against the United States *and* those that destroy retaliating Soviet warheads in flight toward American cities or at least limit the damage these warheads do to American cities. Thus, counterforce weapons include highly accurate ICBMs and SLBMs (which can preempt enemy ICBMs and bombers), antisubmarine ("killer") submarines and other antisubmarine warfare forces (which can destroy Soviet ballistic missile submarines), air defense systems (which can shoot down retaliating Soviet bombers), area-wide antiballistic missile systems (ABM, which can defend cities against retaliating ICBMs and SLBMs), and civil defense (which limits the damage inflicted by Soviet retaliation). Such "defensive" systems as air defense, area-wide ABM, and civil

---

U.S. Policy Said to Focus on Prevailing Over Russians," *The New York Times*, June 17, 1982, p. B17, summarizing Reed; Richard Halloran, "Pentagon Draws Up First Strategy for Fighting a Long Nuclear War," *The New York Times*, May 30, 1982, p. A1, summarizing the secret Administration 5-year defense guidance document; Richard Halloran, "Weinberger Denies U.S. Plans for 'Protracted Nuclear War,'" *The New York Times*, June 21, 1982, p. A5; "Lehman Seeks Superiority," *International Defense Review*, May 1982, pp. 547–548; Richard Halloran, "New Weinberger Directive Refines Military Policy," *The New York Times*, March 22, 1983, p. A18; David Wood, "Pentagon Tames Rhetoric to Offer a 'Softer' Image," *The Los Angeles Times*, March 20, 1983, p. 1; *Annual Report 1983*; and Caspar W. Weinberger, *Annual Report to the Congress: Fiscal Year 1984* (Washington, D.C.: U.S. Government Printing Office, 1983), hereafter *Annual Report 1984*.

defense are really "offensive" in the nuclear context, because they are a vital part of an offensive first-strike system. Second-strike weapons are those that can ride out an enemy attack and retaliate against enemy cities or other "value" (industrial or economic) targets; they include, for example, U.S. Poseidon SLBMs. They need *not* be able to destroy enemy strategic nuclear forces.

In the late 1960s and early 1970s a public consensus formed against counterforce, reflected in the congressional decision to constrain American ICBM accuracy improvements and in congressional hostility toward the proposed ABM system. Some people opposed counterforce on grounds that it increased the risk of war and the risk of wartime escalation. First-strike capabilities on both sides would create a hair-trigger dilemma: whichever side fired first would win, so both sides would be quick to shoot in a crisis.[64] Moreover, conventional war would be much harder to control, since the first side to use nuclear weapons would hold the upper hand, creating a strong temptation to escalate if conventional war broke out.

But the clinching argument was that a counterforce capability simply could not be achieved. According to this view the Soviets, like ourselves, could always take steps—implement countermeasures—to preserve their second-strike capability, because a second-strike capability is so much cheaper to maintain than a counterforce capability. Moreover, the Soviets could not tolerate an American first-strike capability, so they would make sure we never got one, whatever the cost. A second-strike capability is essentially defensive, but a counterforce capability is offensive: a state that can disarm the other side can demand its surrender. Neither superpower could ever let the other get such a capability. Hence, the argument went, American spending on counterforce is futile, because the Soviets will always counter the counterforce the Americans build.

Counterforce came back into fashion in the mid-1970s, with Ford and Carter administration decisions to build major new counterforce systems, chiefly the high-accuracy MX and Trident D-5 (Trident II) missiles. The Reagan Administration has accelerated the Trident D-5 program and added

---

64. On preemptive war, see Thomas C. Schelling, *Arms and Influence* (New Haven: Yale University Press, 1966), pp. 221–259; and Schelling, *The Strategy of Conflict* (New York: Oxford University Press, 1963), pp. 207–254. For another important argument on why counterforce is dangerous, see Robert Jervis, "Cooperation Under the Security Dilemma," *World Politics*, Vol. 30, No. 2 (January 1978), pp. 186–214, also excerpted in Robert J. Art and Kenneth N. Waltz, *The Use of Force*, 2nd ed. (Washington, D.C.: University Press of America, 1983).

new counterforce programs: a modernized continental air defense system, including new F-15 interceptors and AWACS early-warning aircraft; an enlarged civil defense program; and increased research on ABM systems.[65] Administration planning documents suggest a requirement for a second-strike counterforce capability, which could disarm the Soviet Union even after absorbing a Soviet first strike. Presumably a force with this capability could disarm the Soviets more reliably if the United States struck first. A secret Administration "Defense Guidance" paper calls for nuclear forces that "can render ineffective the total Soviet (and Soviet allied) military and political power structure," even if American forces struck second.[66] The Administration envisions attacks on the whole Soviet force structure, including "decapitation" strikes against Soviet political and military leadership: targets would include Soviet "political and military leadership and associated control facilities, nuclear and conventional military forces, and industry critical to military power."[67]

Yet a counterforce capability is much harder to achieve today, because American forces must destroy a much bigger set of Soviet targets. In 1970 the Soviets had 1,800 strategic nuclear warheads; in 1982 there were 7,300.[68] The number of Soviet strategic delivery vehicles (missiles and bombers) has not gone up substantially, but the number of warheads these launchers carry has gone up dramatically (because the Soviets have MIRVed their missiles), so an American first strike must be much more effective to contain the Soviet retaliation to acceptable size. In fact, the Administration's own warning that this Soviet buildup threatens American second-strike capability conflicts with arguments for counterforce: if American second-strike capability is precarious, then a counterforce capability would not seem feasible, since counterforce is much more demanding. Moreover, top priority should go to enhancing the United States' second-strike capability if its retaliatory forces really are not secure, since second-strike capability is the backbone of its defenses.

Hence, the case against the feasibility of a counterforce strategy seems even more persuasive than it was when counterforce was unpopular. More-

---

65. See Kaufmann, SNP 1983, pp. 65–66. Other Administration programs also enhance U.S. counterforce capability, including enhanced nuclear "battle-management" C³I and new nuclear killer submarines.
66. Halloran, "Weinberger Denies U.S. Plans," p. A5.
67. Ibid.
68. Ground Zero, *Nuclear War: What's In It For You?* (New York: Pocket Books, 1982), p. 267, and IISS, *The Military Balance 1982–1983*, p. 140.

over, no new information has appeared to discredit the now-forgotten fear that a first-strike capability on either side would raise the risk of war and escalation. The Administration's commitment to decapitation strikes also seems dangerous, since decapitating the Soviets would leave the United States with no negotiating partner while turning Soviet forces over to Soviet generals and colonels imbued with nuclear warfighting ideas.[69] In such an event, how could the war be stopped?

In the late 1970s the notion arose that counterforce made more sense than before, both because new technology (ICBM accuracy improvements, for example) allegedly made counterforce easier, and because the Soviet counterforce buildup required a symmetrical American response, to retain American "essential equivalence." But by any measure, counterforce is harder to achieve now than fifteen years ago, because the Soviet arsenal is much bigger and better protected. The fallacy lies in counting how many warheads American forces hypothetically could destroy (which has increased), instead of counting how many could not be destroyed (which has also increased), and how much damage these remaining warheads could do to the United States.

The Soviets devote even more effort to strategic nuclear counterforce programs than does the United States, and the Soviet strategic nuclear buildup in the 1970s heavily stressed counterforce. But this does not argue for a simpleminded American imitation of Soviet programs. Rather, the Soviet buildup should have signaled the end of any dreams for a useful American counterforce capability, since this buildup also greatly enhanced Soviet second-strike capability by multiplying the number of protected warheads the United States would have to attack successfully. The most effective response to Soviet counterforce capability is to remove it by enhancing the survivability of American forces. This negates the enormous Soviet counterforce investment, at much smaller cost to the United States.

The Administration's emphasis on counterforce conflicts with its efforts to control the strategic nuclear arms race. Counterforce drives the arms race: neither side can allow the other to gain a meaningful counterforce capability, so counterforce programs on both sides generate answering second-strike programs on both sides, and vice versa. Forces must modernize and arsenals must expand, because neither side can let the other reach its goal. Nuclear arsenals on both sides now vastly exceed overkill because both sides sought

---

69. A source for Soviet military statements on intercontinental thermonuclear war is Joseph D. Douglas, Jr. and Amoretta M. Hoeber, *Soviet Strategy for Nuclear War* (Stanford, Calif.: Hoover Institution Press, 1979).

counterforce capabilities, which bred ever-larger forces, which then created a larger counterforce target set for the other side, which bred still larger forces on the other side.

The nuclear arms race would be best controlled by first controlling counterforce. If the superpowers forswore counterforce, the rationale for nuclear arms-racing would largely disappear, since programs on both sides would no longer create new requirements for the other. Conversely, meaningful arms control is very difficult if the superpowers pursue counterforce seriously, because counterforce programs on both sides force both sides to keep building up. Under these circumstances, arms control agreements merely ratify decisions to build ever-larger arsenals. In short, the Reagan Administration's emphasis on counterforce lessens the possibility that meaningful arms control can be achieved.

What direction should American strategic programs take? Three requirements should take priority. First, American second-strike capability requires reliable, survivable strategic C^3I, so weaknesses in it must be corrected. Second, American force improvements should emphasize "enduring" new systems, since the United States now lacks a satisfactory nuclear delivery system that could survive the unlikely but nevertheless important possibility of months of controlled nuclear war. Third, Minuteman ICBMs eventually must be replaced if the U.S. is to maintain a triad of diverse, secure retaliatory forces at current levels of second-strike capability. An ICBM replacement could perhaps be found more easily if the ICBM force were relieved of its counterforce mission, since this mission reduces the number of ways the missiles can be based. Basing modes might exist that diminish the ICBM "time-urgent, hard-target kill" capability, but that do secure the ICBMs from Soviet preemptive attack (for example, deep burial arrangements[70] or "mini-man" road-mobile small ICBMs). Hence the vulnerability of American forces might be cured more easily if planners put less emphasis on making Soviet forces vulnerable. As a general matter, resources should be shifted from counterforce programs to meet these needs.

OFFENSIVE CONVENTIONAL FORCES AND OPERATIONS
The overall cast of Reagan Administration strategic thought is more offensive than that of past administrations. Thomas Reed, a former Reagan adviser,

---

70. On deep burial see Congress of the United States, Office of Technology Assessment, *MX Missile Basing* (Washington, D.C.: U.S. Government Printing Office, 1981), pp. 269–274.

dismissed the old policy of containment, declaring that the United States now focuses on prevailing over the Soviets.[71] Defense Secretary Weinberger warned against "the transposition of the defensive orientation of our peace-time strategy onto the strategy and tactics that guide us in the event of war."[72]

In nuclear planning the Administration stresses counterforce, while in conventional programs it has adopted a new, more offensive warfighting strategy. Defense Department documents declare that American conventional forces should be "capable of putting at risk Soviet interests, including the Soviet homeland," and emphasize "offensive moves against Warsaw Pact flanks."[73] Navy Secretary John Lehman advocates "getting at the Soviet naval threat at its source."[74] Defense Secretary Weinberger would destory Soviet bombers "by striking their bases" and attack Soviet "naval targets ashore," and maintains that "the principle of non-aggression would not impose a purely defensive strategy in fighting back" against an aggressor.[75] He speaks of a "counteroffensive against [Soviet] vulnerable points . . . directed at places where we can affect the outcome of the war."[76] Most discussion concerns possible strikes against Soviet naval and air bases on the Kola peninsula (northeast of Finland, on the Barents Sea) or at Vladivostok and Petropavlovsk, in East Asia. These bases would be hit by carrier-based aircraft, or possibly by long-range strategic bombers. The Administration has programmed new conventional forces to match this offensive strategy, chiefly two new nuclear-powered aircraft carrier task forces.

Two criticisms can be leveled against this strategy. First, only a huge fleet of carriers could safely attack the Soviet homeland, because Soviet land-based aircraft could destroy a smaller American fleet as it approached. Even

---

71. "Revised U.S. Policy Said to Focus on 'Prevailing' Over the Russians," *The New York Times*; and Reed, "Details of National Strategy," p. 17.
72. *Annual Report 1983*, p. I-16. The *1984 Annual Report* places substantially less emphasis on offensive operations than does the 1983 report. Press accounts indicate that the new Defense Guidance is also more restrained. Yet statements by Administration officials and the direction of the Reagan defense program indicate that basic Administration policy has not changed. The greater restraint of the *1984 Annual Report* may be more a reaction to the public alarm caused by earlier Administration statements than a major change of view. One Administration official explained that in the new Defense Guidance "the words are the only thing that has changed. We just didn't want to get beat over the head by our political enemies." Wood, "Pentagon Tames Rhetoric."
73. Halloran, "Pentagon Draws Up First Strategy," p. 12.
74. "Lehman Seeks Superiority," p. 547.
75. *Annual Report 1983*, p. III-21; *Annual Report 1984*, p. 33.
76. *Annual Report 1983*, p. I-16. See also p. III-21.

with two new carriers, American carrier forces would probably be too weak to mount such a strike. Overall, a counteroffensive strategy is a bottomless pit, since it generates very demanding missions that cannot be achieved without huge expense, if they can be achieved at all. Indeed, the notion of an offensive conventional strategy does not square with Administration warnings of weakness: if America is so weak, how can it think of taking on such ambitious new missions?

Second, a counteroffensive strategy defeats the basic purpose of American conventional forces—the control of escalation. If it succeeds, a counteroffensive would jeopardize assets essential to Soviet sovereignty, or appear to do so, raising the prospect of a Soviet decision to escalate from conventional to nuclear war. For instance, the Soviets base vital elements of their second-strike capability at Murmansk—over half their ballistic missile submarine force and its command apparatus. American strikes against nearby Soviet naval bases and forces could threaten the submarines and provoke desperate Soviet decisions—nuclear strikes against American carriers, for example—if the base could not be defended any other way.[77] The chief purpose of American conventional forces is to provide a buffer between conventional and nuclear war, but an offensive operational strategy would use this force in a way that defeats this fundamental aim.

INTERVENTION FORCES

A significant portion of the American defense effort is now allocated to forces best suited for Vietnam-style or Dominican Republic-style interventions in Third World countries. These forces could be used against the Soviet Union, but they are not ideally suited for that purpose.

Two attributes distinguish intervention forces from others. First, they are highly mobile. Anti-Soviet forces usually need not be highly mobile, since the locations of possible Soviet threats are known, and defending forces usually can be put there in peacetime, as in Western Europe. Clearly the United States needs some mobile forces to deal with the Soviets, especially in the Persian Gulf. The question is, how many? Today the United States has more mobility forces than anti-Soviet contingencies demand, especially more aircraft carriers (unless these are used offensively, in which case it probably does not have enough; see above). Second, intervention forces are

---

77. On the risk of escalation raised by offensive conventional operations, see Posen, "Inadvertent Nuclear War."

lightly armed. Light forces are useful for some anti-Soviet contingencies, for instance, operations against Soviet supply lines in the Iranian mountains. But generally this type of force, best suited for fighting lightly armed opponents (guerrillas, for example), is not appropriate for fighting Soviet forces, which are heavily armed. Again the question is: how many light forces are needed?

Total American mobility forces and unarmored ground forces include the thirteen Navy aircraft carriers, one airborne and one air-mobile Army division, one air cavalry brigade, four regular Army light infantry divisions, Special Forces units, three Marine divisions and associated ships and air wings, airlift and sealift forces, and C.I.A. covert operatives. A war against the Soviets in Europe or the Persian Gulf would productively engage most of these forces, but not all. Some American aircraft carriers (perhaps ten, including those in overhaul) would be required to attack Soviet forces in Iran and guard the Atlantic and Pacific sea lanes, but some carriers would be left over (perhaps three; five with the Reagan program).[78] Possibly six of the nine American light ground divisions would be engaged in Iran or tied down in Norway or Korea, with three left over.

Thus, overall, the United States appears to have substantial superfluous intervention capability, to which the Reagan Administration plans to add even more, with new carriers, new "forcible-entry" amphibious assault ships, and new airlift. The Administration also indicates a revived interest in intervention by rejecting a "one-and-a-half-war" strategy, instead suggesting the United States prepare to fight on several fronts simultaneously.[79] This represents a shift toward intervention, since more "half wars" in addition to Korea would probably be fought in the Third World.

How should the American requirement for intervention forces be assessed? If containment criteria are applied, two questions are paramount: (1) How much would potential Soviet conquests in the Third World enhance Soviet

---

78. A force of ten carriers would give the United States eight carriers for combat missions in wartime, since two carriers would normally be in overhaul. By one estimate, two carriers are required to defend the sea lanes in the Atlantic and two to defend the Pacific sea lane. See Congressional Budget Office, *Navy Budget Issues for Fiscal Year 1980* (Washington, D.C.: CBO, March 1979), pp. 41–42. This would leave four carriers for anti-Soviet missions in the Persian Gulf or the Mediterranean. The wartime requirement for carrier battle groups in the Mediterranean seems questionable, since NATO land-based reconnaissance and fighter aircraft based in Spain, Italy, and Turkey—all NATO members—are capable of covering most of the Mediterranean. This leaves four carriers available for the Persian Gulf area.
79. *Annual Report 1983*, p. I-15.

power? (2) How much would Soviet influence in the Third World increase if the United States were not prepared to intervene? The answers to these questions rest chiefly on three factors: Western dependence on Third World raw materials, the military value of basing rights in Third World states, and the degree of cohesion in the world communist movement. Feasibility should also be kept in mind. At what cost, in dollars and morale, can American forces suppress guerrilla insurgencies in foreign cultures?

First, Western dependence on Third World raw materials should be restudied carefully, not simply assumed. The West should ask how much economic damage Western economies would suffer if they lost access to given supplies from given countries, measuring damage in terms of declining economic growth rates, rising unemployment, higher rates of inflation, and the cost of measures—such as domestic production, product substitution, conservation, stockpiling, or purchase from other foreign suppliers—that would have to be initiated if supplies were lost.[80] Instead, dependence is usually proven by listing raw materials that the West imports, as if trade and dependence were one and the same thing. It is not the volume of trade but rather the cost of halting trade that matters. American dependence on a given country or commodity equals the damage the American economy would suffer if trade in that commodity or with that country were cut off.

In fact, the claim that Western states are dangerously vulnerable to Third World raw material embargoes is quite weak. The United States and its allies depend heavily on foreign oil, but oil is the exception. The Organization of Petroleum Exporting Countries (OPEC) has been the only successful international cartel—a telltale sign that Western dependence on other products is low. The West imports many other products from Third World countries, but most of these materials can be synthesized, replaced by substitutes, or acquired from alternate sources. Otherwise, successful cartels would exist already in those materials as well.

Second, the value of Third World military bases cannot be assessed unless American strategy is spelled out clearly; therefore, the vagueness of current American strategy makes judgment hard. Bases matter if Soviet or Western

---

80. On measuring interdependence, see Kenneth N. Waltz, "The Myth of National Interdependence," in Charles P. Kindleberger, ed., *The International Corporation* (Cambridge, Mass.: M.I.T. Press, 1970), pp. 205–223; and Waltz, *Theory of International Relations* (Reading, Mass.: Addison-Wesley, 1979), pp. 138–160. Patterns of U.S. mineral imports are summarized in Michael Nacht, "Toward an American Conception of Regional Security," *Daedalus*, Vol. 110, No. 1 (Winter 1981), pp. 14–16.

bases in the Third World can affect the United States' ability to execute its overall military strategy. Thus the danger posed by Soviet bases in Third World areas cannot be assessed without knowing how much harder they make American strategy to execute, and this cannot be assessed without knowing what that strategy is.

The effect of the nuclear revolution should be remembered when the strategic importance of the Third World is assessed. The notion that events in Southeast Asia, Southern Africa, or other jungle areas could tip the world balance of power is even more doubtful in a world of second-strike capabilities. Nuclear weapons make conquest much harder, and vastly enhance the self-defense capabilities of the superpowers. This should allow the superpowers to take a more relaxed attitude toward events in third areas, including the Third World, since it now requires much more cataclysmic events to shake their defensive capabilities. Whatever had been the strategic importance of the Third World in a nonnuclear world, nuclear weapons have vastly reduced it.

Finally, the United States should carefully assess how formidable the Soviet threat to the Third World really is. Direct Soviet threats are often exaggerated because Soviet intervention capabilities are deemed larger than they actually are. Likewise, indirect Soviet threats via Soviet revolutionary "proxies" are measured in simplistic fashion.

Cold War experience teaches that the Soviets do not expand via national revolution, but by the force of the Soviet army. Time and again, Soviet influence has proven ephemeral wherever its army was not introduced, even where Soviet "proxies" won control. The notion that Third World leftists are loyal Soviet minions seldom proves correct, except when American policies help make it true, as with Vietnam, Cuba, Nicaragua, and earlier with China.

The bitter nationalisms that tear the Third World make it harder for both the Soviet Union and the United States to establish durable influence. In the end this actually serves Americans' interests, since their chief purpose is to keep the world free from Soviet control, not to rule it themselves. This means the United States should view Third World nationalism as an asset rather than a danger, and that the United States can usually contain the Soviets in the Third World simply by leaving things alone.

Advocates of intervention forces often suggest that the U.S. needs them to halt Soviet "geopolitical momentum," a tide of Soviet influence supposedly sweeping the Third World. In fact Soviet "geopolitical momentum" is a myth; over the past two decades the Soviets have barely held their own ground, even perhaps lost ground.[81] While in the last decade the Soviets have gained influence in Afghanistan, Vietnam, Laos, Cambodia, Ethiopia, Angola, Mozambique, Grenada, Nicaragua, Libya, Cape Verde, and the People's Democratic Republic of Yemen, they have lost influence in China, Japan, Egypt, Indonesia, Sudan, Somalia, Iraq, Guinea, and Equatorial Guinea. Overall, Soviet losses since 1960 probably outweigh Soviet gains.

The debate on U.S. military intervention should not be a matter of hawks versus doves, but of clear strategy. Soviet military power is the principal danger the West faces. American forces should confront this power directly. The United States should realize that it weakens itself and indirectly strengthens the Soviets if it diverts its energy toward less relevant Third World contingencies.

THE LONG CONVENTIONAL WAR

The Reagan Administration has removed the limit on the time American conventional forces must be able to hold a Soviet conventional attack in Europe or the Gulf. Secretary Weinberger warns against the "short war fallacy,"[82] and explains that the United States must prepare to mobilize for a long World War II-style conventional war.[83] This revises the assumption of the 1960s that American conventional forces would only provide a "pause" for negotiation, after which the West would escalate, and puts a bigger demand on American conventional forces.

This shift in strategy may be a reasonable move, but the change must be carried out carefully. First, a long conventional war strategy will not succeed if America's allies do not accept it and design their forces accordingly. Otherwise allied forces in Europe will collapse in a few weeks which would break down the whole NATO defense, even if American forces could fight on. But Western Europe has not accepted the new long-war strategy, nor bought the stocks of ammunition and spare parts necessary to support extended combat. The U.S. cannot make this new strategy work simply by spending more; it also must sell the strategy to its European allies. In short, we need a debate within the alliance on NATO strategy before the U.S. spends more toward a "long war" capability.

---

81. "Soviet Geopolitical Momentum: Myth or Menace? Trends of Soviet Influence Around the World From 1945 to 1980," *Defense Monitor*, Vol. 11, No. 1 (January 1980).
82. *Annual Report 1983*, pp. I-16, I-17.
83. *Annual Report 1983*, pp. I-13, I-14.

Second, American planners should not confuse a requirement for a conventional long-war capability with a prediction that a Third World War would actually be either long or conventional. Today there is a dangerous tendency to speak as if World War III would resemble World War II, on the hopeful assumption that efforts to control the war will succeed. This is a dangerous delusion. We cannot eliminate the risk of nuclear escalation from any East–West conventional war. A global conventional war would present enormous problems of management and coordination. Even during the Cuban missile crisis, American leaders could not fully control, or even understand, all the operations in which American forces were engaged.[84] An East–West conventional war would be vastly harder to manage. American planners should take every step they can to lower the risk of escalation, but they should never believe that these steps make a conventional war easy to control. If they underestimate the risks of nuclear war they invite a frivolous attitude toward war. Moreover, they lose the deterrent benefits of the danger of nuclear war if their declaratory policy leads the Soviet Union to think it can safely use conventional force without risking nuclear escalation. If the risk of escalation is real, American declaratory policy should communicate this clearly.

Third, if American planners take long conventional war seriously, the rest of American strategy should be consistent. Strategies and forces which raise the risk of nuclear escalation should be kept to a minimum. Instead the Reagan defense program emphasizes counterforce and offensive conventional forces and operations, which heighten the risk of nuclear escalation. Thus the Administration plans a long conventional war but then negates this effort with steps that diminish the odds that any war could be kept conventional.

LESS ALLIED CONTRIBUTION

The United States now carries a disproportionate share of the NATO defense spending burden, yet the Reagan defense program would shift the burden even further toward the U.S. In 1980 the United States spent 5.5 percent of its gross national product on defense, while its thirteen NATO allies only

---

84. See John Steinbruner, "An Assessment of Nuclear Crises," in Franklyn Griffiths and John C. Polanyi, eds., *The Dangers of Nuclear War* (Toronto: University of Toronto Press, 1979), pp. 35–40; and Graham T. Allison, *Essence of Decision: Explaining the Cuban Missile Crisis* (Boston: Little, Brown, 1971), pp. 130, 136–143.

spent an average of 3.4 percent of GNP.[85] Among major American allies, only Britain spends nearly as much, 5.1 percent, as the United States. These figures understate the European defense effort by failing to correct for the low salaries that the Europeans pay their conscripted manpower; but even if we eliminate this bias by pricing NATO manpower at American pay scales (which adds 22 percent to European budgets),[86] average European spending comes to only 4.1 percent of GNP, or 75 percent the size of the burden carried by the United States in 1980.

This unequal arrangement arose after World War II, when the United States guarded against the Soviets while the Europeans repaired war damage. Americans assumed that the Europeans eventually would take on the main share of the burden once their economies recovered. No one expected the United States to carry the main burden indefinitely. Yet Europe still carries a lighter load today, even though the West Europeans now have a combined GNP larger than the U.S., their economies grow at a faster rate, and their standard of living is almost as high.

The Reagan defense plan will widen the gap between American and allied defense spending even further. Properly speaking, this decision does not mean the United States takes on a new "mission"—rather, the United States would carry a bigger share of responsibility for existing joint NATO missions—but it adds up to the same thing. In taking on a bigger share of the NATO defense burden the United States asks its forces to perform traditional missions with less allied assistance, which is a more difficult overall task.

If, as planned, the Administration increases American spending to 7.4 percent of GNP, non-United States NATO military spending will dwindle to 56 percent the size of the burden carried by the United States, even if non-United States NATO manpower is priced at American rates (46 percent if it is not). Moreover American willingness to carry such a heavy share of the NATO burden gives other NATO states even less incentive to spend more, so the American share of the NATO burden may grow still heavier if European defense programs stagnate or decline in response to the Reagan program. Because the Americans will do more of the work, the Europeans will have even more reason to take a free ride on the U.S.

In Europe's defense it might be argued that the United States outspends

---

85. IISS, *The Military Balance 1981–1982*, pp. 27–39, 112. Spain, which joined NATO in 1982, is excluded.
86. Sivard, *World Military and Social Expenditures 1981*, p. 37, col. 3.

its allies because it spends more extravagantly, or spends on missions not vital to containment, such as Third World intervention. If the main trouble is American wastefulness, not European lassitude, then the solution is a leaner American defense policy, focused more clearly on the Soviet Union, as European defense policies are. But there is no legitimate reason why the American share of NATO burdens should substantially exceed allied spending in the long run.

Americans' Perceptions of Their Weakness: Built on a Myth

The Administration's defense program has won public approval largely because it could draw upon the widespread myth of American military weakness. If Western forces can in fact achieve their main missions today, what explains this American sense of impotence? Three causes contribute.

First, statistical games substitute for proper measures of national military strength in the public debate about defense. Congressman Les Aspin once described the "Games the Pentagon Plays"—false measures that support Pentagon arguments for preferred policies.[87] These games still confuse and mislead the public on both the size of the Soviet threat and the best solution for defense problems.

In the "numbers game," the sizes of selected Soviet and American forces are compared, always showing the United States lagging. Areas of Western numerical or qualitative superiority are ignored, and differences in the needs of each side are obscured. Thus, we often hear that the Soviets have more tactical aircraft (although American aircraft are much better, and total American tactical air capability is probably greater); more attack submarines (although American submarines are much more capable); more naval warships (although American ships are much bigger, more expensive, and more capable); and so forth. The only question that really matters—"Can the U.S. carry out its strategy?"—is not asked. Yet such misleading analysis is abundant in Secretary Weinberger's *Report to the Congress*, in the Joint Chiefs' *Military Posture* statement,[88] and in newspaper and magazine reporting on defense matters.

In the "trend game," alarming trends are presented without baseline fig-

---

87. "Games the Pentagon Plays," *Foreign Policy*, No. 11 (Summer 1973), pp. 80–92.
88. Organization of the Joint Chiefs of Staff, *United States Military Posture for FY 1983* (Washington, D.C.: U.S. Government Printing Office, 1982).

ures or explanations. Thus we often hear that the U.S. Navy has fallen from 1,000 ships to fewer than 500; it is not explained that the Navy shrank because many ships built for World War II were finally scrapped in the 1960s and 1970s and because the Navy shifted from smaller to larger ships, so it now builds fewer ships of greater tonnage. In fact, the United States has outbuilt the Soviet Union by three to one in warship tonnage since 1960, while NATO as a whole outbuilt the Soviets by nine to two.[89]

In the "go it alone game," Soviet and American forces are compared head to head, as if the United States had no allies and the Soviet Union no other enemies. Thus we often hear of Soviet advantages over the United States in categories where actually NATO holds the lead over the Warsaw Pact, such as military manpower or defense spending. Such comparisons dismiss the success of the entire postwar European and Japanese economic recovery programs, the express purpose of which was to build up American allies so they could defend themselves.

Instead, a proper assessment measures forces against missions, under politically realistic scenarios. Strategic nuclear capabilities on each side are measured by asking how many warheads *can't* each side destroy and what damage can these warheads wreak on the enemy society? American second-strike capability equals the damage surviving American warheads can inflict on Soviet society, while American counterforce capability is the inverse of the damage that surviving Soviet warheads could inflict on American society. Comparing warheads, megatons, throwweights, missiles, and bombers tells us very little if these are not converted into measures of capacity to destroy people and industry. We seldom see such measures, partly because they undercut arguments for counterforce by demonstrating the futility of building more counterforce.

A conventional theater balance cannot be measured without a thorough campaign analysis. At a minimum such an analysis should incorporate data measuring (1) the total firepower available to both sides, (2) the rate at which both sides can mobilize this firepower and move it into the theater of action, (3) the ability of each side to interdict the other's movement, (4) the advantage that geography gives the attacker or defender, and (5) the amount of warning both sides can expect. Yet defense analyses in the press and popular journals almost never discuss defense problems in these terms.

---

89. Congressional Budget Office, *Shaping the General Purpose Navy of the Eighties: Issues for Fiscal Years 1981–1985* (Washington, D.C.: CBO, 1980), p. 44.

Second, the defense debate often confuses political and military factors and too quickly suggests military solutions for political or diplomatic problems. Debates on hardware often turn on differences over the quality of American statesmanship and diplomacy. Thus pessimists often base arguments for more defense spending on scenarios that assume Western statesmen will not use the warning they receive of a Warsaw Pact attack or that assume the United States cannot persuade allies to cooperate in their own defense. Pessimistic scenarios for war in the Persian Gulf, for instance, sometimes assume the European states will not permit American aircraft to refuel in European countries, although vital European intersts would be at stake. A better answer, though, is for American leaders to provide the leadership that these scenarios assume is missing. Moreover, it often turns out that no amount of spending can cure the problems created by weak leadership. America's defense requirements are enormous if we assume its leaders are fools and its allies are malicious or self-destructive. These are problems that more spending cannot easily solve.

Third, American assumptions have shifted from a less demanding to a more demanding grand strategy during the past decade. The drift toward counterforce, intervention, multiple simultaneous contingencies, long conventional war, and offensive conventional operations creates much more demanding military requirements. In our judgment, Western military forces have maintained or even increased their capability to pursue their basic missions over the past decade, but American forces are now measured against harder missions, which makes the U.S. *feel* weaker because the proposed jobs are harder.

What Reforms Make Sense?

Although American capabilities are widely underestimated, American forces nevertheless suffer some real shortcomings. These weaknesses are best alleviated by reforming current forces rather than spending more across the board. Emphasis should fall on selective spending increases, aimed at solving defined problems, or on structural adjustments. In both Europe and the Persian Gulf, relatively inexpensive reforms can make current forces more capable.

With regard to American forces for Europe, five reforms should take priority. First, American weapons design practices need adjustment. The United States still "gold-plates" too much equipment: it passes over cheaper, simpler designs in favor of expensive, complex ones that are only marginally more capable. This happens because the military often demands state-of-the-art in the technology it buys—for instance, the world's first gas turbine engine to make the new M1 tank the fastest in the world. Frequently the military also demands that one weapon be capable of performing several missions; so the Navy's new F-18 fighter must be a superior air-to-air fighter *and* a superior ground attack aircraft. These requirements can drive costs up dramatically. Some analysts estimate that the last 5 percent of performance in American equipment often results in a 50 percent cost increase.[90] This gold-plating leaves the United States without enough equipment in areas where quantity matters more than quality. Gold-plated equipment also makes the readiness problem worse, because its use and maintenance requires scarce, expensive, highly skilled manpower and greater quantities of more costly spare parts.

Unfortunately, the Reagan defense program moves in the direction of more, rather than fewer gold-plated systems—more fancy F-14 and F-15 aircraft, more elaborate SSN-688 "Los Angeles" class nuclear attack submarines, and more nuclear aircraft carrier task forces and their complex Aegis air defense cruisers.[91] Overall, the Administration is moving toward a force that is too complex.

Second, efforts now underway to improve overall combat readiness should be continued. Congress likes to fund glamorous new weapons systems but neglects maintenance for older systems. As a result, much American military equipment is not ready for action on short notice.

In the short run, Reagan programs will improve this situation by increasing fuel and ammunition stocks and improving training and maintenance. These efforts should continue. But in the long run, Reagan programs will make the readiness problem worse, since Reagan forces are so gold-plated they will be even harder to operate and maintain. One result of the Reagan buildup, in fact, may eventually be a new readiness crisis.

Third, more military equipment should be pre-positioned in Europe. Pre-positioning permits the United States to send reinforcements to Europe more quickly, since less equipment must be moved across the Atlantic. This

---

90. Jacques Gansler, *The Defense Industry* (Cambridge, Mass.: MIT Press, 1980), p. 279. For more on gold-plating, see Jack N. Merritt and Pierre M. Sprey, "Negative Marginal Returns in Weapons Acquisition," in Richard G. Head and Erwin J. Rokke, *American Defense Policy*, 3rd ed. (Baltimore: Johns Hopkins University Press, 1973), pp. 486–495.
91. Reagan programs are summarized in *Aviation Week and Space Technology,* April 12, 1982, p. 64.

strengthens the United States in Europe and the Persian Gulf because American airlift and sealift forces are freed for use in the Middle East. The same concept applies to fighter aircraft: the more basing facilities are built in Europe in peacetime, the less equipment must be moved in wartime.

Fourth, the United States should move faster to ready its civilian airlines to transport military equipment and supplies in wartime. Civilian wide-body passenger jets can be modified at modest cost to serve as military cargo planes in wartime. A cargo-convertible "CRAF" (civilian reserve air fleet) is much cheaper than buying a purpose-built military transport aircraft. The Reagan Administration is trying to move forward with CRAF modifications, but the airline industry has not been cooperative. At the same time, however, the Administration plans an expensive new air transport, the C5N. Pressing ahead with CRAF is a better idea.

Finally, Washington should consider shifting more Army manpower from support to combat roles. The "teeth-to-tail" ratio still seems too low. An American combat division with all its support personnel includes roughly 48,000 troops. To deploy comparable numbers of weapons, the Israelis and West Europeans use only 30,000–35,000 soldiers and the Soviet Union only 22,000–25,000. The Soviets probably lack sufficient logistics and support, while we have too much.

Allied reforms and improvements would do even more to strengthen European defense than would American reforms. Four programs should take priority. First, trained West European military reserve manpower should be organized into reserve units, to fill the need for extra forces that can be held back from the front to cope with a possible Warsaw Pact armored breakthrough. Today many of these reserves are used inefficiently, as individual replacements for casualties in units already in action. Restructuring West European reserves should be at the top of the NATO agenda.

Second, the allies' war reserve stocks—ammunition, parts, and replacement equipment—are much lower than those maintained by the United States. They should be increased. Otherwise European forces will collapse early in the war, nullifying the purpose of American stocks. Third, West European ground forces should be armed more heavily. Latest figures indicate they have only half as many major weapons per thousand men as Soviet and American units.[92] Fourth, NATO and Japan should pay their airlines to

---

92. Congressional Budget Office, *U.S. Air and Ground Conventional Forces for NATO: Firepower Issues* (Washington, D.C.: CBO, March 1978), p. 14.

develop cargo-convertible CRAFs. This would increase the potential speed of American reinforcement in Europe and also free American military aircraft capabilities if a simultaneous crisis arose, for example, in the Persian Gulf.

Western capabilities in the Persian Gulf could also be increased at relatively low cost. American intervention forces should be tailored more specifically for Persian Gulf contingencies. The Marines and Army airborne and airmobile units should be better equipped for armored war, with light armored vehicles. More American equipment should be pre-positioned on ships, in Australia, or at the American Diego Garcia base in the Indian Ocean. The NATO allies and Japan should be better prepared to defend themselves, since this frees American military power for the Persian Gulf. American allies should also be prepared to move their own forces into the Gulf if the need arises. The defense of the Gulf is an allied problem: Washington should demand an allied effort. Finally, Washington should quietly discuss pre-positioning equipment in the Persian Gulf states. If Gulf governments do not want a visible American presence, pre-positioning could take the form of extra stocks and equipment for the Gulf states' armies, which Western forces could use in an emergency.

Conclusion

The Reagan Administration proposes some needed new measures, but the overall direction of its defense policy has not been adequately explained, and the scope of its programs seems excessive and ill-directed. This is not to say that the Administration record on defense is all bad. It deserves credit for its efforts to increase short-term readiness, to rationalize procurement with multi-year contracts, to restructure American forces for Persian Gulf defense, and to improve strategic C^3I. But the basic direction of Reagan's defense policy seems mistaken.

The strategy implicit in Administration programs and statements is unrealistically demanding. Insofar as the Administration seems to have a grand strategy, it appears to incorporate requirements for fighting wars of every kind, all at once—global conventional war against an unspecified range of adversaries, offensive conventional operations against the Soviet homeland, and a victorious nuclear war against the Soviets. This is quite a tall order. Both counterforce operations and offensive conventional operations generate open-ended requirements that simply cannot be met.

In fact, press accounts suggest Reagan defense planners believe they cannot achieve their strategy without another enormous military buildup once the current one is completed. The Joint Chiefs of Staff have reportedly warned they would need an additional $750 billion to carry out the missions specified by the Administration, beyond the $1.6 trillion budgeted for defense in the 1984–88 Administration five-year plan.[93] In short, the Administration strategy simply costs too much.

Moreover, the Reagan emphasis on counterforce, conventional offense, and intervention seems inconsistent with containment and with U.S. interest in controlling any war that might break out. Containment suggests a military strategy focused on Eurasia and emphasizing defense, not the global, offense-dominated strategy of the Reagan Administration. Escalation control calls for capable defensive forces and a defensive operational strategy rather than the Reagan strategy. This Administration's emphasis on conventional offense, counterforce, and nuclear warfighting raises the risk that a conventional conflict will escalate to a general thermonuclear war.

Eventually the American public may wonder whether NATO really needs such vast new investments, or why the United States should bear such a heavy share of the NATO burden. Then it may be caught with half-completed programs and a Congress unwilling to fund full readiness for a force that is both too big and too complex. A steady defense policy that avoids boom-and-bust spending cycles, but that will stand up to scrutiny in the long run, is a better idea. A spending spree to exploit a fleeting public panic will not strengthen the country in the end.[94]

In fact, wasteful military spending is itself a national security threat, because it contributes to America's national economic decline. This decline in turn both narrows the economic base from which the U.S. distills its military power and curtails its worldwide economic power. The American share of gross world product has fallen steadily since World War II and seems likely to keep falling in the future. Halting this economic decline is a vital national security goal for the United States. The Administration subverts this goal by damaging the American economy with excessive defense spending.

On the arms control front, the Administration's commitment to counterforce works at cross-purposes with efforts to negotiate new limits with the Soviets. Moreover, the initial Administration Strategic Arms Reduction Talks

---

93. George C. Wilson, "Pentagon: $1.6 trillion will not do job," *The Boston Globe*, March 8, 1982, p. 1.
94. For a list of possible cuts that might be made in the Reagan program, see Kaufmann, SNP 1983, pp. 86–95.

(START) proposal does not seem to constrain counterforce capabilities on either side, so even if the Soviets accepted the Reagan proposal, the risk of war would not be reduced. Arsenals on both sides would be smaller, but they might be more vulnerable, so in a sense the Administration's START proposal is a step backwards, since second-strike capabilities on both sides might be weakened. Instead, the Administration would be better off to pursue an agreement that focused on controlling counterforce systems, as Congressman Albert Gore has suggested.[95] Qualitative arms control is the best route to quantitative arms control. The size of nuclear arsenals is best controlled by limiting the counterforce programs that drive the arms race.

Finally, the Administration deserves criticism for sowing the defense debate with confusion. Its refusal to specify the strategy that requires the Reagan buildup deprives Congress and the public of the tools they need to analyze defense policy. As a result, the whole buildup proceeds with no clear definition of its purpose, no way to judge its necessity, no criteria to judge whether new forces are meeting real needs or leaving real needs unmet, and no logical stopping point. Moreover, those fragments of strategy that the Administration offers often conflict with one another, creating an overall incoherence. Mutually contradictory notions appear in the same statements—for example, in claims that Soviet forces are so strong that the United States requires a major buildup, but so weak that an offensive American strategy is possible.[96]

In addition, this Administration has done even less than its predecessors to make basic defense information available to the public, and its publications have been even more misleading. The 1983 and 1984 Defense Department Annual Reports to the Congress omit basic data contained in previous annual reports such as the relative spending of NATO and the Warsaw Pact, the aggregate tonnages of Pact and NATO fleets, strategic nuclear warhead inventories on both sides, and so forth. Instead, it is filled with alarming charts that imply American weakness but do not clarify where weaknesses really lie.

Public confusion about the basic facts of defense—including an administration's basic goals and strategy—is a major American national security problem. To clarify the defense debate, better public information on defense

---

95. Albert Gore, Jr., "The Fork in the Road: A New Plan for Nuclear Peace," *The New Republic*, Vol. 186, No. 18 (May 5, 1982), pp. 13–16.
96. See, for example, Reed, "Details of National Security Strategy."

is essential. Neither the government nor the major academic institutions are doing enough to make data available to news reporters, students, members of Congress, or other citizens concerned about defense policy. Adequate reference books do not exist, and most writing on defense policy is written by experts, to experts. Defense matters, however, are not too complex for lay persons to understand. They merely seem prohibitive because academic experts and government agencies do so little to explain defense issues in simple terms and make basic facts available in accessible form. The mistakes made by the Reagan Administration began with public confusion about facts of history, hardware, and strategy. Clearing up this confusion is the first step toward better defense policy.

Jousting with Unreality
Reagan's Military Strategy

Jeffrey Record

The Reagan Administration's declared global military strategy, at least as enunciated by Secretary of Defense Caspar Weinberger and Secretary of the Navy John Lehman, is a standing invitation to potential strategic disaster. Although attended by substantial and long overdue real increases in U.S. defense expenditure, what has become known as the strategy of worldwide war almost certainly will be denied the actual fighting power necessary to fulfill its ambitious goals. Worse still, the strategy is militarily unsound, betraying an inadequate appreciation of some of the key lessons of the history of warfare as well as some wishful thinking about future conflicts.

The late Sir B.H. Liddell Hart defined military strategy as "the art of distributing and applying military means to fulfill the ends of policy."[1] Liddell Hart went on to note that

Strategy depends for success, first and most, on a sound *calculation and coordination of the ends and the means*. The end must be proportioned to the total means, and the means used in gaining each intermediate end which contributes to the ultimate must be proportioned to the value and needs of that intermediate end—whether it be to gain an objective or to fulfill a contributory purpose.[2]

Strategy involves choices within the framework of finite resources, and an ability to distinguish between the desirable and the possible, the essential and the expendable. A sound sense of priorities is the essence of a sound strategy. When the United States entered World War II, it pursued a "Germany first" strategy, concentrating the main weight of its military effort against the most powerful and dangerous member of the Axis while initially remaining on the strategic defensive in the Pacific. History has confirmed the wisdom of that strategy, although it entailed some unpleasant choices early in the war against Japan, including the decision to write off the Philippines.

Jeffrey Record is a Senior Fellow at the Institute for Foreign Policy Analysis, Washington, D.C., and author of a forthcoming book on U.S. military strategy.

1. B.H. Liddell Hart, *Strategy* (New York: Frederick A. Praeger, 1967), p. 335.
2. Ibid., p. 336.

International Security, Winter 1983/84 (Vol. 8, No. 3) 0162-2889/84/030003-16 $02.50/0

A strategy whose goals far exceed resources available to implement them is a recipe for defeat. The same may be said of a strategy that fails to adapt effectively to fundamental changes in the national and international political, military, and economic environment. Thus the Third Reich was ultimately doomed by the abyss separating Hitler's virtually unlimited military objectives in Europe and actual German military power. Thus the failure of French strategy in the late 1930s to adapt effectively to the military consequences of the Munich agreement, and to such unfolding technologies as the tank and the airplane, contributed decisively to their swift defeat in 1940.

To be sure, one must be ever mindful of Clausewitz's distinction between "preparations for war" and "war proper," a distinction similar but not identical to that in contemporary military parlance between "deterrence" and "defense." Planning for war—even for the explicit purpose of averting it (deterrence)—is not the same as waging war. The ultimate test of any military strategy is not whether it succeeds in maintaining peace, but whether, in the event of war, it can restore peace on politically favorable terms and at an acceptable cost.

Unfortunately, what has passed for American military strategy during the past two decades has all too often amounted to little more than periodic professions of military desire undisciplined either by an appreciation of the finite limits of U.S. military power or by effective accommodation to fundamental changes in the global geostrategic environment. Since 1945 there admittedly has always been a significant gap between declared U.S. military goals and actual capabilities to fulfill them. The United States in the postwar era has relied heavily on the power of its nuclear arsenal to deter war; it has never possessed the ground, naval, and tactical air power to deliver on all its defense commitments overseas, and certainly not simultaneously.

Realization of stated force goals in the 1960s for "two and one-half wars" (against the Soviet Union in Europe, China in Asia, and a lesser adversary elsewhere) and even, in the 1970s, for "one and one-half wars" (against the Soviet Union in Europe and a lesser adversary elsewhere) has consistently eluded the Pentagon. The "little" half-war in Vietnam directly or indirectly engaged the bulk of U.S. ground and tactical air forces, including units normally withheld in the United States as a strategic reserve;[3] of the 8,744,000

---

3. In 1968, at the height of the Vietnam War, some 10 of the U.S. Army's 19 divisions were deployed in Southeast Asia. Also deployed in the region were 9 of the Air Force's 28 tactical fighter wings. The Korean War of 1950–1953 engaged a total of 9 Army and Marine Corps divisions.

Americans who served on active duty at the time of the Vietnam War, a total of 3,403,000 served in Southeast Asia. Had the Soviet Union chosen to invade Europe in 1968, following its reoccupation of Czechoslovakia, the United States would have been in no position to provide pledged reinforcements for NATO's defense.

This mismatch between U.S. military aspirations and resources, however, was tolerable in the 1960s. The United States still enjoyed a pronounced nuclear superiority over the Soviet Union, dominated the world's oceans, and faced no potential adversary capable of mounting concurrent, decisive assaults on vital American interests in more than one region of the world.

Today's global geostrategic environment is much less favorable. During the past twenty years U.S. military power has sharply declined relative to that of the Soviet Union, which, alone, or in concert with its numerous client states, is now capable of sustaining major conflict on more than one front. America's nuclear superiority has vanished, as has its unchallenged control of the seas. The locus and character of the Soviet threat to the West, a West whose sources of energy are no longer assured, has moreover evolved far beyond that of a direct assault on Europe.

To make matters worse, the relative decline in American military power has been accompanied by an expansion in U.S. military obligations abroad. Following a decade of U.S. retrenchment in Asia heralded by the proclamation of the Nixon Doctrine in 1969 and reversion to a "one and one-half war" standard as the basis for U.S. conventional force planning, U.S. defense commitments overseas were dramatically reinflated in response to the Soviet invasion of Afghanistan and other events in Southwest Asia. The Carter Doctrine, proclaimed in January 1980, imposed on the U.S. military new and exceedingly demanding commitments in a logistically remote area of the world, commitments that remain unaccompanied by requisite expansion in U.S. force levels already overtaxed by traditional obligations in Europe and East Asia. The Rapid Deployment Force, the designated instrument of U.S. military intervention in Southwest Asia, is composed almost entirely of units already committed to the defense of Europe and Northeast Asia.

Reagan's Worldwide War Strategy

The Reagan Administration has inflated U.S. military aspirations still further, again without a commensurate expansion in U.S. military power. While endorsing the Carter Doctrine, the Administration has promulgated what amounts to a three and one-half war strategy. The aims of that strategy were spelled out by Secretary Weinberger in 1982:

Our long-term goal is to be able to meet the demands of a worldwide war, including concurrent reinforcement of Europe, deployment to Southwest Asia and the Pacific, and support for other areas. . . .
Given the Soviets' capability to launch simultaneous attacks in [Southwest Asia], NATO, and the Pacific, our long-range goal is to be capable of defending all theaters simultaneously.[4]

The origins and precepts of the Administration's worldwide war strategy were apparent in the attacks leveled by Reagan supporters against the Carter Administration's defense policies during the 1980 presidential election campaign. President Carter was condemned for having expanded U.S. military obligations overseas without appropriate increases in the defense budget.

The Carter Administration also was criticized for what many Reagan supporters believed was a virtually exclusive force planning focus on the defense of NATO's Central Front at the expense of preparation for combat elsewhere. This focus was censured on a number of grounds, including what many thought to be an implicit assumption that a "one war" with the Soviet Union in Europe would not spill over into other theaters of operations. Writing in 1980, Francis J. West, Jr., who later served in the Reagan Administration as Assistant Secretary of Defense for International Security Affairs, denounced the very concept of "one and one-half wars" as a basis for force planning:

It is currently assumed that the "one war" of the "one and a half war" strategy is limited to a battle on the Central Front and that the United States can prepare (allocate resources) for that war under the assumption that fighting will not spread to other theaters. NATO forces in the Center Region will be so strong that the Soviets will not have sufficient forces to divert to other theaters. Nor will the Soviets start a war except on the Central Front because, if they do, NATO has the escalation option of initiating conventional war in the Center Region. In such escalation, Soviet forces would be caught out of position and the resultant losses, including portions of Eastern Europe, would not, to the Soviets, be worth gains elsewhere. In other words, the essence of the "one and a half war" strategy . . . is that, if the center is strong, that strength will extend the deterrence of conflict to other regions where the military balance is even less favorable.

---

4. Caspar W. Weinberger, *Annual Report to the Congress, Fiscal Year 1983* (Washington, D.C.: U.S. Government Printing Office, 1982), p. III-91.

To assume the "one war" will be mutually restricted (by the United States and by the Soviet Union) to the Central Front of Europe is poor strategy and poorer history, given the course of prior world wars. The Central Front-only strategy is an assumption driven by undue budgetary pressures. To assume that NATO strength on the Central Front can extend deterrence to other theaters is to ignore a decade of trends. The United States, by 1979, had lost the credible threat of escalation dominance. So it was only proper and prudent to build NATO's conventional strength in the Center Region. It was not prudent to assume that this effort . . . spread an umbrella of deterrence over other areas. Soviet strength had grown too powerful for the United States to regain the 1969 balance of power. It has not been strategically sound to neglect NATO's flanks and to discount U.S. strengths outside NATO's land mass . . . as a means of offsetting some Soviet strengths and NATO weaknesses. In sum, the "one war" concept is restrictive in focus and outdated in its concept of extended deterrence.[5]

West's characterization of the Carter Administration's strategic outlook is far from accurate; no one in the Carter Administration ever suggested that a war with the Soviet Union would or could be confined to Europe, and the idea of NATO's starting a war in Europe has never been entertained by any administration. There is no doubt, however, that the Carter Administration did focus heavily on improving the defense of NATO Center, a focus which, in a fiscal environment of attempted austerity, did adversely affect preparation for possible conflict in the Third World and elsewhere outside the NATO Treaty area. There is moreover no question that some prominent Carter Administration officials were "traumatized" by the American experience in Vietnam, and regarded the entire Third World as little more than Vietnam writ large—a place devoid of vital U.S. interests and in which the application of U.S. military power could lead only to trouble.

Nor can it be denied that the central premise of the Reagan Administration's military strategy is that any shooting war with the Soviet Union, wherever it might start, is likely to spread quickly to other theaters of operations:

For many years, it has been U.S. policy to let the investment and planning for our conventional forces be determined primarily by the requirement for fighting a war centered in Europe, and in which NATO forces would be

---

5. Francis J. West, Jr., "Conventional Forces Beyond NATO," in W. Scott Thompson, ed., *National Security in the 1980s: From Weakness to Strength* (San Francisco: Institute for Contemporary Studies, 1980), pp. 324, 326–328.

attacked by the Warsaw Pact. This emphasis recognized that Soviet military forces were concentrated in Central Europe. Preoccupation with the need to be strong in the center led to the mistaken assumption that if the Alliance could meet this largest threat, it would meet lesser ones.[6]

. . . we must recognize that the Soviet Union has enough active forces and reserves to conduct simultaneous campaigns in more than one theater. As a result, we must understand that war could spread to other regions.[7]

A corollary assumption is that other nations hostile to the United States might seek to take advantage of the United States during such a conflict, opening up additional fronts beyond those engaging U.S. and Soviet forces. Secretary Lehman has argued, for example, that in a NATO–Warsaw Pact conflict, Cuban and Cuban-based Soviet forces would seek to interrupt the flow of U.S. reinforcements to Europe, many of which are slated for movement through the Caribbean. Libya, Vietnam, and North Korea also have been cited as potential troublemakers in a worldwide war with the Soviet Union.

In the Reagan Administration's view, the prospect of being confronted by multiple threats simultaneously means that U.S. conventional force planning must reject:

the mistaken argument as to whether we should prepare to fight "two wars," "one and a half wars," or some other such tally of wars. Such mechanistic assumptions neglect both the risks and the opportunities that we might confront. We may be forced to cope with Soviet aggression, or Soviet-backed aggression, on several fronts.[8]

The ambitious objectives of the Administration's worldwide war strategy are not confined simply to meeting the "demands of a worldwide war, including concurrent reinforcement of Europe, deployments to Southwest Asia and the Pacific, and support for other areas. . . ." They extend to that of being able to meet such demands for years, if necessary. Secretary Weinberger has been quite emphatic on this point:

Another fallacy in recent defense policy regarding conventional warfare has been the "short war" assumption—the notion that in planning our strat-

---

6. Weinberger, *Annual Report for Fiscal 1983*, p. I-14.

7. Caspar W. Weinberger, *Annual Report to the Congress, Fiscal Year 1984* (Washington, D.C.: U.S. Government Printing Office, 1983), p. 35.

8. Weinberger, *Annual Report for Fiscal 1983*, p. I-15.

egy and designing our forces we could rely on the assumption that a conventional war would be of short duration. Common sense and past experience tell us otherwise. I have therefore instituted changes in our defense policy to correct this fallacy.

It goes without saying that, should our policy to deter aggression fail and conventional conflict be forced upon us, the United States would bend every effort to win the war as quickly as possible. The two wars in which the United States has fought since the beginning of the nuclear era, however, were both of long duration. Unless we are so strong, or our enemy so weak that we could quickly achieve victory, we cannot count on a war ending within a few months.

. . . Deterrence would be weakened if the enemy were misled to believe that he could easily outlast us in a conventional war. In particular, for a vulnerable and vital region like Southwest Asia, a U.S. strategy that promised our adversaries a "short war" could be an invitation to aggression.[9]

In such a protracted, multi-front war, the United States moreover:

might choose not to restrict ourselves to meeting aggression on its own immediate front. We might decide to stretch our capabilities, to engage the enemy in many places, or to concentrate our forces and military assets in a few of the most critical arenas.

. . . A wartime strategy that confronts the enemy, were he to attack, with the risk of our counteroffensive against his vulnerable points strengthens deterrence. . . . Our counteroffensives should be directed at places where we can affect the outcome of the war. If it is to offset the enemy's attack, it should be launched against territory or assets that are of an importance to him comparable to the ones he is attacking.[10]

The worldwide war strategy's emphasis on counteroffensives against the Soviet Union's "vulnerable points" is exemplified by the Reagan Administration's plans for the U.S. Navy, which is to be expanded by a margin significantly greater than the other services. The Administration seeks a navy of 600 ships and 15 carrier battle groups, which it believes will "restore and maintain maritime superiority over the Soviets."[11] That superiority, however, will be restored and maintained not only through fleet expansion, but also through adoption of a more aggressive warfighting doctrine. As elaborated by Secretary Lehman, the U.S. Navy will seek to "prevail" *simultaneously* over "the combined military threat of our adversaries" in the Pacific, Indian,

---

9. Ibid., pp. I-16, I-17.
10. Ibid., p. I-16.
11. Ibid., p. II-12.

and Atlantic Oceans, including the Norwegian Sea.[12] The Soviet navy is not simply to be bottled up in the constrained waters through which it must pass to reach open ocean; it is to be destroyed at its source by means of U.S. carrier air strikes against ports and naval installations in the Soviet homeland. Never mind that so aggressive a naval doctrine requires bringing the carriers into waters infested with Soviet submarines and well within range of land-based Soviet air power dedicated to the destruction of the U.S. surface navy.

Is Reagan's Strategy Militarily Sound?

The Reagan Administration's worldwide war strategy may be analyzed from two distinct perspectives. First, is the strategy militarily sound? What kind of grade would it receive from Sun Tzu, Clausewitz, or Liddell Hart? Consider the following points.

—The strategy betrays little sense of priorities. The Soviets are to be simultaneously and forcefully engaged on several fronts on or along the Eurasian land mass. The defense of Europe is, of course, important, but in a worldwide war with the Soviet Union, Europe will be only one of several theaters of operations, and not necessarily the decisive one. Prospects for a conclusive counteroffensive in Europe are far less promising than in other regions of the world where the military balance is more favorable to the United States.

Needless to say, such a strategic outlook hardly comforts our NATO allies. It moreover reflects a failure to appreciate the singular strategic importance of Europe to the United States. No area outside North America is as vital to the security and the economic well-being of the United States. In a worldwide war, Soviet conquest of Europe would be the decisive event because it would eliminate America's sole strategically significant foothold on the Eurasian land mass and drive both China and remaining U.S. allies on or along the Eurasian periphery into obsequious accommodation with Moscow. While it is correct to argue that a strong defense of Europe does not necessarily "spread an umbrella of deterrence over other areas," it is dangerous to suggest that those other areas are equal to Europe in importance or that they could be successfully defended in the event of disaster in Europe. Whether

12. *Hearings on the Military Posture and H.R. 5968,* House Committee on Armed Services, 97th Congress, Second Session, 1982, pp. 561–562.

at the tactical, operational, or strategic level, collapse at the center almost invariably produces panic, defeat, or surrender along the flanks.

—The strategy invites a dispersion of limited resources in the presence of a larger, more compact adversary with internal lines of communication, thereby violating the fundamental principle of concentration. "He who attempts to defend too much," once remarked Frederick the Great, "defends nothing." It is one thing to argue the likelihood or even the inevitability of horizontal escalation of a war with the Soviet Union; it is quite another to presume that horizontal escalation would somehow work to the advantage of a defender compelled, as would be the United States with respect to hostilities on the Eurasian land mass, to operate along exterior lines of communication.

Historically, successful operations along exterior lines of communication have in almost every case required a substantial preponderance of force over that of an opponent enjoying interior lines of communication. Ulysses S. Grant's victorious campaign of 1864–1865 against Confederate forces relying on internal lines of communication was based on concurrent advances by Union armies enjoying a crushing local numerical superiority. The decisive instrument of that campaign was Sherman's army, which Grant often called "my spare army." In a worldwide conflict with the Soviet Union, neither the United States nor its allies is likely to have the luxury of a "spare army."

To be sure, the United States did prevail simultaneously on two independent fronts during World War II. It should be recalled, however, that it took four years and a level of defense expenditure that at one point approached 40 percent of the gross national product to achieve victory. As former Chairman of the Joint Chiefs of Staff General David C. Jones has observed, "We had the time and the geographic isolation to mobilize American industry,"[13] two commodities that are not likely to be available to the United States in a future conflict with the Soviet Union.

It should also be recalled that victory in Europe, the primary front, would have been impossible without the assistance of two other world powers, one of whose efforts alone accounted for the destruction of well over one-half of Germany's military forces. In the event of another global conflict, the vast

---

13. David C. Jones, "What's Wrong With Our Defense Establishment?", *The New York Times Magazine*, November 7, 1982, p. 70.

industrial and human resources of one of those powers—the Soviet Union—will be arrayed *against* the United States; and the relative military weight of the other—Great Britain—has dwindled drastically since 1945.

—The strategy seems to presume that the United States will have the initiative from the start—or shortly after the outbreak—of hostilities. While this might be true at sea, the presumption is fundamentally incompatible with the postulation of the Soviet Union as the aggressor. It also reflects inadequate appreciation of the degree to which a properly planned and conducted surprise attack can deprive a defender, even a more powerful defender (which NATO decidedly is not), of the initiative for weeks and even months. As the high commands of numerically superior French and British forces discovered in the German campaign of 1940 against France and the Low Countries, it is difficult to mount counteroffensives with ground and tactical air forces that have been encircled, overrun, or pushed into the sea.

—The strategy presumes that a worldwide war with the Soviet Union would or could be prolonged without nuclear weapons coming into play. In its focus on horizontal escalation the strategy tends to discount the threat of vertical escalation. To be sure, the history of violent conflict among states is littered with short wars that unexpectedly became protracted contests, World War I being perhaps the most prominent example in the present century. Short, operationally decisive conflicts have occurred, however, and with increasing frequency since the dawn of mechanized warfare: the German campaigns of 1939 against Poland and 1940 against Norway and France, the Arab–Israeli wars of 1956, 1967, and 1973, and the Falklands War of 1982 are reminders of how swiftly conclusive events can move on the modern battlefield.

More to the point, history records no instance of war—short or long—between two nuclear armed states. Would not the side that started losing in a massive conventional conflict be sorely tempted to employ nuclear weapons? Is this not the essence of NATO's own doctrine of nuclear first use? Even if nuclear weapons did not come into play, could the United States count on its NATO allies to stay the course in a protracted war with the Soviet Union, a war likely to lead to Europe's utter devastation? And could the United States, which continues to lack even the semblance of a large and rapidly mobilizable defense industrial base (notwithstanding much official rhetoric about the need for one), hold the line in Europe, Northeast Asia, and the Persian Gulf long enough to implement a World War II-style mobilization?

—The strategy presumes that there are Soviet assets beyond the boundaries of their own empire comparable in importance to the ones the Soviets would be attacking in Europe and elsewhere. This is simply not true. As a natural resource-rich and relatively self-sufficient industrial state that has pursued autarky for over six decades, the Soviet Union has no assets beyond the territory it controls today that are as essential to its survival as are, for example, Western Europe and Japan to the United States. Soviet force planners undoubtedly would be willing to trade Cuba for the Federal Republic of Germany, Libya for Norway, or Nicaragua for South Korea.

—The strategy of worldwide war, with its pronounced emphasis on restoration of "maritime superiority" and its naval doctrine calling for direct assaults on Soviet naval bases, encourages the fallacious conclusion that the outcome of the war at sea will be decisive in a global conflict with the Soviet Union. Sea power has always been an essential instrument of preserving vital U.S. security interests overseas, and the Reagan Administration's commitment to fleet expansion is to be heartily welcomed. Yet in a struggle for mastery of the Eurasian land mass it is the land battle—not the naval battle— that will be decisive in the end. As Robert W. Komer has trenchantly observed:

Even if all Soviet ships were swept from the high seas and all Soviet home and overseas naval bases put out of action, could this prevent the U.S.S.R. from . . . overrunning Europe and the Middle East oil fields, emasculating or cowing China, or mounting a land-based missile and air threat to nearby Japan which would dwarf Hitler's 1944 V-1 and V-2 threat to wartime England? Sweeping up the Soviet navy, nibbling at the U.S.S.R.'s maritime flanks, even dealing with Soviet surrogates like Cuba, South Yemen, Ethiopia and Vietnam would hardly suffice to prevent a great Eurasian heartland power like the U.S.S.R. from dominating our chief allies, any more than naval superiority was decisive in defeating Germany in two world wars.[14]

As for Secretary Lehman's warfighting doctrine, it is no less a recipe for the certain disablement or destruction of the very carrier battle groups for which he has long and effectively lobbied. To venture U.S. carrier battle groups close enough to the Soviet Union to launch air strikes on the Soviet navy's home ports is to venture into the jaws of defeat. The punishment to which those groups would be subjected has been graphically surmised by

---

14. Robert W. Komer, "Maritime Strategy vs. Coalition Defense," *Foreign Affairs*, Vol. 60, No. 5 (Summer 1982), pp. 1133–1134.

Admiral Stansfield Turner and Captain George Thibault, Chairman of the Department of Military Strategy at the National War College:

It is hard to believe that thoughtful military planners would actually do this. With modern reconnaissance techniques, such a major force would be detected long before it arrived within striking range of a Soviet base. The Soviets would have time to minimize their forces left in port or on airfields and to put the rest on full alert. By the time the carriers were within 1,600 miles of Soviet air bases, they would be within range of over 90 percent of the U.S.S.R.'s land-based bombers. Yet, the Soviet bases would still be over 1,000 miles beyond the range of carrier aircraft.

Traveling at 25 knots for those last 1,000 miles, the carrier force would be subject to Soviet air bombardment for nearly two days before it was close enough to strike Soviet bases. The force would also be subject to attack by submarines and surface ships with long-range missiles that would have been deployed along the route. In short, we would be fighting the Soviets on their turf at times and places of their choosing, well before we could assume the offensive.

At a point 400 to 500 miles from the Soviet bases, the carriers could finally launch an attack with whatever aircraft were left after two days of Soviet attacks. (Here one must also note the inexorable trend in the last few years to fewer attack aircraft on our carriers, as the need for defensive and support aircraft—such as early warning, antisubmarine and tankers—has increased.) Most Soviet ships and aircraft would have left their bases or airfields when they received warning of the approach of the carriers. Thus, if the carriers wanted to destroy them, the carriers would have to remain in that exposed position and continue attacking long enough to catch the ships and planes that come and go as they require repair, replenishment or refueling—a considerable period of time. Unless nuclear weapons were used, even the attacks on base and airfield facilities would have to be repeated as repairs were made. With the carrier task force in a forward position long enough to do the job correctly, the chance of losing part, if not all of it, would be high simply because the trends of technology give the attacker who employs the new stand-off weapons like Exocet a considerable advantage today.

The loss of three or four of the Navy's 12 to 13 carriers, in what would have to be a gamble to suppress the Soviet Navy in this manner, would be a major catastrophe. No President could possibly permit the Navy to attempt such a high risk effort. There simply would be inadequate fallback forces to handle other threats, especially to the North Atlantic sea lanes.[15]

---

15. Stansfield Turner and George Thibault, "Preparing for the Unexpected: The Need for a New Military Strategy," *Foreign Affairs*, Vol. 61, No. 1 (Fall 1982), pp. 126–127.

—The strategy reveals an insufficient appreciation of the likely forms of Soviet expansionism during the next two decades. To be sure, it would be imprudent, in the wake of the Soviet invasion of Afghanistan, to rule out prospects for further overt cross-border aggression by Soviet conventional forces. Direct aggression, however, has not been nor is likely to be the principal means of Soviet expansionism. The success that Moscow has long enjoyed with politically more subtle, indirect forms of aggression utilizing indigenous and imported surrogate forces suggests an avoidance, where possible, of the inherently greater risks associated with the direct employment of Soviet forces.

Do the Means Match the Ends?

Even were the worldwide war strategy militarily sound, however, there would remain the question that involves the very essence of any strategy— the relationship of ends and means. And it is from this analytical perspective that the strategy has most often and justifiably been condemned. Whatever may be said about the declared goals of the strategy, the stark reality is that the United States does not possess, nor will it in the future, conventional forces sufficient to fulfill those goals. As Senator Sam Nunn has noted, "[the Reagan Administration's] military strategy far exceeds our present and projected [military] resources,"[16] a judgment that is widely shared within the Pentagon. Testifying before the Senate Armed Services Committee in 1982, Under Secretary of Defense Fred Iklé stated flatly that:

Even an increase in U.S. military investments as high as 14% per year, continued throughout the decade, would not close the gap in accumulated military assets between the U.S. and Soviet Union until the early 1990s. That is a bleak outlook, implying either further deterioration in our security or a need for a defense increase considerably steeper than what the Administration now proposes.[17]

Earlier, then Army Chief of Staff Edward C. Meyer voiced his conclusion that "We are accepting tremendous risks with the size of forces that we have

---

16. Speech before the Georgetown Center for Strategic and International Studies, Washington, D.C., March 18, 1982.
17. Statement before the Senate Armed Services Committee, February 26, 1982, p. 3.

to do what we have pledged to do."[18] In their annual posture statement for fiscal year 1984 the Joint Chiefs conceded that:

With regard to these global responsibilities, U.S. forces are obviously not available to defend everywhere against every threat at all times. . . . Because our current forces are insufficient to take on all tasks simultaneously, general strategic priorities and the specific circumstances and forces available at the time will govern force employment.[19]

The magnitude of the mismatch between aspirations and resources is reflected in the huge disparity between extant and projected conventional force levels on the one hand, and those believed by the Joint Chiefs of Staff (JCS) necessary to provide reasonable assurance of fulfilling the objectives of the worldwide war strategy. In 1982 the JCS recommended conventional force levels that would have cost an estimated $750 billion more than the $1.6 trillion requested in the Administration's fiscal year 1982 five-year defense plan, which itself represented a major increase in U.S. defense expenditure over that of previous years.[20]

In 1983, during preparation of the fiscal year 1985–1989 Defense Guidance, the JCS recommended, again unsuccessfully, large increases in the numbers of active-duty ground force divisions, carrier battle groups, Air Force fighter wings, and long-range air transports.[21] Table I shows the differences between those forces on hand in 1983; forces planned for 1989; and forces recommended for 1989 by the JCS.

What is immediately striking is how little the Reagan Administration is actually buying in the way of additional conventional forces, notwithstanding its conscious inflation of U.S. conventional force obligations and success to date in obtaining significant real increases in defense expenditure. The Administration plans no increases in the number of active-duty Army and Marine Corps divisions, despite the fact that at least four additional Army divisions would be required to permit that service to fulfill its responsibilities in Southwest Asia without jeopardizing its ability to reinforce Europe as

---

18. Testimony before the Senate Armed Services Committee, February 2, 1982.
19. *United States Military Posture FY 1984* (Washington, D.C.: Department of Defense, 1983), p. 6.
20. George C. Wilson, "U.S. Defense Paper Cites Gap Between Rhetoric, Intentions," *The Washington Post*, May 27, 1982.
21. Richard Halloran, "New Weinberger Directive Refines Military Policy," *The New York Times*, March 22, 1983.

Table I. Proposed U.S. Conventional Force Level Increases, 1983–1989.

Category of Force	Forces on Hand 1983	Forces Planned by DoD for 1989	Forces Recommended by JCS for 1989
Active Army Divisions	16	16	23
Marine Amphibious Forces	3	3	4
Navy Carrier Battle Groups	13	15	24
Air Force Fighter Wings	24	27	44
Long-Range Air Transports	304	348	1,308

Source: Richard Halloran, "New Weinberger Directive Refines Military Policy," *The New York Times,* March 22, 1983.

planned.[22] The Air Force is to receive but three new tactical fighter wings, and less than 50 additional long-range air transports for a total of 348, despite the Pentagon's assessment that almost four times that many are needed to meet the acute strategic mobility requirements of a multi-front worldwide war. The Navy is to receive two more carrier battle groups for a total of 15, although Secretary Lehman's warfighting doctrine would require no fewer than 24 groups. Even the once-touted goal of a 600-ship navy now appears to be in jeopardy, what with the combination of spiraling unit costs and mounting Congressional opposition to sustaining annual real increases in the defense budget averaging 9.2 percent[23] in the face of massive federal deficits and high unemployment.

There is in fact no assurance that the Congress, which in 1983 slashed in half the 10.5 percent real defense spending increase requested by the Administration for fiscal year 1984, will fully fund any of the "modest" conventional force-level increases proposed in the Administration's five-year defense plan.

Even were the Congress to accede fully to the Administration's request, it is doubtful whether the five-year plan contains sufficient money to finance

22. See *Rapid Deployment Forces: Policy and Budgetary Implications* (Washington, D.C.: Congressional Budget Office, 1983). Also see Jeffrey Record, *The Rapid Deployment Force and U.S. Military Intervention in the Persian Gulf* (Washington, D.C.: Institute for Foreign Policy Analysis, 1981).
23. As requested in the proposed defense budget for fiscal years 1982–1986.

planned increases in U.S. conventional force levels. A 1982 analysis sponsored by the conservative Heritage Foundation concluded that unrealistic cost planning and force development decisions are not only endemic within the Defense Department but also will rob the Administration of much of the force increases anticipated under its five-year defense plan.[24]

No less questionable is whether the all-volunteer force could adequately man those force levels, especially in an environment of economic recovery that substantially reduced levels of unemployment. Even in such an environment, the all-volunteer force in the coming decade will still confront a continuing absolute and relative decline in the size of that segment of the American male population between the ages of 18 and 26.

In sum, the Reagan Administration's declared military strategy is not only militarily defective. It is also foolishly ambitious, betraying an unbridgeable abyss between aspirations and resources. Indeed, if strategy is the calculated relationship of ends and means, the strategy of worldwide war is not a strategy at all.

---

24. George W.S. Kuhn, "Ending Defense Stagnation," in Richard N. Holwill, ed., *Agenda '83* (Washington, D.C.: The Heritage Foundation, 1982), pp. 69–114.

Measuring the European Conventional Balance

Coping with Complexity in Threat Assessment

Barry R. Posen

$\mathbf{I}$f NATO is to invest its scarce resources wisely in the coming years, if it is to choose intelligently from the menu of possible conventional improvements,[1] it must begin with a careful assessment of the current NATO–Warsaw Pact military balance in Central Europe. Such assessments can only provide useful program guidance

This article is a substantially revised version of "Competing Views of the Center Region Conventional Balance," in Keith A. Dunn and William O. Staudenmaier, eds., *Alternative Military Strategies for the Future* (Boulder, Colo.: Westview Press, forthcoming). The author wishes to thank all of the friends and colleagues who provided comments on various drafts of this essay. He also wishes to thank the Council on Foreign Relations and the Rockefeller Foundation for their financial support. The author alone is responsible for the content of this essay.

Barry Posen is an Assistant Professor in the Department of Politics and the Woodrow Wilson School at Princeton University and the author of The Sources of Military Doctrine: France, Britain, and Germany between the World Wars *(Ithaca: Cornell University Press, 1984).*

1. The wide range of possible improvements may be loosely grouped into three categories: those of the "military reformers," who advocate a host of tactical, organizational, and hardware changes that would improve conventional capabilities without major spending increases; those of the NATO (and Pentagon) bureaucracy, which has made a battery of proposals (such as the Long Term Defense Plan) simply to buy a lot more of what we have been buying; and those of a group of technology-minded individuals who advocate investments in "new" technologies (usually called "emerging technologies" or "E.T."). For a critical discussion of the possible tactical implications of the military reformers' prescriptions for ground warfare, see John J. Mearsheimer, "Maneuver, Mobile Defense, and the NATO Central Front," *International Security*, Vol. 6, No. 3 (Winter 1981/82), pp. 104–122. For the best example of how the reformers' ideas have crept into official U.S. Army doctrine, see U.S. Army, *FM 100-5, Operations* (August 20, 1982). The reformers are also keenly concerned about weapons design. Their principal criticism of current U.S. weapons design philosophy is that it strives for technological parameters that are too far removed from the actual circumstances of *both* peacetime and wartime military practice. For a useful reform perspective on the technology of ground warfare, see Steven Canby, *The Alliance and Europe: Part IV, Military Doctrine and Technology*, Adelphi Paper No. 109 (London: International Institute for Strategic Studies, 1974/75), pp. 34–41. On aerial technology, see Jack N. Merritt and Pierre M. Sprey, "Negative Marginal Returns in Weapons Acquisition," in Richard G. Head and Ervin J. Rokke, eds., *American Defense Policy*, 3rd ed. (Baltimore: Johns Hopkins University Press, 1973), pp. 486–495. On the Long Term Defense Plan, see Harold Brown, *Annual Report of the Department of Defense, Fiscal Year 1981* (Washington, D.C.: U.S. Government Printing Office, 1980), pp. 47–49, 215. For arguments in favor of "emerging technologies," see *Strengthening Conventional Deterrence in Europe*, Report of the European Security Study (New York: St. Martin's Press, 1983).

International Security, Winter 1984/85 (Vol. 9, No. 3) 0162-2889/84/030047-42 $02.50/1
© Barry R. Posen.

if they focus on the most dangerous threats faced by the Alliance, and capture as fully as possible the efforts NATO has already made to deal with those threats. Most assessments, unfortunately, are too simplistic, relying heavily on simple "bean counts" and failing to take adequate account of the many other variables involved. This analysis will explain what some of these other variables are and how they may be combined into a model that will provide a more realistic balance assessment and a basis for evaluating possible improvements.

The Problem

The distinctive characteristic of military competition in Central Europe is the large concentration of mechanized ground forces on both sides, supported by substantial numbers of attack helicopters and fighter aircraft. Most assessments give the Warsaw Pact credit for quantitative superiority in these assets. These are the same kinds of forces that are associated with the major blitzkrieg operations of the last half-century: the German invasions of Poland, France, and the Soviet Union in World War II; the Israeli victory over the Arabs in 1967; and the Israeli counterattack across the Suez Canal in 1973. Western scholars and political leaders have tended to fixate on the powerful offensive potential of Soviet armored forces, thus creating fears that a convential war in Europe could end in a quick NATO defeat. If the Soviets believe that they can achieve victory with conventional forces alone, then overall deterrence of Soviet aggression is surely undermined. As John Mearsheimer has pointed out, in the world of *conventional* deterrence, it is confidence in quick, cheap victory that causes the aggressor to attack.[2] In NATO's case, Soviet confidence in a speedy conventional victory may also undermine the deterrent effect of the Alliance's nuclear weapons, providing hope to the Pact that NATO could be overrun before a decision to use nuclear weapons were taken.

In spite of the prevailing fears and perceptions, however, not all of the military history of the last fifty years confirms the hypothesis that armored forces enhance the offense's chances of success. Individual battles such as Kursk and the Bulge in the Second World War and the Israeli defense of the Golan Heights in 1973 all suggest that armored assaults can be stopped—

---

2. John J. Mearsheimer, *Conventional Deterrence* (Ithaca: Cornell University Press, 1983), pp. 23–66.

that mechanized *defenders* can also turn in impressive performances. Indeed, the German army's overall performance during the second half of World War II, when it was substantially outnumbered, is testimony to the defensive potential of even *partially* mechanized forces.

A survey of the history of armored warfare also suggests that the place to begin any assessment of the current NATO–Warsaw Pact military balance is the so-called "breakthrough" battle. Armored attackers customarily have concentrated their best resources on narrow sectors of their enemy's front, hoping to achieve a degree of quantitative superiority that could cause a major rupture in the defense line. Such ruptures permit the deep exploitations associated with the classical German, and Israeli, practice of blitzkrieg, and the encirclements associated with German and Soviet operations on the Eastern Front during World War II. This essay, however, does not deal explicitly with the exploitation phase, but focuses on NATO's initial capability to keep it from arising.[3]

Most analyses of warfare in the Central Region of Europe correctly assume a front of roughly 750 kilometers (km) and further assume that the Soviets will attempt to break through in a small number of areas where the terrain and the road net are particularly suitable for armored warfare. The map of the Central Region in Figure 1 shows the four most attractive breakthrough sectors. Most analysts agree that the Pact will mount at least one major attack in the North German plain, considered to be the best corridor. One will almost surely be launched in the Fulda Gap, if only to tie down the powerful U.S. V Corps. The Göttingen corridor running through the German III Corps sector just north of the Fulda Gap is somewhat more attractive as a third choice than the Hof corridor. Each of these corridors is roughly 50 km wide.

In spite of the often cited Soviet numerical superiority in Europe, most analyses of potential Soviet attacks expect that the Pact will have to concentrate its efforts on these three or four rather well-defined breakthrough sectors since the Pact's quantitative advantage over NATO is not great enough to permit it to greatly outnumber Western forces everywhere. Thus, the successful breakthrough battle is the key to a quick Pact victory, and thwarting Pact breakthrough efforts becomes NATO's primary conventional

---

3. If breakthroughs do occur, operational reserves are necessary to combat the adversary's exploitation or encirclement efforts. NATO should, therefore, maintain sufficient "operational reserves" to counterattack in the event that the adversary manages to achieve a clean breakthrough.

Figure 1. Most Likely Axes of Advance in a Warsaw Pact Attack Against NATO

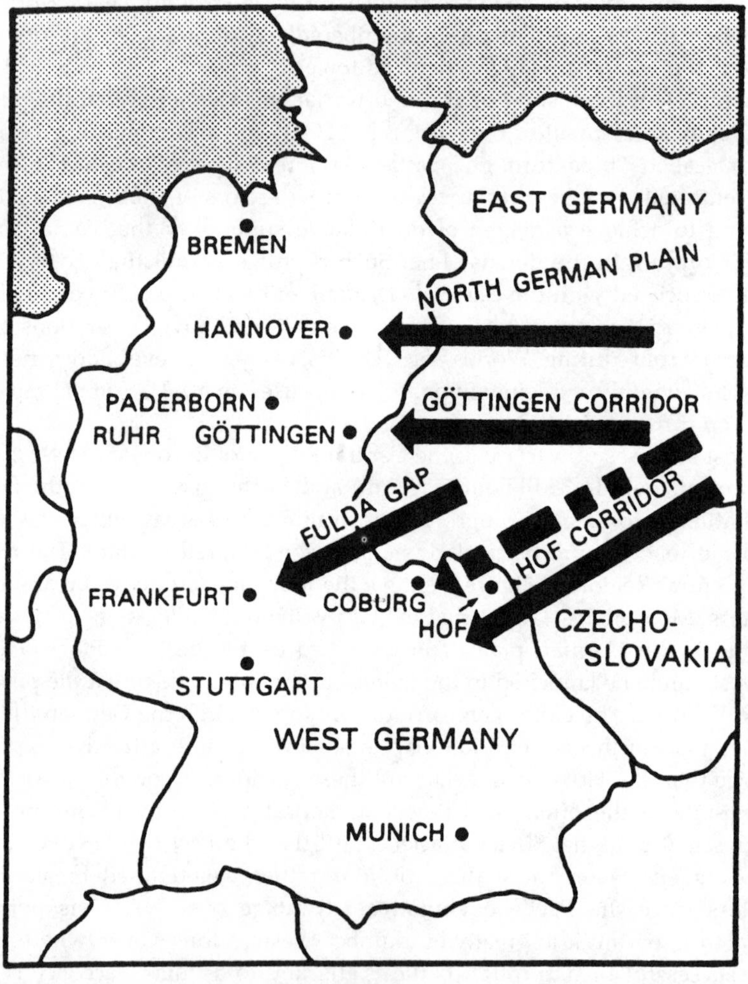

SOURCE: John J. Mearsheimer, "Why the Soviets Can't Win Quickly in Central Europe," *International Security*, vol. 7, no. 1 (Summer 1982), p. 21.

military task. If NATO can achieve this in war, it may ultimately be able to mobilize its superior economic power against the Pact. If the Soviet Union can be made to believe in peacetime that NATO has this capability, then overall deterrence is enhanced. This analysis, therefore, concentrates upon the relative ability of NATO and the Warsaw Pact to cope with the demands imposed by multiple breakthrough battles.

NATO vs. Pact Doctrine

How does the breakthrough battle figure in each side's general war plans? Every military organization, explicitly or implicitly, has a theory of victory, a notion of the combination of human and material resources and tactics that it believes is most likely to produce success on the battlefield. This theory of victory is the organization's military doctrine.

The Warsaw Pact's and NATO's military doctrines, which determine how each alliance builds and organizes its military forces, are quite different from each other. At the most *general* level, the Pact prefers large numbers of major weapons and formations (often called "tooth") over training, the experience of military personnel, logistics, and the command, control, communications, and intelligence (C^3I) functions broadly defined. (Logistics and C^3I are often referred to as "tail.") Additionally, it prefers ground forces to tactical aviation, although the Soviet Union does have substantial tactical air capability. NATO, on the other hand, prefers a more balanced mix of tooth and tail, shows greater interest in the training and experience of its personnel, and places greater emphasis on tactical airpower.

In terms of military operations, Pact doctrine tends to extol the advantages of the offense. This is fairly explicit in Soviet military writings. On the other hand, partly as a function of the Alliance's political orientation but also because of the lessons it has drawn from the school of military experience, NATO tends towards a more balanced view of the relative advantages of defensive and offensive tactics. This view is more implicit than explicit in NATO doctrine, which as a whole tends to be less formal than that of the Pact. Particularly at the level of the small unit engagement, Western military thinkers have long held that the defense has a substantial advantage—one that can be turned into an overall strategic defensive advantage through careful planning and the skillful conduct of military operations.[4]

---

4. On the defender's tactical advantage, see John J. Mearsheimer, "Why the Soviets Can't Win Quickly in Central Europe," *International Security*, Vol. 7, No. 1 (Summer 1982), pp. 15–20, especially footnote 30. The now superseded July 1976 version of the U.S. Army's basic field manual, *FM 100-5, Operations*, included some explicit statements on the extent of numerical inferiority that the defender could accept and still expect to hold successfully. In describing the tasks of a defending general, it asserts, "As a rule of thumb, they should seek not to be

The net result of these differences is that the Warsaw Pact generates military forces that, at least at first glance, look substantially more formidable than those of NATO. Although official comparisons of NATO and Warsaw Pact defense spending have consistently shown NATO outspending the Pact by varying degrees ($360 billion vs. $320 billion in 1982 according to a recent Department of Defense estimate[5]), the tendency in both official and unofficial balance assessments has been to highlight Pact advantages in tanks, guns, planes, or divisions. The possibility that NATO's higher spending might be generating less visible, but equally important, elements of military capability seldom receives much consideration. Instead, NATO's superiority in the spending comparisons and apparent equality or near-equality in manpower[6] are ignored, or explained away with relatively cursory arguments.[7]

---

outweighed more than 3:1 in terms of combat power. With very heavy air and field artillery support on favorable terrain, it may be possible to defend at a numerical disadvantage of something like 5:1 for short periods of time" (p. 5-3). Somewhat ambiguously, these ratios are said to apply "at the point and time of decision" (p. 3-5). The document also holds that on the offense, U.S. generals should strive for "concentrated combat power of about 6:1 superiority" (p. 3-5). In general, then, the Field Manual seems to hold that defenders can fight successfully if outnumbered 3:1, and may be able to do so if outnumbered as much as 5:1. The new version of the Field Manual is silent on these numerical ratios. It does, however, seem to imply that, given certain tactical advantages held by the defender, the attacker must muster numerical superiority at a small number of times and places of his choosing. See *FM 100-5* (1982), pp. 8-5, 8-6, 10-3, 10-4.

5. U.S. Department of Defense, *The FY 1984 DOD Program for Research, Development and Acquisitions*, Statement by the Honorable Richard DeLauer, Undersecretary of Defense for Research and Engineering, 98th Congress, 1st session (March 2, 1983), p. I-7.

6. International Institute for Strategic Studies, *The Military Balance 1983–84* (London: IISS, 1983), pp. 125–126. According to the IISS counting rules employed in the preceding editions, the Warsaw Pact fields 4.7 million men to NATO's 5.4 million. In 1983, IISS credits the Soviet Union with an additional 1.5 million men, bringing the Pact total to 6.2 million. The manpower ratio is thus either 1.15:1 in the Pact's favor, or 1.15:1 in NATO's favor. Unfortunately, IISS offers no explanation for why it has changed its counting rules.

7. Richard DeLauer argues that the Soviet Union somehow has a lower cost of doing business than the United States or NATO. This argument is almost certainly based on the Central Intelligence Agency (CIA) dollar model which prices Soviet activities at the rate that it would cost the United States to accomplish them in exactly the same way that the Soviets do. Pact manpower is largely valued according to U.S. wages and maintenance costs for individuals of equal rank and experience. If Soviet manpower costs in dollars appear lower than NATO's, it should be a function of the relatively smaller professional non-commissioned officer and officer cadre in the mass conscription Pact militaries, not of greater Soviet efficiency. Moreover, what is publicly known about Soviet maintenance practices, for instance, suggests that they are less efficient than those of the West. When priced according to the dollar model, these inefficiencies emerge as a higher cost of doing business, making the Pact effort appear to be greater than it would if it allocated its resources more efficiently. See DoD, *The FY 1984 DOD Program for Research, Development and Acquisitions*, pp. 1–9. On the CIA methodology, see Central Intelligence Agency, National Foreign Assessment Center, *Soviet and US Defense Activities, 1970–79: A Dollar Cost Comparison* (Washington, D.C.: Central Intelligence Agency, 1980).

Although the investment (i.e., major procurement) spending of NATO compared to the Pact

In effect, then, NATO tends to buy military forces according to its own theory of victory, its own military doctrine. Analysts, however, have tended to assess the military balance according to a different—the Soviet—theory of victory. Adopting Soviet criteria for measuring the balance will always make the West look bad in comparison to the Pact, short of very substantial increases in NATO defense spending and manpower, because NATO organizes and procures its forces according to quite different criteria. Indeed, if NATO were to try to build a military force that would redress the imbalance portrayed by its current assessments, yet build that force according to its own military doctrine, it would have to increase its spending lead over the Pact still further, and probably keep even more men under arms. The fact that the Reagan Administration's substantial increases in defense spending have done very little, and will do very little, to change the numbers of tanks, guns, and planes in military units that have provided the basis for so many pessimistic assessments of the balance in Europe supports this judgment.

NATO's political and military leaders consistently have allocated scarce economic and demographic resources according to a particular military doctrine. In spite of assaults by dedicated military reformers, this pattern of resource allocation continues.[8] The only conclusion that can be drawn from

---

is only somewhat lower (roughly 113 to 135 billion dollars in 1981), the argument is often advanced that NATO's procurement spending is less efficient than the Pact's. Caspar W. Weinberger, *Annual Report of the Department of Defense, Fiscal Year 1984* (Washington, D.C.: U.S. Government Printing Office, 1983), pp. 21–23. (I have crudely estimated Japan's investment spending and subtracted it from the "NATO plus Japan" figure offered by Weinberger.) These Pact investment figures are probably a little high, as the CIA recently concluded that its previous estimates in this area were wrong, and that Soviet procurement spending did not grow very much from 1976 to 1984. See "Soviets Seen Slowing Pace of Arming," *The Washington Post,* November 20, 1983, p. A-14. The efficiency argument has an element of plausibility, since more Pact production is concentrated in big Soviet plants than NATO production is in any plants. Still, more than a sentence is required. The Pact, indeed the Soviet Union itself, tends to produce several different types of the same weapon simultaneously. For instance, somewhere in the Pact, three or four medium tanks (T-55, 62, 64, and 72) have been in production over the last several years. Moreover, the Pact seems to have as much difficulty as NATO does in writing off unsuccessful weapons. The SU-7 and 9 fighters have never seemed particularly impressive, for instance. Finally, it has long been believed that the Soviet Union is less efficient than the West in most areas of industrial production. Why should the advantages of scale economies totally wipe out the West's historical advantages in managerial skills and production efficiency? If arguments to the effect that NATO's spending superiority is virtually irrelevant to the military balance, indeed that it produces a net military inferiority of substantial proportions, are to be taken seriously, then proponents must make their arguments more thoroughly than they have.

8. Canby, *The Alliance and Europe,* pp. 15–41, offers the clearest critique. Recent events illustrate that not much has actually changed. In the mid-1970s, Senator Sam Nunn of Georgia succeeded in getting the Seventh Army in Europe to trade off some support for combat assets—creating two new combat brigades in Europe. Since then, the U.S. Army has effectively reversed the Senator's reforms. The "Division '86" reorganization has reduced the number of maneuver

this situation is that NATO planners believe that their theory of military outcomes is correct. It may be prudent planning to ask what *could* happen if most of NATO's fundamental decisions about the allocation of its military resources proved to be wrong, and to buy some insurance against this possibility. Absent *convincing* arguments that *most* of NATO's military decisions have been wrong (and I believe that the arguments that have been made fall well short of this standard), these "worst-case" analytical exercises should never stand alone. Rather, they should accompany analyses that capture the expected positive military impact of the fundamental doctrinal assumptions that guide NATO's defense decisions. If they do not, they portray such pessimistic outcomes of a NATO–Pact conflict that they make improvements in conventional capabilities seem pointless, and, if believed by NATO's adversaries, may undermine the conventional component of its deterrent posture. Therefore, estimating the consequences for NATO if its current military doctrine is correct is as important to a comprehensive assessment of the military balance as assessments that assume the superiority of Pact doctrine. Moreover, by disaggregating NATO's relatively inexplicit military doctrine into subcomponents directly related to military outcomes, critical attention can be better focused upon them. Such attention will permit clearer thinking about the adequacy of NATO's current doctrine and may reveal that some aspects seem less plausible than others.

Factors in Thorough Balance Assessment

Public discussion of the conventional balance in Europe often focuses on simple force comparisons that fail to include factors that will be vital to the outcome of any real battle. The Secretary of Defense's current Annual Report, for example, asserts that: "Measures of total combat potential, which take into account both numbers and quality of weapons, show that Warsaw Pact forces in the Central Region of Europe have improved by more than 90% from 1965 to the present, while NATO forces advanced by less than 40%. . . . Overall, the shift in the conventional balance has posed new challenges

---

battalions in the European-based divisions from eleven or twelve each, down to ten. Recently, the Army has announced its intention to disband one of the independent brigades based in Europe. The net loss is at least seven maneuver battalions, more than the six battalions contained in the Nunn brigades. Meanwhile, total Army manpower in Germany has risen by nearly 20,000 men.

to our ability to offset the Soviets' quantitative superiority with our qualitative superiority, and has raised serious questions about our ability to halt a Soviet advance."[9] Such simplistic analysis represents only the beginning of a complete threat assessment. At least six other variables must be taken into account before we arrive at a reasonable appraisal of relative battlefield capabilities. Analyses that exclude these factors are incomplete and unrevealing, and provide no meaningful basis for NATO planning. These variables are:

1) RELATIVE MILITARY CAPABILITIES OVER TIME. At what rate can both sides move military forces into the battle area along the inter-German and Czech–West German border? What is the likely combat capability of these forces when training, maintenance, command and control, leadership, and quantity and quality of weaponry are taken into account?

2) THE EFFECT OF TACTICAL AIR FORCES ON THE GROUND BATTLE. Many public assessments of the balance simply leave out "tacair,"[10] and official assessments often give each side equal credit for tactical air effectiveness. In either case, possible advantages that NATO might hold in this area are unaccounted for.

3) FORCE-TO-SPACE (AND HENCE FORCE-TO-FORCE) RATIOS. Implicitly, or explicitly, the adversary is often given credit for an ability not only to close his many divisions to the battle area quickly, but to actually concentrate them on small segments of the front to achieve the very high local offense-to-defense force ratios that could produce breakthroughs. Yet, historically, armies have found that there is a limit to how much force can be concentrated in a given space. If NATO can achieve some level of density of its ground forces across the front, then it should be difficult for the Pact, even with more forces overall, to achieve very high ratios in selected breakthrough sectors.

4) ATTRITION RATES. At what "pace" or "level of violence" will the battle proceed? What kinds of casualties is the adversary willing to take? Does "friction" place some limits on the pace at which the battle can be forced? Historically, short periods of very intense combat can be identified in which

9. Caspar W. Weinberger, *Annual Report of the Department of Defense, Fiscal Year 1985* (Washington, D.C.: U.S. Government Printing Office, 1984), p. 24.
10. See, for example, Pat Hillier and Nora Slatkin, *US Ground Forces: Design and Cost Alternatives for NATO and Non-NATO Contingencies* (Washington, D.C.: Congressional Budget Office, 1980), pp. 25–26.

one side or both suffered 10 percent or worse attrition to armored fighting vehicles per day. On the other hand, rarely are battles of this intensity sustained for more than a few days.

5) EXCHANGE RATES. How many destroyed armored fighting vehicles must NATO suffer in order to kill a Pact vehicle? Given the Pact superiority in numbers of major weapons, NATO must achieve favorable exchange rates in order to defeat the Pact. If the exchange rate is not in the 2:1 range in NATO's favor, then the Alliance could find itself in trouble. Favorable exchange rates are not uncommon for defenders fighting on their own ground, particularly if that ground has been prepared with field fortifications, obstacles, and mines. Indeed, an often quoted rule of thumb suggests that the defender can hold at an engaged force ratio of 3:1 in favor of the offense. This would be consistent with a 3:1 exchange rate.

6) ADVANCE RATES. There is a tendency to assign fairly fast advance rates to Pact forces, several tens of kilometers per day in some cases. Some of this tendency can be attributed to Soviet military literature, which *calls for* very high advance rates. There has also been a tendency to simply assume that the high advance rates characteristic of armored warfare's headier historical successes would be replicated by the Soviets. Finally, crediting the Pact with very large forces and very high force ratios in breakthrough sectors tends to produce relatively fast forward movement according to some widely employed dynamic analytical techniques, such as the Lanchester square laws. On the other hand, even with armor pitted against armor, and often with high force ratios, modern mechanized armies have frequently found forward movement against determined defenders to be very difficult.

These six variables can be combined into a model that provides a more realistic approach to comparing forces, for it will include quantitative and other factors in precisely the way the one-dimensional comparisons do not. One such model, known as the "Attrition–FEBA Expansion Model," provides the framework for the subsequent analysis.[11]

This model (a noncomputerized analytical framework) assumes that, at the outset of war, NATO populates the front evenly and tries to hold what forces it can in reserve. The Pact similarly populates the less important sectors of

---

11. The Attrition–FEBA Expansion Model illustrates the stresses imposed on Pact and NATO forces depending on the values assigned to these six variables. FEBA is an acronym for "Forward Edge of the Battle Area." I am deeply indebted to Dr. Richard Kugler, who devised this model, for explaining it to me. The uses to which it has been put in this essay are my responsibility alone.

the front, but concentrates to the extent that it can in the three breakthrough sectors. Also, it is assumed that, as the Pact's breakthrough effort begins to move in NATO's direction, each side tries to move forces into the flanks of the penetrating salient at a density equal to that achieved on the nonbreak-through parts of the front (see Figure 2).

The model tests the adequacy of each side's forces to meet the demands of these multiple breakthrough battles. Once some assumptions are made about attrition, exchange rates, the role of "tacair," movement rates, and force-to-space ratios, a curve can be generated that shows each side's military requirements starting out with the first day of the war, then rising with the accumulated consequences of daily attrition and the need to populate a FEBA that expands as a function of the forward movement of the breakthrough salients. This requirements curve for each side can be compared to each side's mobilization curve to test the adequacy of its forces. At some point, if the defending forces are inadequate to fulfill their requirements, the defense finds itself having to defend with an ever-shrinking force-to-space ratio—that is, fewer and fewer defensive forces are available to hold the line. The

Figure 2. Simple Model of a Warsaw Pact Breakthrough Effort

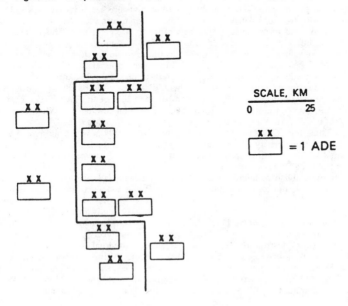

consequence is that the attacker can muster the large local force ratios in his favor that could produce a clean breakthrough. If the defender has not already ordered a general withdrawal to "shorten the front," he may soon suffer a catastrophic rupture of the line, followed by a classical armored exploitation. Since the defender's reserves have been exhausted by the requirement of defending an expanded FEBA, he is not in a position to combat the exploitation. The offense, on the other hand, may find his breakthrough effort stalling as a function of insufficient reserves to sustain high intensity combat at the front of his penetrating salients or to defend the flanks of those salients from the defender's likely counterattacks.[12]

---

12. The Attrition–FEBA Expansion Model uses Armored Division Equivalents (ADEs) as the common basic unit for comparison: "The ADE is a relative measure of effectiveness of ground forces based on quantity and quality of major weapons. This measure—which is widely used within DOD for ground force comparisons—is an improvement over simple counts of combat units and weapons; however, it does not take into account such factors as ammunition availability, logistical support, training, communications, and morale." Caspar W. Weinberger, *Report on Allied Contributions to the Common Defense* (Washington, D.C.: U.S. Government Printing Office, 1983), p. 36. The ADE scoring system used in this essay is summarized in Mako, *U.S. Ground Forces*, Appendix A, pp. 105–125. For example, a U.S. armored division based in Germany is worth nearly 1.1 ADEs, an average German armored division .72 ADEs, and a Soviet armored division in East Germany .9 ADEs. In terms of real divisions, roughly 110 Soviet and East European formations are included in Figures 3, 4, and 6. Independent regiments, brigades, and divisions equivalent to nearly 50 U.S. or West German divisions are included for NATO. NATO's forces look a little stronger relative to the Pact when forces are measured in ADEs than when selected weapons categories, such as numbers of tanks, are compared. This is because NATO tends to buy a different mix of weapons than the Pact, weapons that receive less attention in public comparisons. It is also worth noting that infantry soldiers do not contribute much to a formation's ADE score. Yet, NATO armies "buy" proportionately more infantry than Pact armies. Infantry soldiers are expensive for Western armies, where manpower is often scarce. Thus, the NATO choice to invest in this area would seem to reflect a different judgment about the importance of infantry to mechanized combat than that of the Pact. This difference may simply be a function of tradition, but it may also reflect a tactical insight. Whatever the reason, much of NATO's combat manpower is not contributing as much to the ADE score as the Pact's manpower. Thus, the ADE system may still fail to capture fully NATO's alternative view of the appropriate mix of weaponry for mechanized formations. See Mako, *U.S. Ground Forces*, p. 37, for an estimate of the length of front an ADE should be able to cover with confidence.

The "Force Needs" curves are derived as follows. In Figure 3, NATO needs one ADE per 25 km of front to establish a defensive line. The Pact needs one ADE per 25 km to tie down NATO's forces in the nonbreakthrough sectors. The Pact manages to concentrate two ADEs per 25 km in each of three 50-km breakthrough sectors for a total of twelve ADEs involved in breakthrough operations. Thus, for 750 km of front, NATO needs thirty ADEs to start; the Pact needs thirty-six to start. If twelve Pact ADEs on breakthrough sectors are willing to accept 10 percent attrition per day, they lose 1.2 ADEs. If the Pact-to-NATO exchange rate is 1.5:1, NATO loses .8 of an ADE to destroy the Pact forces. To generate the total demand for additional forces imposed by the day's action, the forces needed to populate the "expanding FEBA" must be calculated. Here, it is assumed that the Pact manages to advance 5 km per day, producing 30 km of additional FEBA (i.e., two flanks, 5 km long, for each of three penetrations). Both NATO and the Pact need another 1.2 ADEs to populate the flanks of the penetrating sectors. Thus,

This model of hypothetical military confrontation in Central Europe will be used to illustrate the sensitivity of the outcome of such a battle to assumptions that are either consistent with the caricature of Soviet doctrine often used for balance assessments (referred to here as the "Soviet" doctrine) or with the very different military doctrine that appears to guide the way NATO builds its forces (referred to here as the "NATO" doctrine). This model highlights the interrelated effects of several aspects of combat between NATO and the Pact about which there is substantial uncertainty. If we resolve all these uncertainties in favor of the Pact's military doctrine, we can produce the pessimistic portrayal of the outcome of a conventional clash in Europe that has been common over the last decade. On the other hand, if we resolve these uncertainties in favor of NATO's military doctrine, the Alliance appears to be capable of preventing a successful Pact breakthrough.

Limitations of Model-Building

Before turning to an analysis of what we learn about the NATO–Warsaw Pact balance by employing the "Attrition–FEBA Expansion" model, it is necessary to note the limitations of this or any model that attempts to approximate the vast and unpredictable complexities of the battlefield.

First, like all models, this one does not generate predictions for the outcome of a war in the Central Region. There are simply too many uncertainties for any model to capture, certainly too many for a model to capture with high confidence. This model illustrates the adequacy of forces of a given capability to cope with particular sets of military demands. The values assigned to the six variables discussed above determine the demands imposed and the amount of capability present to deal with those demands. Thus, the model does not portray a particular battlefield outcome in terms of forces destroyed or territory lost. Rather, it says, "Depending on how well the adversary performs in combat in the likely breakthrough sectors, NATO should or

---

the Pact's total additional force requirement after a day of combat is 2.4 ADEs. NATO's is 2 ADEs. Each side's demand for forces rises at this constant daily rate, producing the slope of the "Force Needs" curves. This same basic procedure is applied in Figure 4. Aside from changing the attrition, exchange, and movement rates, the major change is the factoring in of armored vehicles killed by "tacair." NATO's estimated average daily number of "tacair" armored vehicle kills is converted to an ADE score and subtracted from the total daily attrition that the Pact is willing to accept. NATO must pay to kill the rest of the Pact's ground force loss for the day in the coin of its own ground forces. The damage done by Pact "tacair" is added to this attrition to arrive at NATO's daily loss rate.

should not be able to forestall a catastrophic rupture of its defense line with or without a major withdrawal across the front."

Several additional caveats are in order. The model is a substantial abstraction from reality. Breakthrough sectors are not exactly 50 km wide; attrition does not occur at a steady rate; the offense does not move forward at a steady rate; all offensive efforts are not equally successful, or necessarily successful at all. Moreover, in real combat, divisions do not "fight to the finish" as assumed here; rather, they fight until they are down to 50–70 percent of their initial strength and then they are pulled out of the line for rest and refitting. Additionally, not all the attrition is taken in breakthrough sectors; some occurs on "quiet" sectors of the front. Finally, this model does not make any complicated tactical assumptions. As any student of armored warfare knows, defenders and attackers do not merely attempt to populate the flanks of penetrations. Rather, the defender tries to counterattack into the flanks of the penetration to pinch it off, while the attacker tries to widen the hole in the enemy line.

The model also does not deal well with the fluid warfare that would probably characterize a Pact attack after only a few days of mobilization, one that would likely catch most NATO forces before they were able to form a coherent defense line—in other words, a surprise attack. Such an attack would pit about three dozen Soviet and East German divisions against various U.S., West German, French, and other NATO forces, equivalent in strength to roughly two dozen U.S. mechanized divisions. This fighting would, at least initially, take the form of mobile warfare, in which NATO's small, ready, forward-deployed, covering forces (equivalent to a few armored brigades), supported by some portion of NATO's tactical aircraft, would fight a running battle of delay to enable the rest of NATO's standing forces to form a rough defense line several tens of kilometers back from the inter-German border. The model would only become useful as an analytical tool if and when such a line were established. NATO's forces might also try to mount some quick, sizable counterattacks during this covering force battle, in order to exploit some of the coordination and logistics problems that would surely attend the Pact's efforts to mount an attack with such little preparation time.[13]

---

13. While it is true that, if Polish and Czech Category I divisions joined the Soviet and East German attack, the Pact could outnumber NATO in firepower assets (ADEs) by as much as 2:1, both sides would experience problems getting into action with only a few days of mobilization.

Assigning Values in the Attrition–FEBA Expansion Model

These caveats aside, the Attrition–FEBA Expansion Model illustrates the effects of various assumptions about NATO–Warsaw Pact military capabilities and the course of combat on NATO's ability to forestall a Pact breakthrough. But how are we to assign specific values to the variables captured by the model? In principle, one could assign values based upon a historical survey of many battles; or upon an intensive examination of a few battles that one believes to be sufficiently similar to a NATO–Warsaw Pact clash to be instructive; or upon the application of dynamic models; or upon the use of military rules of thumb or planning factors. To some extent, the analysis presented here relies upon all of these methods.

The values of the variables that place demands on the forces—buildup rates, tactical air power, force-to-space ratios, attrition rates, exchange rates, and advance rates—can be set by the user as he or she sees fit. The only

---

To assess relative performance under these circumstances, a thorough comparative assessment of the peacetime readiness for combat of each side's ground and tactical air forces is essential, as well as an assessment of how many days would be required for each to overcome its deficiencies. The circumstantial evidence is that NATO's standing forces are substantially readier for combat than those of the Pact, but data available in the public domain do not permit a high-confidence judgment.

Several pieces of evidence are suggestive, however. Since NATO outspends the Pact, but the Pact "out-invests" NATO, it follows that NATO outspends the Pact on people, operations, training, maintenance, and the like. In 1981, NATO roughly outspent the Pact by 35 percent in these areas, using the CIA dollar model (see footnote 7). Since the Pact is credited with more major items of equipment in active inventory than the West, it follows that its "readiness" spending per unit of equipment is a good deal lower. What is known about Soviet maintenance and training practices supports this judgment. Similarly, assigning NATO some military credit for its greater peacetime manpower committed to the command and support area suggests an initial *capabilities* ratio less favorable to the Pact than is commonly supposed. As Figure 3 illustrates, under this assumption the Pact-to-NATO capabilities ratio after seven days of Pact mobilization and no NATO mobilization is little better than 1.3:1. These points lead one to suspect that NATO is "readier" for combat on a day-to-day basis than the Pact and has already built some cushion into its military structure against the possibility that the Pact will have a seven-day mobilization lead.

In the net, however, the available data tell us little about the speed with which each side could transition to combat. A balance assessment that compares relative NATO and Warsaw Pact peacetime readiness for combat would be an essential tool for testing the Alliance's vulnerability to surprise attack. Short of such a comprehensive assessment, one can only venture the judgment that the facts available do not suggest that the Pact should have high confidence that a short-preparation attack, aimed at suprising NATO, would produce decisive results.

On the readiness of Pact units for short warning attacks, see William W. Kaufmann, "Defense Policy," in Joseph A. Pechman, ed., *Setting National Priorities: Agenda for the 1980s* (Washington, D.C.: Brookings, 1980), p. 300; and William W. Kaufmann, "Nonnuclear Deterrence," in John D. Steinbruner and Leon V. Sigal, eds., *Alliance Security: NATO and the No-First-Use Question* (Washington, D.C.: Brookings, 1983), pp. 59, 70.

requirement is that the reasons for the user's judgments on these matters be explicit. Since these variables affect one another, the user should also work out plausible relationships among them. For instance, it seems unlikely that low attrition rates and high offense-defense exchange rates would produce much retreat by the defender.[14] In applying the model, variables were set according to the two different doctrines employed by the Alliance: the "Soviet" doctrine often used for balance assessment, and the "NATO" doctrine that in fact seems to drive NATO's force planning.

BUILDUP RATES

Estimates of relative Pact and NATO military buildup rates include two areas of uncertainty that strongly affect possible military outcomes. For the Pact, the major question is the speed with which partially manned, low-readiness Soviet and East European divisions can be mobilized, brought to a standard of training that will permit them to operate effectively in combat, and moved to the front. For NATO, the major question is whether or not the Alliance's propensity to allocate greater manpower to command and support than the Pact produces any military benefit.

The standard Pact buildup curve usually employed in public analyses was first published by the Department of Defense (DoD) in 1976.[15] Although the published chart contained no actual numbers on its time and force axes, subsequent published information can be used to reconstruct those numbers. This information is provided in Figure 3. Adding this to knowledge of how the ADE scoring system worked at that time allows one to estimate which Pact divisions were included by the DoD.[16] Unless the DoD curve included

---

14. This is in sharp contrast to the most widely used dynamic analytical technique—the Lanchester Square Law. The equations that capture the Law do explicitly relate force ratios and attrition rates, once some assumptions are made about the number of forces engaged in a battle and their effectiveness. An exchange rate can be derived from the calculation. Analysts have also derived movement equations consistent with the Law. It is important to note, however, that those who use the equations must make several judgments about the values assigned to the key variables—particularly the forces included in the engagement, their effectiveness, and the relationship between the attrition suffered by the defender and his propensity to withdraw. In that sense, the Lanchester technique is nearly as dependent upon the analyst's "military judgment" as is the model suggested here. For a clear explanation of the Lanchester Laws and how to use them, see William W. Kaufmann, "The Arithmetic of Force Planning," in Steinbruner and Sigal, eds., *Alliance Security*, pp. 208–216.
15. U.S. Department of Defense, *A Report to Congress on U.S. Conventional Reinforcements to NATO* (Washington, D.C.: U.S. Government Printing Office, 1976), Chart IV-1, p. IV-3, cited in Richard K. Betts, *Surprise Attack: Lessons for Defense Planning* (Washington, D.C.: Brookings, 1982), p. 182.
16. William P. Mako, *U.S. Ground Forces and the Defense of Central Europe* (Washington, D.C.: Brookings, 1983), pp. 108–125.

Figure 3. A NATO Defeat: NATO/Warsaw Pact Military Capabilities and Requirements Over Time if NATO's Doctrine Is Incorrect

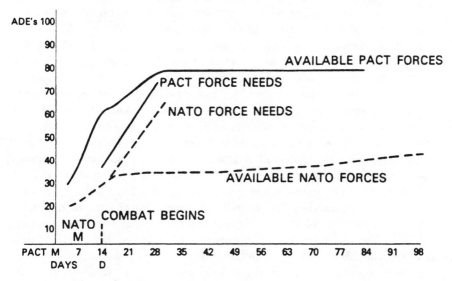

SOURCE: Derived from US Department of Defense, OSD, "A Report to Congress on U.S. Conventional Reinforcements to NATO" (June, 1976), chart IV-1 (cited in Richard K. Betts, *Surprise Attack: Lessons For Defense Planning* [Washington: The Brookings Institution, 1982], p. 182); William Mako, *U.S. Ground Forces and the Defense of Central Europe* (Washington: The Brookings Institution, 1983), pp. 42, 134; and author's estimates.

Assumptions Summary:

— No Pact build-up delay for post-mobilization training
— No NATO credit for greater command and support efforts
— One ADE per twenty-five km for NATO; Pact puts one ADE per twenty-five km in minor sectors, two ADEs per twenty-five km in breakthrough sectors. NATO needs thirty ADEs to start; Pact needs thirty-six to start.
— Daily Pact attrition in breakthrough sectors—10 percent
— Daily NATO attrition in breakthrough sectors—13 percent
— Exchange Rate - - Pact:NATO 1.5:1
— Pact advance rate in breakthrough sectors, five km/day
— Each side's tactical air force and ground based air defenses neutralize the effectiveness of the other's air force on the ground battle

Category I divisions from the Far East (not often done to my knowledge), this estimate projected the arrival of roughly nineteen Category II divisions to the battle area by M+14 and thirteen to fourteen Category III divisions by M+21. Nine low-readiness Czech and Polish Category III divisions were considered available by M+7. While the assembly and delivery of these forces in such a short time is plausible, most public assessments of the combat capability of these divisions under conditions of rapid mobilization and deployment suggest that they would not be particularly effective. Yet, assigning these divisions equivalent combat capability to Category I divisions is common practice in many analyses of the NATO–Pact balance.[17]

Published estimates indicate that the Soviets (and their East European allies) would likely subject these mobilized divisions to intensive refresher training before committing them to combat: thirty to forty-five days for Category IIs, ninety days or more for Category IIIs.[18] There are two major reasons for such estimates. First, Soviet Category II and III divisions are manned at "cadre" strength, perhaps an average of 50 percent for the former and 25 percent for the latter. The cadre of these divisions are not all seasoned professionals. Perhaps one-half or more are themselves conscripts, serving their obligatory two-year term of service. Some are in their first six months of service and, like many Soviet conscripts, receive basic training in their combat units. Since these divisions have quite a bit of equipment, much conscript time is spent in basic vehicle maintenance, not in field training. Similarly, because the divisions are only partially manned, thorough training of officers and enlisted men at all levels is not always possible.

Second, upon mobilization, these divisions would be "fleshed out" with reservists that have completed their two-year term of service and returned to civilian life. Unlike U.S. National Guard or Israeli reservists, these people do not know each other. Most receive no annual refresher training. Because of the many generations of equipment in the Soviet inventory, mobilized reservists may receive equipment different from that with which they originally trained. Category II and III divisions seldom call up large numbers of conscripts for major exercises.[19] This is in sharp contrast to U.S. or Israeli reservists who receive thirty to forty-five days of individual and unit training

---

17. This is effectively what was done in the DoD 1976 buildup curve and in the CBO buildup estimates in 1980. It is also the implication of most of the public "bean-count" comparisons of NATO and Warsaw Pact holdings of various kinds of military equipment. The 1982 edition of the Luns Report is a good example: Joseph Luns, Secretary General of NATO, *NATO and the Warsaw Pact: Force Comparisons* (Brussels: NATO, 1982).

18. Irving Heymont and Melvin Rosen, "Foreign Army Reserve Systems," *Military Review*, Vol. 53, No. 3 (March 1973), pp. 84–85; David C. Isby, *Weapons and Tactics of the Soviet Army* (London: Jane's, 1981), p. 28; Jeffrey Record, *Sizing Up the Soviet Army* (Washington, D.C.: Brookings, 1975), pp. 21–22.

19. On the peacetime organization and training of low-readiness Category II and III divisions, see testimony of the Defense Intelligence Agency in U.S. Congress, Joint Economic Committee, *Allocation of Resources in the Soviet Union and China—1981*, Hearings before the Subcommittee on International Trade, Finance, and Security Economics, 97th Congress, 1st session, part 7, 1982, p. 199.

per year with the people and the units that they will accompany into battle. It is worth noting that, even given this level of annual activity, Israeli reservists were not particularly effective during the first few days of the 1973 war. Moreover, close observers of the Guard and U.S. Army Reserve suggest that a month or more of postmobilization refresher training is required.[20] The long postmobilization training periods suggested above reflect these shortcomings.

My estimate of Soviet postmobilization training is more favorable to the Soviet Union than those cited above. The mobilization curve in Figure 4 gives the Category IIs thirty days of training and the Category IIIs sixty days. It appears that the DoD mobilization curve does not bring U.S. National Guard divisions to the front until M+60. Allowing thirty days for mobilization and shipment to Europe, these troops could have thirty days to train, if arrangements had been made in advance to facilitate this, so that they would not be further delayed.[21]

This slow Pact buildup stands in sharp contrast to the curves published by DoD in 1976 and used in several subsequent studies. These projections of a relatively fast Soviet buildup rate are consistent with a "Soviet theory" of victory, i.e., the collection of hardware is what counts, not the human organization. Moreover, the standard Pact buildup models seem to credit the Soviets with a willingness to expend lives with great profligacy. This may be true, but credit should then be taken for greater Western effectiveness against these divisions. Finally, fast buildup rates for low-readiness Soviet divisions often cloak a hidden assumption: the Pact does in fact take a month or more to retrain these divisions, but Western intelligence misses this extraordinary activity, Western leaders prove too frightened to take any military response to such actions, or consensus takes too long to build. Given the tremendous publicity that attended Soviet efforts to ready *some* divisions for action against Poland in 1981 and the recent public disclosures of the amount of technical warning Western intelligence had of Soviet preparations for the

---

20. Mako, *U.S. Ground Forces*, p. 83, quotes Martin Binkin's estimate of fourteen weeks to prepare a U.S. reserve division for combat, but judges this estimate to be pessimistic.

21. I have not added any delay for roundout battalions and brigades assigned to fill out active U.S. Army divisions. Nor has any special delay been factored in for refresher training for German Territorial Army Units, which are somewhat similar to U.S. Guard and Reserve units. Since the Pact is not in a position to attack before M+30 and the Germans are fighting at home, these units would probably have time for some refresher training before commitment to battle. Finally, the Army's XVIIIth Airborne Corps, effectively three divisions and their support units worth roughly 3.4 ADEs, are assumed to be tied up in a non-European contingency. See Mako, *U.S. Ground Forces*, p. 133.

Figure 4. A Successful NATO Defense: NATO/Warsaw Pact Military Capabilities and Requirements Over Time if NATO's Doctrine Is Correct

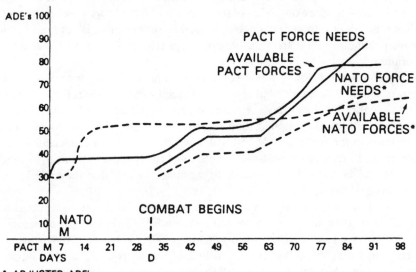

* ADJUSTED ADE's

SOURCE: Derived from US Department of Defense, OSD, "A Report to Congress on U.S. Conventional Reinforcements to NATO" (June, 1976), chart IV-1, p. IV-3 (cited in Richard K. Betts, *Surprise Attack: Lessons For Defense Planning* [Washington: The Brookings Institution, 1982], p. 182); William Mako, *U.S. Ground Forces and the Defense of Central Europe* (Washington: The Brookings Institution, 1983), pp. 42, 134; and author's estimates.

Assumptions Summary:
— Category II divisions delayed an additional thirty days, Category III divisions sixty days for post-mobilization training
— NATO ADE strength is multiplied by 1.5 for command and support efforts
— One adjusted ADE per twenty-five km for NATO; Pact puts one ADE per twenty-five km on minor sectors, 1.5 ADE per twenty-five km on breakthrough sectors. NATO needs thirty adjusted ADEs to start (twenty real ADEs). Pact needs thirty-three to start.
— Daily attrition, Phase I—Breakthrough Sectors
  Pact 7.5 percent; 57 percent of casualties caused by NATO tacair
  NATO* 4.3 percent; 45 percent of casualties caused by Pact tacair
— Daily attrition, Phase 2—Breakthrough Sectors
  Pact 7.5 percent; 27 percent of casualties caused by NATO tacair
  NATO* 5.8 percent; 29 percent of casualties caused by Pact tacair
— Pact: NATO exchange rate 2:1
— Pact advance rate 2km/day
*NATO attrition is assessed against the adjusted ADE score

invasion of Czechoslovakia in 1968 and the Afghan invasion of 1979 (both smaller affairs than that projected here), the argument that NATO leaders will not know about Soviet preparations seems suspect.[22] If American and European planners believe that the West could lose a war because its political leaders are likely to be too concerned with provocation to order mobilization or too militarily ill-informed to understand that NATO must compete with Soviet partial mobilization efforts (i.e., refresher training for Category IIs and IIIs), then the task is to educate the leaders. Finally, it may be possible to design partial mobilization efforts for NATO that would be sufficiently un-provocative to win political approval.

My NATO buildup curves, both the standard and adjusted versions, rely heavily on the buildup schedule developed by William Mako,[23] whose schedule is roughly consistent with the curve published by DoD in 1976. The major difference between the two is that DoD's criteria for readiness seem to be less stringent than Mako's. Like DoD and unlike Mako, I assume that all forward-based NATO forces are effectively "ready" on M-Day, even though this clearly simplifies what must surely be more complicated reasoning on the part of DoD. The principal change, however, has been to assign an effectiveness multiplier to the NATO ADE score. This multiplier is not as-signed for weapons quality, which is ostensibly handled in the ADE meth-odology, nor for personnel quality, which is difficult to measure. The mul-tiplier is simply applied for greater numbers of people performing command, intelligence-reconnaissance, maintenance, and supply functions.

Nearly ten years ago, in an essay that remains one of the more useful primers on differences between NATO and Warsaw Pact strategy, tactics, and organization, Steven Canby highlighted NATO's emphasis on the com-mand and support areas.[24] He devised a system for comparing the total number of combat, combat support, and combat service support people, inside and outside the divisional organization, needed to generate a fighting force of a given size. While his numbers are somewhat dated, they are good enough for our purposes here. Using an average West European division as base, Canby estimated that the NATO allies needed roughly 40,000 men to field and support a given number of individuals in front-line combat roles in

---

22. Kaufmann, "Defense Policy," in Pechman, ed., *Setting National Priorities*, p. 300, estimates that it takes the Soviets months, rather than weeks, even to organize a small military operation.
23. Mako, *U.S. Ground Forces*, p. 134.
24. Canby, *The Alliance and Europe*, pp. 3–4, 10, and footnote 10.

wartime. Given prevailing Soviet practices, the Pact would have only allocated 21,500 people to the same task. A similar comparison was made for peacetime U.S. and Soviet divisions, which yielded 41,000 for the United States and 21,500 for the Soviets. Thus, on the average, it took NATO roughly twice as many people to field a front-line force of a given size as it did the Pact. Because Canby's methodology is a bit opaque, it is worth looking at the current figures in a somewhat different way as a check. Adapting figures from the *Military Balance 1983–84,* we see that the United States now allocates roughly 34,000 men *per ADE* in Germany, the German Army 31,000, and the Soviet Army 24,000 per ADE deployed in Eastern Europe. This yields an average peacetime NATO superiority of 1.33:1. The wartime superiority would probably grow in the direction suggested by Canby, since much of the American and German reserve structure is devoted to support. Given the large number of divisions that the Soviets are said to man on mobilization, it seems unlikely that their support-to-combat ratio would grow at quite the same rate. Finally, a comparison of the organizational charts of current first-class Soviet and U.S. divisions shows that *within* the divisional organization, the United States allocates about 1.5 times as many people to command and support per ADE as the Pact. These numbers and ratios are all, of course, quite rough, but they are indicative of how NATO allocates its personnel and its financial resources.[25]

Canby, of course, argues that whatever the difference, the West should receive no special credit for these assets. Rather, by organizing their forces to achieve greater initial firepower, the Pact will simply swamp NATO's smaller forces before these support assets become useful. In this formulation, these support assets are seen primarily as "long-war" capabilities. In spite of Canby's arguments and substantial pressure from such reformers as Senator Sam Nunn, little has changed in the Central Region since Canby's analysis. Instead, the U.S. Army has managed to reverse many of the "tooth-to-tail" reforms imposed on it by the Nunn amendment, and NATO's military leaders remain committed to rich command and support assets. Since most public assessments of the military outcome of an East–West war do not project a particularly long NATO effort, one can only deduce that NATO's military leaders believe that these command and support assets would play a signif-

---

25. See Kaufmann, "Nonnuclear Deterrence," pp. 55–58. On Soviet and U.S. divisions, see Defense Intelligence Agency, *Soviet Divisional Organizational Guide* (Washington, 1982); and U.S. Army Armor School, *U.S. Army Armor Reference Data,* Vols. I and III (Fort Knox, Ky., 1981).

icant role in a short war as well. A careful examination of the history of armored warfare does reveal that the supply and maintenance of mechanized forces have been a consistent problem, although historical accounts do not reveal much about the details of the appropriate combat-to-support ratio.

In sum, as a function of NATO's efforts in the command and support areas, a multiplier of 1.5 is applied to NATO's ADE score to take into account the increased combat effectiveness that NATO's military leaders presumably expect from their efforts.[26] (The median between the high ratio of 2:1 and the low of 1.35:1 would be 1.67:1. Thus, a 1.5 effectiveness multiplier seems a conservative way to take credit for NATO's greater support efforts.) Balance assessments that do not try to account for these factors are implicitly admitting the correctness of Canby's arguments. If this is true, then NATO must ask itself whether it can afford to compete with the Soviet Union if it does not make efforts to change its structure. Consistent with the respect for Soviet organization implicit in balance assessments that do not take credit for NATO's support and command efforts, NATO should imitate its adversary. If, however, NATO's military professionals remain committed to doing

---

26. The Lanchester Square Law provides an argument for taking some credit for NATO's superior personnel investment in the command and support areas. The law captures, arithmetically, the effect of concentration on military outcomes. Put simply, as most military commanders have long realized, the side that manages to *concentrate* more forces on the actual battle will achieve a substantial advantage. The question is not who has more, which some users of the law seem to believe, but who concentrates more. Concentration should depend not merely on the availability of weapons, but also on the ability to find the places where they can best be employed and get forces there in fighting shape. Achieving concentration should, in short, depend on an appropriate balance between "concentrators" and "concentratees." NATO views about this balance clearly differ from Soviet views. If NATO is right, then it should be able to make the Lanchester process work better for its "smaller" force than the Pact should for its larger force.

Taking credit for support assets provides an avenue for including NATO's war reserve stocks, equipment held outside of units to replace damaged vehicles that cannot be repaired in the forward areas. NATO tries to keep its divisions in combat at full strength in contrast to the Pact intention of pulling out and replacing the whole division. While the European allies do not have large war reserve stocks, U.S. stocks, particularly of tanks, seem to be quite large. The U.S. Army is currently credited with roughly 12,000 usable tanks in its inventory. Harold Brown, *Annual Report of the Department of Defense, Fiscal Year 1982* (Washington, D.C.: U.S. Government Printing Office, 1981). Yet, by a generous counting procedure, there are barely enough armored units in the Army to swallow up 7,000 of them, leaving 5,000 as war reserve stocks. These 5,000 tanks are worth nearly six ADEs and are never counted in balance assessments. One of the purposes of the U.S. support structure is to keep these tanks flowing into units so that they can remain near their designated strength and to keep damaged tanks flowing to the rear where they can be fixed. It is difficult to predict how long this stockpile would last in war. The average Israeli "total loss" rate in 1973 (tanks utterly destroyed) was about a half percent per day of the total original force. At this rate, the U.S. stockpile could keep its nominal 7,000 tank operational force at full strength for four months of relatively serious combat.

business in their traditional fashion, then they should be asked to explain
and to take account of the benefits that they derive that the Soviets do not.

THE EFFECTIVENESS OF TACTICAL AIR POWER

Frequently, public assessments of the Central Region military balance do not
account for the possible influence of NATO's tactical air forces ("tacair") on
the ground battle.[27] NATO, however, allocates substantial funds to aircraft
with ground attack capability and to special ground attack ordnance. My
analysis takes credit for NATO's tactical air investments in a simple and
straightforward way, not to show how well they *will* do, but to show the
kinds of outcomes that might be produced if they do as well as NATO's
persistent investments in the area seem to imply.

While public comparisons of relative NATO and Pact "tacair" investments
are not available, one may deduce from several facts that NATO probably
makes a greater effort than the Pact. American spending on "tacair" has
nearly equaled the Soviets' over the last ten years.[28] U.S. allies, who themselves seem to spend a good deal on "tacair," contribute substantially more
to NATO's total defense spending than the East European states do to Pact
total spending.[29] As Joshua Epstein has argued, Pact efforts in the training
and support of its "tacair" assets are significantly less than those of the
United States.[30] It seems unlikely that a different pattern would prevail in
overall NATO–Pact comparisons.

NATO has made a substantial financial effort to produce aircraft and
weapons devoted specifically to close air support (CAS). With the exception
of the still small number of "Frogfoot" aircraft, Pact tactical fighter-bombers
are not well suited to this mission. Moreover, the Pact seems more concerned
with attacking NATO's tactical nuclear assets and airbases than with using
"tacair" to affect the ground battle. Moreover, Epstein demonstrates that,
even given assumptions about Soviet Frontal Aviation's performance that

---

27. See Hillier and Slatkin, *U.S. Ground Forces*; Mako, *U.S. Ground Forces*; and Dan Gans, "Fight
Outnumbered and Win," Part 1, *Military Review*, Vol. 60, No. 12 (December 1980), pp. 31–45.
28. Central Intelligence Agency, National Foreign Assessment Center, *Soviet and US Defense
Activities, 1970–79: A Dollar Cost Comparison*, SR 80-1000J (Washington, D.C., January 1980), p.
10.
29. IISS, *Military Balance, 1983–1984*, pp. 125–126; and U.S. Department of Defense, *The FY 1984
DOD Program for Research, Development and Acquisitions*, Statement by Honorable Richard De-
Lauer, Undersecretary of Defense for Research and Engineering, 98th Congress, 1st session,
March 2, 1983.
30. Joshua Epstein, *Measuring Military Power: The Soviet Air Threat to Europe* (Princeton: Princeton
University Press, 1984), pp. 96–98.

are relatively favorable to the Warsaw Pact (e.g., three sorties per day), the Pact would probably only complete 44 percent of its counternuclear, counterairfield missions before virtually exhausting itself in the middle of the sixth day of combat. A recent Brookings study offers a similar estimate of the Pact's likely performance.[31]

My assessment of relative NATO–Warsaw Pact tactical air influence on the ground battle jumps off from the preceding two assessments. Simply put, NATO and the Pact are given credit for their known CAS assets—attack helicopters and fighter aircraft specifically configured for antiarmor operations in close proximity to friendly ground forces.[32] Thus, this analysis is conservative in that it does not try to account for the contribution that hundreds of other NATO aircraft configured for bombing missions could make to the ground battle. Effectiveness, sortie rate, and attrition rate values are assigned to these aircraft, to produce an estimate of how many armored vehicle kills each side could achieve in Phase I and Phase II of the "NATO doctrine" case.[33] (See Table 1.) The principal tactical assumption is that both sides allocate all their CAS assets to the breakthrough sectors. This is unlikely to be fully achieved in practice, but it is a sensible way to use the aircraft.

For the first phase of the conflict, NATO is given credit for U.S. reinforcing aircraft. Neither the Pact nor NATO is given credit for reinforcing attack helicopters, since unclassified numbers on attack helicopters are not very reliable.[34]

---

31. Ibid., Appendix C, pp. 243–245, especially Table C-9, p. 245; Kaufmann, "Nonnuclear Deterrence," pp. 76–77.

32. For NATO, I count 300 A10s, 100 A7s (with GE 30mm gun pods), 100 German Alphajets, and 400-odd armed helicopters. For the Pact, I count 800-odd armed helicopters; see footnote 34. The rest of NATO and Pact aircraft are presumed to be absorbed in a hugh air battle consisting of air-to-air, airfield suppression, and SAM suppression activities. The sum total of all these efforts allows each side's CAS assets to operate at the relatively high attrition and low effectiveness assumed in this analysis. It is my judgment that these assumptions are favorable to the Pact.

33. The "tacair" formula is straightforward. For each sortie the total number of aircraft leaving base is multiplied by .95 (i.e., 5 percent attrition) and then by the kill rate to come up with a total kill per sortie. Those aircraft that have survived the sortie (i.e., 95 percent) are run through the equation for the next sortie. Second sortie survivors are run through the third, etc.

34. The numbers used are drawn from the Luns Report (1982) and include combat helicopters in the region in peacetime. The numbers are somewhat favorable to the Pact; the report is favorable to the Pact across the board. See Luns, *NATO and the Warsaw Pact (1982)*, Figure 2. This report assigns 400 attack helicopters to NATO and 700 to the Pact in peacetime. IISS, *Military Balance, 1983–84*, p. 139, assigns 805 to NATO and 786 to the Pact. IISS includes French assets, while the Luns Report does not. Which Pact helicopters are being counted in both sources is unclear. I have given NATO credit for only 400 armed helicopters and the Pact 800 for the sake of conservatism.

Table 1. The Tactical Air Efforts

	Phase I		Phase II	
	NATO	**Pact**	**NATO**	**Pact**
Aircraft				
Fixed Wing	500	0	350	0
Helicopter	400	800	250	800
Total	900	800	600	800
Attrition	5%	5%	5%	5%
Kills/Sortie	.5	.25	.5	.25
Sortie Rate Per Day	2	1	1.5	1

In the second phase of the battle, the Pact is permitted to replace all losses incurred during the first phase (400 helicopters), and NATO is allowed to replace two-thirds (400 helicopters and fighters) of its Phase I losses of 600 aircraft. On the NATO side, this would be achieved by bringing in some of the remaining 500 attack helicopters in U.S. operational units, by stripping helicopters and aircraft from the training base and maintenance pipeline (currently planned), and by battle-damage repair.[35]

The 5 percent attrition per sortie assumed here is high by historical standards for Western air forces.[36] One-quarter to one-half a vehicle killed per sortie is in the historical range of performance. The West has been assigned a higher kill rate primarily on the grounds of superior weaponry. The General

35. This level of replacement is consistent with the number of CAS aircraft candidates remaining in both sides' inventories. For example, although the United States has 476 A10s and 700 Cobra attack helicopters in units, it appears to have roughly 687 A10s and 1,000 Cobras in inventory. See relevant sections of *Annual Report of the Department of Defense*, Fiscal Years 1978, 1982, 1983, and 1984 for the sources of these numbers. The difference between what is in units and what is in the inventory is presumably used for training or is in the maintenance pipeline. Plans exist to tap these sources in wartime. The Pact is permitted its level of replacement to account, at least in part, for the very large number of "armed" helicopter assets credited to them by several sources. For instance, although IISS only seems to count the Soviet Union's 800-odd MI24s of all kinds as attack helicopters, it also suggests that some portion of the 1,500 MI8 troop transports assigned to the Soviet Air Force should be considered as armed. This is consistent with *Jane's All the World's Aircraft, 1982–83* (London: Jane's, 1983) entries for both helicopters.
36. Congressional Budget Office, *Navy Budget Issues for FY 1980* (Washington, D.C.: Congressional Budget Office, 1979), pp. 98, 102–103. U.S. Navy attrition over North Vietnam between 1965 and 1973 was .1 percent. Israeli Air Force attrition during the 1973 war was .8 percent. Israeli A4s, whose missions most closely approximated NATO's CAS missions, suffered 1.5 percent. Historically, U.S. air commanders were willing to accept sustained 5 percent attrition during World War II and Korea, if the mission was perceived to be important.

Electric 30mm antiarmor cannon on U.S. fixed wing aircraft and the TOW antitank guided missile on U.S. attack helicopters should be more effective than the Swatter missile which most Soviet attack helicopters still carry according to public sources.[37] Finally, NATO is assigned a higher sortie rate on the grounds of greater maintenance efforts and greater ruggedness of aircraft over helicopters. During the battle's second phase, NATO's sortie rate is lowered on the assumption that spare parts inventories will be reduced, and wear and tear on the aircraft will have made them more subject to failure. The Pact's sortie rate remains constant.

The damage in armored fighting vehicles destroyed can be calculated and converted to an average number of ADEs destroyed per day for a fourteen-day campaign in Phase I and a twenty-one-day campaign in Phase II of the battle. (An ADE equals roughly 1,200 combat vehicles, including self-propelled and towed artillery weapons.) For ease of comparison, the total number of ADEs destroyed in the campaign is divided by the total number of days in the campaign to come up with an average number. (See Table 2.) This obscures the fact that "tacair" would probably do better early in the campaign than later, when high aircraft losses will have cut the number of sorties being flown per day.

Taking credit for NATO's investments in CAS aircraft and armaments as well as training and maintenance suggests that these assets could make a substantial contribution to stopping Pact breakthrough efforts, if properly employed. NATO's "tacair" destroys roughly nine Pact ADEs in five weeks of combat, while Pact "tacair" gets credit for destroying roughly four NATO ADEs. Put another way, NATO "tacair" destroys Pact ground forces equivalent to nearly one-half of all Soviet forces stationed in East Germany in peacetime.

Table 2. The Tactical Air Contribution

	Phase I		Phase II	
	NATO	**Pact**	**NATO**	**Pact**
Sorties Flown	13,000	7,000	9,200	10,000
AFVs Killed	6,500	1,950	4,600	2,500
ADEs Killed	5.4	1.6	3.8	2.1
Average Enemy Killed Per Day	.4	.12	.18	.1

37. *Jane's All the World's Aircraft*, MI8 and MI24 entries.

FORCE-TO-SPACE RATIOS

How much force does a defender require to hold a given sector? How much force can the attacker concentrate in a given breakthrough sector? The "Soviet" and "NATO" cases illustrate different assumptions about these values. A close examination of the admittedly sparse information on these questions turns up an important insight. Simply put, given the number of forces that NATO already has, it may be extremely difficult for the Pact to achieve the high offense-to-defense ratios (greater than 3:1) that experience suggests are necessary to achieve breakthroughs.

Among those who have discussed the preferred defensive force-to-space ratio, the prevailing assumption seems to be that roughly one ADE is required to hold every 25 km of front. Mako settles on this figure, although he quotes some retired U.S. officers to the effect that a U.S. armored or mechanized division, armed with modern weaponry (worth perhaps 1.1–1.3 ADEs), should be able to hold 30 to 60 km of front (i.e., as little as .5 or as much as one ADE could be needed to defend 25 km).[38] If William Kaufmann's methodology for assessing divisional firepower is converted to ADEs, he appears to assume that between .75 and one ADE would be required to hold 25 km of front.[39] David Isby suggests that the Soviets would assign one Motor Rifle Division (.66–.76 ADE) to defend 25 km of front.[40] The appropriate "conservative figure" would then appear to be one ADE per 25 km of front.

Because NATO has only thirty real ADEs at Pact M+14 (Pact D-Day), a literal application of this conservative planning factor plays into the hands of the Pact armored offensive, as many students of armored warfare have observed. In effect, many NATO forces would be pinned down, "conservatively" defending sectors that are not the victims of major breakthrough efforts, while those that are the victims would find themselves short of the tactical and operational reserves that might stop a breakthrough from happening or restore the situation if it occurred.

---

38. Mako, *U.S. Ground Forces*, pp. 36–37, especially footnote 18. See, also, the most widely quoted discussion of the defender's force-to-space requirements: B.H. Liddell Hart, *Deterrent or Defense: A Fresh Look at the West's Military Position* (New York: Praeger, 1960), pp. 97–109. Liddell Hart observed that the defender's force-to-space requirement, measured in manpower in divisions, has been dropping in this century. He also observed that the level of quantitative superiority that the attacker must enjoy if he is to achieve a successful breakthrough has been rising. Citing U.S. and British experience in World War II, he noted that superiorities between 3:1 and 5:1 were required, with some attacks failing at ratios of 10:1.
39. Kaufmann, "Nonnuclear Deterrence," pp. 62, 210.
40. Isby, *Weapons and Tactics of the Soviet Army*, pp. 20, 38.

In the "NATO" case, operational reserves become available as a function of the effectiveness multiplier assigned to NATO ADEs. This case assumes one *adjusted* ADE per 25 km, .66 of the real ADE.[41] The command, reconnaissance, and logistics assets assigned to NATO forces should affect the amount of space that they can control. For example, the ammunition-handling capability of an average U.S. or West German division permits a far greater daily ammunition expenditure than that of a comparable Soviet division. Supply and maintenance assets should also affect the overall attrition that NATO divisions suffer, since these assets should provide NATO a superior capability to repair damaged vehicles or replace them from war reserve stocks.

This assumption leaves NATO defending within the one-half to one ADE per 25 km range cited above and is consistent with Isby's estimates for Soviet defending forces. Thus, NATO puts two-thirds of its forces in the line (with each division in the line holding a small tactical reserve), and one-third of its forces in operational reserve. This is lower than Liddell Hart's prescription that one-half of the defender's forces be held in reserve, higher than the one-fourth that appears to be NATO's intention, and equal to the one-third figure attributed to Canby.[42]

There is even less in the open literature on the question of appropriate *offensive* force-to-space ratios. How much force can the attacker pack into a given segment of the front in his efforts to achieve the very high force-to-force ratios that are often thought to be the key to the successful armored breakthrough? In general, the impression has been created that the achievement of very high force-to-space ratios is relatively simple and that the adversary certainly intends to do so.

---

41. This force-to-space ratio is substantially higher than that enjoyed by the Israeli 7th armored brigade in 1973, which successfully defended roughly 20 km of front on the Golan Heights with less than one-quarter of an ADE, no major reserves (other than the brigade's organic reserve), and virtually no CAS. This brigade was outnumbered 4:1 or worse. This was not, of course, a comfortable position, and Colonel Janush Ben-Gal (now Major General retired) was aided by prepared positions and Syrian unimaginativeness. Even with these advantages, the brigade was nearly exhausted after 2.5 days. Its performance, however, is exemplary of the impressive defensive potential of modern armored forces. At least 300 tanks plus other armored fighting vehicles were damaged, destroyed, or captured by the 7th Brigade. See Trevor N. Dupuy, *Elusive Victory: The Arab-Israeli Wars, 1947–1974* (New York: Harper and Row, 1978), pp. 437–461. By comparison to the 7th Brigade, the standard suggested here would leave a U.S. or West German division with two brigades forward, each on 19 km fronts, backed by one brigade in reserve. In the breakthrough sectors, such a force would receive substantial air support and could be reinforced rather quickly by reserves that are withheld in the "NATO" case.
42. Mako, *U.S. Ground Forces*, pp. 37–38.

While it is true that Soviet doctrinal literature calls for very high offense-to-defense ratios in breakthrough sectors, on the order of 4–6:1 in tanks and artillery, the available evidence on how the Pact would set up a breakthrough attack casts doubt on its ability to achieve such ratios easily. These high ratios may be achievable, but they will likely occur on only a few very small 4 or 5 km segments of the front.[43] Thus, successful attacks in these sectors would take the form of narrow "wedges" driven into the NATO line. Whether or not these "wedges" would produce a catastrophic failure of the defense line depends upon the defending division commander's ability to bring tactical reserves quickly to bear on the engagement. He has these reserves available, so the question may ultimately be one of competent leadership.

Figure 5 illustrates the kinds of major efforts the Soviets seem to envision. It appears that a four-division Soviet or Pact Army and some attached Army and Front artillery would be tasked against a 50 km breakthrough sector, like that assumed in the model. Apparently, the Soviets would put two divisions forward and hold two in reserve. Other estimates suggest either slightly wider Army sectors; three divisions forward, and only one in reserve; or a five-division Army. To capture the full potential utility attributed to the divisions in reserve, the "Soviet" case factors this entire force into the battle for every day of combat, roughly four ADEs.

In the "NATO" case, the Pact is assumed to be slightly less successful at concentration than assumed above; it achieves only three ADEs in engaged combat power on any 50 km of front. This partially reflects the Soviets' apparent intention to hold a substantial part of its force in reserve. It also reflects the difficulty of managing such a high concentration of capabilities in such a small area. For instance, during November of 1944, in its attempt to reach the Roer River, the U.S. XIX Corps attempted a concentration similar to that assumed by the Soviet case. The commanders on the scene found their position to be very cramped, and it was necessary to withhold one-half of the armored division for several days until more space could be opened by the Corps' advance. It is also worth remembering that this concentration was achieved under conditions of total air superiority, and against an enemy that was short of ammunition and thus could afford little harassing artillery fire.[44]

---

43. See, for example, Isby, *Weapons and Tactics of the Soviet Army,* p. 38.
44. While one example is scarcely definitive, the XIX Corps' attempt to concentrate one armored and two infantry divisions plus fifteen-odd nondivisional artillery batteries on a 16 km front is

Figure 5. Breakthrough Attack Deployments (Tank Units)

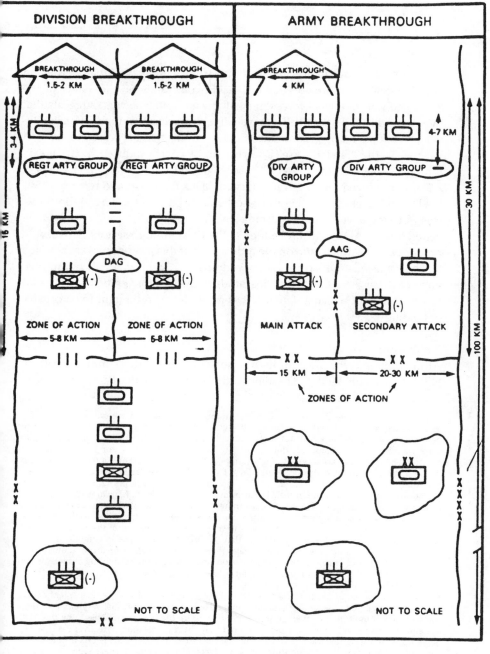

SOURCE: US Army, FM 71-2; *The Tank and Mechanized Infantry Battalion Task Force* (June 30, 1977), p. 5–12.

NATO's existing ability to cover the front at densities that permit an effective defense, coupled with real world constraints on the ability of the Pact to concentrate large forces in small breakthrough sectors, suggests that the Pact will, *at least initially*, have difficulty achieving high offensive-to-defensive force ratios in *either* the "Soviet" or the "NATO" case.

Thus, in the "Soviet" case, a force ratio of 2:1 is produced in the breakthrough sectors. In the "NATO" case, a ground force ratio in real ADEs of 2.25:1 is produced, although in adjusted ADEs the force ratio remains 1.5:1. NATO and Pact "tacair" should also be factored into the force ratio, however.[45] Using a very simple formula, NATO and Pact "tacair" can be converted into an ADE score and added to the breakthrough sectors. This would produce a "real" force ratio on the order of 2:1. If this procedure were adopted for the adjusted ADE score, the ratio drops to 1.4:1. It is worth noting that none of these force-to-space ratios produce force-to-force ratios near the 3:1 rule of thumb at which a defender has generally been thought to be capable of holding.

ATTRITION RATES

Attrition rates in the breakthrough sectors are a key variable in the Attrition–FEBA Expansion Model. The daily attrition rate that the Pact is willing to

---

instructive. These three divisions had, at minimum, 6,500 vehicles of all types and probably more. Actual combat vehicles, however, probably added up to no more than 1,500–2,000, worth between one and one-and-a-half ADEs. Additionally, two infantry divisions and a cavalry group were waiting "in the wings" on the Corps' left flank. The Official History reports that the commanders found the situation extremely cramped. The 2nd Armored division had to withhold half its strength from the battle for several days. This level of concentration is roughly consistent with that attributed to the Pact in the "Soviet" case, and thus one ADE per 12.5 km would seem a good theoretical maximum. On the XIX Corps assault, see Charles B. MacDonald, *The Siegfried Line Campaign* (Washington, D.C.: U.S. Government Printing Office, 1963), pp. 521–522. At first glance, it appears that a higher force-to-space ratio was achieved by the British in their GOODWOOD offensive out of the Normandy perimeter. A close examination of the forces involved and the course of battle, however, suggests that the British were unable to commit their third division to the fray and were forced to engage their first two armored divisions sequentially. Once spread out and engaged, these two divisions (with roughly 1,200 fighting vehicles or an ADE) took up about 12 km of front. See John Keegan, *Six Armies in Normandy* (New York: Viking, 1982), pp. 183–219, especially p. 218.

45. For purposes of aggregation, I simply treat these aircraft as tanks, since helicopters armed with anti-tank guided missiles and cannon-equipped aircraft are basically just very mobile direct-fire weapons. I multiply my average-sorties-per-day figure (derived from Table 1) by the ADE system's defensive weighting for tanks (55). I multiply that by a weapons effectiveness factor to come up with a weighted value that can then be converted to an ADE score. As a function of the different kill rates that I assign the two CAS fleets, NATO's effectiveness score is one and the Pact's is .5. Sorties are scored, rather than aircraft, because actual battlefield presence is the output to be measured.

suffer ultimately is a key determinant of NATO's daily ground force needs. Varying the attrition rate is a way of representing how much Pact commanders and their troops are willing to suffer on a sustained basis. Additionally, it is a way of representing the effects of "friction" on the Pact offensive. How much can the attacker suffer, even if he wants to? I have chosen two values for the sustained breakthrough sector attrition rate: 10 percent for the "Soviet" case and 7.5 percent for the "NATO" case.

Tank attrition rates provide a useful starting point for estimating overall ADE attrition rates. Tanks make up one-half of the ADE score for NATO divisions and one-half or more for Pact divisions. Three sources of data for sustained, front-wide, tank attrition are employed: two from real wars and one from a recent unclassified projection of tank attrition in a NATO/Pact war. Table 3 compares these attrition rates with those of the "NATO" and "Soviet" cases from the Attrition–FEBA Expansion Model. To arrive at the front-wide attrition figure, breakthrough sector casualties are added to an estimate of the casualties taken in the minor sectors: 1 percent per day.

Table 3. Frontwide Attrition Rates[a]

Source	Victim	Daily Rate	Comments
U.S. Army Official History[b]	U.S.	2%	Tanks, Battle of the Bulge, First and Third Armies, 14 days
Author's Estimate[c]	Israel	2%	20-Day War, 1973, tanks, one-half reparable
Author's Estimate	Arabs	3%	20-Day War, 1973, tanks
Cordesman[d]	Pact	3.3%	D + 12–32, tanks
	NATO	2.77%	D + 12–32, tanks
"Soviet" Case	Pact	4%	ADEs
"Soviet" Case	NATO	3.5%	ADEs
"NATO" Case	Pact	2.8%	ADEs
"NATO" Case	NATO	1.7%	Adjusted ADEs, Phase I

[a] Percent of engaged/committed forces at original strength.
[b] Hugh Cole, *The Ardennes: Battle of the Bulge* (Washington, D.C.: U.S. Government Printing Office, 1965), p. 664.
[c] These estimates are based on Trevor N. Dupuy, *Elusive Victory: The Arab–Israeli Wars, 1947–1948* (New York: Harper and Row, 1978), p. 609; Shlomo Gazit, "Arab Forces Two Years After the Yom Kippur War," in Louis Williams, ed., *Military Aspects of the Israeli–Arab Conflict* (Tel Aviv: University Publishing Projects, 1975), pp. 188, 194.
[d] Daniel Gans, "Fight Outnumbered and Win," pp. 24–33, as cited by Anthony H. Cordesman, "The NATO Central Region and the Balance of Uncertainty," *Armed Forces Journal International*, July 1983, pp. 36–37, Table Six.

The "Soviet" case assumes higher front-wide attrition rates than those experienced by the Israelis or the Arabs in the 1973 war, which was viewed at the time as a very high-attrition war by historical standards. The "NATO" case applies slightly lower values to the "attacker" and the "defender" than those prevailing in the 1973 war. It seems plausible that, in the 1973 war, Arab and Israeli attrition rates were partly driven by the need for Middle East belligerents to achieve their military objectives with great speed, in order to beat the truce usually imposed by the superpowers. Neither NATO nor the Pact would be under such pressure. On the other hand, of course, weaponry has improved since that war, and some would argue that the Soviets will press the pace of the war in order to somehow forestall NATO's resort to nuclear escalation. The attrition suffered by the Alliance in the "NATO" case is a good deal lower than Anthony Cordesman's estimates, but it is consistent with U.S. Army experience during an intense World War II battle against a competent adversary at the Battle of the Bulge. Several Pentagon experts on armored vehicle attrition were skeptical that attackers would accept *sustained* 10 percent attrition in breakthrough sectors. Some simply doubt that the battle could be forced at such a pace on a sustained basis.

EXCHANGE RATES

Exchange rates are an equally difficult problem to discuss. As noted earlier, given Pact superiority in numbers of weapons, NATO must achieve favorable exhange rates if it is not simply to be worn down into defeat. There seems to be general agreement, however, that the defender should enjoy favorable exchange rates. Table 4 represents a range of possible exchange rates derived from experience and from the judgments of professional defense analysts.

None of these values can be taken as definitive. Factors of troop quality, leadership, terrain, and terrain preparation would all figure in determining the exchange rate of an actual battle. Nevertheless, consistent with the view that Soviet doctrine is superior to NATO's and the view that offense is somehow a "better" posture than defense implicit in that doctrine, a relatively gentle 1.5:1 exchange rate is imposed on the Soviets in the "Soviet" case. This still assumes some advantage for the tactical defender, although not very much.

The "NATO" case assumes a slightly more favorable exchange rate, 2:1. This is still a good deal less than the Israelis enjoyed in 1973 and a good deal less than many professional estimates available.

Table 4. Exchange Rates

Source	Exchange Rate	Comments
Author's Estimate[a]	Arab–Israeli, 3:1	1973 War, tanks, Israel outnumbered 2:1, Israel on both defense and offense.
Author's Estimate[b]	Syria–Israel, 4.5:1	Golan Heights, 1973, tanks, 1st five days, Israel outnumbered by at least 3:1 for much of the fighting, Israel mainly on defense.
Cordesman[c]	Pact–NATO, 3.2:1	Tanks, Pact outnumbers NATO 2.7:1, theater-wide.
Dunnigan[d]	Offense–Defense, 4–6:1	Offense outnumbers defense 2–3:1, tactical engagement.
Interviews	Offense–Defense, 3–6:1	Consistent with the view that the defender, armed with modern weaponry, can hold outnumbered 3–6:1.

[a] These estimates are based on Trevor N. Dupuy, *Elusive Victory: The Arab–Israeli Wars, 1947–1948* (New York: Harper and Row, 1978), p. 609; Shlomo Gazit, "Arab Forces Two Years After the Yom Kippur War," in Louis Williams, ed., *Military Aspects of the Israeli–Arab Conflict* (Tel Aviv: University Publishing Projects, 1975), pp. 188, 194.

[b] This estimate is based on Dupuy, *Elusive Victory,* pp. 437–461; and Chaim Herzog, *The War of Atonement: October 1973* (Boston: Little, Brown, 1975), pp. 55–127. Both accounts agree that by the end of the fourth day of combat, the two Israeli armored brigades that had withstood the initial Syrian attacks were left with less than two dozen operable tanks. This would imply that roughly 200 tanks had suffered enough damage to be viewed as casualties. Not all of these were seriously damaged, and some tanks from reinforcing brigades were also casualties, but 200 seems a good rough estimate of losses for this phase of the battle. Herzog reports that, for one reason or another, the Syrians left nearly 900 tanks on the Golan Heights in their retreat. Some of these had been abandoned in operable condition (p. 127). Thus a 4.5:1 exchange rate for this phase of the battle would seem a fair estimate.

[c] Anthony H. Cordesman, "The NATO Central Region and the Balance of Uncertainty," *Armed Forces Journal International,* July 1983, pp. 36–37.

[d] James F. Dunnigan, *How To Make War* (New York: William Morrow, 1982), pp. 39–40.

ADVANCE RATES

Advance rates during breakthrough operations have also not received a thorough public discussion, although one analyst has compared historical advance rates with those found in published Soviet writing. Perhaps the most definitive conclusion that can be gleaned from a quick historical survey is that sustained advances of 15–20 km per day are possible against a disorganized, erratic, and uncoordinated defense.[46] This estimate, however, is in

46. Jeffrey Record's dated, but still useful, examination of historical armored advance rates notes that some Soviet guidelines call for sustained advances of over 100 km per day. "Armored

sharp contrast to the 100 km or more per day found in some Soviet literature. Since the Attrition–FEBA Expansion Model tests NATO's ability to prevent breakthroughs during stressful assaults, the question is: what is a reasonable rate of advance for a determined breakthrough effort?

Jeffrey Record notes that during the breakthrough battle at Sedan in 1940, it took the German XIX Panzer Corps (1st, 2nd, and 10th Panzer divisions) some four days to crack the French defense line near Sedan for an average daily advance of about 6 km per day.[47] The "Soviet" case assumes a 5 km daily rate of advance. Such an assumption would be consistent with the hypothesis that a NATO–Pact quantitative and qualitative gap similar to that which existed between the best-armed and best-trained mechanized formations of the German army and a mixed bag of largely unmechanized, active and reserve, French infantry divisions will prevail in the breakthrough sectors. This would seem a pessimistic assessment of the quality and quantity of NATO's military forces.

The "NATO" case makes movement rate assumptions more consistent with the tougher defensive actions of World War II. The U.S. First and Ninth Armies' efforts to reach the Roer River, after the Siegfried Line had been partially breached, may be taken as representative of such actions. The area opposite the Ninth Army's XIX Corps was rolling, open country, dotted with small villages. The Germans had taken three weeks to prepare the area with earthworks and belts of mines. This sector would be similar to the more topographically attractive breakthrough sectors along the inter-German border. Since the "Soviet" case assumes that at least a month is required for the Pact to train and move forward the Category II divisions needed to support a big attack, NATO would have as much time to prepare the terrain for defense as the Germans did. Although the Allies enjoyed complete air superiority, reasonably good (though not great) flying weather, outnumbered the Germans by at least 5:1, and had a very high offensive force-to-space ratio, the advance rate for the XIX Corps was barely one km per day, for a three-week period.[48] Low rates of advance also prevailed in the First Army sectors, especially in the highly defensible Hurtgen forest. Similarly, low advance rates and high attrition rates were experienced by the U.S. and

---

Advance Rates: A Historical Inquiry," *Military Review*, Vol. 53, No. 9 (September 1973), p. 63. For advance rates against scattered opposition, see pp. 65–66.
47. Ibid., p. 64.
48. MacDonald, *The Siegfried Line Campaign*, pp. 397, 409–410, 520, 577, Maps VII and VIII.

British forces in their efforts to break out of the Normandy bridgehead in early to mid-July 1944.[49]

In order not to appear excessively optimistic, despite these historical examples, the Soviets are given credit in the "NATO" case for a sustained 2 km rate of advance—this with a real force ratio, including "tacair," below 2:1, and an adjusted force ratio below 1.5:1. Both of these ratios are in stark contrast to the 3:1 offense-defense superiority traditionally cited as acceptable to the defense, the 4–6:1 ratio that I have encountered among experts, and the 5:1 force ratios that U.S. and British forces usually needed to dislodge the Germans in World War II. Thus, allowing the Pact a *sustained* forward movement rate of 2 km per day in all three breakthrough sectors is not a particularly optimistic assumption from NATO's perspective.

Lessons of the Model

In sum, using standard military judgments and historical analogies, it is possible to estimate some plausible alternative values for the seven variables discussed here. Each of these variables is, for a variety of reasons, very difficult to gauge with confidence. The analysis above describes one possible way of using these variables to model an assessment of the Warsaw Pact

---

49. Martin Blumenson, *Breakout and Pursuit* (Washington, D.C.: U.S. Government Printing Office, 1961), pp. 175–176, 194. Extrapolation from past military engagements to possible future battles between NATO and the Warsaw Pact is an exercise that requires much care. In general, I have chosen to examine recent battles in the Middle East and World War II battles on the Western Front because both involve most of the same basic kinds of ground and air forces that would be employed in a NATO–Pact war.

Middle East combat is especially interesting because the belligerents employ virtually the same weapons and much of the same tactics and organization as are found in Central Europe today. One must, of course, be sure to account for the great qualitative disparity that seems to prevail between Israeli officers and enlisted men and those of that country's Arab adversaries.

Careful study of World War II battles in Western Europe between Anglo–American forces and those of Germany offers somewhat different advantages and disadvantages. Clearly, the equipment was a good deal more primitive than that which we field today, but all the basic elements of current military forces were present. Combat in Europe in 1944 occurred on nearly as large a scale as would prevail today. By 1944, as a function of the casualties that Germany had suffered and the experience that the British and Americans had accrued, the qualitative disparity between the officers and enlisted men of the German army and those of the Allies was probably the smallest that has prevailed between mechanized armies anywhere. Historians do seem to agree, however, that the Germans still enjoyed a meaningful degree of superior military leadership. Much of the terrain fought over in 1944 is quite similar to that along the inter-German border today. In gross terms, the Allies enjoyed a substantial materiel superiority over the Germans, which far exceeded the level of superiority attributed to the Pact today. Thus, it is my judgment that German defensive successes against the Allies are quite relevant to assessing the course of future conflict between NATO and Warsaw Pact.

conventional threat to Europe. Using a similar model, one could have used numbers different from those chosen here, but for the purposes of illustration, these numbers seem to represent sound choices.

Using these explicit judgments for the reasons explained in the preceding sections, what do we learn about the NATO–Warsaw Pact balance?

Figures 3 and 4 (pp. 63, 66) portray the results of applying "Pact" and "NATO" military doctrine respectively to assessing NATO's ability to cope with a conflict in the Central Region today. Figure 3 illustrates the application of Soviet doctrine and is broadly consistent with more pessimistic assessments of the balance. The figure shows the rapid development of a rather dangerous situation for NATO, one that would ultimately lead either to the loss of Germany or to nuclear escalation. The Pact manages to close its low-readiness Category II and III divisions to the battle area in short order. They are assigned full credit for their assigned weaponry, without reference to combat readiness or supportability. I do assume, however, that the Pact would need at least two full weeks to ready itself for an attack of this magnitude. NATO mobilizes seven days after the Pact, and receives no credit for the larger command and support apparatus with which it manages, maintains, and supplies its combat equipment. The Pact concentrates large forces and imposes a sustained, violent battle in the key breakthrough sectors, effectively neutralizes NATO tactical air capabilities, and prevents NATO from achieving a particularly favorable exchange rate. Additionally, the Pact achieves fairly high rates of advance in the breakthrough sectors.

Under these circumstances, after two weeks of combat, NATO finds itself trying to hold 45 km sectors with each remaining ADE of firepower.[50] The Pact, on the other hand, still has enough forces left to populate the whole front and the flanks of each salient at one ADE per 25 km, and has two ADEs per 25 km poised for a fresh effort in each breakthrough sector. Given this situation, NATO is clearly in trouble. Either it will have already ordered a general withdrawal to shorten the total defense line (i.e., eliminate the shoulders of the major penetrations), or it will have suffered, or be on the verge of suffering, a breach in the line. Such a breach could produce disruptive, deep, blitzkrieg-style penetrations into NATO's rear areas. More con-

---

50. This is in sharp contrast to the 25 km per ADE that some analysts view as a conservative average strength that NATO should try to achieve along the Central Front. See, for example, Mako, *U.S. Ground Forces*, p. 37, based on his interview with analysts in the Office of the Secretary of Defense.

servatively, the Pact could aim for envelopments of major NATO formations and their subsequent annihilation. In either case, NATO would face disaster. Thus, NATO would likely opt for early withdrawal across the front, allowing a general Pact advance that could ultimately result in the loss of Germany. As such a process unfolded, some NATO military leaders would no doubt request authorization for the use of nuclear weapons.

Figure 4 illustrates a very different outcome. In my view, this seems a more accurate portrayal of the pattern of conflict than does the preceding case. Here, as a consequence of the relative unreadiness of Pact Category II and III divisions, and as a function of taking some credit for NATO's efforts in the areas of command and support (i.e., NATO's ADE score is multiplied by 1.5 in order to represent the increased effectiveness that should result from greater efforts in these areas), the overall capabilities ratio over time looks very different from what the conventional wisdom would suggest. Figure 6 illustrates the conventional view of the capabilities balance over time and an adjusted view. Figure 4 also credits NATO's tactical aircraft with markedly greater success against Pact ground forces than Pact aircraft enjoy

Figure 6. Pact/NATO Capability Ratios Over Time; Mobilization Only–No Attrition

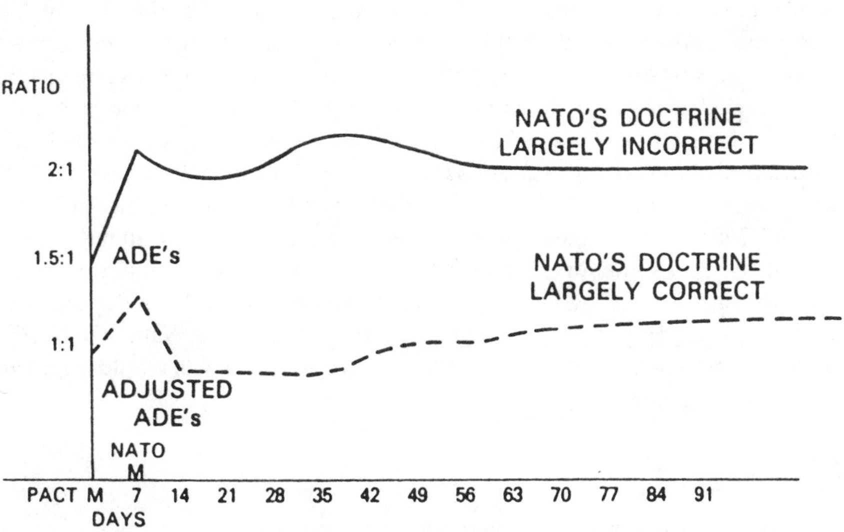

SOURCE: Derived from Figures 3 and 4

against NATO's ground forces. Reflecting available information on Pact intentions and historical experience, the Pact is credited with a lower offensive concentration in the breakthrough sectors. A more favorable exchange rate, reflecting the advantages often credited to the defense by military planners and commentators, is also assumed. Consistent with all of the preceding assumptions, and with a good deal of American and British experience fighting the Germans in World War II, a slower advance rate in the breakthrough sectors is factored into the model.

With these assumptions, NATO appears capable of coping successfully with Pact efforts to achieve catastrophic breakthroughs. The Pact is capable of mounting a good-sized attack at M+30, which it could sustain for roughly two weeks before it would find itself short of reserves. NATO's mobilization lags the Pact's by seven days, but the Alliance would possess sufficient reserves to cope with the Pact advance without having to initiate a general withdrawal. The Pact would resume the offensive two weeks later once its Category III divisions were ready for action, but NATO forces would still be strong enough to deal with the penetrations without resorting to a general withdrawal. As a result, NATO should not be particularly vulnerable to a major rupture of the line. In this second phase of the battle, as a function of unreplaced aircraft attrition and lower sortie rates, NATO ground forces would have to work harder and take more casualties than they did in the first phase of the battle. Both the Pact and NATO would begin running short of forces to sustain this pace of battle after three weeks, and it seems likely that a period of reduced activity would set in. Finally, the outcome portrayed here is a little artificial, since NATO's reserves in the first phase of the battle would probably allow it to counterattack successfully and thus hold the Pact to an even slower rate of advance than that assumed. Similarly, the "surplus" of NATO's available forces over its needs for most of the battle suggests that, even if the Pact somehow managed to convert one of its salients into a clean breakthrough, NATO would have operational reserves to throw against the Pact's exploitation effort. Several uncommitted ADEs would remain to NATO until the last week of heavy fighting, when the Pact itself would begin to run short of forces.

Conclusion

Figures 3 and 4 portray the very different implications for NATO in the Central Region that arise from a comprehensive application of Pact and

NATO doctrine. If assumptions consistent with the notion that most of the Pact's allocation decisions are right and most of NATO's are wrong are factored into a balance assessment, one can produce a very pessimistic portrayal of NATO's military prospects. If, however, assumptions consistent with NATO's pattern of resource allocation are factored into a balance assessment, things look better (see Figure 4). If these assumptions are further combined with an assessment of the constraints that would govern the employment of Pact forces, a conservative application of military rules of thumb, and some inferences from Western military experience, NATO's prospects seem much brighter.

Under relatively conservative assumptions, NATO's forces appear adequate to prevent the Pact from making a clean armored breakthrough. The ground forces of the Alliance seem large enough to hold the Pact to breakthrough-sector force ratios that are much lower than those that soldiers and military commentators have thought necessary to produce success. If the Pact is given credit for an ability to make NATO withdraw at a slow pace that is consistent with the low force ratio, *and* Pact units are forced to pay a relatively modest price to do so (i.e., a two-to-one exchange rate), NATO still appears capable of containing the penetrations and preventing breakthroughs. Moreover, as was noted earlier, NATO still would have sizable uncommitted reserves for much of the battle, which could counterattack a successful breakthrough if it occurred.

Clearly, if NATO's doctrine is correct (and I have tried to show that this is at least plausible), its forces are much more likely to defend successfully than is widely perceived to be the case. The question then is whether NATO has chosen the correct doctrine. If not, then huge new investments spent the same old way cannot rectify whatever defense problems the Alliance may actually have. If the doctrine is correct, then major new investments in capabilities may not be necessary. Rather, investments should be carefully directed towards buying more insurance in the areas of greatest uncertainty.[51]

The practice of building forces according to a theory of victory that NATO's military planners apparently believe and then assessing their capabilities

---

51. For some specific recommendations for improving NATO's conventional forces, see, for example, Barry R. Posen and Stephen Van Evera, "Defense Policy and the Reagan Administration: Departure from Containment," *International Security*, Vol. 8, No. 1 (Summer 1983), pp. 39–42; and Barry R. Posen, "Competing Views of the Center Region Conventional Balance," in Keith A. Dunn and William O. Staudenmaier, eds., *Alternative Military Strategies for the Future* (Boulder, Colo.: Westview Press, forthcoming).

according to a very different theory of victory can only confuse NATO's political leaders and publics about the state of the military balance and what should be done to improve it. The principal result of this practice is that NATO's current position in conventional forces is made to appear very poor and the investments needed to repair the situation are made to appear very great. While this behavior might help promote some extra investments that could ultimately provide a useful margin of military safety, they may also obscure the progress that NATO has already made, and make modest improvements that lie within the realm of political and economic feasibility appear pointless to those who must find the resources. Similarly, the practice also inhibits clear thinking about NATO's future military efforts. Pessimistic portrayals of the military balance may divert scarce political and economic resources to speculative military ventures that promise quick and easy solutions to NATO's seemingly insurmountable difficulties. To some extent, NATO is already falling victim to these pitfalls.

Finally, one-sided portrayals of the conventional balance may have a pernicious effect in political crises. It is surely true that, if the Pact mobilizes, trains, and assembles its Category II and III divisions and NATO does not respond in some fashion, then the Alliance will shortly find itself in a very dangerous military situation. If, however, NATO's political leaders are convinced that no amount of mobilization will make the Alliance competitive with the Pact, then they will be more inclined to delay in a crisis, out of fear that any military action will not only appear provocative, but will not improve NATO's chances in war anyway. In short, whatever the motives, failure to account fully for the Alliance's current military effort in a NATO–Pact balance assessment has costs. These costs are not always immediately visible, nor are they necessarily incurred by those who engage in such assessments, but they are real—and they may be high.

Why the Soviets Can't Win Quickly in Central Europe

John J. Mearsheimer

In light of the emergence of strategic parity and NATO's manifest lack of enthusiasm for tactical nuclear weapons, the importance of the balance of conventional forces in Central Europe has increased significantly in the past decade.[1] Regarding that balance, the conventional wisdom is clearly that the Warsaw Pact enjoys an overwhelming advantage. In the event of a conventional war, the Soviets are expected to launch a *blitzkrieg* that will lead to a quick and decisive victory.

The implications of this specter of a hopelessly outgunned NATO are significant. Certainly, NATO's behavior in a major crisis would be influenced by its view of the conventional balance. Furthermore, one's perception of the conventional balance directly affects his or her view of the importance of both strategic and tactical nuclear weapons for deterrence in Europe. *The New York Times*, for example, endorsed the controversial neutron bomb as a means to counter NATO's perceived inferiority at the conventional level.[2]

The fact of the matter is that the balance of conventional forces is nowhere near as unfavorable as it is so often portrayed to be. In fact, NATO's prospects for thwarting a Soviet offensive are actually quite good.[3] Certainly, NATO

The author wishes to thank the following people for their helpful comments on earlier drafts of this essay: Robert Art, Mary Mearsheimer, Stephen Meyer, Barry Posen, and Jack Snyder.

John J. Mearsheimer is a Research Associate at Harvard University's Center for International Affairs. This article is based on a chapter in his forthcoming book, The Theory and Practice of Conventional Deterrence.

1. Recognition of this is clearly reflected in the annual *Posture Statements* of the Secretaries of Defense for the past ten years. Also see: Helmut Schmidt's October 1977 speech before the International Institute for Strategic Studies, a copy of which can be found in *Survival*, Vol. 20, No. 1 (January/February 1978), pp. 2–10; and *White Paper 1979: The Security of the Federal Republic of Germany and the Development of the Federal Armed Forces* (Bonn: Federal Minister of Defence, September 4, 1979), p. 112, hereinafter cited as *1979 German White Paper*. Very importantly, the Soviets have also shown increased interest in the possibility of a conventional war in Europe. See Colonel Graham D. Vernon, *Soviet Options For War In Europe: Nuclear or Conventional?* National Security Affairs Monograph 79–1 (Washington D.C.: National Defense University, January 1979).
2. "The Virtues of the Neutron Bomb," Editorial, *The New York Times*, March 30, 1978, p. 32.
3. It should be noted that since the early 1960s there have been a handful of studies which have concluded that NATO has the capability to defend itself against a conventional attack by the

International Security, Summer 1982 (Vol. 7, No. 1) 0162-2889/82/010003-37 $02.50/0

does not have the capability to *win* a conventional war on the continent against the Soviets. NATO does have, however, the wherewithal to *deny* the Soviets a quick victory and then to turn the conflict into a lengthy war of attrition, where NATO's advantage in population and GNP would not bode well for the Soviets.[4]

The aim of this article is to examine closely the Soviets' prospects for effecting a *blitzkrieg* against NATO. In analyzing this matter, two closely related issues must be addressed. First, one must determine whether the Soviets have the force structure, the doctrine, and the raw ability to implement this strategy. In other words, do the Soviets, when viewed in isolation, have the capacity to effect a *blitzkrieg*? Secondly, when NATO's defense capabilities and the theater's terrain are considered, what then are the prospects for Soviet success? It may very well be that the Soviet military is well-primed to launch a *blitzkrieg*, but that NATO in turn has the capability to thwart it.[5]

Any assessment of the NATO–Pact balance is dependent on certain as-

---

Warsaw Pact. See, for example, Alain C. Enthoven and K. Wayne Smith, *How Much Is Enough?* (New York: Harper and Row, 1971), chapter 4. In 1973, the *Washington Post* reported that "a major new Pentagon study," which had been "two years in the making," concluded that NATO could defend itself. See Michael Getler, "Study Insists NATO Can Defend Itself," *Washington Post*, June 7, 1973, pp. 1, 20. Since NATO has spent considerably more money on defense than has the Pact since 1973 (see former Secretary of Defense Harold Brown's *FY 1982 Posture Statement*, Appendix C-12, which is entitled "Comparison of NATO and Warsaw Pact Total Defense Costs") and since there have been no significant changes in the force levels of each side since 1973, there is no reason to believe that the conclusions of this study are outdated. Actually, Harold Brown's four *Posture Statements* (FY 1979–FY 1982) describe a situation where NATO stands a reasonable chance of thwarting a Warsaw Pact offensive without resorting to nuclear weapons. Such a viewpoint, however, is hardly commonplace.

4. There are a variety of other reasons why the Soviets would want to avoid a war of attrition. Obviously, they would not want to suffer the tremendous costs associated with a lengthy conventional war. Second, the Soviet Army is not configured for a long war. Although the Soviets could remedy this problem, the fact remains that they have not. Third, because of the Sino-Soviet split, the Soviets must consider the possibility of a war on two fronts. Even if there was not an imminent threat of war with China, a war of attrition in the West would threaten to weaken the Soviets to the point where they might think themselves vulnerable to a Chinese attack. Fourth, there is the real threat of unrest among the non-Soviet armies as well as the populations of the East European states, should the Pact find itself engaged in a bloody war. (See A. Ross Johnson et al., "The Armies of the Warsaw Pact Northern Tier," *Survival*, Vol. 23, No. 4 [July/August 1981], pp. 174–182.) Finally, there is the danger that nuclear weapons will be used if the Soviets do not win a quick and decisive victory. Also see fn. 65.

5. This study does not consider the impact of air forces on the balance. Although it is possible that NATO's airpower will not have the decisive influence on the land battle that many expect, it is clear that the air balance, when qualitative and quantitative factors are considered, does not favor the Pact. See Carnegie Panel on U.S. Security and the Future of Arms Control, *Challenges for U.S. National Security, Assessing the Balance: Defense Spending and Conventional Forces*, A Preliminary Report, Part II (Washington D.C.: Carnegie Endowment for International Peace, 1981), pp. 69–73.

sumptions made about the preparatory moves both sides take before the war starts. Among the many that might be considered, three scenarios are most often posited. The first of these is the "standing start" attack,[6] in which the Soviets launch an attack after hardly any mobilization and deliver a knock-out blow against an unsuspecting NATO.[7] This is not, however, a likely eventuality. First of all, without significantly improving the readiness of their standing forces, the Soviets would not have the capability to score a decisive victory. Instead, they would have to settle for capturing a portion of West German territory. Such a limited victory is hardly an attractive option.[8] Secondly, for a war in Europe to become a realistic possibility, there would have to be a significant deterioration in East–West relations. Given such a development, it is very likely that both sides will take some steps, however limited, to increase the readiness of their forces. It is difficult to imagine a scenario where an alert Pact catches NATO completely unprepared.

---

6. The two most prominent examples of this viewpoint are General Robert Close, *Europe Without Defense?* (New York: Pergamon, 1979) and U.S., Congress, Senate Armed Services Committee, *NATO and the New Soviet Threat*, report by Senators Sam Nunn and Dewey F. Bartlett, 95th Cong., 1st Sess. (Washington D.C.: GPO, January 24, 1977), hereinafter cited as *Nunn-Bartlett Report*. For the best critique of this scenario, see Les Aspin, "A Surprise Attack On NATO: Refocusing the Debate," a copy of which can be found in *Congressional Record*, February 7, 1977, pp. H911–H914.

7. It should be emphasized that, given NATO's intelligence-gathering capabilities, the Pact would not be able to mobilize its forces in any significant way without being detected—thus taking away the element of surprise. Therefore, the notion of "an immense blitzkrieg preceded by little warning" (*Nunn-Bartlett Report*, p. 16) or a "gigantic operation [that] would have the advantage of complete surprise" (Robert Close, "The Feasibility of a Surprise Attack Against Western Europe," study prepared for the NATO Defense College, February 24, 1975) is unrealistic. A massive surprise attack is a contradiction in terms.

8. With an attack from a standing start, the Soviets would not be able to employ all of the Pact's 57⅓ standing divisions. Undoubtedly, they would rely on the 19 Soviet divisions stationed in East Germany and the 5 Soviet divisions stationed in Czechoslovakia. However, they probably would not upgrade these divisions significantly prior to an attack for fear that this would tip off NATO. Given that non-Soviet divisions in the Pact are three-quarters or less manned and that alerting them of a forthcoming offensive might lead to a security breach, it is highly unlikely that these forces would be used for a surprise attack. This would leave the Pact with 24 Soviet divisions, which would be striking against NATO's 28 divisions. The 24:28 ratio would shrink even further if translated into either armored division equivalents or divisional manpower. Although NATO's forces would not be in their forward positions in this scenario, the Pact would still have to defeat these forces to gain a decisive victory. This is hardly likely given the balance of forces that attend this scenario and the fact that the Pact would not overrun NATO's forces *at the outset* of this conflict. Instead, a majority of NATO's forces would be located behind their forward defensive positions, where they would have ample time to identify the Pact's main thrusts. A number of analysts point out that such a short-warning attack will invariably result in a limited victory. See, for example, Aspin, "A Surprise Attack On NATO," pp. H912–H913; Alain Enthoven, "U.S. Forces In Europe: How Many? Doing What?" *Foreign Affairs*, Vol. 53, No. 3 (April 1975), pp. 517–518; and General James H. Polk, "The North German Plain Attack Scenario: Threat or Illusion?" *Strategic Review*, Vol. 8, No. 3 (Summer 1980), pp. 60–66.

The second scenario is a more realistic and more dangerous one. Here, in the midst of a crisis, NATO detects a Pact mobilization, but does not mobilize its forces for a fear of triggering a Soviet attack.[9] Surely, if NATO fails to respond quickly to a Pact mobilization as posited in this second scenario, the Pact would soon be in a position to inflict a decisive defeat on NATO.

In the third scenario, NATO's mobilization begins immediately after the Pact starts to mobilize. Here, the Pact does not gain an overwhelming force advantage as a result of NATO's failure to mobilize. It is with this third scenario that I shall concern myself in the present essay. The focus will thus be on a conflict in which both sides are alerted and where neither enjoys an advantage as a result of the other's failure to mobilize.

This is not to deny that strategic warning and especially the political decision to mobilize are important issues. They certainly are and they will have a significant influence on the outcome of any future conflict in Europe. The assumption on which I base the following analysis is that strategic warning and mobilization are acted upon by NATO; the raw capabilities of the opposing forces will thus be examined under those clearly defined conditions.

Before directly assessing Soviet prospects for launching a successful *blitzkrieg*, we must examine briefly the balance of forces on the Central Front and the doctrines of the two sides.

The Balance of Forces on the Central Front

The Pact has 57⅓ divisions located in Central Europe, while NATO has 28⅓, giving the Pact slightly more than a 2:1 advantage in divisions.[10] Comparing

---

9. For an excellent discussion of this matter, see Richard K. Betts, "Surprise Attack: NATO's Political Vulnerability," *International Security*, Vol. 5, No. 4 (Spring 1981), pp. 117–149. Also see his "Hedging Against Surprise Attack," *Survival*, Vol. 23, No. 4 (July/August 1981), pp. 146–156.

10. These figures are taken from Robert L. Fischer, *Defending the Central Front: The Balance of Forces*, Adelphi Paper No. 127 (London: IISS, 1976), p. 8. Fischer's calculations are based on the assumption that the Pact has 58⅓ divisions in Central Europe. Actually, the Soviets recently removed a division from East Germany, leaving 57⅓ divisions. Since the Soviets have increased the size of their remaining divisions somewhat and since my argument does not rest on precise calculations (see fn. 20), this minor discrepancy raises no problems. Regarding the balance of divisions on the Central Front, also see James Blaker and Andrew Hamilton, *Assessing the NATO/Warsaw Pact Military Balance* (Washington D.C.: Congressional Budget Office, December 1977) and *The Military Balance, 1980–1981* (London: IISS, 1980). Although the Fischer and Blaker/Hamilton studies are somewhat dated, there have been no shifts in the force levels on either side which would alter the figures in these studies in any significant way. It should be noted

numbers of divisions, however, gives a distorted view of the balance, since this measure does not account for the significant differences, both qualitative and quantitative, among each nation's divisions. There are generally two alternative ways of assessing the balance. One is to focus on the manpower on each side, while the other is to compare weaponry.[11]

MANPOWER

Robert Lucas Fischer, in his 1976 study of the conventional balance in Europe (which is, unfortunately, one of the few comprehensive studies done on that subject), notes that NATO has 414,000 men in its divisions, while the Pact has 564,000.[12] With this measure of divisional manpower, the Soviet advantage shrinks to 1.36:1. Fischer calculates that when overall manpower levels on the Central Front are considered, the Pact's advantage shrinks even further to 1.09:1. This is because NATO has traditionally had more men assigned to combat units which are not organic to divisions. Since the study was issued, the Pact has added approximately 50,000 men, raising the overall advantage in manpower to 1.15:1—hardly an alarming figure.[13] In the British Government's recent *Statement on Defence Estimates, 1981*, the Soviets are given an advantage in overall manpower of 1.2:1.[14] Under the category of "soldiers in fighting units," the Soviets are again given a 1.2:1 advantage. These figures are clear evidence that NATO is not hopelessly outnumbered.[15]

---

that throughout this article, French forces are counted in the NATO totals. Regarding this assumption, see *1979 German White Paper*, p. 118.

11. It should be emphasized that the available data base on the conventional balance is a relatively primitive one. Certainly, there are a number of simple assessments where, for example, numbers of tanks or numbers of divisions are counted. There are, however, very few comprehensive studies of the balance in which analysts attempt to examine the balance of forces in a detailed manner. This is especially true with regard to weaponry. There is an acute need for studies which attempt to look at all the weapon systems on each side, and at all of the various indexes by which their effectiveness is measured, and then make some overall judgment about the balance. This article will not attempt such a net assessment of forces on the European front. Its purposes are, rather, more limited: to rebut on their own terms the many critics who claim that NATO's numerical inferiority has made it hopelessly vulnerable to defeat by a Soviet *blitzkrieg*.

12. See Fischer, *Defending the Central Front*, pp. 10–15.

13. This increase has been reflected in the annual *Military Balance*. Also see Robert Shishko, *The European Conventional Balance: A Primer*, P–6707 (Santa Monica, Calif.: Rand Corporation, November 24, 1981), p. 18.

14. Quoted in Shishko, *ibid.*, p. 18.

15. It should be noted that if the entire French Army were counted, instead of just the French forces stationed in West Germany, NATO forces *would* outnumber Pact forces. See Blaker and Hamilton, *Assessing the NATO/Warsaw Pact Military Balance*, p. 11.

Perhaps the most important problem with comparing manpower levels, however, is that it does not account for weaponry.

WEAPONS

It is not difficult to compare numbers of specific weapons on each side. For example, the Pact has approximately a 2.5:1 advantage in tanks and about a 2.8:1 advantage in artillery.[16] Such comparisons, however, do not take into account qualitative differences within the same category of weapons (i.e., NATO's artillery is significantly better than Pact artillery); nor do they deal with the problem of comparing different categories of weapons (i.e., tanks vs. artillery). To counter this problem, the Defense Department has devised a system of weighing weapons within the same category as well as across different categories.[17] Three principal characteristics of each weapon are considered: mobility, survivability, and firepower. Using this system, the Defense Department weighs all the weaponry in every division on the Central Front and then arrives at a composite figure, known as armored division equivalents (ADEs), for both NATO and the Warsaw Pact. Unfortunately, the number of armored division equivalents on each side is classified. Very importantly, however, the ratio is not. Looking at standing forces, the Pact has a 1.2:1 advantage.[18] Again, it is clear that NATO is not hopelessly outnumbered.

REINFORCEMENT AND MOBILIZATION

Now, consider the critical matter of comparative reinforcement capabilities. Although NATO's reinforcement capability is not as great as the Soviets' in an absolute sense, NATO has the potential to keep the overall ratio of forces very close to the pre-mobilization ratio. The notion that the Soviets can rely

---

16. These figures are from Shishko, *The European Conventional Balance*, p. 18.
17. For further discussion of the concept of armored division equivalents, see Blaker and Hamilton, *Assessing the NATO/Warsaw Pact Military Balance*; and U.S. Army Concepts Analysis Agency, *Weapon Effectiveness Indicies/Weighted Unit Values (WEI/WUV)*, Study Report CAA–SR–73–18 (Bethesda, Maryland: U.S. Army Concepts Analysis Agency, April 1974).
18. Regarding the balance of armored division equivalents, see Pat Hillier, *Strengthening NATO: Pomcus and Other Approaches* (Washington D.C.: Congressional Budget Office, February 1979), pp. 53–57; and Pat Hillier and Nora Slatkin, *U.S. Ground Forces: Design and Cost Alternatives for NATO and Non-NATO Contingencies* (Washington D.C.: Congressional Budget Office, December 1980), pp. 23–24. It should be noted that this figure was calculated on the basis of 58⅓ Pact divisions and not 57⅓ divisions (see fn. 10). Also, it is not possible to ascertain whether NATO and Pact non-divisional assets have been incorporated into this 1.2:1 ratio. If not, the ratio would shift further in NATO's favor when they were added to the balance.

on some massive second echelon that NATO cannot match is a false one. However, the ratio of forces in any future mobilization will be heavily influenced by the timeliness with which each side starts to mobilize. If NATO begins mobilizing its forces before the Pact does, or simultaneously with the Pact, then the force ratios will remain close to the 1.2:1 (in armored division equivalents) and 1.36:1 (in divisional manpower), the ratios which obtained before mobilization.[19] If NATO starts mobilizing a few days after the Pact, then the balance of forces should approach but not exceed a 2:1 ratio in the very early days of mobilization and then fall to a level close to the pre-mobilization ratios. But once the gap in mobilization starting times reaches seven days (in the Pact's favor), NATO begins to face serious problems, problems which become even more pronounced as the mobilization gap widens further. As noted, the assumption here is that NATO starts mobilizing immediately after the Pact, thus ensuring that the overall force ratios never reach 2:1, and, in fact, remain reasonably close to the pre-mobilization ratios.

NUMBERS AND STRATEGY: THE CRITICAL CONNECTION

It should be emphasized that there are definite limits to the utility of measuring force levels. After all, even a cursory study of military history would show that it is impossible to explain the outcome of many important military campaigns by simply comparing the number of forces on each side. Nevertheless, it is clear that if one side has an overwhelming advantage in forces, that glaring asymmetry is very likely to lead to a decisive victory. In essence, the larger force will simply overwhelm the smaller one as, for example, the Germans did against the Poles in September 1939. The previous analysis of the balance of forces in Europe indicates that the Soviets do not enjoy such an overwhelming advantage. They do not have the numerical superiority to simply crush NATO. In a conventional war in Europe, whether or not the Soviets prevail will depend on how they employ their forces against NATO's defenses. In other words, success will be a function of strategy, not overwhelming numbers. This is not to deny that the Soviets would be better

---

19. See Fischer, *Defending the Central Front*, pp. 20–25 and Hillier, *Strengthening NATO*, pp. 53–57. Also see Hillier's more recent study (*U.S. Ground Forces*), where he makes the highly questionable assumption that the Soviets will have 120 divisions in Central Europe after 30 days. Even then, the overall ratio of armored division equivalents never exceeds 2:1 (see p. 24 of his study). In fact, at its peak, the ratio for the 120 division figure is 1.7:1.

served with an overall advantage in armored division equivalents of 1.8:1 rather than, say, 1.2:1. But regardless of which ratio obtains, ultimate success will turn on the issue of strategy. More specifically, success will depend on the Soviets' capability to effect a *blitzkrieg*.[20]

Doctrine

NATO's forces are divided into eight corps sectors which are aligned in layer-cake fashion along the inter-German border (see Figure 1).[21] There are four corps sectors each in Northern Army Group (NORTHAG) and Central Army Group (CENTAG). There are also German and Danish forces located in Schleswig-Holstein, which is adjacent to the northern portion of the Central Front.

NATO's forces are arrayed to support a strategy of forward defense. In other words, to meet a Pact offensive, the forces in each of NATO's corps sectors are deployed very close to the border between the two Germanies. The objective is to meet and thwart an attack right at this boundary. Political as well as military considerations dictate the choice of this strategy. A number of defense analysts in the West, however, argue that NATO's chances of thwarting a Pact attack are negligible as long as NATO employs a forward defense. They claim that the Soviets can mass their forces at points of their choosing along NATO's extended front, achieve overwhelming force ratios, and then blast through NATO's forward defense. It would then be very easy to effect deep strategic penetrations, since NATO has few reserves which could be used to check the Soviets' armored spearheads. These analysts favor a maneuver-oriented defense.[22] The subsequent discussion will address the charge that NATO's strategy of forward defense is fundamentally flawed.

---

20. This discussion of the importance of strategy highlights the key point that my argument does not depend on precise calculations about the balance of forces. In other words, whether or not the balance of armored division equivalents is 1.2:1 or 1.3:1 is not, in and of itself, of great consequence. Of course, there is no doubt, as just noted in the text, that there is an important difference between a balance of 1.2:1 and 1.8:1. See the discussion in fns. 33 and 61.
21. A corps normally controls from 2–3 divisions as well as a number of non-divisional assets. In NATO, corps are comprised of forces from only one nation.
22. For a discussion of the views of the maneuver advocates, see my "Maneuver, Mobile Defense, and the NATO Central Front," *International Security*, Vol. 6, No. 3 (Winter 1981/1982), pp. 104–122.

Figure 1. NATO Corps Sectors West Germany

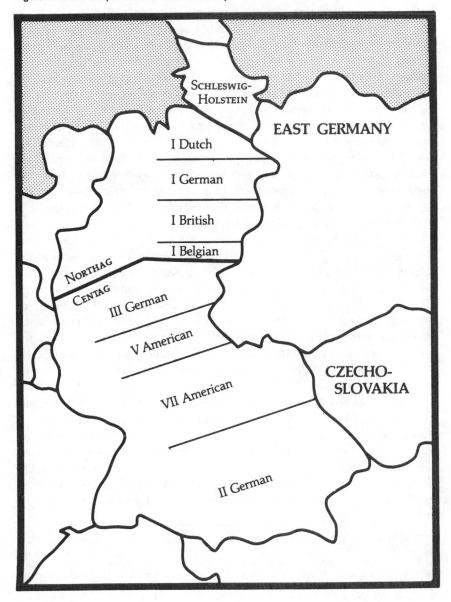

SOVIET BLITZKRIEG STRATEGY

How do the Soviets plan to fight a non-nuclear war in Europe? What, in other words, is their doctrine for fighting a conventional war? Western analysts often assume that the Soviets have a neatly packaged doctrine for fighting a conventional war. As will become evident, this is not the case. The assumption here is that they will employ a *blitzkrieg*.[23] This strategy calls for the attacker to concentrate his armored forces at one or more points along the defender's front, pierce that front, and race deep into the defender's rear. The aim is to avoid a broad frontal attack and, instead, to drive a small number of powerful armored columns into the depths of the defense. Although it may be necessary to engage in a set-piece battle to accomplish the initial breakthrough, a high premium is placed on avoiding further battles of this sort and, instead, following the path of least resistance deep into the opponent's rear. Of course, the tank, with its inherent flexibility, is the ideal weapon for implementing such a strategy.

The *blitzkrieg* is predicated upon the assumptions that the defender's army is geared to fighting along a well-established defensive line, and that the defender has a vulnerable communications network located in its rear. This network would be comprised of numerous lines of communication, along which move supplies as well as information, and key nodal points which join these various lines. Destruction of this central nervous system is tantamount to destroying the army. The attacker, therefore, attempts to pierce the defender's front and then drive *deep* into the defender's rear, severing lines of communication and destroying key junctures in the communications network as he proceeds.

Although the Soviets do not use the term *blitzkrieg*, it is clear that they pay serious attention to the question of how to effect a *blitzkrieg* against NATO. They continually emphasize the importance of massing large tank forces on narrow fronts, breaking through NATO's forward defenses, and then racing deep into NATO's rear so as to bring about the rapid collapse of NATO's forces. Furthermore, the Soviets have shown considerable interest in studying the lessons of their 1945 offensive against the Japanese Army in Man-

---

23. Despite the frequency with which the term *blitzkrieg* is used, there is no systematic study of this military strategy. It will be discussed at length in my forthcoming book, *The Theory and Practice of Conventional Deterrence*. Also see B.H. Liddell Hart, *Memoirs*, Vol. 1 (London: Cassell, 1967), pp. 64–65; *HDv 100/100, Command and Control* (Bonn: Ministry of Defence, September 1973), chapter 27; and Edward N. Luttwak, "The Operational Level of War," *International Security*, Vol. 5, No. 3 (Winter 1980/1981), pp. 67–73.

churia.[24] That operation was a classic *blitzkrieg*. Although the focus here is on the Soviets' capability to effect a *blitzkrieg*, there *is* an alternative strategy that the Soviets might employ. They could employ their forces as they did against the Germans on the Eastern Front in World War II.[25] Instead of relying on deep strategic penetrations to bring about the collapse of the German Army, Soviet strategy called for wearing the German Army down by slowly pushing it back along a broad front. Massive firepower is the key ingredient in this strategy of attrition.

There is no doubt that the Soviets want to use a *blitzkrieg* strategy in any future war in Europe. There is, however, growing doubt in the Soviet Union as to whether this is possible on the modern battlefield.[26] This matter has been debated at length in Soviet military journals. Despite such attention, apparently no clear consensus has emerged on this issue. The important question, which will be addressed later, is: what effect does this doctrinal uncertainty have on the Soviets' ability to effect a *blitzkrieg*?

Soviet Prospects for Effecting a Blitzkrieg in Central Europe

By choosing a forward defense strategy, NATO has effectively determined that a war in Europe will be won or lost along the inter-German border. It is thus imperative that NATO thwart the Pact in those initial battles along the border. This point is clearly reflected on the opening page of *FM 100-5*, which spells out basic U.S. Army doctrine: "the first battle of our next war

---

24. See John Despres, Lilita Dzirkals, and Barton Whaley, *Timely Lessons of History: The Manchurian Model for Soviet Strategy*, R–1825–NA (Santa Monica, Calif.: Rand Corporation, July 1976); Lilita I. Dzirkals, *"Lightning War" In Manchuria: Soviet Military Analysis Of The 1945 Far East Campaign*, P–5589 (Santa Monica, Calif.: Rand Corporation, January 1976); and Peter Vigor and Christopher Donnelly, "The Manchurian Campaign and Its Relevance to Modern Strategy," *Comparative Strategy*, Vol. 2, No. 2 (1980), pp. 159–178.

25. For a good description of Soviet strategy against Germany, see Erich von Manstein, "The Development of the Red Army, 1942–1945," in *The Soviet Army*, ed. B.H. Liddell Hart (London: Weidenfeld and Nicolson, 1956), pp. 140–152.

26. See Christopher N. Donnelly's *very important* article, "Tactical Problems Facing the Soviet Army: Recent Debates in the Soviet Military Press," *International Defense Review*, Vol. 11, No. 9 (1978), pp. 1405–1412. This article challenges the widely held belief that the Soviets have developed a well-knit strategy for defeating NATO (see the sources cited in fn. 79 for evidence of this belief). Also see A. A. Grechko, *The Armed Forces Of The Soviet Union*, trans. Yuri Sviridov (Moscow: Progress Publishers, 1977), p. 160; Phillip A. Karber, "The Soviet Anti-Tank Debate," *Survival*, Vol. 18, No. 3 (May/June 1976), pp. 105–111; V. Kulikov, "Soviet Military Science Today," *Strategic Review*, Vol. 5, No. 1 (Winter 1977), pp. 127–134; and Vigor and Donnelly, "The Manchurian Campaign."

could well be its last battle. . . . the U.S. Army must, above all else, *prepare to win the first battle of the next war."*[27] If the Soviets win those initial battles and penetrate with large armored forces deep into NATO's rear, NATO's fate is sealed, since it has neither the reserve strength necessary to counter such penetrations, nor the strategic depth which would allow for retreat and the establishment of a new front.

To determine whether the Soviets can successfully launch a *blitzkrieg* against NATO's forward defense, two key questions must be answered. First, can the Soviets achieve the necessary force ratios on their main axes of advance so that they can then open gateways into NATO's rear? In other words, given the deployment of NATO's forces as well as the terrain, how likely is it that the Soviets will be able to repeat the German achievement opposite the Ardennes Forest in 1940? Is it true, as advocates of a maneuver-oriented defense claim, that the Pact can choose any point on the NATO front and achieve the superiority of forces necessary to effect a breakthrough? The answer to these questions will largely be determined by matching NATO's deployment pattern, which is well known, against those deployment patterns which would most likely be used as part of a Soviet *blitzkrieg*.

Second, if the Soviets are able to tear open a hole or two in NATO's defensive front, will the Soviets be able to exploit those openings and penetrate into the depths of the NATO defense before NATO has a chance to shift forces and slow the penetrating spearheads? Effecting a deep strategic penetration in the "fog of war," when the defender is doing everything possible to seal off the gaps in his defense, is difficult and requires a first-rate army. How capable is the Soviet Army of accomplishing this difficult task? Although it is not possible to provide definitive answers to these questions, there is good reason to believe that NATO is capable of thwarting a Soviet *blitzkrieg* and turning the conflict into a war of attrition.

THE INITIAL DEPLOYMENT PATTERNS

When considering Soviet deployment patterns for a conventional European war, the most basic question is: how will the Soviets apportion their forces across the front? More specifically, will the Soviets disperse their forces rather evenly across the front, mounting attacks along numerous axes, or will they concentrate their forces at one, two, or three points along the inter-German

---

27. *FM 100-5: Operations* (Washington D.C.: Department of the Army, July 1, 1976), p. 1-1.

border? In many of the accounts by Western analysts, it is assumed that a Soviet offensive will be a multi-pronged one. For example, John Erickson expects that they will attempt "eight to ten breakthrough operations."[28] In effect, NATO will be faced with numerous attacks across its entire front. Equally important, it is frequently assumed that the Soviets will achieve overwhelming superiority in forces on *each* of these avenues of attack.

It is possible that the Soviets might choose to launch an offensive along multiple axes of advance. This would be consistent with their doctrine for fighting a nuclear war in Europe, where the emphasis is on keeping the attacking forces widely dispersed so that they are not vulnerable to nuclear attacks. However, such a deployment pattern would hardly facilitate employment of a *blitzkrieg*, simply because it would be virtually impossible for the Soviets, given the present overall balance of forces, to achieve overwhelming force ratios on any of the axes. This can be demonstrated by looking at a *hypothetical* but realistic model of the Central Front.

Let us assume that the Pact has 64 armored division equivalents while NATO has 32; in other words, the Pact has a 2:1 force advantage across the front.[29] Furthermore, assume that the Soviets plan to employ a multi-pronged attack, aiming to strike along six main axes. In keeping with the dictates of a forward defense, NATO divides its 32 divisions evenly among its eight corps sectors (see Figure 2). It is usually assumed that to overwhelm the defense, an attacking force needs more than a 3:1 advantage in forces on the main axes of advance; assume, then, in the first instance, that the Soviets decide that they require a 5:1 advantage.[30] They would therefore need 20

28. John Erickson, "Soviet Breakthrough Operations: Resources and Restraints," *Journal of the Royal United Services Institute*, Vol. 121, No. 3 (September 1976), p. 75. Also see the scenario described by John Hackett et al., *The Third World War: A Future History* (London: Sidgwick and Jackson, 1978), p. 127.

29. It should be emphasized that in light of the balance of standing forces in Central Europe (1.2:1 in terms of armored division equivalents) and the fact that NATO has the capability to match the Pact as it brings in reinforcements, this 2:1 force advantage is a conservative figure. Unless otherwise specified, the unit of measurement in all subsequent discussion of force ratios is armored division equivalents.

30. The Soviets emphasize the importance of achieving overwhelming superiority on the main axes of advance in a conventional war. See V. Ye. Savkin, *The Basic Principles of Operational Art and Tactics* (Moscow, 1972), trans. U.S. Air Force (Washington D.C.: GPO, 1976), pp. 119–152, 201–229 and A.A. Sidorenko, *The Offensive: A Soviet View* (Moscow, 1970), trans. U.S. Air Force (Washington D.C.: GPO, 1976), chapter 1. Based on the lessons of World War II, the Soviets estimate that "a decisive superiority . . . [is] 3–5 times for infantry, 6–8 times for artillery, 3–4 times for tanks and self-propelled artillery, and 5–10 times for aircraft." Sidorenko, p. 82. These ratios are consistent with the American Army's view on the matter. See *FM 100-5*, p. 3-4.

Figure 2. Initial Distribution of NATO Divisions

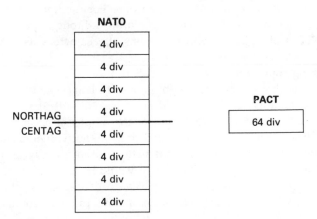

divisions per axis, which would allow them only three main axes of advance[31] (see Figure 3). Moreover, they would be quite vulnerable to NATO in the remaining five corps sectors.

If we assume that the Soviets require only a 4:1 advantage on the main axes, they would then need 16 divisions per axis. This would allow them only four main axes; however, they would not have any forces left with which to defend the remaining corps sectors (see Figure 4). If the Soviets were to aim for the projected six axes, they would be able to place approximately ten divisions on each main axis (see Figure 5). This would give them a force ratio on each axis of 2.5:1, which is hardly satisfactory in light of the widely recognized assumption that an attack requires more than a 3:1 ad-

---

31. This *hypothetical* model is based on the important assumption that the Soviets can only place one main axis in each corps sector. As will become evident in the subsequent discussion, the terrain features along the inter-German border force the attacker to think in terms of a single axis per corps sector. Moreover, in light of the length of the various NATO corps sectors and the length of front the Soviets allot their attacking divisions and armies, it is most likely that the Soviets would locate only one axis in each corps sector. For a discussion of Soviet attack frontages, see Christopher Donnelly, "The Soviet Ground Forces," in *The Soviet War Machine*, ed. Ray Bonds (New York: Chartwell, 1976), pp. 166–170; John Erickson, "Soviet Theatre-Warfare Capability: Doctrines, Deployments and Capabilities," in *The Future of Soviet Military Power*, ed. Lawrence L. Whetten (New York: Crane, Russak, 1976), p. 148; and fn. 58 and the attendant text of this article.

Figure 3. Distribution of Forces When Soviets Desire 5:1 Advantage

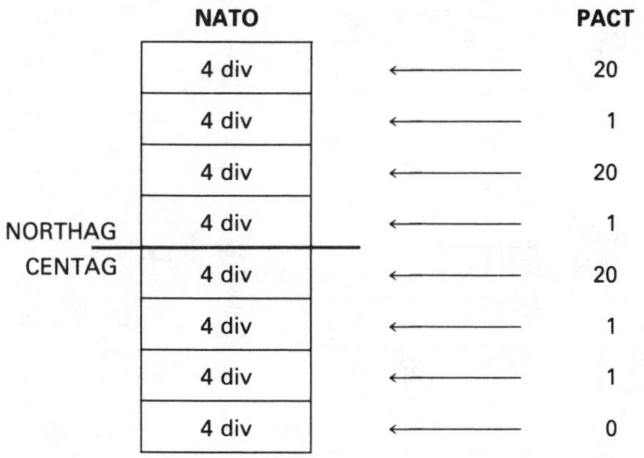

	NATO		PACT
	4 div	←	20
	4 div	←	1
	4 div	←	20
NORTHAG	4 div	←	1
CENTAG	4 div	←	20
	4 div	←	1
	4 div	←	1
	4 div	←	0

vantage on each main axis to succeed. Obviously, the more axes you have, the smaller the advantage you achieve on each axis. Finally, the point is reached, in this case with eight main axes of advance, where the distribution of forces on each axis is the same as the overall 2:1 ratio (see Figure 6).

It is apparent from this *hypothetical* model that as long as NATO keeps the overall force ratio under 2:1, it is impossible for the Soviets to have 6–10 axes

Figure 4. Distribution of Forces When Soviets Desire 4:1 Advantage

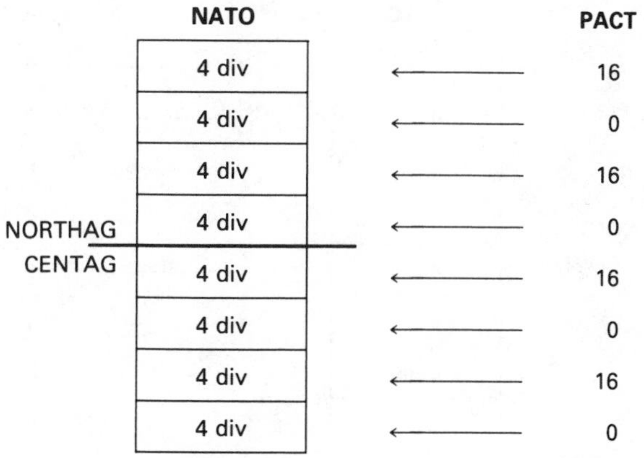

	NATO		PACT
	4 div	←	16
	4 div	←	0
	4 div	←	16
NORTHAG	4 div	←	0
CENTAG	4 div	←	16
	4 div	←	0
	4 div	←	16
	4 div	←	0

Figure 5. Distribution of Forces When Soviets Aim for 6 Main Axes

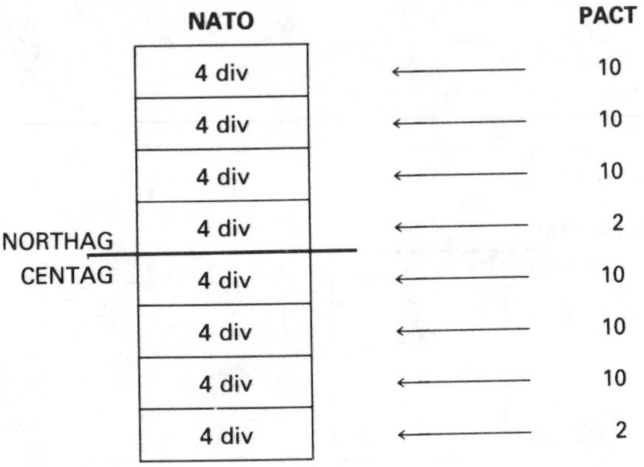

	NATO		PACT
	4 div	←	10
	4 div	←	10
	4 div	←	10
NORTHAG	4 div	←	2
CENTAG	4 div	←	10
	4 div	←	10
	4 div	←	10
	4 div	←	2

of advance and at the same time have an overwhelming advantage in forces on each axis (i.e., a ratio of 4:1 or more). They just do not have a great enough overall force advantage to allow them to spread out their forces on numerous widely dispersed axes. The matter of force ratios aside, from NATO's viewpoint, a multi-pronged attack is the most desirable Pact deployment pattern. Then, NATO, whose forces are evenly spread out along

Figure 6. Distribution of Forces When Soviets Aim for 8 Main Axes

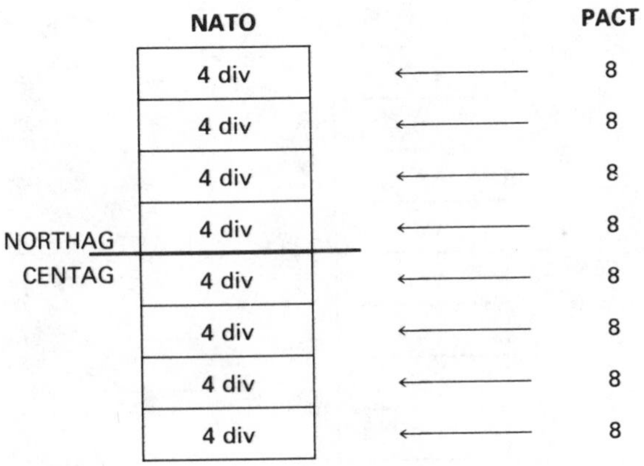

	NATO		PACT
	4 div	←	8
	4 div	←	8
	4 div	←	8
NORTHAG	4 div	←	8
CENTAG	4 div	←	8
	4 div	←	8
	4 div	←	8
	4 div	←	8

a wide front, does not have to concern itself with shifting forces to counter massive concentrations of force by the Pact. From NATO's perspective, a multi-pronged attack results in a propitious meshing of the offensive and defensive deployment patterns.[32]

If the Pact does choose to employ a multi-pronged attack, it will, at best, end up pushing NATO back across a broad front, similar to the way the Soviets pushed the Germans westward across Europe in World War II. This is not a *blitzkrieg*, but a strategy of attrition. If the Soviets hope to defeat NATO with a *blitzkrieg*, they will have to concentrate massive amounts of armor on one, two or, at most, three major axes of advance. This raises the obvious questions: where are those axes likely to be? and how well-positioned is NATO to deal with the most likely Pact deployment patterns? More specifically, are NATO's forces positioned so that they can: first, stymie the initial onslaughts on the various potential axes of advance; and secondly, provide the time for NATO to move reinforcements to threatened positions, and, in effect, erase the temporary superiority in forces that the Pact has achieved by massing its forces at specific points?[33] These questions are best answered by closely examining, corps sector by corps sector, both the terrain and the deployment of NATO's forces.

---

32. Frequently, the claim is made that the Soviets will monitor progress along the various axes and move second-echelon armies (those forces moving up from the Western Soviet Union) onto the axes where they are making the most progress. This is hardly conducive to effecting a *blitzkrieg*. First, NATO will also be moving its reinforcements onto those same axes since that is where the Pact is threatening a breakthrough. Moreover, it takes time to move second-echelon forces into an attacking position, time during which NATO will make important adjustments. A *blitzkrieg*, by effecting a rapid breakthrough and then immediately exploiting it, seeks to deny the defender the time to make such adjustments. Finally, the divisions in the Pact's second-echelon armies will not be the Pact's most capable divisions. The 26 divisions in Central Europe, and specifically the 19 Soviet divisions in East Germany, are the best divisions in the Pact. They will have to make the key breakthroughs and conduct the deep strategic penetrations. The second-echelon armies may be of crucial importance in a war of attrition, but they will not play a major role in a *blitzkrieg*.

33. The assumption here is that, even if the Pact has only a small overall force advantage, it can still establish a significant superiority on at least one axis. NATO must then shift its forces so as to re-establish the overall balance at the points of main attack before the Pact is able to effect a deep strategic penetration. When one considers that it is widely accepted that the attacking forces need more than a 3:1 advantage at the points of main attack (see fn. 30 and the attendant text), and that the overall balance will be significantly less than 3:1, one sees that NATO will be in excellent shape if it has the capability to stop the initial onslaughts and then shift NATO forces to threatened points. Some analysts argue that, if the overall balance of forces is greater than 1.5:1, NATO's chances of accomplishing this task will be slim. See Hillier, *Strengthening NATO*; Hillier and Slatkin, *U.S. Ground Forces*, chapter 2; and James Schlesinger's *FY 1976 and 197T Posture Statement*, p. III-15. See also the discussion of this matter in fn. 61.

It is most unlikely that the Pact would place a major axis of advance in either the far north or the far south of the NATO front. In the south, this would preclude a major attack against II German Corps, simply because it would not result in a decisive victory. The Allies could afford to lose almost the entire corps sector, reaching back to the French border, and they would still be able to continue the war. Moreover, the mountainous terrain in this part of Germany is not conducive to the movement of large armored forces. In the north, a major offensive against Schleswig-Holstein is unlikely. Although the terrain is not mountainous in this sector there are still enough obstacles (bogs, rivers, urban sprawl around Hamburg) to hinder the movement of a large armored force. Furthermore, a Pact success in this region would not constitute a mortal blow to NATO. The main body of NATO's forces would still be intact and capable of conducting a vigorous defense.

CHANNELING FORCES: THE PACT'S AXES OF ATTACK IN CENTAG

The Soviets are most likely to locate their main attacks along the front stretching from the I Dutch Corps Sector in the north to the VII American Corps Sector in the south. Let us first consider the three key corps sectors in CENTAG (III German, V U.S., and VII U.S.). Generally, the terrain in the CENTAG area is very obstacle-ridden. Besides being a mountainous region, it has numerous rivers and forests. Consequently, there are a small number of natural avenues of attack in CENTAG. Actually, there are three potential axes on which the Soviets are likely to attack.

The most threatening of the three possibilities would be an attack from the Thuringian Bulge through the Fulda Gap, aimed at Frankfurt (see Figure 7). Except for the Fulda River, the terrain on this axis should not greatly hinder the movement of large armored forces. Importantly, this axis cuts across the "wasp-waist" or the narrowest section of Germany. The distance from the inter-German border to Frankfurt is a mere 100 km. Frankfurt, because of its central location in Germany's communications network, would be a most attractive target. Capturing Frankfurt would effectively cut Germany in half, and given the importance of north-south lines of communication, would leave NATO's forces in southern Germany isolated.

The second potential axis of advance is located in the sector covered by the III German Corps. The attacking forces would move through the Göttingen Corridor, just south of the Harz Mountains. The industrialized Ruhr is located due west of Göttingen. Although the terrain on the western half of this axis (between Paderborn and the Ruhr) is suitable for the large-

Figure 7. Most Likely Axes of Advance in a Warsaw Pact Attack Against NATO

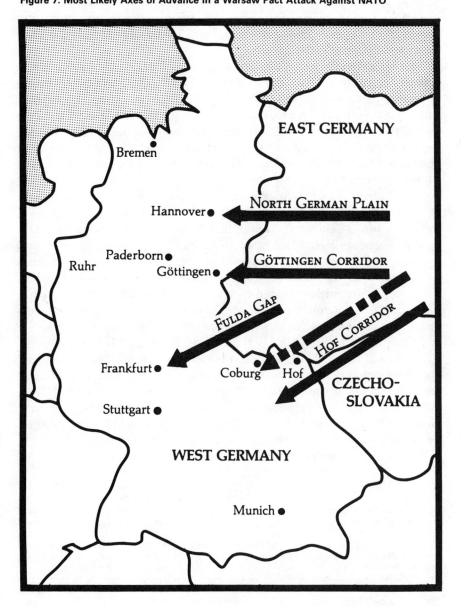

scale employment of tanks, the terrain on the eastern half of the axis, which the attacker must traverse first, is not obstacle-free. There are a number of forests in the region, and the attacking forces would have to cross the Leine River and then the Weser River.

There is a third potential axis of advance in CENTAG, although it is less attractive than the axes which run through the Fulda Gap and the Göttingen Corridor. This axis runs from Bohemia through the area around the city of Hof toward Stuttgart: the Hof Corridor.[34] The terrain that an attacking force would have to traverse there is considerably more obstacle-ridden than the terrain along the other axes. Moreover, Stuttgart is a far less attractive target than either Frankfurt or the Ruhr. Aside from these three axes, there are no attractive alternatives.

NATO's forces in CENTAG should be able to contain a major Soviet attack in this region. There are only a limited number of potential axes of advance, each of which is quite narrow and well defined and each of which NATO is well prepared to defend. Moreover, NATO has contingency plans to shift forces to combat Soviet efforts designed to achieve overwhelming force ratios at the points of main attack.[35] NATO's prospect of successfully halting a Soviet attack are further strengthened by the terrain, which not only limits the number of potential axes, but also channels the attacking forces across the width of Germany. In other words, the potential axes of advance are rather narrow and do not allow the attacker to spread his forces after the initial breakthrough.[36] In 1940, once the Germans crossed the Meuse River, they came upon the open, rolling plains of northeastern France, which was ideal terrain for armored forces. This would not be the case in CENTAG, where the attacking forces would be canalized by terrain throughout their movement across Germany. This should contribute to NATO's prospects for stopping a Soviet penetration before a decisive blow can be landed.

Another reason for optimism is that the NATO corps sectors in CENTAG

---

34. This axis could be shifted somewhat by moving the axis of advance 50 km to the west of Hof, toward the city of Coburg. Therefore, one could argue that there are actually two potential axes of advance in the U.S. VII Corps Sector.
35. Furthermore, given the sophisticated intelligence-gathering devices in the service of NATO forces, it should be possible to locate the Pact's main forces as they move to concentrate for the attack. Certainly, NATO should know where to look for Soviet troop concentrations.
36. It should be noted, however, that the Göttingen Corridor only covers the eastern half of West Germany. (It is approximately 100 km in length.) To the west of Paderborn, the terrain is open and generally well suited for armored warfare.

are manned by German and American Forces, which are the best in NATO.[37] Furthermore, there are reinforcements in CENTAG. The United States has pre-positioned materiel for two divisions in CENTAG's rear.[38] Also, French and Canadian forces (three small French armored divisions and one Canadian brigade) are located in CENTAG and can serve as an operational reserve for this half of NATO's defense.[39]

THE NORTH GERMAN PLAIN: OPEN ROAD FOR A PACT ADVANCE?
Now, consider NATO's prospects for containing a Soviet attack directed against NORTHAG. It is widely held that NATO is more vulnerable in this region than in CENTAG. The terrain in NORTHAG, because it is not mountainous and covered with forests, is generally held to be more favorable to the movement of large armored formations. Frequent reference is made to the suitability of the North German Plain for a *blitzkrieg*.[40] Secondly, there are doubts about whether the Dutch and the Belgians, and even the British, have the capability to withstand a Soviet attack. There is only one German Corps Sector in NORTHAG and there is no U.S. Corps Sector, although pre-positioned materiel for a U.S. Corps, which will serve as an operational reserve for NORTHAG, is being deployed near Bremen.[41] Notwithstanding

---

37. In terms of the quality of the fighting forces, it is widely recognized among NATO military leaders that the German Army is the best in Europe, the Soviets included. Regarding equipment, the German and American Armies are the best equipped in NATO.
38. This equipment for U.S. forces is commonly referred to as POMCUS (pre-positioned materiel configured to unit sets). In a crisis, the United States will fly the designated units (only the troops) to Europe, where the necessary equipment will be waiting for them. POMCUS solves the difficult problem of rapidly transporting a unit's equipment across the Atlantic. A POMCUS division is expected to be ready to fight 10 days after mobilization. For a discussion of POMCUS, see Hillier, *Strengthening NATO*.
39. It should be noted that the Germans are in the process of significantly upgrading the fighting capability of their Territorial Army. The core of this force is six armored infantry brigades, although there are numerous other units (including six more armored infantry brigades) which are being upgraded. See *1979 German White Paper*, pp. 154–156.
40. For example, see Close, *Europe Without Defense?*, p. 172; John M. Collins, *U.S.–Soviet Military Balance* (New York: McGraw-Hill, 1980), pp. 312–314; Hackett et al., pp. 101–102; and Richard D. Lawrence and Jeffrey Record, *U.S. Force Structure in NATO* (Washington D.C.: The Brookings Institution, 1974), p. 28. For an excellent discussion of this matter, which directly challenges this view, see Polk, "The North German Plain Attack Scenario."
41. This corps will comprise three divisions. It is important to note that only two brigades will actually be stationed in Europe. These two brigades will serve as forward elements for two of the divisions, the remainder of which will be flown in from the U.S. All of the third division will be stationed in the United States. The POMCUS (see fn. 38) for one of these three divisions is in place. The POMCUS for the remaining two is presently being deployed (see *FY 1983 Posture Statement*, pp. III-96–III-97). The presence of these three POMCUS divisions in NORTHAG, plus

that NATO is more vulnerable in this region than in CENTAG, the prospects for thwarting a major Soviet attack in NORTHAG are quite good. The terrain is not obstacle-free by any means and, as will become clear, the Belgian and Dutch Corps Sectors are not the weak links that they are often said to be.

NORTHAG covers a front of only 225 km while CENTAG defends a front that is more than two times as long (500 km).[42] Appropriately, the corps sectors in NORTHAG are smaller than those in CENTAG. The I Belgian Corps occupies the southernmost and smallest sector in NORTHAG, measuring only 35 km. Approximately one-third of the front is covered by the Harz Mountains, while the terrain throughout the depth of the corps sector is laden with obstacles. Belgium's two divisions, small as they are, are adequate for defending this short front in the initial stages of an attack.[43] Although it is unlikely that the Pact would place a main axis through this corps sector, if it did, forces from the III German Corps, immediately to the south, could be moved north to reinforce the Belgians, and forces from the U.S. Corps in reserve could be moved forward.

The North German Plain, above the Belgian Corps Sector, is covered by the I British and I German Corps. There is widespread agreement that the Pact will place a single main axis against NORTHAG and that that axis will be located on the North German Plain. Although there are no mountains and few forests in this region, there are obstacles in both the German and British Corps Sectors. In the British Corps Sector, there is significant urban sprawl centered on Hannover, which is located in the heart of this corps sector.[44] Armored forces simply will not be able to move rapidly through those urban

---

the two POMCUS divisions in CENTAG, highlights how important it is that NATO begin mobilizing its forces immediately in a crisis.

42. Polk, "The North German Plain Attack Scenario," p. 61. It is somewhat difficult to reach a precise agreement on these distances because one can measure either: the actual contour of the inter-German border; the straight-line distance of the corps sector front; or some combination of the two.

43. The matter of force-to-space ratios will be discussed later in greater detail. It is generally agreed that a brigade can hold a front of 7–15 km (see fn. 52 and the attendant text). Since the Belgians have four brigades in their corps sector (a good portion of which is covered by the Harz Mountains), they should be able to hold 35 km of front long enough for NATO to bring in reinforcements.

44. See Paul Bracken, "Urban Sprawl and NATO Defence," *Survival*, Vol. 18, No. 6 (November/ December 1976), p. 256; and *FM 100-5*, p. 14-17. The Soviets are fully cognizant of the difficulties of conducting offensive operations in urban areas. See C.N. Donnelly, "Soviet Techniques for Combat in Built up Areas," *International Defense Review*, Vol. 10, No. 2 (1977), pp. 238–242. For a general discussion of the terrain in NORTHAG, see Polk, "The North German Plain Attack Scenario," pp. 61–62.

areas that NATO chooses to defend. Since urbanization continues in this area, it will become increasingly difficult, if not impossible, to avoid large-scale urban fighting in the event of war. There are also a number of rivers in the British sector. The terrain in the I German Corps Sector, on the other hand, is covered, in large part, by the Lüneberger Heath, which is a formidable impediment to the rapid movement of masses of armor. It is for this reason that the North German Plain is usually identified with the British Corps Sector.

The British Army of the Rhine (BAOR) is comprised of four small divisions, a force that is adequate for covering the 70 km corps sector front.[45] There are, however, 13 brigades—or four and one-third formidable divisions—in the I German Corps Sector.[46] Aside from the fact that these German forces are more than adequate for defending their assigned corps sector, they can be rapidly moved to the south to augment the BAOR and, of course, they can also move northward to help the Dutch. This contingent in the I German Corps Sector represents the largest concentration of forces in all of the sectors. Given its central location in NORTHAG as well as the excellent north-south lines of communication in that region, this force is a formidable instrument for thwarting a Pact attack across the North German Plain.[47] Furthermore, there will be an American Corps, part of which is already deployed, in NORTHAG's rear.[48] In sum, NATO *has* the wherewithal to deal with a Pact attack across the North German Plain.

Finally, there is the Dutch Corps Sector, which is manned by two Dutch divisions. Should the Soviets place a main axis through this sector, the Dutch

---

45. There are the equivalent of seven brigades in the BAOR. Assuming that a brigade can cover a front of 7–15 km (see fn. 52 and the attendant text), the BAOR should be able to hold its front long enough for NATO to bring in reinforcements.

46. Furthermore, those 13 brigades are ten percent "over strength." Daniel Schorr, "The Red Threat And NATO Today," *Norfolk Virginian-Pilot*, October 2, 1978, section 1, p. 19. Also see Polk, "The North German Plain Attack Scenario," p. 61.

47. The German forces are divided among three corps sectors and Schleswig-Holstein. None of these sectors are adjacent to each other (see Figure 1), which means that the Germans, by bumping forces up or down the line, can move German brigades into every non-German corps sector on the front. When an attacking force executes a *blitzkrieg*, the attacker's flanks are usually vulnerable. The Soviets would have to keep in mind that if they penetrate into the rear of a non-German corps, the Germans will undoubtedly drive into their exposed flanks, attempting to sever the penetrating forces from their base.

48. Furthermore, German units from CENTAG can be moved to NORTHAG. See Ulrich de Mazière, *Rational Deployment of Forces on the Central Front*, Study Prepared for the Western Economic Union, April 2, 1975, p. 40. There are also the forces in the German Territorial Army (see fn. 39), a portion of which will undoubtedly be assigned to NORTHAG in a conflict.

forces, like their British and Belgian counterparts, should be capable of defending their front in the initial stages of the conflict. Then, forces from the adjacent I German Corps can be moved north to assist the Dutch. Moreover, the American Corps will be located directly to the rear of the Dutch Sector. The terrain within the Dutch Corps Sector is not conducive to the rapid movement of armored forces. In addition to the Elbe River, which forms the inter-German border in this sector, a number of other rivers, canals, and bogs are liberally sprinkled throughout this sector. The Lüneberger Heath, which is such a prominent feature in the adjacent I German Corps Sector, extends northward across the Dutch Sector. To add to the woes of the attacker, there is significant urban sprawl around Bremen and Bremerhaven.[49] Finally, even if the attacking forces were able to penetrate through this sector rapidly, it is unlikely that NATO would be mortally wounded. Certainly, NATO would feel the loss of the ports in northern Germany. However, since the attacking forces would exit Germany into the northern part of the Netherlands, NATO would still have access to the most important Belgian and Dutch ports.

FORCE-TO-SPACE RATIOS

There are a number of additional points concerning Soviet and NATO deployment patterns that merit attention. The discussion has so far focused on the matter of the Pact's achieving overwhelming superiority on specific axes of advance. However, when examining prospects for a breakthrough at the point of main attack, one cannot simply focus on the *balance* of forces. It is also necessary to consider *force-to-space ratios*, or the number of divisions that the defender requires to *hold* a specific sector of territory.[50] If a defender can comfortably hold 100 km with four divisions, then even if the attacker has 24 divisions, that attacker will have to sacrifice a significant number of his 24 divisions before he finally wears the defender down to the point where he can effect a penetration. Obviously, this would be a time-consuming as well as a costly process, during which the defender can bring in reinforcements. There is an important factor which complicates the attacker's task in such a situation: the "crossing the T" phenomenon.[51] Simply put, there is not

---

49. See Bracken, "Urban Sprawl and NATO Defence," p. 256 and *FM 100-5*, p. 14-17.
50. For an excellent discussion of this concept, see B. H. Liddell Hart, *Deterrent or Defense* (New York: Praeger, 1960), chapter 10.
51. Although originally a naval concept (see George Quester, *Offense and Defense in the International System* [New York: John Wiley, 1977], p. 92), "crossing the T" also applies to land warfare.

enough room for the attacker to place all of his 24 divisions at the point of attack. He must therefore locate a portion of his divisions in subsequent echelons behind the attacking forces, where their impact on the battlefield will be minimal while the first echelon is engaged. In essence, the defender is in the enviable position of being able to deal with the attacker's forces on a piecemeal basis. How do these abstract considerations relate to the European Central Front?

It is generally agreed that a brigade can hold a front approximately 7–15 km long.[52] With 7 km, which is obviously the more desirable figure, a brigade should be able to hold its position for an extended period of time before it needs reinforcement. As the figure approaches 15 km, the defender should be able to cope with the initial onslaughts without any problem. However, it will be necessary to bring in reinforcements after a day or so since the attacker's forces will have begun to wear down the defender by then. Since the length of the NORTHAG front is 225 km, if one assumes that each brigade could hold 15 km, then a minimum of 15 brigades would be needed to cover the front. There are actually 30 brigades within the four NORTHAG corps sectors.[53] Given that there are 30 brigades and a 225 km front, this means that each brigade will have to cover 7.5 km, which is extremely close to the most desirable force-to-space ratio for a brigade.

Now, let us assume that NATO deploys its 30 brigades along the NORTHAG front in the traditional "two brigades up, one back" configuration. This would leave 20 brigades to cover 225 km (each brigade would have to cover 11 km), with 10 brigades in immediate reserve. This leaves NATO in very good shape. Two other important points are in order. First, because there are a number of obstacles along the NORTHAG front, NATO would

---

52. Regarding the optimum number of km which a brigade can hold, it is difficult to come up with an exact figure. This is because such a force-to-space ratio varies according to the size and quality of the forces on each side as well as the nature of the terrain. Recognizing that this problem exists, it is generally estimated that a brigade can hold 7–15 km of front. These figures are based on discussions with American, German, and Israeli military officers as well as: J. R. Angolia and Donald B. Vought, "The United States Army," in *The U.S. War Machine*, ed. Ray Bonds (New York: Crown, 1978), p. 74; Hillier and Slatkin, *U.S. Ground Forces*, p. 25; Liddell Hart, *Deterrent or Defense*, chapter 10; Hans-Joachim Löser, "Vorneverteidigung der Bundesrepublik Deutschland?" *Österreichische Militärische Zeitschrift*, Vol. 18, No. 2 (March/April 1980), p. 121; and U.S. Army Training and Doctrine Command, *Division Restructuring Study*, Phase 1 Report, Executive Summary, Vol. 1, Fort Monroe, VA, March 1, 1977, p. 3.
53. There are: 6 brigades in the I Dutch Corps Sector; 13 brigades in the I German Corps Sector; the equivalent of 7 brigades in the I British Corps Sector; and 4 brigades in the I Belgian Corps Sector. These figures are from de Mazière, "Rational Deployment of Forces," pp. 11–12.

not have to worry about covering every section of the 225 km front. Second, the American Corps in NORTHAG's rear, when fully operational, will provide an additional nine brigades. Also, there are at least six armored infantry brigades in the German Territorial Army that could be assigned to NORTHAG.[54] In short, NORTHAG does not have force-to-space problems.[55]

The length of the CENTAG front is 500 km. Assuming 15 km per brigade, 33 brigades would be required to cover this front. NATO has 33 brigades in the four CENTAG corps sectors, a figure which is hardly alarming in light of the obstacle-ridden terrain along this portion of the NATO front and the fact that the brigades in these corps sectors are the heaviest in NATO and therefore will have the least amount of trouble covering 15 km of front.[56] Furthermore, there are 21 brigades (including the French, but not including the German territorials) available for reinforcement in CENTAG's rear.[57]

"CROSSING THE T" IN EUROPE

Consider briefly the "crossing the T" phenomenon, which further highlights the problems that the Soviets will have breaking through NATO's forward positions. In one of the U.S. Army's standard scenarios for a major Soviet attack against one of the two U.S. Corps Sectors in CENTAG, a Soviet force of five divisions is pitted against two American divisions.[58] In the opening battle, three Soviet divisions attack across about 40 to 50 km of front against

---

54. See the discussion of the German Territorial Army in fn. 39.

55. It should be noted that after a lengthy mobilization involving both sides, NATO's position, regardless of what the overall balance of forces looked like, would be extremely favorable on force-to-space ratio grounds. In other words, with regard to having adequate forces to cover the entire front, NATO's position, which is favorable before mobilizing, improves even more as large numbers of additional forces are moved to the Central Front.

56. There are: 7 brigades in the III German Corps Sector; 7 brigades in the V U.S. Corps Sector; 7 brigades in the VII U.S. Corps Sector; and 12 brigades in the II German Corps Sector. These figures are from de Mazière, *ibid.*, pp. 12–13.

57. Also, given the nature of the terrain along the inter-German border in CENTAG, NATO would not have to be very concerned with protecting sizeable segments of the front. The 21 brigades include a Canadian brigade and 3 French divisions (6 brigades) stationed in West Germany as well as 2 American-based divisions (6 brigades) with POMCUS in CENTAG and 4 French divisions (8 brigades) stationed in France.

58. See U.S., Congress, Senate Armed Services Committe, *Hearings on Department of Defense Authorization for Appropriations for Fiscal Year 1981 (Part 5)*, 96th Cong., 2nd Sess. (Washington D.C.: GPO, 1980), pp. 3053–3078. It should be noted that the Americans would actually have two and one-third divisions, not two divisions, in each of their corps sectors. This discrepancy is a result of the fact that the armored cavalry regiment that would be in each corps sector is not counted in this scenario.

two U.S. divisions.[59] The remaining two Soviet divisions are held in immediate reserve. Thus, in that opening battle the ratio of forces directly engaged
is 3:2 in the Pact's favor, not 5:2. (It should be noted that these ratios would
be even more favorable to NATO if they were translated into armored division equivalents.) Of course, the key question is: can those three Soviet
divisions so weaken the two American divisions that the remaining two
Soviet divisions will be able to effect a breakthrough? In this regard, the
matter of force-to-space ratios is of crucial importance. Since two divisions,
or six brigades, are defending 40–50 km, each of these powerful American
brigades will be holding approximately 7 km. Without a doubt, the Soviets
would have a great deal of difficulty penetrating that American front.

Now, let us assume that the Soviets start with ten or even fifteen divisions,
instead of the five employed in the above scenario. Only a very few of these
additional divisions could be placed at the point of main attack, simply
because there would be limited room on the front to accommodate them.
They would have to be located *behind* the attacking forces, where they would
have little impact on the initial battles.[60] Certainly, the forces in each NATO
corps sector should be capable of blunting the initial Soviet attack and providing adequate time for NATO to shift forces from other corps sectors and
its operational reserves to threatened points along the front.[61]

---

59. It should be noted that these three attacking divisions would not be spread out evenly
across the 40–50 km of front. They would concentrate at specific points along that front.
60. The Soviets could attempt to spread their forces out and attack across a broad front.
However, this would lead to serious problems. First of all, the terrain along the inter-German
border is such that the natural avenues of attack are relatively narrow and well defined. Second,
and more importantly, once the attacking forces are spread out, the key principle of concentrating forces on narrow fronts to effect a breakthrough is violated. Not surprisingly, all evidence
indicates that the Soviets intend to concentrate their attacking forces on narrow fronts, placing
large numbers of their divisions in echelons behind the main body of attacking divisions. (See
the sources cited in fns. 31 and 72.) It should be noted that over the past decade the United
States has devoted considerable attention to developing weaponry specifically designed to attack
second and third echelon forces. (See, for example, the discussion in the document cited in fn.
58.)
61. It was noted in fn. 33 that a number of defense analysts argue that NATO must prevent the
overall ratio of forces on the Central Front from exceeding 1.5:1 in the Pact's favor. Once this
occurs, it becomes easier for the Pact to achieve overwhelming force advantages at specific
points along the front. Although it is certainly desirable to keep that overall ratio at 1.5:1 or less,
it seems clear from the foregoing discussion that even if the overall ratio reaches 2:1 (which is
certainly a worst case assumption, with NATO mobilizing immediately after the Pact) and the
Pact thus achieves overwhelming superiority on two or three axes, NATO should be able to
hold at those points of main attack long enough to allow NATO to shift its forces and establish
ratios at these points that reflect the overall 2:1 ratio. However, it is clear that NATO would

In sum, given the initial deployment patterns of both NATO and the Pact, it appears that NATO is reasonably well deployed to meet a Soviet *blitzkrieg*. Although both Pact and NATO deployment patterns have been examined, attention has been focused, for the most part, on examining *NATO*'s capability to thwart a *blitzkrieg*. Now let us shift the focus and examine, in detail, *Soviet* capabilities.

Soviet Capabilities for Blitzkrieg Warfare

To ascertain whether the Soviet Army has the capacity to effect a *blitzkrieg*, it is necessary to examine that Army on three levels. First, one must consider how the Soviet Army is organized. In other words, are the forces structured to facilitate a *blitzkrieg*? Second, it is necessary to consider doctrine, a subject that has already received some attention. Finally, there is the matter of raw skill. Assuming that the problems with force structure and doctrine are minimal, is the Soviet Army capable of performing the assigned task? There are, of course, no simple answers to these questions. They are nonetheless extremely important questions which have received little serious attention in the West, where it is all too often assumed that the Soviets have only strengths and no weaknesses.

Since almost all the Pact divisions that would be used in a European war are either armored or mechanized infantry, it seems reasonable to assume that the Pact is appropriately organized to launch a *blitzkrieg*. On close inspection, however, there are potential trouble spots in the Pact's force structure. Over the past decade, Soviet divisions have become extremely heavy units. Western analysts pay a great deal of attention to the large and growing number of tanks, infantry fighting vehicles, artillery pieces, rocket launchers, surface-to-air missiles, air defense guns, anti-tank guided missiles (ATGMs), and assorted other weapons that are found in Soviet as well as other Pact divisions.[62] Past a certain point, however, there is an inverse relationship between the mass and the velocity of an attacking force. As the size of the attacking force increases, the logistical problems as well as the command and control problems increase proportionately. Then, it becomes very difficult to

---

have significant problems should the overall ratio surpass 2:1. See *FY 1982 Posture Statement,* p. 74.
62. See, for example, Richard Burt, "Soviet Said To Add To Its Bloc Troops," *The New York Times,* June 8, 1980, section 1, p. 4.

move that force rapidly—an *essential* requirement for a *blitzkrieg*, where the attacker is seeking to strike deep into the defender's rear before the defender can shift forces to deal with the penetrating forces. Although the notion is perhaps counterintuitive, bigger divisions are not necessarily better divisions when an attacking force is attempting to effect a *blitzkrieg*.[63]

Consider now the matter of doctrine. As noted earlier, it is not possible to determine exactly how the Soviets plan to fight a conventional war in Europe. This is because the Soviets themselves are not sure; there is presently doctrinal uncertainty in their military circles. Certainly, they continue to emphasize the necessity of rapidly defeating NATO, should a war in Europe break out. The Soviets recognize, however, that it is becoming increasingly difficult to do this, especially because of the proliferation of ATGMs.[64] Moreover, they are well aware of how these organizational problems compound their task. They realize that it will be difficult to effect deep strategic penetrations against prepared defenses.[65] Although there has been a considerable effort to find a solution to this problem, if anything, the Soviets appear to be moving closer to a strategy of attrition. This is reflected in their growing reliance on artillery and dismounted infantry.[66] There is no evidence that the Soviets have made a conscious decision to fight a war of attrition. Instead, it appears that they are being inexorably drawn in this direction by their

---

63. See the comments of the former German General Balck on this matter in General William E. DePuy, *Generals Balck and von Mellenthin On Tactics: Implications For NATO Military Doctrine*, BDM/W–81–077–TR (McLean, VA: The BDM Corporation, December 19, 1980), pp. 46–48.

64. See the sources cited in fn. 26, especially Donnelly's "Tactical Problems," which examines in detail Soviet thinking on strategy and tactics in a European land war. Also see his "Soviet Tactics for Overcoming NATO Anti-Tank Defenses," *International Defense Review*, Vol. 12, No. 7 (1979), pp. 1099–1106. For a general discussion of ATGMs and the *blitzkrieg*, see my "Precision-guided Munitions and Conventional Deterrence," *Survival*, Vol. 21, No. 2 (March/April 1979), pp. 68–76.

65. Christopher Donnelly writes, "[I]f the victory is not achieved quickly, the Russians believe, no meaningful victory can be achieved at all. It is not surprising, therefore, that Soviet officers have applied themselves to the problem of how to ensure their rapid rate of advance in war. . . . What is of particular interest is that no single straightforward answer to this problem has yet emerged and that it is still the subject of intense discussion." Donnelly, "Tactics for Overcoming," p. 1099. He then goes on to say that, "In general, their identification and dissection of the problem is excellent. Their suggestions as to what should be done usually appear quite sound, but are often tinged with lack of confidence or an excess of bland enthusiasm, hiding uncertainty. Sometimes they are contradictory in detail." *Ibid.*, p. 1100.

66. See Christopher Donnelly, "Modern Soviet Artillery," *NATO's Fifteen Nations*, Vol. 24, No. 3 (June–July 1979), pp. 48–54; Donnelly, "Tactical Problems"; Donnelly, "Tactics for Overcoming"; and Karber, "Anti-Tank Debate."

efforts to neutralize the growing firepower, both ground-based and air-delivered, available to NATO.

BLITZKRIEG AND THE NUCLEAR BATTLEFIELD

The Soviets continue to pay serious attention to the possibility that NATO will use nuclear weapons. Thus, they devote much time to training for a nuclear war which, by their own admission, would be fundamentally different from a conventional war and would require a different doctrine. For example, unlike a *blitzkrieg*, where the armor is concentrated in massive formations, the armor would be widely dispersed across the front so as not to present NATO with lucrative targets for her nuclear weapons.[67] Moreover, given the firepower provided by nuclear weapons, piercing NATO's front would not *require* the high concentration of forces that is necessary to achieve that objective in a conventional conflict. This highlights the point that the role of artillery would be greatly diminished on a nuclear battlefield. The upshot of this is that the time and resources the Soviets spend on preparing their forces to fight a nuclear war are time and resources that could be spent training those forces to fight a conventional war. In a crisis, the Soviets will be faced with an acute dilemma: whether to prepare their forces for a nuclear war or a conventional war. In this regard, NATO's plethora of tactical nuclear weapons serves a valuable purpose. The nuclear-conventional dichotomy aside, the Soviets still have not found a satisfactory strategy for fighting a conventional war. As long as they are not confident that they have a sound doctrine for inflicting a rapid and decisive defeat on NATO, the Soviets are not likely to initiate conflict in a crisis.

SOVIET TRAINING AND INITIATIVE

Finally, there is the question of whether the Soviet Army has the necessary raw skills. An army that intends to implement a *blitzkrieg* must have a highly flexible command structure as well as officers and NCOs at every level of the chain of command who are capable of exercising initiative.[68] A *blitzkrieg* is

---

67. See Savkin, *The Basic Principles of Operational Art and Tactics*, chapter 3. Also see V.D. Sokolovskiy, *Soviet Military Strategy*, ed. Harriet Fast Scott, 3rd ed. (New York: Crane, Russak, 1968).
68. These distinguishing characteristics are readily apparent in both the Israeli and German armies. See Dan Horowitz, "Flexible Responsiveness and Military Strategy: The Case of the Israeli Army," *Policy Sciences*, Vol. 1, No. 2 (Summer 1970), pp. 191–205; DePuy, *Generals Balck*

not a steamroller: success is ultimately a consequence of able commanders making rapid-fire decisions in the "fog of battle" which enable the attacking forces to make the crucial deep strategic penetrations. Should the Soviets attack NATO, there is a chance that the Soviets will open a hole or holes in the NATO front. Naturally, NATO will try to close those holes and seal off any penetrations as quickly as possible. The key question is: can the Soviets exploit such opportunities before NATO, which is well prepared for such an eventuality, shuts the door? In this battle, the crucial determinant will not be how much firepower the Soviets have amassed for the breakthrough; success will be largely the result of highly skilled officers and NCOs making the decisions that will enable the armored spearheads to outrun NATO's defenses. A *blitzkrieg* depends on split-second timing since opportunity on the battlefield is so fleeting.

There is substantial evidence that Soviet officers and NCOs are sadly lacking in individual initiative and, furthermore, that the Soviet command structure is rigid. Christopher Donnelly notes:

It is hard for a western officer to appreciate what a difficult concept [initiative] this is to reconcile with a normal Soviet upbringing. There has never been a native Russian word for initiative. The idea of an individual initiating unilateral action is anathema to the Soviet system. The Soviet army has always considered as one of its strengths its iron discipline and high-level, centralised command system combined with a universal tactical doctrine. The run-of-the-mill officer, particularly a sub-unit officer, has never had to do other than obey orders.[69]

The Soviets are keenly aware of the need for initiative and flexibility, and they go to great lengths to stress the importance of these qualities in their military journals.[70] These are not, however, attributes which can be willed into existence. Their absence is largely the result of powerful historical forces.[71] Fundamental structural change in Soviet society and the Soviet

---

and von Mellenthin on Tactics, pp. 16–23, 54–55; Erich Von Manstein, *Lost Victories* (Chicago: Regnery, 1958), pp. 63, 284; and *HDv 100/100* (especially p. 10-2).
69. Christopher Donnelly, "The Soviet Soldier: Behavior, Performance, Effectiveness," in *Soviet Military Power and Performance*, ed. John Erickson and E.J. Feuchtwanger (Hamden, Conn.: Archon Books, 1979), p. 115. Also see Joshua M. Epstein, "Soviet Confidence and Conventional Deterrence in Europe," *Orbis*, Vol. 26, No. 4 (Spring 1982).
70. Interestingly, Donnelly notes that when the Soviets discuss the problem of achieving a quick victory on the battlefield, "Not infrequently, the panacea of 'initiative' is invoked as a *deus ex machina.*" Donnelly, "Tactics for Overcoming," p. 1100.
71. See Norman Stone, "The Historical Background of the Red Army," in Erickson and Feuchtwanger, *Soviet Military Power and Performance*, pp. 3–17.

military would be necessary before there would be any significant increase in flexibility and initiative.

Certainly analysts in the West argue that the Soviets have obviated this problem by relying on "steamroller tactics at the divisional level." Steven Canby, one of the leading proponents of this view, writes:

Steamroller tactics, at the divisional level, are characterized by a relatively inflexible command system and a rigid system of echeloned forces. . . . As formations are exhausted by fighting they are replaced rapidly by other echelons. . . . By maintaining momentum with large numbers of formations, Soviet forces plan to saturate enemy defences and offset the need for flexibility and initiative at the company level, where their tactics tend to be rigid. Having large numbers available gives higher commanders considerable flexibility.

Combat divisions and *even armies* can be used like drill tips on a high-speed drill—to be ground down and replaced until penetration occurs. [Emphasis mine][72]

There are major problems with this approach. First, the Pact does not have the overall superiority in forces needed for such "steamroller tactics." The notion that the Pact has an overwhelming superiority of forces which would allow it to expend forces in such a manner does not square with reality.[73] Secondly, the process of removing shattered divisions from the front and replacing them with fresh divisions is a complex and time-consuming task. Thirdly, even if such "steamroller tactics" enable the Pact to open a hole in NATO's front in the initial stages of the conflict, the Pact forces still must effect a deep strategic penetration while NATO is moving forces into its path. This is a most demanding task and requires both flexibility and initiative. Continued use of "steamroller tactics" after the breakthrough battle will not suffice.[74]

---

72. Steven Canby, *The Alliance and Europe: Part IV, Military Doctrine and Technology,* Adelphi Paper No. 109 (London: IISS, 1974/5), pp. 10–11. Also see John Erickson, "Soviet Ground Forces and the Conventional Mode of Operations," *Journal of the Royal United Services Institute,* Vol. 121, No. 2 (June 1976), p. 46.

73. This is reflected in the overall force ratios presented in this study.

74. What is particularly ironic about Canby's views on a Soviet offensive is that he criticizes NATO for preparing for a firepower-oriented battlefield while the Pact "is oriented towards an armoured-style conflict based on manoeuvre." He goes on to say, "[T]his means the United States fights battles to wear down opponents. The Soviet Union fights battles to *avoid* further battles." Steven Canby, "NATO: Reassessing the Conventional Wisdoms," *Survival,* Vol. 19, No. 4 (July/August 1977), p. 165. This view of Soviet strategy hardly squares with his discussion on using divisions and *even armies* in support of "steamroller tactics."

Other deficiencies in the Soviet Army cast doubt on the Soviets' capacity to launch a successful *blitzkrieg*. For example, the Soviets have significant problems with training.[75] Overreliance on training aids and simulators is a factor often cited, and there is widespread feeling that the training process does not satisfactorily approximate actual combat conditions. Training is of special importance for the Soviets since their army is comprised largely of conscripts who serve a mere two years. Moreover, since new conscripts are trained in actual combat units, more than half of the troops in the 19 Soviet divisions in East Germany are soldiers with less than two years of experience. At any one time, a significant number of those troops is either untrained or partially trained. It should also be noted that Soviet soldiers are deficient in map reading, a skill which is of much importance for an army attempting to launch a *blitzkrieg*.[76]

Finally, one must consider the capabilities of the non-Soviet divisions, which comprise approximately half of the Pact's 57⅓ standing divisions. Although the Soviet divisions will certainly perform the critical tasks in any offensive, the non-Soviet divisions will have to play a role in the operation. Otherwise, the size of the offensive would have to be scaled down significantly. One cannot say with any degree of certainty that the East Europeans would be militarily incapable of performing their assigned task or that they would not commit themselves politically to supporting a Soviet-led offensive. The Soviets, however, would have to give serious consideration to the reliability of the East Europeans.[77] If the Soviets indeed pay such careful attention to the lessons of the Great Patriotic War as is widely claimed, they recall what happened opposite Stalingrad in 1942 when the Soviets were able to inflict a stunning defeat on the Germans by ripping through those sectors of the front covered by the Rumanians, the Hungarians, and the Italians.[78]

---

75. See Donnelly, "Soviet Soldier," pp. 117–120; Keith A. Dunn, "Soviet Military Weaknesses and Vulnerabilities: A Critique Of The Short War Advocates," memorandum prepared for Strategic Studies Institute, U.S. Army War College, Carlisle Barracks, PA, July 31, 1978, pp. 15–16; Herbert Goldhamer, *Soviet Military Management at the Troop Level*, R–1513–PR (Santa Monica, Calif.: Rand Corporation, May 1974), chapters 2–4; Leon Gouré and Michael J. Deane, "The Soviet Strategic View," *Strategic Review*, Vol. 8, No. 1 (Winter 1980), pp. 84–85; and Karber, "Anti-Tank Debate," p. 108.
76. Dunn, "Soviet Military Weaknesses," pp. 16–17.
77. See Johnson et al., "The Armies of the Warsaw Pact" and Dale R. Herspring and Ivan Volgyes, "Political Reliability in the Eastern European Warsaw Pact Armies," *Armed Forces and Society*, Vol. 6, No. 2 (Winter 1980), pp. 270–296.
78. As John Erickson notes, it is very unlikely "that any non-Soviet national force would be alloted an independent operational role on any scale." Erickson, "Soviet Military Capabilities in

Although the Soviet Army has important deficiencies, it would still be a formidable opponent in a war in Europe; the Soviet Army is not by any means a hapless giant. Neither, however, is it an army which is well prepared to defeat NATO with a *blitzkrieg*. The shortcomings noted in the foregoing cast extreme doubt on the claim that the Soviets have the capability to launch a *blitzkrieg* with confidence of success. The Soviet Army is definitely not a finely tuned instrument capable of overrunning NATO at a moment's notice. To claim, then, that the Soviets have "adopted and improved the German *blitzkrieg* concept"[79] has a hollow ring. Most importantly, the evidence indicates that the Soviets recognize these shortcomings and their implications for winning a quick victory.

Conclusion

Even if one were to discount these weaknesses of the Soviet Army, the task of quickly overrunning NATO's defenses would be a very formidable one. A Pact offensive would have to traverse the obstacle-ridden terrain which covers almost all of Germany and restricts the movement of large armored units. Moreover, there is good reason to believe that NATO has the wherewithal to thwart such an offensive. In short, NATO is in relatively good shape at the conventional level. The conventional wisdom which claims otherwise on this matter is a distortion of reality. Since, as former Defense Secretary Donald Rumsfeld noted, "the burden of deterrence has once again fallen on the conventional forces," this is welcome news.[80]

Two very important caveats, however, are in order. First, NATO must provide for the continuation of ongoing improvements in its force structure. There is no evidence that the Soviet effort to modernize her forces in Central Europe is slowing down. Therefore, NATO must continue to make improvements if it is to maintain the present balance. It is absolutely essential, for example, that deployment of the American Corps in NORTHAG be com-

---

Europe," *Journal of the Royal United Services Institute*, Vol. 120, No. 1 (March 1975), p. 66. This could lead to problems for the Soviets because it forces them to disperse their own divisions, thus limiting the number available for the principal attacks.

79. Canby, *The Alliance and Europe*, p. 9. This view is also reflected in: Eugene D. Bétit, "Soviet Tactical Doctrine And Capabilities And NATO's Strategic Defense," *Strategic Review*, Vol. 4, No. 4 (Fall 1976), p. 96; Erickson, "Soviet Ground Forces," p. 46; and Daniel Gouré and Gordon McCormick, "PGM: No Panacea," *Survival*, Vol. 22, No. 1 (January/February 1980), p. 16.

80. *FY 1978 Posture Statement*, p. 85.

pleted. It is also imperative that the Belgians, the British, and the Dutch continue to modernize and upgrade their conventional forces. More specifically, these forces, especially the British, must increase the firepower of their individual brigades. The Germans, for their part, must maintain their commitment to developing a formidable Territorial Army. At a more general level, NATO should make a greater effort to prepare the terrain in West Germany so as to further compound the attacker's problems. And, the Allies need to place more emphasis on improving the sustainability of their forces.

Although none of these improvements require significant increases in defense spending, there is cause for concern over their implementation. The various policy disputes that have plagued the Alliance over the past few years (neutron bomb, TNF modernization, Afghanistan, and Poland) have markedly weakened Alliance cohesion. Once again there is serious talk in the United States about greatly reducing the American commitment to Europe.[81] And although there is no direct evidence yet that the Reagan Administration wants to scale back the American commitment to Europe, it is apparent from the Administration's first *Posture Statement* that it is primarily interested in spending defense dollars on strategic weaponry and the Navy.[82] Even in the American Army, which was very much a Europe-oriented force in the 1970s, there is growing interest in preparing for contingencies outside of Europe.[83] If the Administration has to cut back projected defense spending for the next five years, it is likely that the NATO portion of the budget will come under attack.

Of course, there are danger signs on the other side of the Atlantic as well. Given the state of Britain's economy and her decision to purchase the expensive Trident missile, one cannot help but wonder if the British Army will not suffer in the future allocation of scarce resources.[84] Unfortunately, the

---

81. See for examples: David S. Broder, "Rising Isolationism," *Washington Post,* January 13, 1982, p. 23; Morton M. Kondracke, "Talking Ourselves Into Breaking Up the Alliance?" *Wall Street Journal,* January 7, 1982, p. 21; Ronald C. Nairn, "Should the U.S. Pull Out of NATO?" *Wall Street Journal,* December 15, 1981, p. 30; and Stansfield Turner, "A New Strategy for NATO," *New York Times Magazine,* December 13, 1981, pp. 42–49, 134–136.
82. See *FY 1983 Posture Statement.*
83. See, for example, General Edward Meyer's (the Army Chief of Staff) comments in Richard Halloran, "$40 Billion Is Urged To Modernize Army," *The New York Times,* November 30, 1980, p. 33.
84. For an excellent discussion of the problems the British face as a result of a weak economy and the purchase of Trident missiles, see Lawrence Freedman, "Britain: The First Ex-Nuclear Power?" *International Security,* Vol. 6, No. 2 (Fall 1981), pp. 80–104.

British economy is not the only European economy that has fallen on hard times. Even in Germany, defense spending has been curtailed because of economic considerations.[85]

It seems reasonable to assume that in the next few years, NATO will have some difficulty holding the line against attempts to cut back spending for the conventional defense of Europe. If such efforts were to succeed, NATO's present capability to defend against a Soviet offensive would be seriously eroded. Given the widespread recognition that parity obtains at all levels of the nuclear equation, and given the need for a conventional deterrent which flows from nuclear parity, such a development would be a mistake of grand proportions. What is particularly ironic about this threat of lost momentum at the conventional level is that it is due, in part, to the popular misconception that Western forces are hopelessly outnumbered at the conventional level. The reason is simple: if one believes that the disparity in conventional forces is very great, then what is the point of continuing to spend precious resources on a hopeless cause? Those Allied leaders who continually denigrate NATO's substantial conventional capability are, in effect, undermining popular support for continued spending on NATO's conventional forces.[86]

Two other points regarding this popular misconception about the conventional balance in Europe bear mentioning. First, for the purposes of deterring a Soviet attack in some future crisis, it makes absolutely no sense to emphasize that should the Soviets attack, an easy victory would await them. Second, should there be a war in Europe, that message will not help and may very well threaten the resolve of NATO's fighting forces. As Senator Sam Nunn once remarked, "If our American fighting men ever conclude that high levels of this Government have them deployed on a strategy that is inevitable failure, then nothing could destroy military morale of our country quicker."[87] No one wants to die for a lost cause. Fortunately, the conventional wisdom is wrong; NATO presently has the capability to thwart a Soviet attack. Unfortunately, too few people recognize this.

The second caveat concerns warning time and mobilization. Given NATO's

---

85. For a pessimistic assessment of the future of the German military, see John Vinocur, "Study by Bonn Foresees Trouble for the Military," *The New York Times*, February 9, 1982, p. 12.
86. This is not to deny that NATO has legitimate deficiencies which Allied leaders have a responsibility to point out and to rectify.
87. See U.S., Congress, Subcommittee on Manpower and Personnel of the Senate Armed Services Committee, *Hearings on NATO Posture And Initiatives*, 95th Cong., 1st Sess. (Washington D.C.: GPO, August 3, 1977), p. 20.

present intelligence capabilities and the Pact's force structure, there is little doubt that NATO would detect a full-scale Pact mobilization almost immediately. Obviously, NATO must ensure that it maintains this capability. Problems arise, however, in circumstances where the Pact pursues a limited mobilization which is somewhat difficult to gauge. Although there are real limits as to how much mobilization the Soviets can achieve before tipping their hand, NATO needs to be especially sensitive to such an eventuality. Moreover, NATO must be prepared to respond to a limited mobilization, even if the evidence of such a mobilization is somewhat ambiguous. This leads to the critical problem of mobilization.

This article highlights how important it is that NATO mobilize its forces immediately after the Pact begins its mobilization. A favorable balance of forces in a crisis will be a function of political as well as military factors. As Richard Betts notes in his very important article on this subject, "Even if intelligence monitoring can ensure warning, it cannot ensure authorization to respond to it."[88] Therefore, it is essential that NATO's political and military leaders carefully consider the various mobilization scenarios that they may face in a crisis. The real danger is that NATO's leaders will not agree to mobilize in a crisis for fear that such a move might provoke a Soviet attack. The risk of pushing the Soviets to preempt can be reduced, however, by avoiding certain provocative moves and by clearly communicating one's intentions to the other side. Nevertheless, the risk of provoking a Soviet attack by initiating NATO mobilization can never be completely erased. That risk, however, must be weighed against the far greater danger that if NATO does not mobilize, the capability to defend against a Pact attack will be lost. Moreover, once the Pact achieves a decisive superiority because of NATO's failure to mobilize, it would be not only difficult, but very dangerous for NATO to attempt to redress the balance with a tardy mobilization. Seeing that process set into motion, the Pact would have a very strong incentive to attack before NATO erased its advantage. In short, it is essential that NATO plan for ways to mobilize that do not provoke a Soviet attack, but, at the same time, ensure that NATO does not lose its present capability to defend itself effectively against a Soviet offensive.

---

88. Betts, "Surprise Attack," p. 118.

Uncertainties for the Soviet War Planner

Benjamin S. Lambeth

During the years when American strategic superiority overshadowed Soviet power, most Western observers tended to dismiss Soviet military doctrine as an anachronism. Its stress on such themes as preemption and victory, given the incapacity of Soviet forces to lend them credibility, was generally interpreted as little more than routine military incantation. The true measure of Soviet strength was felt to lie in such observables as the Soviet backdown during the Cuban Missile Crisis and Moscow's indisposition to challenge the United States to a race for strategic preeminence immediately thereafter. Under these circumstances, the bombast of Soviet pronouncements tended to resonate with hollow tones. Aside from occasional voices urging a more concerned view of Soviet ambitions, the consensus held that the Soviets had finally come to recognize their place in the nuclear relationship and could be counted on to conduct themselves with circumspection.

Since that time, the pendulum of U.S. assessments has swung from complacency to near-alarm as a result of the steady gains in Soviet force modernization over the past 15 years. Although Soviet doctrine itself has remained largely unchanged since the 1960s, the force posture has moved toward such close congruence with that doctrine that many commentators are now convinced that the Soviet leaders actually believe they are within reach of being able to fight and win a nuclear war. This image of Soviet robustness has fostered growing concern that the Soviet leaders may see a lucrative connection between their achievement of parity and their potential for assertive behavior at the expense of the West. A prominent journalist not normally given to brooding over the Soviet threat, for example, voiced concern well over a year before the invasion of Afghanistan that the Soviets might eventually "talk themselves into the most dangerous of all positions: the self-intoxicating position of believing that they can get away with anything."[1]

Benjamin S. Lambeth is a Senior Staff Member of the Rand Corporation, specializing in Soviet political and military affairs. He served previously in the Office of National Estimates and Office of Political Research, Central Intelligence Agency.

---

1. Joseph Kraft, "Russia's Winning Streak," *The Washington Post*, May 4, 1978.

International Security, Winter 1982/1983 (Vol. 7, No. 3) 0162-2889/83/030139-28 $02.50/1

In principle, such concern over Soviet military programs and conduct is both proper and long overdue. At the same time, we must take care not to overdramatize Soviet prowess. Not only would an exaggerated image of Soviet strength engender needless Western paralysis in the face of Soviet misbehavior, it would also undermine acceptance by the American public of the argument that feasible improvements in the U.S. defense posture will make a difference; without public support, essential improvements will be impossible. Furthermore, such an image would be contradicted by long-standing evidence of Soviet leadership conservatism and risk-aversion.

In isolation from political context, Soviet doctrinal rhetoric projects a stark image of singularity of purpose. On closer examination, however, the message transmitted by this rhetoric is not quite as threatening as it first sounds. For one thing, Soviet leaders view the world just as darkly as Americans do. Having never fought a nuclear war and thus lacking any experience at it, they appreciate that strategic planning operates in a realm of vast obscurity. Moreover, although Soviet forces and concepts reflect an undeniable combat orientation, their principal purpose remains deterrence rather than war. The fact that, through tradition and preference, the Soviets have sought security in hedges against failures of deterrence rather than in stability through "mutual assured destruction" in no way bespeaks any underlying disposition to put those hedges to the test.

Most assessments of Soviet capability emphasize elements that contribute to Soviet strength. By contrast, vulnerability analysis remains undeveloped in strategic research.[2] This essay aims to provide an exploratory venture in the latter direction. It seeks to illuminate some of the unknowns, uncertainties, and doubts that would be likely to temper Soviet incentives to use force in any confrontation laden with risks of nuclear war. Some of these concerns find occasional expression in Soviet military writings. Others are observable in characteristic modes of Soviet crisis behavior. Their net effect is to portray an adversary less assured of its combat virtuosity than a superficial review of its doctrine and forces might suggest. These sources of anxiety and doubt in Soviet planning are the focus of the following discussion. Its objective is to explore a variety of factors conducive to Soviet strategic nervousness that place the more strident refrains of Soviet doctrine in a less distressing light.

---

2. See, however, Major General Jasper A. Welch, Jr., USAF, "The Role of Vulnerability Analysis in Military Planning for Deterrence and Defense of Invasion Threats to NATO" (unpublished paper, June 1976).

The result should help reduce the image of Soviet strength projected by the raw evidence of Soviet force development down to the more manageable proportions it deserves.

Ambivalence in Soviet Doctrine and Style

The most obvious indication of uncertainty in Soviet force planning can be found in the important qualifications contained in Soviet military doctrine itself. In Soviet parlance, doctrine is commonly defined as a set of organized views on "the nature of contemporary wars that might be unleashed . . . against the Soviet Union and on the resultant demands, which flow from such views, for the preparation of the country and its armed forces for war."[3] Not surprisingly, Soviet writings display more confidence on the second score than the first. Where such matters as the basic nature of the security dilemma and the required concepts and hardware for dealing with it are concerned, the Soviets show little confusion. In their view, although the destructiveness of nuclear weaponry has made major war highly unlikely, it nonetheless remains possible because the opposing social systems have irreconcilable incompatibilities. This possibility must be duly accommodated in Soviet defense planning. A force capable of merely inflicting punitive retaliation following an enemy attack is considered insufficient because it is unreliable and could fail to compel enemy restraint in a crisis precisely when it was most needed. From the Soviet perspective, the only sensible foundation of national security is a force capable of decisively seizing the initiative at the brink of war and actually fighting toward specific political and military objectives. Such a posture is not only likely to offer the strongest guarantee of continued deterrence; it will also provide the military wherewithal that would be needed for coping responsibly should deterrence fail.

In contrast to these certitudes about the imperatives of weapons procurement, Soviet commentary on what a nuclear war might actually look like is highly imprecise. Soviet authorities manifest unresolved feelings about such crucial but imponderable questions as how such a war might be triggered in the first place, how long it might last, whether it would be containable at the conventional level, how rapidly it would escalate to theater nuclear operations, what dynamics the transition to intercontinental warfare would entail,

---

3. Lieutenant General I. Zavialov, "On Soviet Military Doctrine," *Krasnaia zvezda*, March 30, 1967.

and, most of all, what the endgame would look like in terms of American behavior and ultimate Soviet prospects for victory. Soviet military spokesmen have been consistently frustrated in their efforts to grapple with these issues since their discourse on strategic nuclear matters began in the 1950s.

In practical terms, all doctrine does for Soviet planners, aside from prescribing broad guidelines for force procurement, is to indicate the most sensible modes of combat in the best of all worlds. Because of its irresolution about the precise contours a war might assume and its appreciation that things could go badly despite the best efforts of the leadership to control events, doctrine scarcely offers a hard prediction of how the Soviets would actually respond, or much comfort in the way of "instant courage" for Soviet strategic decision-makers.

To suggest this, of course, is not to deny the importance of doctrine as a reflection of Soviet strategic logic or as a factor significantly affecting the way the Soviets go about force development and modernization. Nor, most emphatically, is it to deprecate the threat to U.S. interests posed by recent Soviet force improvements or to "excuse" them on the ground that they somehow constitute a legitimate outgrowth of Soviet paranoia.[4] Nonetheless, we must be careful not to misread Soviet doctrine as a categorical predictor of Soviet behavior. The Soviet armed services can readily accept injunctions about the need for large weapon inventories with not only equanimity but enthusiasm, so long as they do not impose an intolerable drain on resources or provoke the United States into determined offsetting measures. Doctrinal insistence on preemption as the only key to Soviet survival, however, would probably

---

4. This point warrants elaboration. Some analysts have downplayed the significance of the Soviet buildup on the ground that it has been driven more by legitimate security concerns than by aggressive hegemonial ambitions. In the words of one such proponent, "the firmly rooted Russian–Soviet sense of insecurity . . . has very likely bred a natural inclination to overcompensate and overinsure on security matters." Because of this underlying motivation, he argues, the resultant Soviet quest for strategic advantage "should not be interpreted in a totally offensive threatening light" and "need not be destabilizing if [properly] understood." Dennis Ross, "Rethinking Soviet Strategic Policy: Inputs and Implications," *The Journal of Strategic Studies*, Vol. 1, No. 1 (May 1978), pp. 4–5. Pushed to the extreme, such formulas amount to apologetic pleas to "pity the poor Russians" because of their unfortunate historical experiences. This viewpoint may have logical attractions, but it ignores the severe consequences the fruits of perceived Soviet "insufficiency" can have for vital Western interests. Whether or not recent Soviet policy has had "aggressive" underpinnings, Moscow's insistence on forces capable of assuring absolute security for the Soviet Union necessarily implies an unacceptable condition of absolute insecurity for everybody else. It is one thing to *explain* Soviet behavior as a manifestation of security. It is something quite different to *condone* such behavior solely on the strength of the explanation. Whatever the motivations for continued Soviet force improvement, the capabilities for coercive diplomacy they permit can scarcely escape the concern of responsible Western planners.

find less ready acceptance in the crisis deliberations of political leaders ultimately responsible for decisions about war and peace. Those leaders would be disciplined by an appreciation of the severe opportunity costs of miscalculation and of the proclivities of best-laid plans to go astray.

The ambiguity of formal doctrine as a guide to Soviet action is matched by strong tendencies toward restraint and caution in Soviet political–military style. In his account of the Soviet political character written in the early 1950s, Nathan Leites advanced the proposition that, when all the returns are examined, "the Politburo's question for any major operation is whether it is required or impermissible . . . rather than whether it is tough or easy."[5] This proposition suggests a Soviet standard of behavior fundamentally unlike that familiar to most Westerners and touches the heart of the reason why the Soviets have failed to develop sophisticated "theories" of coercive diplomacy comparable to those prevalent in U.S. strategic discourse. Although the Soviets are masters of opportunism, they have avoided indiscriminate muscle-flexing. Instead, their tendency has been to talk tough as a matter of practice, yet to reserve actual intervention for cases where they have supreme interests at stake, a high probability of U.S. noninvolvement, and a comfortable prospect of success with moderate investment of military capital.[6]

Given this Soviet instinct to avoid meddling in areas where intervention could threaten to boomerang and to engage militarily only after weighing the costs of inaction against the possibility for success with an economy of force, it is hardly surprising that the Soviet leaders were so perplexed by the piecemeal and ultimately disastrous American involvement in Vietnam. Everything we know about the Soviet philosophy of intervention suggests that they saw the initial U.S. decision to escalate as a headlong leap into a quagmire and the ultimate U.S. acceptance of defeat as a testament to Americans' lack of "seriousness" about war, neither of which they would likely countenance in their own military conduct. In contrast to U.S. experience, the Soviets have generally regarded military power primarily as a static

---

5. Nathan Leites, *A Study of Bolshevism* (Glencoe, Ill.: The Free Press, 1953), p. 34.
6. A considerable body of literature on Soviet crisis comportment generally supports the notion that despite their frequent rhetorical excesses, Soviet political leaders have pursued risk-minimizing strategies more or less regardless of variations in the East–West military balance. See, in particular, Hannes Adomeit, *Soviet Risk-Taking and Crisis Behavior: From Confrontation to Coexistence*, Adelphi Paper, Number 101 (London: International Institute for Strategic Studies, 1973); and Jan F. Triska and David D. Finley, *Soviet Foreign Policy* (New York: Macmillan, 1968), pp. 310–349. See also Jack L. Snyder, *The Soviet Strategic Culture: Implications for Limited Nuclear Options*, R-2154-AF (Santa Monica, Calif.: The Rand Corporation, September 1977), pp. 13–15.

guarantor of deterrence on terms congenial to Soviet diplomatic interests, and only marginally as an instrument for underwriting adventures not deemed essential to the preservation of Soviet security.

What, then, of the Soviet decision to emplace ballistic missiles in Cuba in 1962? A critic of the thesis outlined above might argue that Khrushchev's gambit was a gesture totally out of keeping with the idea that Soviet conduct has been characteristically risk-averse. A reasonable reply would be that Khrushchev's initial calculations were probably based on an honest belief that he could get away with his move, given previous U.S. irresolution in Vienna and at the Bay of Pigs, and that the real demonstration of Soviet crisis behavior came only after the U.S. imposition of a naval blockade made it clear that he had grossly underestimated the intensity of the American response.

The Soviet concept of security has always featured a prominent element of expansionism. Yet Soviet leaders from Lenin onward have repeatedly shown sublime faith that time is on their side. As a consequence, they have been reluctant to "push" history with attempts to reap political gains on the cheap before the natural convergence of the right conditions. In the case of the Cuban crisis, Khrushchev, in all likelihood, genuinely felt he had tested the waters and found them safe. Once he realized that the American commitment to getting the missiles out was greater than his own interest in keeping them in, he immediately reverted to a strategy of prudent loss-cutting by withdrawing the offending weaponry in return for a face-saving U.S. guarantee not to invade the island.

In each phase, the initial deployment and the ultimate backdown alike, he acted with characteristic Soviet rationality, "pushing to the limit" (in Leites's formulation) where he perceived an opportunity to do so at low cost, yet yielding to U.S. resistance when he discovered, doubtless to his astonishment, that the game was not worth the gamble. In the bill of particulars brought against him by his successors, his cardinal sin was probably not so much his failure to stand firm in the face of American opposition (which would have been gravely foolhardy under the circumstances) as his colossal misjudgment of the American temper that caused the Soviet Union to suffer such humiliation. In the Soviet system, no less than in the criminal underworld and other communities based on unmoderated power, mistakes of that magnitude are rarely forgiven, not so much for reasons of callous insensitivity but precisely because of the threat they pose to the institutions they represent.

Sources of Soviet Strategic Anxiety and Doubt

Probably to its credit, the Soviet Union has never developed refined theories about the use of strategic power in coercive diplomacy comparable to such Western notions as "compellence," graduated escalation, and selective nu-clear options. The Soviets regard such concepts as dangerous usurpations of the proper role of military power—namely, the prompt securing of objectives deemed essential to the national interest but unattainable through less ex-treme measures. As Soviet reluctance to commit forces beyond the immediate periphery of Soviet hegemony attests, these sorts of objectives have, at least until now, remained extremely limited. These narrow circumstances (the Hungarian and Czechoslovak invasions of 1956 and 1968, the Sino–Soviet border clashes of 1969, and the ongoing Afghanistan operation) have entailed what the Soviet leadership considers intolerable pressures on its own door-step. They have also been distinguished by a very low probability of U.S. military opposition.

The caution that has tended to deter Soviet leaders from indulging in adventures of dubious necessity or prospect for success would probably assert itself forcefully in a future confrontation where direct superpower combat loomed as a serious possibility. It would also be reinforced by several important operational concerns regarding the many ways Soviet plans could become upset due to weaknesses in such areas as combat readiness, com-mand and control, alliance solidarity, and military morale. Such sources of hesitancy would be especially likely to counsel Soviet restraint in crises where Soviet leaders were convinced that continued inaction or carefully measured exploratory probing, whatever their long-term political costs, would promise less risk than would proceeding with dramatic initiatives that could backfire in unexpected ways. Although it would be imprudent to overstate this point, it seems reasonable to suggest that these elements of anxiety and uncertainty could exert a powerful self-deterrence in future crises short of one where Soviet decision-makers were so convinced that major war was coming that *some* decisive preemptive move was required.

The Soviets are uniquely prone to approach–avoidance conflicts in crisis decision-making because of divergent strains in their political culture. On the one hand, their offensive military orientation, their belief in the commanding importance of initiatives, and their compulsion to check undesirable trains of events before they become unmanageable incline them toward rejecting pas-sivity and treating forceful preemption as the supreme measure of leadership rectitude. On the other hand, their faith in the inevitability of socialism, their abhorrence of momentary acts that might threaten to undo their existing gains, their tendency to draw sharp distinctions between the desirable and the necessary, and their associated confidence that time is on their side impose a powerful braking influence on their willingness to seek radical solutions when events might be safely left to continue for another day.

These conflicting pressures have saddled the Soviet leadership with dilemmas probably far more deeply felt than comparable influences on the crisis decision-making of Western political leaders. Even in Hungary and Czechoslovakia, where perceived necessity and the local balance of forces strongly supported positive action and offered confident prospects for Soviet success, the decision to intervene was preceded by excruciating rumination over potential risks and costs, in which arguments for delaying were strong and the final choice was anything but foreordained.[7] In light of that experience, similar indecision could be expected to weigh on Soviet policymakers with vastly greater effect in any challenge where the Soviet Union stood at the brink of full-scale combat involvement with U.S. forces. In such a case, the preeminent Soviet concern would probably not be over the threat of a "credible first strike," or any of the other niceties of American strategic parlance, so much as over the more undifferentiated specter of "just plain war," to use Thomas Schelling's apt formulation.[8] Given this prospect, Soviet planning, at least initially, would probably emphasize identifying and evaluating those uncertainties about Soviet military performance and the possible interplay of uncontrollable variables that would threaten the success of *any* Soviet option, rather than detailed force capabilities and exchange ratios in specific scenarios. At this level of policy deliberation, with the basic question of war or peace yet undecided, the weight of evidence from past Soviet behavior suggests that consideration of prospective gains would be overshadowed by contemplation of the various things that could go awry.

---

7. In the case of Hungary, Khrushchev recounted that, until the final decision to invade was consolidated within the Party Presidium, "I don't know how many times we changed our minds back and forth." *Khrushchev Remembers*, ed. and trans. Strobe Talbott (Boston: Little, Brown, 1971), p. 148. As for Czechoslovakia, Brezhnev related after the event that one major concern among diverse Politburo members was that "this step would threaten the authority of the Soviet Union in the eyes of the people of the world." Jiri Valenta, *Soviet Intervention in Czechoslovakia, 1968: Anatomy of a Decision* (Baltimore: Johns Hopkins University Press, 1979), p. 142.
8. Thomas C. Schelling, *Arms and Influence* (New Haven: Yale University Press, 1966), pp. 98–99.

This is not to say that in all crises involving the possibility of war with the United States, the Soviets would invariably find themselves mired in immobility. Much would depend on the situation, its proximity to Soviet lines of communication, its relevance to Soviet security interests, and the balance between political stakes and military risks. Much would also hinge on authoritative Soviet assessments of U.S. seriousness and capacity for concerted action. The Chinese expression for "crisis"—a compound of the words "danger" and "opportunity" (*wei-chi*)—neatly captures the conundrum that would beset Soviet leaders in contemplating any direct use of military force against the United States. Obviously they would feel conflicting pressures toward boldness and caution. Their choice would probably hinge as much on what they thought they could get away with as on any detailed assessment of comparative strategic strengths.

Nonetheless, in any Soviet–American confrontation where major escalation appeared possible, Soviet deliberations would be strongly influenced by numerous concerns generally muted in peacetime. The following remarks will survey some of the uncertainties that could generate worry in the minds of Soviet decision-makers if they embarked on a potentially dangerous course, yet still commanded some initiative and could make the outcome go either way. These should be read neither as confident forecasts of Soviet caution in all circumstances nor as an exhaustive account of every conceivable source of concern that might counsel Soviet restraint. Rather, they should be regarded as an abbreviated checklist of fears that could arise in any circumstance where Soviet military forces might actually be required to fight. Although these anxieties scarcely vitiate the importance of doctrinal verities or diminish the seriousness with which those articles should be viewed by Western planners, they suggest that Soviet elites are far less confident than an isolated reading of their doctrinal professions might indicate.

OPERATIONAL CAPABILITIES OF SOVIET FORCES
Apart from uncertainty about such poorly understood aspects of weapons phenomenology as electromagnetic pulse and fratricide and other technical imponderables of force performance that afflict all nuclear states, the Soviet leadership probably senses a whole range of deficiencies in its arsenal that are unobservable to the West yet figure significantly in Soviet planning. Just to cite one example, we assume that Soviet authorities command fairly accurate knowledge of their ICBM force's reliability as a result of their extensive

experience with operational training launches.[9] We are necessarily less certain about the extent of confidence that knowledge inspires, but it may be less than comforting to decision-makers who are obliged to worry about worst cases and would have to shoulder the responsibility for their mistakes. Various sources indicate that ostensibly "no-notice" Soviet operational readiness inspections are carefully stage-managed so that all participants earn high marks.[10] If this practice is widespread throughout the Soviet military, it provides Soviet planners with not only a good feel for what their forces can do under controlled peacetime conditions, but also with grounds for legitimate concern about the degradations they might encounter in a combat situation marked by confusion and a requirement for improvising under duress. If global war appeared a foregone conclusion, such uneasiness might urge prompt preemption while adequate time remained to bring Soviet forces to full readiness under the cover of secrecy. In most situations, however, it would more likely engender profound distress reminiscent of Khrushchev's legendary "smell of burning in the air" at the height of the Cuban crisis.[11] Professional soldiers, if not their civilian superiors, are the least confident of their preparedness the closer they edge toward war. Such foreboding would probably afflict Soviet commanders as intensely as it would comparable military elites the world over.

Similar sorts of brooding, easily sublimated in peacetime yet difficult to suppress in crises, might also surface in connection with Soviet nonnuclear forces. Despite their extensive investments in air defense, we know from the testimony of Lieutenant Victor Belenko that the Soviets have little confidence in the ability of their front-line interceptors to deal with the U.S. low-altitude bomber threat.[12] For many force categories, Soviet planners may not have developed certain theoretically feasible employment options occasionally attributed to them in worst-case Western threat assessments, such as the use

9. Unlike the United States, the Soviet Union routinely conducts ICBM tests and training firings from operational silos. As of early 1974, it had carried out approximately one hundred such launches. See Secretary of Defense James Schlesinger, *Annual Defense Department Report, FY 1975* (Washington, D.C.: U.S. Government Printing Office, March 4, 1976), p. 56.
10. See Herbert Goldhamer, *The Soviet Soldier: Soviet Military Management at the Troop Level* (New York: Crane, Russak, 1975), pp. 116–124.
11. "Khrushchev's Report on the International Situation," *Current Digest of the Soviet Press*, Vol. 14, No. 51 (January 16, 1963), p. 7.
12. John Barron, *MiG Pilot* (New York: McGraw–Hill, 1980), p. 72.

of bombers on one-way missions against the United States. In his memoirs, Khrushchev graphically recounted the derision that met proposals to have the BISON recover in Mexico from bombing missions against U.S. targets. This casts at least some suspicion on more recent Western intimations that the BACKFIRE might be slated for similar one-way missions terminating in Cuba.[13]

These and other indicators are, of course, merely straws in the wind and scarcely constitute conclusive evidence of Soviet shortcomings. All the same, they remind us that Soviet decision-makers know themselves far better than the Americans know them and are likely to be far more sensitive to their operational inadequacies than they are frequently given credit for. How these perceived inadequacies would affect Soviet crisis behavior would depend on Soviet judgments about the nature of the strategic imperatives. They could never be completely ignored and might constitute major factors advising restraint if the necessity for decisive military action had not been clearly established in the minds of the Soviet leaders.

OPERATIONAL CAPABILITIES OF U.S. FORCES

Just as U.S. policymakers tend to exaggerate Soviet strengths, so may the Soviets exaggerate the Americans'. Henry Kissinger has likened both superpowers to "heavily armed blind men feeling their way around a room, each believing himself in mortal peril from the other whom he assumes to have perfect vision."[14] This characterization not only reflects the Americans' occasional urge to overstate unpleasant turns of Soviet behavior as components of a coherent "master plan"; it also reflects both countries' tendency to view their opponent's strategic developments in the gloomiest light while deprecating their own considerable advantages in the process. The Soviets have deep admiration for American technological prowess. This contributes to a Soviet perspective on U.S. weaponry at substantial odds with their general contempt for U.S. strategic doctrine and concepts. As a consequence, Soviet

---

13. On the matter of the BISON, Khrushchev noted: "This plane failed to satisfy our requirements. It could reach the United States, but it couldn't come back. Myasischev [the designer] said the Mya-4 could bomb the United States and then land in Mexico. We replied to that idea with a joke: 'What do you think Mexico is—our mother in law? You think we can simply go calling anytime we want? The Mexicans would never let us have the plane back.'" *Khrushchev Remembers: The Last Testament* (Boston: Little, Brown, 1974), p. 39.
14. Henry A. Kissinger, *White House Years* (Boston: Little, Brown, 1979), p. 552.

threat assessments could well be colored by an unconscious propensity to attribute larger-than-life performance capabilities to American military forces.

At first glance, such a suggestion runs counter to the popular notion that, because of the vast dissimilarities between American and Soviet societies, the Soviets enjoy the twin advantages of secrecy to cloak their own operational deficiencies from Western intelligence purview and freedom to scrutinize every detail of U.S. strategic capabilities like an open book. Yet Moscow's image of American power resulting from this so-called "information asymmetry" may not be nearly so confidence-inspiring as this stark depiction would have us believe. Much has been made about the amount of damaging military data Americans freely provide the Soviets through such open sources as annual Posture Statements, Congressional testimony, technical journals, and press reports. As a result of this hemorrhage of information, so the argument goes, it would take an obtuse Soviet observer indeed not to be able to piece together a mosaic of U.S. programs, capabilities, and plans with a degree of exactitude that Western analysts are only rarely capable of replicating for the Soviet Union, even with the most rigorous and sophisticated intelligence collection techniques.

Although the difficulty of protecting military information in a democratic society is a proper concern of U.S. defense planners and undoubtedly exacts some toll in the effectiveness of the American military posture, there are plausible grounds for wondering whether it uniformly provides advantages to those Soviet officials responsible for keeping track of American force developments. The Soviet military bureaucracy is highly stratified and compartmentalized, and unimpeded data flow is anything but routine. Given the pervasiveness of an acute "left hand knoweth not" syndrome through the Soviet defense community, one can fairly ask how capable its evaluation network is to filter information about U.S. capabilities and draw appropriate connections. The Soviet intelligence subculture has long been known to harbor profound distrust of open-source material on the grounds that it could constitute purposely distorted "disinformation." Instead, it has tended to rely on hard-copy data secured through classic espionage channels as the only authoritative sources of insight into enemy capabilities and plans. Coupled with Moscow's traditional stress on uprooting enemy "secrets" as the ultimate proof of intelligence virtuosity and the KGB's reputed disdain for analysis (which a former Soviet officer once dismissed as "a job for lieutenants and women"), this trait suggests that the Soviet Union may be less effective in assimilating evidence about U.S. strengths and weaknesses than the darker fears of some Americans might suggest.[15]

If there is any truth to this notion, high-level Soviet defense officials may regard U.S. capabilities as being far less imperfect than Americans are frequently inclined to view them. To note only one possibility, the Soviets are probably less impressed by the much-heralded "Minuteman vulnerability problem" than most U.S. defense analysts, since they apparently retain considerable faith in hardened silos to protect their own ICBMs and show little concern—at least yet—about the need for new basing modes to accommodate the impending hard-target capabilities of MX and Trident. If Soviet decision-makers derive any comfort at all from this impending U.S. liability, it probably stems more from U.S. expressions of anxiety over it than from any independent technical evaluations of their own counterforce capabilities. Soviets, like Americans, tend to be fixated by worst-case projection in their contingency planning. It is thus probable that their own uncertainties about how successful a Soviet disarming attack might be, rather than vicarious reassurance from U.S. nervousness about Minuteman survivability, would play the commanding role in any Soviet consideration of the first-strike option in a crisis.

The effect of this Soviet approach to threat assessment is far from congenial to U.S. interests as far as peacetime force planning is concerned, because it probably accelerates rather than moderates Soviet force improvement activities. Yet during a grave crisis in which the Soviet Union's livelihood lay at risk, it could induce caution rather than boldness in military initiatives that could backfire catastrophically in the event of miscalculation. The broad chasm that separates perceptions of Soviet capability on the part of professional intelligence specialists from the more basic images held by senior officials is a characteristic feature of American defense politics.[16] In the Soviet Union, such disparity is probably even more pronounced because of the rigid

---

15. According to one authoritative account, although "the KGB strives to verify the authenticity of stolen documents and the accuracy of agent reports," it completely lacks "any independent body of professional analysts who attempt to distill the underlying meaning and import from intelligence." John Barron, *KGB: The Secret Work of Soviet Secret Agents* (New York: Reader's Digest Press, 1974), pp. 76–77.

16. As Henry Kissinger has observed, "One of the key problems of contemporary national security policy is the ever-widening gap that has opened up between the sophistication of technical studies and the capacity of an already overworked leadership group to absorb their intricacy." Quoted in E.S. Quade and W.I. Boucher, eds., *Systems Analysis and Policymaking: Applications in Defense* (New York: American Elsevier Publishing Company, 1968), p. v.

compartmentalization and hierarchical structure of the Soviet policy apparatus. Accordingly, those party authorities who would be held responsible for gross errors of judgment in a crisis would probably be more disposed to give U.S. capabilities the benefit of the doubt than would intelligence experts commanding a more finely grained appreciation of deficiencies in the U.S. military posture.

AMERICAN RATIONALITY UNDER PRESSURE

One of the more ironic sources of Soviet hesitation in past times of East–West tension has been Moscow's bewilderment at the often cryptic character of American conduct. As a result of their ideological convictions and the abiding constancy of purpose they have inspired, Soviet leaders have come to follow a definite logic in their own political behavior over the years and to acquire a clear set of derivative expectations about the forms of comportment their "capitalist" adversaries ought to observe. Just as conservative Western analysts have been tempted to interpret the most unconnected Soviet moves as parts of a coherent "grand design," so the Soviets have had their own compulsions to perceive all facets of U.S. foreign behavior as being unswervingly inimical to Soviet security interests.

It has long been a familiar cliché that the Soviets would prefer to deal with hardcore Wall Street bankers than romantic liberals in their relations with the United States, because the former are at least conditioned to act in the predictable fashion Soviet *apparatchiks* are schooled to expect. Liberals, by contrast, have frequently adopted policies out of phase with Soviet expectations and thus highly perplexing in their underlying motivations. The numerous instances of inconsistency and vacillation in U.S. behavior during the Carter years directly occasioned the undoubtedly genuine Soviet expressions of frustration over the so-called "zigs and zags" of U.S. policy and probably fostered great uncertainty about how the United States might respond to future Soviet policy initiatives. Despite the embarrassment of riches nominally available to Soviet intelligence analysts, the Soviet estimator responsible for forecasting future U.S. behavior probably has no easier lot than his American counterpart.

Although Soviet doctrinal writings have long underscored the tactical virtues of preemption at the edge of war, their associated image of "victory" (both theater and intercontinental) has hinged on the tacit assumption that the United States would be unable or unwilling to muster an effective retaliation. If the Soviets have been reassured in their defense planning by the notion that nothing succeeds like success, they cannot have escaped the collateral axiom that nothing fails like failure. Their doctrinal refrain that nuclear weapons now permit the achievement of fundamental strategic aims at the very outset of an unrestricted war ultimately entails making a virtue of necessity, for it almost *requires* those objectives to be attained as a precondition of victory. The rational response for the United States in the wake of a massive Soviet counterforce attack would almost have to be a rejection of counter-city retaliation in favor of using surviving forces to try to bargain for a reasonably acceptable postwar settlement from a position of severe military disadvantage. Yet it is far from clear that a U.S. leadership driven by confusion, desperation, and inflamed passion for revenge would choose (or be able) to exercise such supremely disciplined self-control.

In the unlikely case that U.S. unpredictability caused the Soviets to be concerned that the United States might initiate the large-scale use of nuclear weapons, the Soviet urge to preempt would probably overwhelm any arguments for hesitancy. In most circumstances, however, the Soviets would have little cause to fear such a U.S. move (at least at the intercontinental-war level). Any Soviet decision to preempt would accordingly have to account for the possibility that the United States might respond by executing the countervalue portion of the Single Integrated Operational Plan (SIOP)—or worse yet, launch the entire component of its nonreserve forces under assessment of incoming attack—with all the consequences such a possibility would imply for Soviet prospects for success. Even though such a U.S. response under conditions of adversity might leave the Soviet Union with a favorable outcome in purely military terms, Soviet decision-makers would have to inquire searchingly whether such an outcome would constitute any practical "victory" worth having, given the far greater rewards that would accrue from not triggering such devastation in the first place.

At the height of the Vietnam War, President Nixon remarked that the United States had a vested interest in cultivating an image of unpredictability.[17] Carried to extremes, such an attitude could risk provoking just the sort of Soviet impulsiveness it was intended to prevent. Within limits, however,

---

17. After his departure from office, the former president expanded this point into a general principle of strategic diplomacy: "International relations are a lot like poker—stud poker with a hole card. . . . Our only covered card is the will, nerve, and unpredictability of the President— his ability to make the enemy think twice about raising the ante. . . . If the adversary feels that you are unpredictable, even rash, he will be deterred from pressing you too far. . . . We should not make statements that we will never launch a preemptive strike. Whether or not we would ever exercise that option, we should always leave open the possibility that in extreme circumstances we might." Richard M. Nixon, *The Real War* (New York: Warner Books, 1980), pp. 253–256.

U.S. efforts to exploit the "rationality of irrationality" principle by stressing the inevitability of retaliation and alluding periodically to launch-on-warning as a last-ditch nuclear option could reinforce deterrence, so long as they were not substituted for continued investments in U.S. strategic capability. Even though the most ardent American enthusiasts of "assured destruction" might doubt whether such a threat would actually be consummated, there is enough evidence that things could go the other way to make Soviet first-strike proponents unsure about testing their luck. Soviet doctrine may emphasize such principles as surprise, momentum, and victory, but it does not commit Soviet leaders to modes of action that would go against common sense. Insofar as the Soviets can not *count* on U.S. passivity in situations where logic would suggest it as the only sensible alternative, their doctrinal rhetoric must provide them cold comfort at best.

THE DANGER OF DISORIENTATION AND DERAILMENT

Nathan Leites has observed that "Bolsheviks intensely fear their own disposition toward fear."[18] Although this assessment was ventured during the 1950s when inferiority and enemy encirclement were the entirety of Soviet historical experience, it remains valid and continues to explain much of the Soviet Union's distinctive style of military behavior. Much of the bravado in Soviet doctrine can be read as reaction against Moscow's feelings of insecurity and doubt, as can the "gigantism" of Soviet weapons programs stressing size and brute force (exemplified by the SS-18) and the pursuit of numerical abundance in armored vehicles and fighter aircraft, which would sustain high attrition in modern combat. Indeed, almost every feature of Soviet doctrine, arms acquisition, and manpower recruitment lends itself to partial explanation as evidence of Soviet overinsurance against the possibility of wartime events unfolding in unexpected ways.

To a certain extent, such concerns are generic to all military commanders regardless of their ideology or political culture. They are particularly influential in Soviet planning, however, because of the Soviet Union's adherence to an operational doctrine that relies so heavily on initiative and surprise. It is not uncommon to encounter expressions of mild resentment in Western circles over the Soviet Union's apparent luxury to choose the time and complexion of any war it might fight. Yet along with that luxury goes a burden of responsibility unique to holders of offensively oriented doctrines

18. Leites, *Study of Bolshevism*, p. 38.

to weigh the prewar situation with extraordinary prescience, since the chances of success are heavily bound up with the correctness of planning assumptions and opportunities for regrouping are likely to be few and far between. Countries on the receiving end that are politically bound to defensive and reactive strategies have options for flexibility generally denied to those who would start a war. In many cases, the defender might need only be capable of disrupting the attacker's designs to forestall defeat.

None of this has been lost on the Soviets, and evidence of the unease it inspires can be found across a broad range of Soviet military writing and planning activity. Soviet articles on military training and troop management brood over the danger of *rasteriannost'* ("losing one's bearings") in the heat of the battle.[19] Concern over getting caught up in a train of events that cannot be controlled has long preoccupied Soviet commanders and political officers. This respect for the corrosive influence that uncontrolled events could exert on leadership voluntarism was neatly captured in a high-level Soviet political injunction over a decade ago that "the time has long passed when a general could direct his troops while standing on a hill."[20] It goes far toward explaining the unusual stress on redundancy in Soviet command and control arrangements. It also accounts for the preoccupation shown by Soviet commanders and training officers over the difficulty of maintaining motivation and discipline among rank-and-file troops to endure the dislocations that would attend any battlefield use of nuclear weapons. There is little indication of concern over the political loyalty of the armed forces (even though that loyalty may attach more to national than to party symbols), but there is ample evidence of Soviet uncertainty over the extent to which those forces could sustain adequate performance under conditions of unprecedented duress. As a consequence, routine training patterns show signs of an acutely felt need to assure such performance in the event of war through peacetime psychological conditioning and example-setting.[21]

---

19. A representative example of this fixation may be seen in the remark by Army General Pavlovskii that a major objective in the training of officers must be to ensure that "they do not lose their bearings when events develop unfavorably." *Krasnaia zvezda*, February 13, 1974. Also pertinent is the following editorial comment that "of active deeds in battle, capable above all is the man who knows how to subdue not only the feeling of fear—that assertion is hardly distinctive—but also the feeling of *rasteriannost'*." *Krasnaia zvezda*, January 24, 1974.

20. Major General V. Zemskov, "An Important Factor for Victory in War," *Krasnaia zvezda*, January 5, 1967.

21. A detailed and sophisticated marshalling of evidence from Soviet source materials bearing on this concern may be found in Nathan Leites, *What Soviet Commanders Fear from Their Own Forces*, P-5958 (Santa Monica, Calif.: The Rand Corporation, May 1978).

This preoccupation has origins running back to the earliest days of the Bolshevik Revolution and has persisted as a dominant theme in Soviet military education ever since. The "quality of commanders," one may recall, figured prominently among Stalin's five "permanently operating factors" affecting the outcome of war,[22] and inspirational leadership remains a critical precondition of victory in the current Soviet litany of operational desiderata. As early as the 1930s, Soviet training doctrine depicted "political steadfastness and moral attitudes" as indispensable ingredients of operational effectiveness and affirmed the vital importance of assuring that "whatever the difficulties, the army knows what it is fighting for."[23] As a consequence, much of the party's political work in the armed forces has been directed less toward fulfilling watchdog roles (as is often assumed in the West) than toward what Timothy Colton has called the "internalization of civic virtue" among troops that would bear the brunt of losses in combat.[24]

Unfortunately for Soviet planners, merely recognizing the importance of discipline and pursuing measures to instill it can provide little assurance that the results will weather the test of war, particularly one where nuclear weapons might be involved. The Soviets harp about morale, yet fear losing it just when it would be most urgently needed. Their reported policy of whole-unit replacement in the event of major battlefield losses to nuclear effects testifies to their determination to avoid contaminating fresh troops with the resignation that would afflict the survivors of any such catastrophe.[25] Nonetheless, despite their efforts to inculcate strong moral fiber among their troops and their associated measures to contain the more corrosive effects of nuclear shock on unit performance, the specter of confusion, defeatism, and even mass desertion must be an enduring source of uncertainty to any Soviet commander or decision-maker who would have to count on Soviet ground forces to secure victory.

A related malaise that periodically crops up in Soviet military writing

---

22. The other four included the stability of the rear, the morale of the army, the quantity and quality of divisions, and the armament of the army. For discussion, see Herbert S. Dinerstein, *War and the Soviet Union* (New York: Praeger, 1962), pp. 6–8; and Raymond L. Garthoff, *Soviet Military Doctrine* (Glencoe, Ill.: The Free Press, 1953), pp. 34–35.

23. V.K. Triandafillov, *Kharakter operatsii sovremennykh armii* [The operational character of modern armies] (Moscow: Voenizdat, 1932), pp. 50–63.

24. Timothy J. Colton, *Commissars, Commanders, and Civilian Authority: The Structure of Soviet Military Politics* (Cambridge: Harvard University Press, 1979), p. 71.

25. See Colonel A.A. Sidorenko, *The Offensive* (Moscow: Voenizdat, 1970), translated and published by the U.S. Air Force, p. 143.

concerns the perils of overconfidence and the danger that inadequate flexibility at the threshold of war could draw the Soviet Union into a cul-de-sac from which graceful extrication would be impossible. Western analysts often miss this factor and look solely to the surface manifestations of doctrine for insight into Soviet assumptions and expectations. Although it is hardly routine in Soviet discourse on operational matters, one can find sufficient warnings about the dangers of *shapkozakidatel'stvo* ("misplaced belief in the prospect of an easy victory") in Soviet writings to demonstrate that the Soviets do not necessarily believe in the self-fulfilling quality of their doctrinal prescriptions. This applies with particular force to the controversial question of whether the Soviet leadership confidently "thinks it could fight and win a nuclear war."[26] It is a far cry from traditional Soviet military thought to say that Soviet officials are so self-assured that they are prepared to contemplate threats against bedrock U.S. interests in cases other than those where Soviet survival lay equally at risk. Even in dire emergencies where "striking first in the last resort" was the Soviet leadership's least miserable option for attempting to control rapidly unravelling events, Soviet deliberation over such a decision would still be dominated by the most awesome doubt about the future of the socialist vision.

At almost every level of conventional force employment, Soviet commentary emphasizes the importance of such critical intangibles as leadership, awareness, and flexibility, none of which can be counted on in adequate measure at the proper time. It is common to find criticisms of commanders who allow their crews to train repetitively in stereotyped scenarios where targets, terrain features, and the disposition of the "enemy" are all well known in advance, yet who persuade themselves that their impressive results would be repeated in a combat environment.[27] Whether comparable concerns attach to higher-level exercises involving nuclear forces is not ascertainable

---

26. Richard Pipes, "Why the Soviet Union Thinks It Could Fight and Win a Nuclear War," *Commentary*, Vol. 64, No. 1 (July 1977).

27. A candid illustration may be seen in the following comment by the Soviet air commander for the North Caucasus Military District: "Once we investigated a case where a team of experienced pilots carried out a bombing mission which was rated very low. . . . In this case, the pilots had been flying the same routes for a long time and had only worked out the combat problems for their own range under normal target conditions. They did not work out the tactical background. In training, the pilots imitating the target fly only on a straight line, without changing altitude or speed. . . . These people are assuming that the simulated enemy air defense system has been destroyed, but they have simply not thought out the situation. How can someone go into real combat without the necessary skills?" Lieutenant General of Aviation G. Pavlov, "The Inexhaustible Reserve," *Krasnaia zvezda*, August 4, 1976.

from Soviet writings, but it would scarcely be surprising given the Soviet penchant for training across the board in highly routine and unimaginative ways.

A final source of uncertainty involves the appreciation by many Soviet commanders of the potential cost of overcentralization that pervades the Soviet armed forces from the General Staff down to field units. This uncertainty is closely linked with the broader problems associated with the Soviet Union's offensively oriented doctrine discussed above. The Soviet command structure is stratified almost to ossification, with each echelon highly dependent on authority from above and little allowance provided for initiative at lower levels. This hierarchical quality of Soviet military life affects planning and operations in equal measure and heavily influences Soviet military performance. It has the virtue of providing an environment in which roles and missions are carefully allocated in advance and plans can be put into operation with maximum orderliness and singularity of purpose.

Unfortunately, this strength can also constitute a paralyzing weakness when command and control links have been broken, original plans have been derailed, and improvisation becomes required to salvage some measure of control from a rapidly eroding situation. As long as events unfold as anticipated, centralization and command integration can compensate for insufficiencies in the more tangible ingredients of military power. Yet, highly orchestrated war plans requiring careful coordination for mission effectiveness have had a rich record of becoming snarled beyond repair.[28] In the face of such a possibility, one of the least likely sources of versatility and strength would be to have principals on the front line who had been programmed never to think for themselves.

A glimpse of the penalties that can ensue from such overcentralization and inflexibility was displayed in the July 1970 air battle between Soviet and Israeli pilots over the Suez Canal, in which five MiG-21s were destroyed with no Israeli losses in an intense engagement lasting less than five minutes. The day before, Soviet-flown MiGs had attacked and damaged an Israeli A-4 on a deep interdiction sortie near the Egyptian airfield at Inchas. The Israelis sought retribution by launching a diversionary feint. As expected, the MiGs rose to the bait and were promptly engaged by eight Israeli F-4s and Mirages.

---

28. Particularly notable in this regard are the well-known failures of the German Schlieffen Plan and the British amphibious assault on Gallipoli during World War I, both of which involved elaborate schemes that were impressive in concept yet foundered in execution because of various deficiencies in leadership. See B.H. Liddell Hart, *The Real War, 1914–1918* (Boston: Little, Brown, 1930), pp. 46–49, 159–174.

As described in various published accounts, the Soviet formation rapidly broke up in confusion and chaos once the first MiG was shot down. Throughout the engagement, the Soviets showed little evidence of air combat proficiency or air discipline. Having presumably been trained solely for radar intercepts against passive targets, they simply found themselves out of their element once they became unexpectedly caught in a hard-maneuvering visual fight in which the initiative was no longer theirs.[29]

Naturally, one must guard against overgeneralization from such an isolated example. Yet the inflexibilities that caused those Soviet aircrews to experience such a rude lesson in tactical surprise were precisely of the sort that regularly elicit criticism throughout Soviet military articles on operational training to this day. Such criticism is particularly visible in Soviet commentary on matters pertaining to pilot training, but it addresses a cultural trait that probably exists to some degree at all levels of Soviet military activity and constitutes one of the most deep-seated weaknesses of the Soviet armed forces.

Other Uncertainties

The sources of uncertainty in Soviet operational planning examined above apply mainly to questions affecting the performance of Soviet forces and command structures under the strains that would accompany any superpower showdown involving risk of major war. They encompass those concerns that would most immediately bedevil high-level Soviet planners tasked with recommending whether, when, and how to commit Soviet forces to major actions involving danger of nuclear escalation.

Beyond these operational–tactical sources of hesitancy is a broader array of nightmares that might give equal or greater pause to Soviet civilian leaders. Each higher-order concern could be extensively explored in a separate inquiry. This discussion merely identifies them and briefly indicates how they might constrain Soviet assertiveness at the brink of war.

APPRECIATION OF SOVIET COMBAT INEXPERIENCE

Prior to Afghanistan, the Soviet armed forces had never fought on any respectable scale in their entire postwar history. Their only significant involvement had been against neighboring "allies" in policing actions featuring

---

29. For a rare first-hand account of this engagement, see Zeev Schiff, *A History of the Israeli Army* (San Francisco: Straight Arrow Books, 1974), pp. 199–202. Additional details may be found in "Israel: Preparing for the Next Round," *Air Enthusiast*, Vol. 1, No. 7 (December 1971), p. 344.

little risk of military opposition. Soviet spokesmen have gone to remarkable lengths in recent years to express grudging admiration for the operational seasoning U.S. armed forces acquired in Vietnam and that which the Israelis have gained in their various combat trials in the Middle East.[30] The Soviet Union, for better or worse, has enjoyed no comparable opportunity to test its mettle against a determined adversary since its triumph over Nazi Germany in the Great Fatherland War. Although the Afghanistan episode may yet remind the Soviets what it means to live with casualty lists on a daily basis, it is scarcely likely to provide much of an opportunity for gauging how Soviet forces would perform in high-intensity combat against a technologically sophisticated adversary like the United States. Undoubtedly, the Soviets have gained some instructive baseline data about operational resource management through their various power-projection activities in recent years, but there is a limit beyond which these fringe experiences (and such routine peacetime practices as summer training exercises) cannot replicate the demands and uncertainties of sustained military conflict. This inexperience must inspire nagging unease in the minds of Soviet decision-makers, especially those who do not routinely concern themselves with military matters. It may assume heightened significance if the Soviet Union eventually proves to be as inept at counterinsurgency warfare in Afghanistan as the United States seems to have been in Southeast Asia.[31]

CONCERN OVER PREMATURE NUCLEAR WEAPONS RELEASE
The Soviets are at least as obsessive about nuclear weapons control as their American counterparts are. The alert rate of Soviet nuclear forces is generally believed to be far lower than that of the United States.[32] In the Warsaw Pact forward area, nuclear weapons may not even be collocated with, let alone mated to, their delivery systems in peacetime.[33] And, even for periods of tension, it is far from explicit what measures might threaten to remove

---

30. See Drew Middleton, "Soviet Officers Said to Admire American Army," *The New York Times,* December 19, 1977.
31. See Kenneth H. Bacon, "Russian Army Has Been Good But Not Perfect in Combating the Insurgents in Afghanistan," *The Wall Street Journal,* April 24, 1980.
32. John Newhouse, *Cold Dawn: The Story of SALT* (New York: Holt, Rinehart and Winston, 1973), p. 23. See also Robert Berman and John Baker, *Soviet Strategic Forces: Requirements and Responses* (Washington, D.C.: The Brookings Institution, forthcoming).
33. Thomas W. Wolfe, *Soviet Power and Europe: 1945–1970* (Baltimore: Johns Hopkins University Press, 1970), p. 487; and Jeffrey Record, *U.S. Nuclear Weapons in Europe: Issues and Alternatives* (Washington, D.C.: The Brookings Institution, 1974), p. 37.

nuclear weapons from the direct supervision of the Soviet national command authorities. During the Cuban crisis, for example, it was never clear whether nuclear warheads were actually emplaced on the island alongside the missiles.[34] In peacetime, responsibility for nuclear weapons security is reportedly not assigned to operational commands but instead is vested in the KGB, an independent civilian institution.[35]

These and related indicators suggest that Soviet nuclear arms are scarcely poised on a hair trigger. On the contrary, the Soviet nuclear arsenal appears to be so securely disciplined by party authority as to raise a legitimate question whether the Soviet decision-making apparatus is actually capable of supporting the requirement for timely preemption reflected in formal Soviet strategic doctrine. During the terminal phase of the party–military debate over institutional roles following Khrushchev's ouster, an authoritative party spokesman reminded the armed forces that nuclear weapons were so laden with political importance that the party could never allow them "to escape its direct control."[36] Given the unique instabilities of the Soviet political system, many reasons beyond command and control could account for this insistence on civilian monopoly over nuclear armaments at all times. One may be a justifiable leadership concern that premature release of such armaments in a crisis might jeopardize not only Soviet national security but continued party preeminence as well.

TRUSTWORTHINESS OF SOVIET "FRATERNAL ALLIES"

Western analysts generally assume that Soviet forces alone would bear the *initial* burden of air and ground operations in a European conflict. At the same time, a major role in the ensuing phases of combat would probably be

---

34. At the time the crisis broke, the missile launch sites were nearing completion, but only 42 MRBMs had been delivered and none of the IRBMs had been introduced. Moreover, although nuclear weapons storage bunkers were in various stages of construction, the missiles were far from operationally ready when the dismantling of the sites began. In *Essence of Decision: Explaining the Cuban Missile Crisis* (Boston: Little, Brown, 1971), Graham Allison reports that MRBMs had not been observed with warhead sections during their shipboard transportation (p. 103). All of this involves compound speculation, and none of it should be taken to suggest that the Soviets were not prepared to introduce nuclear weapons once their overall deployment effort succeeded. Nonetheless, the notion that they were in no hurry to move nuclear warheads prematurely to Cuba is consistent with general evidence of Soviet concern over the maintenance of close nuclear command and control.
35. Oleg Penkovskiy, *The Penkovskiy Papers* (New York: Doubleday and Company, 1965), p. 331. See also Barron, *KGB*, p. 15, and Allison, *Essence of Decision*, p. 110.
36. Major General V. Zemskov, "An Important Factor for Victory in War," *Krasnaia zvezda*, January 5, 1967.

assigned to various indigenous Warsaw Pact forces. Since the prospect and character of their support would depend heavily on the circumstances that occasioned the war in the first place, they have been topics of intense speculation in Western defense circles ever since the Warsaw Pact was first constituted. The Soviet leadership could never be completely confident of effective Pact support in any circumstances that directly threatened independent East European security interests.[37] Any plan to commit Soviet forces against NATO that required organized Pact involvement as a precondition of success would entail a particularly thorny Soviet decision as a consequence of this uncertainty. Most East European elites are beholden to Soviet power and support for their continued tenure, but they are scarcely obliged to squander their political fortunes or otherwise sacrifice the interests of their domestic constituencies in blind obeisance to Soviet ambitions.[38]

THE THREAT OF MILITARY BONAPARTISM

Since the dismissal of Marshal Zhukov in 1957, the Soviet military has never even remotely challenged the preeminence of party rule. Nonetheless, its interests are frequently at odds with those of the civilian party apparatus and it does command a monopoly on arms. During the 1960s, Western analysts of Soviet party–military relations tended to characterize the two organizations as natural rivals because of their divergent interests and images of how best to deal with Soviet security.[39] More recently, it has become apparent that this tension principally reflected transitory incompatibilities between Khrushchev and his marshals and that party and military interests in fact now overlap a great deal. Persisting differences typically remain limited to matters of resource allocation and show little evidence of deeper contention over institutional roles and power distribution within Soviet society.[40]

---

37. For one of the few serious attempts to examine this commonly expressed but rarely documented proposition in detail, see Dale R. Herspring and Ivan Volgyes, "Political Reliability in the East European Warsaw Pact Armies," *Armed Forces and Society*, Winter 1980, pp. 279–296. See also A. Ross Johnson, Robert W. Dean, and Alexander Alexiev, *East European Military Establishments: The Warsaw Pact Northern Tier*, R-2417/1-AF/FF (Santa Monica, Calif.: The Rand Corporation, December 1980).
38. See, for example, Eric Bourne, "Kremlin Allies Grumble over Afghan War," *The Christian Science Monitor*, June 4, 1980.
39. This thesis was most prominently expounded by Roman Kolkowicz, *The Soviet Military and the Communist Party* (Princeton: Princeton University Press, 1967).
40. See, for example, William E. Odom, "The Party Connection," *Problems of Communism*, September–October 1973, pp. 12–26; and Odom, "Who Controls Whom in Moscow," *Foreign Policy*, Number 19 (Summer 1975), pp. 109–123.

All the same, the Soviet Union remains a nonpluralistic social organism with no formal mechanism for the orderly transfer of political power. Accordingly, in times of leadership transition or external stress, the military could play a major role in domestic politics either by throwing its weight behind its favored contender or directly insinuating itself into the processes of decision-making in cases that threatened its image of Soviet security interests. Because the party enjoys no natural tradition of civilian rule and lacks the constitutional legitimacy of elected governments in Western democratic societies, it might face the added problem of having to worry about its *internal* sources of support alongside the choices and dilemmas imposed by external events.

Would the armed forces be disposed to supplant party authority in the event of a nuclear crisis in which the domestic instruments of social control had fallen apart and the survival of the regime lay in the breach? Perhaps not, given almost everything we know about their past patterns of political conduct. Yet, such a situation would be unprecedented in Soviet experience, and the party leadership could never know for sure.

INTERNAL NATIONALIST INSURRECTIONS

An associated question that could beset Soviet leaders in an incipient wartime situation concerns ethnic forces that might threaten to fragment the Soviet Union. The USSR is not a naturally cohesive nation–state but a quasi-imperial conglomeration of diverse cultures held together far more by Soviet power than by any feelings of national identity. The Slavic component of the Soviet armed forces might indeed fight to the finish for "Mother Russia" in most conditions of national crisis, but similar devotion could hardly be counted on from those non-Russians who increasingly constitute the majority of Soviet military manpower.[41] Soviet leaders have long been sensitive to the threat of insurgent nationalist movements within Soviet borders as a consequence of external encouragement. Indeed, a major component of their rationale for moving into Afghanistan was a felt need to head off any prospect, however remote, of radical Muslim fundamentalism infecting Soviet Central Asia. In recent years, Western defense writings have suggested that the United States might have much to gain by capitalizing on Soviet ethnic rivalries and thus fragmenting the Soviet Union politically in the event of

---

41. See S. Enders Wimbush and Alex Alexiev, *The Ethnic Factor in the Soviet Armed Forces*, R-2787 (Santa Monica, Calif.: The Rand Corporation, March 1982).

war.[42] Although there are severe difficulties concerning how one might actually carry out such a plan to significantly influence war outcomes, even the slightest hint of such reasoning in U.S. planning would cause acute discomfort in the minds of the Soviet leaders. After all, one of their predominant goals in any crisis would be the preservation of the Soviet state. This interest would scarcely be served by actions that threatened to unleash internal forces beyond the ability of Soviet domestic power to contain.

THE YELLOW PERIL

Perhaps the most deeply rooted fear of Soviet leaders and ordinary Russians alike is the specter of a billion Chinese on the southern flank of the Soviet Union, armed with nuclear weapons and animated by consuming anti-Soviet hatred, major territorial claims against the USSR, and global ambitions aimed at undercutting Soviet influence and presence. The Soviet leadership is acutely concerned about the prospect of a two-front war and could never be assured that the Chinese would not try to capitalize on a Soviet–American confrontation, either as an ally of the United States or independently, with a view toward exploiting the Soviet Union's predicament. The urgency of Soviet concern over China's propensity for irrationality that was felt at the height of the Cultural Revolution has almost surely abated dramatically now that Mao has departed and a more secular and moderate leadership has assumed the reins of power. At the same time, China remains a natural enemy of the Soviet Union in a way the United States never has been. The thought least likely to inspire composure in the minds of the Soviet leaders is the prospect of being reduced to China's stature and thus prey to Chinese revanchism as the necessary price for strategic "victory" in a war with the United States.

Concluding Warnings

After all is said and done, a great deal of uncertainty remains about Soviet strategic uncertainty. There is much we do not know (and cannot know)

---

42. Colin Gray, for example, has noted the potential deterrent value of a U.S. targeting plan aimed expressly at critical Soviet social control mechanisms whose widespread disruption during the course of a war might allow "the centrifugal forces within the Soviet empire to begin to bring that system down from within." "Soviet Strategic Vulnerabilities," *Air Force Magazine*, March 1979, p. 64. See also the reference to possible use of nuclear weapons "to achieve regionalization of the Soviet Union" in Walter Pincus, "Thinking the Unthinkable: Studying New Approaches to a Nuclear War," *The Washington Post*, February 11, 1979.

about how Soviet leaders would act in the face of a major test. Uncertainty can cut two ways, depending on how the Soviet leadership perceives the risks and stakes of a situation. It can counsel circumspection and hesitancy— but it can also provide strong incentives toward forceful action aimed at seizing the initiative, defining the rules of engagement according to Soviet preference, and dominating events before they have a chance to slip irretrievably out of grasp.

An example of the latter phenomenon might be sought in the hypothetical case of a major European war in which nuclear weapons had not yet been used, yet where things were plainly going badly for NATO. A sweeping Soviet conventional victory could contain the seeds of disaster in that it would threaten to trigger NATO nuclear escalation as a last-ditch move to forestall utter military defeat. Such a prospect would be almost certain to give Soviet decision-makers compelling grounds for theater nuclear preemption, a major move entailing manifold implications the Soviets might genuinely prefer to avoid.

Conversely, in a conventional war in which NATO had succeeded in disrupting Moscow's offensive momentum, the Soviets themselves could feel powerful urges to raise the ante with nuclear escalation to head off the possiblity of not only losing the military campaign but also watching their East European empire crumble away in the process. If nuclear employment appeared unavoidable sooner or later, the Soviets might well see good reasons for *starting* with nuclear operations and forgoing the conventional phase altogether.

This uncertainty is why, in reasoning far more conclusive than indications drawn from Soviet force posture or doctrine, it is so hard for Western analysts to generate persuasive scenarios for a NATO contingency involving solely conventional arms. However gratifying it may be intellectually, U.S. planners and researchers who indulge in elaborate exercises of manipulating fighter sortie rates, tank exchange ratios, and comparable battlefield minutiae as though the analytical problem simply entailed a grand replay of World War II with modern technology are living in a world of sublime unreality. Soviet incentives for nuclear weapons use, to the extent they would be felt at all, would stem less from doctrinal preference than from operational necessity. If the Soviet leaders felt any mental conflict whatever in such a predicament, it would, in all likelihood, turn on the question of whether to go to war in the first place, not on whether they had a choice between conventional or nuclear options.

Whatever way Soviet decision-makers choose to resolve such uncertainties will depend heavily on the particular crisis they face. In the remote event the Soviets decided the time was right for a full-fledged invasion of Europe and had carefully planned for such an attack in advance, they would also have reconciled themselves to the possibility of a broader superpower war and accepted the risks of such a war as a fair price for the fruits of theater victory. In such a case, there would be little the United States and NATO could usefully do in the way of threat manipulation and "intrawar bargaining." The operational challenge for the West would reduce simply to fighting the war as well as possible and hoping the Soviets had misjudged their chances for success. In the more likely event that both superpowers found themselves inadvertently caught in a conventional skirmish that neither side was eager to pursue, however, there might be considerable room for the sorts of uncertainties discussed here to help lead the Soviets toward some face-saving settlement before the point of no return had been reached.

Conventional Strategy | *Richard K. Betts*

New Critics, Old Choices

American conven-
tional strategy and force structure are now subject to more scrutiny than at
any time since the early 1960s. The passing of U.S. nuclear superiority—no
longer cushioned as it was in the early 1970s by hopes for détente or success
in Mutual and Balanced Force Reductions negotiations—has raised the sali-
ence of conventional defense for the West. Hawks who fear Soviet intentions
and doves who seek a rationale for a nuclear no-first-use policy are united
in the search for more credible conventional deterrence. Recent increases in
military spending and reinvigoration of forward commitments, however,
have not been matched by a clear official articulation of whether or how
strategic concepts might be revised. The Reagan Administration has placed
more emphasis on naval power but has not presented a compelling plan for
improving the ability of land forces to fulfill their primary missions. Without
improving NATO ground forces, all the aircraft carriers in the world would
not stop the Soviet army from overrunning Europe.

This combination of change in the importance of conventional strategy and
continuity in official conceptions has left a large opening for critical analysts
outside the Defense Department. The so-called "military reform" movement
has seized prominence in the debate, but the movement is polymorphous
and often discordant. One thing reformists agree on is the inadequacy of
"business as usual" approaches to defense. As the first section of this essay
will suggest, there is much merit in such criticism, especially when it highlights the astrategic quality of standard analyses oriented to calculating the
"balance" of military power.

To an unfortunate degree, however, reformist critiques have made an
impression by resorting to hyperbole, overlooking dilemmas, and fixating on
stark conceptual alternatives that rarely stand up to the practical requirements
of fielding a large, variegated force committed to meet multiple contingencies.
Those who focus on innovation in strategy often confuse heuristic arguments
with policy prescriptions, because they suffer from insensitivity to political

*Richard K. Betts is a Senior Fellow at the Brookings Institution and lecturer at Columbia and Johns
Hopkins universities. Part of this article draws on a section of a paper presented at the Annual Conference
of the Leonard Davis Institute for International Relations of the Hebrew University of Jerusalem in June
1982. Thanks for helpful comments on the original manuscript are due to Asa A. Clark, Joseph Collins,
Jeffrey McKitrick, Thomas McNaugher, and John Oseth.*

International Security, Spring 1983 (Vol. 7, No. 4) 0162-2889/83/040140-23 $02.50/0

constraints (or simple disdain for them). Those who focus on technology point out the costs of undisciplined sophistication, but go overboard, and many of them implicitly foster the dangerously alluring illusion of a military "free lunch"—better defense for less money. Valuable as gadflies have been, it is time to step back and subject the critics to criticism, and to admit the unedifying but real merits of some conventional wisdom. But first it is useful to explore an area where conventional analyses of conventional forces are weakest.

Threat Assessment and Myths of the "Balance"

Modern reconnaissance and electronic monitoring permit a historically un-precedented degree of accuracy in determination of the quantities and phys-ical qualities of enemy military forces. Yet analysis is too often abused and debate degraded by epistemological errors. The crudest and most common is comparison of particular elements abstracted from integrated capability as a whole—for example, comparison of numbers of tanks without reference to anti-tank weapons; numbers of artillery tubes without reference to tactical aircraft that may be used for similar missions; numbers of ships without consideration of tonnage and unit capability; numbers of nuclear warheads without attention to yield; or defense expenditure totals of the superpowers without mention of the overall totals of the two alliance systems. This ap-proach can lead to a meaningless inductive basis for defining requirements. Desirable forces are simply aggregated, which offers no basis for planning because available resources—except at the margins—are determined deduc-tively, from the political balance between visceral mood about the threat and pressures against increased taxation, deficits, or reductions in domestic pro-grams. The crucial defense budget debates in Washington hinge on the desirable percentage change for the aggregate budget; this is not a measure calibrated to the actual military balance.

To provide a more useful estimate of requirements, given the pressures against potentially endless aggregation, the most relevant—albeit difficult—form of analysis is net assessment: comparison of the full panoply of capa-bilities available to both sides in a prospective encounter. Relative power, not absolute power, is the only meaningful measure of the adequacy of a conventional force. Too much of what passes for criticism in security debates glosses over this obvious point. For example, those doves who simply decry the precipitous increase in Third World military expenditures, or the "record" growth in U.S. defense spending projected by the Carter and Reagan administrations, do not demonstrate that either phenomenon is wasteful or dangerous. Data on absolute levels of military investment do not show that Third World countries have bought more than they need to defend against local enemies, or that the U.S. expenditures will produce more than would be needed to defend against Soviet attacks, or that the world would be more peaceful if there were less total military spending but greater imbalances in relative capabilities. At the other extreme those hawks who, for example, simply decry the massive growth in Soviet naval capabilities do not demonstrate that this causes Western maritime inferiority (as opposed to diminished superiority) because it ignores the earlier baseline. The Soviet naval buildup proceeded from next to nothing in blue-water operational capability. On the other hand, the quantitative balance does not speak for itself either. Geographic asymmetries give Soviet and American naval forces different missions. The military significance of whatever balance obtains varies widely depending on objectives and strategy.

Much of what passes for net assessment, however, is a narrow focus on static orders of battle—the observable and quantifiable constituents such as manpower and equipment—or dynamic simulations of combat engagement. The numerous subjective or intangible factors such as campaign strategy, operational doctrine, training, morale, or command competence receive shorter shrift, yet these factors (unless material imbalance is overwhelming) almost always do more to determine the outcome of battle than the numbers of troops and distribution of weapons. This point is illustrated by the German campaigns of World War II, the Israelis in 1956 and especially 1967, and, more recently, the South Atlantic War, in which a numerically inferior force of British Marines with little fire support quickly rolled up the well-entrenched Argentinian garrison on the Falkland/Malvinas Islands.

The reason for the tendency to focus on the more visible balance of forces is akin to "the principle of the drunkard's search." Although it is procrustean, concentrating on what is clear and quantifiable rather than what is murky and uncertain *appears* to allow more rigor and confidence in the estimate. Moreover, despite its limitations, the quantitative balance must remain an important element in discussion because it is the closest thing we have to a simple index of relative power. Much discussion has to rely on shorthand measurements. But shorthand calculations imprison the relevance of estimates within narrow assumptions about specific operational missions which may not correspond to actual priorities in war. This problem is aggravated by the fact that major wars are usually fought with new technologies untested in previous large-scale combat. Consider this assessment of the relative import of battleships and aircraft carriers written by a naval officer on the eve of Pearl Harbor:

The power of aviation is increasing, but . . . the strength of the battle line is still the decisive factor. . . . a battleship would begin an engagement with about 1,200 heavy projectiles; it would require 1,200 bombing planes to carry in a single flight 1,200 1-ton bombs, which are comparable in destructive power. As planes improve this ratio will decrease, but when planes can carry 3 1-ton bombs it will still take 400 planes to equal a single battleship in hitting power for the duration of an engagement.[1]

For attacking coastal targets on land, this assessment of the battleship's advantage was quite reasonable; it was simply irrelevant to the more critical decisive battles at sea in 1942.

More comprehensive assessments are necessarily more complex and scenario-dependent. Any more complex evaluation is scenario-dependent. While scenarios clarify issues at the micro-level, they confuse them at the macro-level; overall strategy must handle multiple scenarios, and the hypothetical permutations and combinations are endless. The problem with holding subjective variables in abeyance is that estimates of the quantifiable balance can easily provide analytical ammunition for both sides in U.S. defense debates, because either can temper the significance of the balance by appealing selectively to other considerations. Those who debunk alarmist views of the Soviet threat can point to areas of overwhelming U.S. advantage, such as in long-range logistical capacity and power projection forces for intervention in Third World regions. Despite dramatic growth in Soviet projection forces, they contend, the Russians would still have only weak options for contesting Western military action in Latin America, Africa, and the Pacific basin. Opponents can counter that in parts of the Middle East—a more likely and important scene of confrontation—the USSR's geographic proximity neutralizes U.S. superiority in airlift, sealift, and aircraft carrier striking power.

Those who see Warsaw Pact power in Central Europe as overwhelming point to the large disparity in ground forces that would exist even after

1. Captain W.D. Puleston, USN, *The Armed Forces of the Pacific: A Comparison of the Military Power of the United States and Japan* (New Haven: Yale University Press, 1941), pp. 178–179. On "the drunkard's search" see Abraham Kaplan, *The Conduct of Inquiry* (San Francisco: Chandler, 1964), pp. 11, 17–18. The metaphor refers to the old joke about the drunkard who looks for his house key under a street lamp not because he thinks he lost it there, but because the light is better.

NATO mobilization. Their opponents, however, cite mitigating factors: improbable cohesion of the Eastern alliance, questionable skill levels and esprit among Soviet troops, long mobilization (and hence longer warning time) necessary to mount an attack with more than fifty or sixty divisions, and the military advantage of a defensive posture, which allows NATO units to hold off larger numbers of offensive forces. If one assumes that NATO mobilizes and reinforces, force-to-space ratios make it difficult for the Soviets to funnel enough divisions into narrow sectors to achieve breakthrough.[2] The pessimists can counter by citing asymmetries in the vulnerability of rear areas that favor the Warsaw Pact,[3] severe doubts about the political capability of NATO to reach a decision for mobilization in response to warning, lack of sufficient operational reserves to contain a penetration, and the strategic advantage of the initiative for the attacker (the option to focus effort, to exploit deception and innovative plans, and to choose the timing, locale, and mode of engagement) which may neutralize the tactical advantage of the defense.[4]

At a very simple level of analysis, assessments of the balance are the least unsatisfactory indicator of which side has the advantage because the quantitative data are firmer than the data on intangible factors. Serious investigation, however, should take such assessments as the starting point for analysis, not the answer to what capabilities are adequate for defense. Otherwise, evaluations must rest on the dubious assumption of the equivalence of imponderables (that is, that the various advantages in subjective factors are about evenly distributed between the two sides and cancel each other out). Or, even more riskily, the U.S. assessment would have to assume that most of the subjective variables favor the West. Given the huge uncertainties on these questions, however, the only way to hedge in a direction that minimizes risk is to compensate for the unknowns by overinsurance in the quantitative elements, to provide a cushion against bad luck or unexpectedly high enemy competence. This is the solution that Moscow appears to have chosen in regard to the area of highest military priority for both superpowers—the Central Front in Europe.

U.S. planners, therefore, must either accept higher risk (by resting on one

2. John Mearsheimer, "Why the Soviets Can't Win Quickly in Central Europe," *International Security*, Vol. 7, No. 1 (Summer 1982), pp. 26–29.
3. Robert Shishko, *The European Conventional Balance: A Primer*, P-6707 (Santa Monica: Rand Corporation, November 1981), p. 21.
4. Richard K. Betts, *Surprise Attack: Lessons for Defense Planning* (Washington, D.C.: Brookings Institution, 1982), pp. 9–10, 12–16.

of the above assumptions) than the Soviets do, or they must arrive at a more complex assessment of how the fuzzier factors stack up. As examples of the difficulty in reaching definitive judgments of the subjective issues I will briefly mention some considerations in regard to one: the relative advantages of tactical defensive operations and strategic initiative for the attacker.[5] Uncertainty about coalition solidarity in wartime probably favors NATO. But even if just one or two countries in the Western alliance—for example, Belgium or the Netherlands—opt out of mobilization, critical difficulties in covering the front would arise. Moreover, because Soviet troops comprise a large majority of Pact forces and are more heavily equipped than many NATO units, with surprise they might outnumber and outgun the West even if they attacked alone after incomplete mobilization. But their advantage would not be sufficient to overcome a reinforced and entrenched defense (that is, a NATO front line augmented by U.S. POMCUS[6] divisions that had time to deploy and prepare fortified positions during the warning period) unless the Soviets used uncharacteristically bold and innovative tactics. Therefore NATO's greatest vulnerabilities are probably: (1) political indecision in response to warning indicators which could delay alert and coordination of the defense (especially if several "cry wolf " false alerts in a gradually evolving crisis dulled sensitivity); (2) an adventurous Soviet attack plan that, for example, launched air strikes well *before* the ground offensive was ready, in order to disrupt the U.S. airlift, interdict sea ports, wreck POMCUS depots, and short-circuit Western communications; and (3) deceptions that could mask the main axes of Soviet advance, preventing NATO's limited mobile reserves from moving efficiently to the critical sectors.

Judging by most historical precedents, the first vulnerability is quite plausible. The second is not thoroughly consistent with what is known of Soviet doctrine which stresses careful preparation and mass and condemns adventurism (although the doctrine does also emphasize surprise), but it is certainly conceivable. The third is unlikely given the technical capabilities of modern intelligence surveillance mechanisms, unless there is a combination of bad weather and novel Soviet means of spoofing. In any case, the position of initiative gives the Soviets more options for resolving the uncertainties on

---

5. Part of the following draws on ibid., pp. 170–188, 199–207.
6. Prepositioned Overseas Materiel Configured to Unit Sets. These are equipment stocks in depots in Germany, to which divisions can be airlifted from the continental United States. Without prepositioned equipment, the units would have to move by sea, which takes much longer.

preferred terms, for setting the conditions of engagement and focusing an attack on NATO's weak points, if they are willing to take high risks and mount operations in ways unheralded by previous evidence in their military writings and exercises. Any decision to resort to war, though, presupposes radical action. Thus some elements in this collection of uncertainties favor NATO, and some Moscow. Which way they tilt overall depends largely on faith, though the net result probably favors the USSR. A sterile assessment based on the quantifiable balance of forces, however, provides no answers about the effect of these considerations on the question of which side would achieve its objectives in war.

If the balance were the problem, the solution would be simple: deploy more weapons and increase manpower until the balance is even, or favors the West. Some doves, focusing on NATO strengths and Soviet weaknesses, believe this could be done with modest increments of investment. Hawks believe the increments would have to be massive. The latter thus have a greater incentive to increase power by changes in strategy and tactics.

Strategic Romanticism

The importance of subjective factors and initiative has been recognized by reformist critics. Until recently, civilian contributions to conventional strategy have been much sparser than to nuclear strategy (largely because palpable experience with the former made clear its daunting complexity, while the purely hypothetical nature of nuclear strategy made it seem susceptible to analysis by logical deduction). Civilian analyses of conventional forces rarely ventured beyond the static balance. The most eloquent figure in the new school is the *enfant terrible* of strategic studies, Edward Luttwak, who has performed a great service by brutally exposing the sterile, ahistorical, and mechanistic quality of much American defense analysis.[7] The exposé, however, sometimes goes overboard and is limited by its own monomania. Strategic thinking is implicitly conveyed as an autonomous art, a genie that should drive defense planning, unhobbled by managerialists. As Luttwak

---

7. Examples of Luttwak's arguments are "On the Meaning of Strategy . . . for the United States in the 1980s," in W. Scott Thompson, ed., *National Security in the 1980s: From Weakness to Strength* (San Francisco: Institute for Contemporary Studies, 1980); and "Why We Need More 'Waste, Fraud, and Mismanagement' in the Pentagon," *Commentary*, Vol. 73, No. 2 (February 1982), pp. 17–30.

waxes at one point, "the Way of Strategy [*sic*] is not given to all."[8] His criticism reveals severe debilities—such as the simplistic focus on "the balance"—but then often caricatures and misconstrues the dominance of economists, systems analysts, and astrategical micro-managers in U.S. defense planning, and it promotes an almost mystical apotheosis of strategy as a vocation.

The attack on managerial methodologies confuses principle and practice and fails to grapple with the problem of opportunity cost. The function of systems analysis is to estimate investment tradeoffs, allowing the most effective mix of combat power to be obtained from the aggregate resources available—which are always finite. Eliot Cohen attacks systems analysis for its pretensions to determining "how much is enough" for defense.[9] This critique has some validity for the 1960s, but is exaggerated. First, it takes too seriously the claims of early practitioners. Even in the McNamara period, despite official declarations to the contrary, the defense budget ceiling was set independently, according to general predispositions about threat and competing budgetary demands. In an ingenious exposition Arnold Kanter reveals that arbitrary financial constraints, civilian controls, and outcomes actually differed far less between the 1950s and 1960s than folklore maintains.[10] The real utility of systems analysis is to highlight tradeoffs deductively, within the expenditure ceiling.

Second, Cohen overestimates the influence of systems analysts. Even in the heyday of the 1960s it is difficult to find many programs whose fate was primarily determined by the "Whiz Kids." At best their judgments are usually only one of several competing inputs to decision, and most of the time they are less influential than the advice of other interest groups. (The most prominent example of a program that was warped by McNamara's approach—the TFX/F-111 fighter project—actually contradicts another of Cohen's criticisms, that systems analysis ignores the incalculable advantages of versatility in a weapon and promotes single-mission systems. The TFX fiasco was due in

---

8. "Why We Need More 'Waste, Fraud, and Mismanagement,'" p. 25.
9. Eliot Cohen, "Systems Paralysis," *American Spectator*, Vol. 13, No. 11 (November 1980), pp. 23–27.
10. Arnold Kanter, *Defense Politics: A Budgetary Perspective* (Chicago: University of Chicago Press, 1979), pp. 74–78, 82–93. The premier example of quasi-memoir accounts that inflate the role of systems analysis is Alain Enthoven and K. Wayne Smith, *How Much is Enough?* (New York: Harper & Row, 1971).

large part to systems analysts' pressure to widen the capability of the plane.) Even if the criticisms are valid for the 1960s, before systems analysis was reined in, how instructive is it to beat a horse that has been dead for fifteen years?

Third, the wrongheaded quests for narrow efficiencies that the critics lament are regrettable, but are only examples of the bad cost-effectiveness calculation. And the criticism does not offer any forthright definition of what alternate mode of assessment guarantees fewer bad decisions, other than the experience and intuition of professional soldiers. There is no clear evidence that the overall force structures developed before or after the period when the role of systems analysis was greatest were "better" in terms of the match between available resources and effective power than those of the 1960s. If seasoned strategists have made proportionally fewer unwise program trade-offs *within a finite budget* than the McNamara regime did, the fact remains to be demonstrated. The *clear* examples are those that *add* extra capabilities rather than those that explicitly give one up to gain another—in short, cases where hard choices could be avoided.

The alternative to crude economic reductionism is not to do without such calculations. Rather it is to make them better or, as the critics imply, to do them intuitively, or by another name ("strategic thinking"), or by default. Like Tartuffe who was surprised to find that he had been speaking prose all his life, strategists who make choices between alternatives (rather than simply adding all desirable capabilities together) practice systems analysis without realizing it.

This point is obscured by some of the critics' assertion that efficiency and military effectiveness are contradictory. This is true only where "efficiency" is defined quite narrowly. The elementary economic reality of opportunity cost means that for each inefficient program, some other useful element of combat power is forgone. Luttwak cites the strategic benefit of inefficient production in a hypothetical case[11]—and in this case he may be correct—but does not state what other capability he wants to give up for that benefit. The real logic of this line of criticism is an argument for a higher resource ceiling, to allow acquisition of more of all sorts of things. This may be a valid goal but it is a separate issue from how to determine choices within a constrained budget. Resource ceilings are determined by vague senses of threat and acceptable risk, not by strategy; rather strategy must put the available re-

---

11. "Why We Need More 'Waste, Fraud, and Mismanagement,'" p. 22.

sources to work in the best combination of outputs. Visionary strategists who gloss over opportunity cost have a usefulness as limited as that of mechanistic managers who don't understand the vagaries of war. Rather than flagellate inept systems analysts, critics aiming to change policy might more profitably link their strategic thought to the corpus of serious organization theory that explains the impediments to rational action by complex institutions. But while managerialists can be criticized for not having read Xenophon, Clausewitz, or Douhet, those who venerate strategy give no indication that they have read Cyert, March, or Simon. Thus they are subject to the same joke told about analytic propensities of the professional fraternity they criticize: two professional economists are marooned on a desert island (in the days before flip-tops) and find a can of beer—when one asks, "What shall we do?" the other cogitates and says, "First, assume a can opener."

In railing against managerialism, systems analysis, and the "bookkeeping" approach to defense policy, critics have implicitly enshrined bold and creative strategic thought as an independent solution, and strategy as the factor to which other constraints must be adapted. Luttwak argues, "only a fully strategical appraisal can yield a valid answer. Beginning at the level of *national strategy*, one must proceed level by level to the intended theater strategies, to the operational methods . . . all the way down to the tactics of specific forces in particular situations."[12] This sort of pure "strategism" is heuristically valuable but is a prescription for thought, not policy. Like the focus on quantitative balance assessments, it neglects critical mitigating factors. Foremost are political constraints that are essential (rooted in the U.S. Constitution), not peripheral. In a nation that has never faced imminent extinction or threats that admit of no ambiguity, one cannot expect the polity to adapt to strategy; rather strategy must adapt to the polity. The polity must respond to threats if it is to survive, but the mode of response—strategy—will be pushed, pulled, and squeezed by competing theories and interests; coherence may emerge if the process is well managed but it will always be suboptimal according to the logic of any particular philosopher king. *Apolitical strategy is no improvement over astrategic economics.*

Strategic innovation depends on the social and political milieu. The German blitzkrieg was attributable not just to the genius of Manstein and Guderian or the superior tradition and ethos of the German army; the army originally resisted the 1940 Manstein Plan as too adventurous and it was

---

12. Ibid., p. 20 (emphasis in original).

Hitler's direct personal intervention that made its implementation possible. The Prussian military reforms of earlier times were also *societal* reforms.[13] Napoleon's genius would have loomed lower in military history were it not for the *levée en masse* made possible by the French Revolution. Do current critics propose a cultural revolution or constitutional change to make radical reform possible? If so, what sorts, and how are they to be brought about? Despite critics' frequent invocation of the need to consider non-technical and social factors, there is thin attention at best to these questions, aside from exhortations to take the Soviet threat more seriously, and when there is it sometimes takes the counterproductive form of sneering at the effeteness of American society.

Realistic strategic analysis must be interdisciplinary, not a field in its own right. Focusing on military genius in concepts as the key to strategy, and implicitly viewing resource management or political constraints as distractions, is neither empirically realistic nor normatively legitimate. Doing so makes criticism either curmudgeonlike or wistfully romantic. Romance may be a necessary condition for an ideal marriage but it is not a sufficient one; strategism may be a necessary contribution to improvement of American defense but it is also insufficient.

In strictly military terms pure strategism rejects modernity almost as much as it embraces it. The conventional forces of today's superpowers are too complex and their commitments too diverse and contradictory to allow full subordination of strategy to genius in campaign planning. Just as the theories of Adam Smith or Karl Marx, intellectually powerful as they are, can no longer sufficiently explain the functioning of post-industrial technocratic economies, neither Clausewitz nor Jomini can sufficiently guide modern strategy. Changes in technology, logistics, and costs per unit of combat capability make management as vital as leadership and bookkeeping as vital as inventiveness in operational concepts. Because the West is in the defensive and reactive position, it must emphasize long-war capabilities more than Moscow (only an offensive or preemptive doctrine is conducive to banking on a short conflict and such a change is still foreclosed by U.S. and—even more—allied public opinion). And because the United States itself is blessed by large buffers of water it is cursed by huge mobility requirements if it is to aid allies. Thus logistics is more central to American strategy than to that of

---

13. I am indebted to Barry Posen and Congressman Newt Gingrich for reminding me of these points.

most other great powers in history. Logistics more than anything requires efficient management. There is an old joke that amateurs talk strategy and professionals talk logistics. This is unfair, but efficient logistics for modern forces require the sorts of systems analysis "bookkeeping" at which critics sneer.[14] Consider the tradeoffs that have to be calculated in integrating "intrinsic" logistics (elements inherent in hardware design) with "extrinsic" alternatives deriving from "processes of support structure."[15]

Napoleon faced awesome logistical challenges but they were simpler to grasp intellectually—involving mainly food, a few types of ammunition, and (with limited exceptions) campaigns that were less than intercontinental—than those that face U.S. planners today. Even Patton and MacArthur had less complexity to manage than today's SACEUR or CINCPAC to deal with force structures dependent on a raft of high-technology weapons, communication systems, and phased global mobility operations. The increased prominence of managerial concerns is less an aberration of national style than a reflection of the secular trends in modern technology and potential geographic scope of war that have driven up the tail-to-teeth ratio in force structures. Smaller military establishments such as Israel's can escape some of this complexity, or larger ones like the USSR's can drown it with less efficient mass, but the United States can do neither. For American planning, management that deprecates strategy is sterile and strategy that deprecates management is helpless.

One basic problem in disparaging the U.S. emphasis on managerial skill and techniques is that making strategy the independent variable implies that force structure and weaponry can be dependent variables, developed to fit strategy. This is proper in principle but has been infeasible in practice. Modern weapons have long lead times from conception to deployment (five to fifteen years) and changes in force structures tend to proceed glacially because adaptability varies inversely with complexity. Luttwak and others recognize this, and are not naive about tailoring weaponry to doctrine. And of course it is possible to go further in that direction. Innovative attempts

---

14. Attempts at excessive calibration of logistical operations in the fog of war is of course unrealistic. See Martin Van Creveld, *Supplying War: Logistics from Wallenstein to Patton* (New York: Cambridge University Press, 1977), pp. 202–210, and Betts, *Surprise Attack*, pp. 185–187. That sort of unrealism, however, is only pseudo-efficiency, not an argument against the importance of management.
15. Colonel Elbridge P. Eaton, USAF, "Let's Get Serious About Total Life Cycle Costs," *Defense Management Journal*, Vol. 13, No. 1 (January 1977), p. 3.

such as the Army's "High Technology Test Bed"[16] are desirable experiments, although more ambitious projects such as the "Concepts Based Requirements System"—attempting to direct technological development to doctrine for battles in the year 2000[17]—seem too much like an exercise in crystal-ball planning. Modern technology has too much of a life of its own to be pressed into service on that time scale without sacrificing potential benefits (through doctrinal adaptation) from scientific serendipity.[18]

A more fundamental problem obstructs strategism. For the United States since World War II, changes in strategy—or, less charitably, "strategic fads"— often outpace changes in *both* weaponry and force structure. For example, Western deterrence before the Korean War rested almost entirely on the U.S. Strategic Air Command. Soon, however, NATO shifted to planning for serious conventional defense—the Lisbon meeting in 1952 decided on force goals of 96 divisions and 9,000 aircraft to be reached by 1954. But less than two years later the Eisenhower Administration's "New Look" shifted to the massive retaliation strategy, which pushed the Army toward reorganization around the assumption of tactical nuclear war (recall the Pentomic division). Scarcely later than this alteration had shaken down, the Kennedy flexible response strategy shifted back to prolonged conventional operations. As the Vietnam War wound down, the Army was driven to reemphasize the NATO mission, and the "heavy" force structure appropriate for it. No sooner had this reorientation solidified than anxiety about the Persian Gulf and the need for a Rapid Deployment Force (RDF) compelled attention to novel structures and lighter equipment. By the time the RDF finally becomes viable it is not unlikely that change in strategic priorities or threat fixations will be working in another direction. Whatever ideal Pattonesque strategist critics have in mind will have to engage novel threats with forces determined largely by criteria other than those of the strategy of the moment.

Practitioners of strategism can respond by saying "Exactly! That's the problem. American defense is incoherent because leaders don't know what they want." The problem, however, cannot be solved by better military education

---

16. See Lieutenant Colonel Huba Wass de Czege, "Toward a New American Approach to Warfare," in *The "Military Reform" Debate: Directions for the Defense Establishment for the Remainder of the Century*, Senior Conference XX (West Point: U.S. Military Academy, June 1982), pp. 61–62.

17. Ibid., p. 61.

18. Richard K. Betts, "Innovation, Assessment, and Decision," in Betts, ed., *Cruise Missiles: Technology, Strategy, Politics* (Washington, D.C.: Brookings Institution, 1981), p. 9.

or appointment of officials with a more subtle flair for the "Way of Strategy." Nor is the problem simply cultural (which would make it irremediable, since only disaster can bend a liberal culture to military requirements). It is, however, almost as deeply rooted as culture. The problem lies in the juncture between the American political system and the ambiguity of conventional military requirements for a superpower in a world of both nuclear risks and changing commitments. Ambiguity fosters diverse notions of deterrence and defensive options, while democratic politics makes the dominance of any view ebb and flow. Only if U.S. administrations had the duration and consistency of the Soviet Politburo, or if Americans really saw their survival as being tenuous, could there be much more persistent congruence between U.S. strategy and force structure, and thus more room for subtle tuning of doctrine and tactics to strategic guidance.

One solution for bringing strategy and structure into alignment in this context is to emphasize flexibility in structure through long-range mobility and versatility in weaponry. This requires maximal efficiency in resource allocation and calculation of tradeoffs between technical alternatives, because versatility goes hand-in-hand with sophistication and cost, and transport investments are made at a cost to combat equipment. As with logistics, efficient calculations require the cost-effectiveness methodologies and management systems that are denigrated as "bookkeeping," because calculations in this realm are more scientific than artful.

Critics can counter that there is another alternative—to emulate the Russian solution by developing new prototypes in greater numbers, with more frequency, so choices can be made more often and forces modernized steadily rather than episodically. Some argue that the Soviet approach successfully subordinates weapons acquisition to doctrine.[19] Or there is the option to

---

19. Colonel Richard G. Head, USAF, "Technology and the Military Balance," *Foreign Affairs*, Vol. 56, No. 3 (April 1978), pp. 544–563. Critics also argue that the Russians manage to develop and deploy several new types for each one the U.S. does—for example, T62, T64, T72 (and almost T80) tanks during the ten years it took to turn out the U.S. M-1. Major Jeffrey McKitrick maintains, however, that this difference is overrated. During this period "the M60 was upgraded to the M60A1, M60A2, and M60A3 with design improvements in engines, ammunition, suspension systems, range-finding equipment, and night-fighting equipment resulting at each step in a tank with greater capabilities than its predecessor. Further the three 'new' Soviet tanks . . . were not always different tanks. The T62 was basically the same tank as the older T55 except for the main gun. The T64 was new, but the T72 followon was again basically the same as its predecessor." Debunking the horror stories about cost overruns for the M-1, McKitrick reports that the Army's Director of Weapons Systems says the price of the M-1 at the time of deployment, with inflation discounted, was within 5 percent of the first projection. "A Military Look at Military Reform," *Comparative Strategy*, Vol. 4, No. 1 (forthcoming; manuscript quoted).

compensate quantitatively with higher force levels, avoiding risky choices in trying to squeeze the best from each defense dollar, relying on a cushion of size and diversity from slop in investment. Because of geography, however, the Soviets do not need to divert resources from combat formations to long-range mobility and logistics to the same extent as the United States. So even with equal spending direct U.S. combat power would be less. In any case, the solution of washing out uncertainties through higher military expenditures runs into the basic problem with strategism—it is less practicable (in peacetime) in a democracy than in an autocracy.

As a source of power potential the West's economic superiority is more than offset by the East's administrative superiority, even discounting the recent weakness of capitalist economies and the spectre of global financial crisis. The Soviet system can subordinate competing demands to strategy, and has been able to produce steady, long-term increases in military investment. Because U.S. defense budget changes are determined more by broad swings in public and Congressional mood than by consistent strategic planning, they fluctuate much more. Even under circumstances most propitious for raising defense spending—the election of a hawkish president in 1980—it is clear that U.S. defense budgets will not rise to levels that would establish conventional superiority or parity in Europe. It does no good for critics to argue that cost is not a barrier because we spent a far larger proportion of GNP on defense in the 1950s (this was before the revolution in welfare and entitlement program budgets) or the 1960s (when the economic pie expanded fast enough to increase both guns and butter). If Ronald Reagan cannot succeed in exacting more than incremental military increases from the polity, no administration will, short of an epochal crisis.

It would be naively fatalistic to assume that this condition is immutable. But it is only realistic to recognize that domestic politics determines military options far more than expert strategic analysis does. Until pro-defense critics offer a pathbreaking *domestic* strategy to secure more solid and enduring support for defense allocations, all the military strategic genius in the world will be scarcely more relevant to policy than any other sort of wishful academic philosophy, and scarcely more helpful than concentrated managerial efforts to maximize effective use of available resources.

Despite its limitations strategism still performs a vital role as an irritant in defense debate, goading leaders to remember that good management is a necessary but not sufficient condition for military planning. The ideal solution would be to mold the defense planning process so that the distinct levels of analysis could be coherently combined. Democracy in a generic sense does not preclude this, but the unique character of American democracy makes it quite difficult. The essence of the Constitution is the dispersion of power and turnover of leadership, whereas coherent planning requires both concentration and consistency of authority. A more integrated military staff system that reduced the centrifugal influence of the separate services would help. Indeed, the reason that systems analysis in the Office of the Secretary of Defense burgeoned in the 1960s was that there was no comparable center of integrative analysis within the military. Were the United States to have a genuine and effective General Staff, there would be less need and less excuse for concentrating assessment of cross-service tradeoffs in the hands of civilian managers (although given the competitive balance of power between the separate services, special pleading would persist and some autonomous civilian analytical discipline would still be helpful). General Staff types of organizational solutions, however, have been proposed often but have traditionally been anathema to Congress, which normally prefers to constrain the executive by dividing it and to deal directly with the separate services. The putative fear of a Man on Horseback, used as an excuse for precluding a General Staff, is more a rationale for maintaining legislative clout than for protecting the nation. Recently the climate in Congress has become markedly more receptive to reform and centralization of the JCS system, but the proposals considered stop short of a full-blown General Staff system.

Doctrinal Fetishism

The American political system and the complexity of modern technology and military organization conspire to make force composition only loosely responsive to specific strategies. The only clear way to reverse this trend is to attack it as one would the Gordian Knot—by frontal assault on fundamental trends and assumptions in military planning and weapons production. Two groups of iconoclasts have visibly promoted such approaches since the late 1970s. But the danger to guard against in the Gordian Knot approach is being left with what Alexander had after he cut the knot—a loose bunch of string no more useful than the original mess.

One group deals in terms of operational doctrine, arguing that ground and air operations should be oriented much more to the canons of maneuver and agility than to the emphasis on firepower and attrition that they charge has governed American doctrine. The principal public exponents have been Luttwak, John Boyd, William Lind, Steven Canby, and Jeffrey Record. They have argued that such reorientation is the only way to reconcile the constraints that limit the size of Western forces with hope for successful conventional defense against Soviet hordes. Maneuverist critics often couple their doctrinal diagnosis with assertions that the U.S. military has a steady record of operational failure ever since the Inchon landing of 1950. This hyperbolic combination exaggerates both the merits of maneuver and the obtuseness of American commanders. Few of the critics bother to point out that MacArthur, the strategist they revere, caused a debacle at the Yalu when the propensity for high risks that had yielded success at Inchon produced the longest retreat in U.S. military history. The larger strategic disappointments in Korea and Vietnam were not due to doctrinal deficiencies half so much as to political constraints against escalation and the inherent disadvantages of a status quo power in *un*conventional war. Tactics in Vietnam, in fact, *were* dominated by maneuver (insofar as maneuver is identified with movement—a definition with which some of the reformists quarrel, though unconvincingly, as I will argue below). Airmobile warfare, "vertical envelopment" by helicopters, was a remarkable innovation and became the staple of ground operations. The only way maneuver might have been more sweeping and decisive was through an invasion of North Vietnam, which would have been as reckless and irresponsible as the policy of prosecuting more limited war in the South. Military leaders can be criticized for not resigning in the face of political constraints which, though proper, precluded sensible strategy and made lasting military success improbable, and for not appreciating the inappropriateness of conventional forces for an unconventional revolutionary war, but it is inaccurate to charge them with not utilizing maneuver to the degree that was operationally feasible.

Here again the intellectual vulnerability of the critics derives from addressing strategy and doctrine autonomously, without clarifying the political context and constraints which govern them, and also from fuzzy definitions of doctrinal concepts. There are indications that maneuverist criticisms have been taken to heart in the Army's latest revision of its basic operations manual, FM 100-5.[20] Skeptical observers, however, view the change as largely cosmetic ("more or less multiplying the number of times the word 'maneuver' appears by two," as one suggested to me), half meant to coopt the critics.

---

20. See Lieutenant Colonel Huba Wass de Czege and Lieutenant Colonel L.D. Holder, "The New FM 100-5," *Military Review*, Vol. 62, No. 7 (July 1982), pp. 53–70.

The problem is that contrasting maneuver and firepower is a bit like contrasting hitting and fielding in baseball—both are necessary components for success, one can be emphasized over the other only by a matter of degree, and in an integrated campaign the emphasis in the mix may not appear very stark. This problem is underlined by the appreciable limitations of maneuver doctrine for defensive operations, especially on the Central Front in Europe. (Given the vagaries of terrain in Germany and the extent to which mobile defense would have to surrender the advantages of prepared positions, Mearsheimer argues that such a change in doctrine would increase risks and ease the Soviets' tasks. McKitrick also points out that maneuver requires more fuel and less ammunition than defensive operations, but the logistics for moving fuel on the battlefield are more difficult than for ammunition.)[21] There are also substantial arguments for the case that revolutionary technological developments linking data collection and transmission to new types of ordnance will make firepower a far more dominant factor on the European battlefield of the near future.[22]

There is also an implicit question about whether full exploitation of maneuver at the operational level would not imply a generally more offensive strategy. The Army's new AirLand Battle 2000 concept is explicit about application of firepower—emphasis on interdiction and second-echelon targeting—but, at least in public explanations, the novel forms of maneuver envisioned seem to be primarily tactical. Could grander-scale emphasis on maneuver logically be separated from plans for very deep and sustained counterattacks into East Germany and Czechoslovakia? Samuel Huntington has advocated such a revision of conventional deterrence strategy.[23] This aim would probably require substantial increases in NATO force levels (though Huntington believes reorganization and reorientation might suffice), and it would certainly require a diplomatic coup. The consensual glue holding NATO together, especially today as political strains within the alliance have intensified, is the sacred premise that the organization is purely defensive. It is true that there is no inconsistency between defensive policy and offensive

21. John J. Mearsheimer, "Maneuver, Mobile Defense, and the NATO Central Front," *International Security*, Vol. 6, No. 3 (Winter 1981/1982), pp. 123–143; McKitrick, "A Military Look at Military Reform."
22. Neville Brown, "The Changing Face of Non-Nuclear War," *Survival*, Vol. 24, No. 5 (September/October 1972), pp. 211–213.
23. Samuel P. Huntington, "The Renewal of Strategy," in Huntington, ed., *The Strategic Imperative: New Policies for American Security* (Cambridge: Ballinger, 1972).

military strategy. The Soviets and Israelis have recognized this very clearly. However, it is hard to see how even very adept diplomacy could convince NATO governments, let alone fractious European publics, that this notion is anything but revolutionary and frightful.

Most of the pro-maneuver critics have skirted this issue—although recommendations to increase the NATO teeth-to-tail ratio and ape Soviet emphasis on short-war capabilities would seem, logically, to imply decisive offense, since nothing else could *militarily* bring the war to a conclusion before the tail collapsed. Perhaps it is not necessary to resolve the issue, especially if political impediments might be finessed by masking strategic implications with discussion in tactical terms. When it comes to elucidation of the maneuver critique at even this more limited level, however, the prescriptions turn out to be quite vague. When Army spokesmen maintain that maneuver has been a vital element in doctrine all along, some critics resort to very expansive definitions of the concept, arguing that maneuver is more than "movement."[24] When defenders of more traditional approaches try to pin down the critics, they are faced with arguments that seem to identify maneuver with unspecified sorts of creativity, excellence, or any sort of sensible ingenuity in command:

Operations and tactics follow no formulas. . . . The real defeat is the organizational/mental/systemic breakdown caused by the enemy's realization that the situation is beyond his control. . . . maneuver warfare is not a new formula, but a replacement for formulas. . . . since we cannot offer a formula, a certain degree of abstraction is necessary. . . . our goal is not a commander with a mental "checklist," but one with what the Germans call "a feeling in the tips of his fingers" . . . a thought process rooted in a *Gestalt* . . . mental reference points, not rules. . . . The key to success is less often a brilliant plan than the ability to innovate rapidly under severe pressure. . . . *agility*.[25]

This sort of slippery abstraction could be a prologue to reformed doctrine, but it is far short of a prescription. *Mystique is no substitute for formulas.* All the preceding desiderata tell a commander is that he should be smart, quick, and ready to take advantage of opportunities in whatever undefined way is appropriate. Who could quarrel with that? At such a level of discussion the critique is immune to refutation.

---

24. William Lind does identify maneuver with movement, but also argues more forcefully than some other critics that attrition and maneuver are diametrically opposed types of warfare. "The Case for Maneuver," in *The "Military Reform" Debate*, pp. 19–20.
25. Ibid., pp. 20, 22, 26–29, 32.

The maneuver advocates have performed a valuable service by pushing debate beyond assessment of the static balance and refocusing attention on operational doctrine and the need to find ways of grabbing back the initiative in an engagement rather than resting on reactive defensive concepts. But they have done so by functioning as one pole in a dialectic, not by providing a synthesis. The useful impact of their service will be a nuance rather than a revolution.

Technological Reaction

Another group of critics has helped the defense debate by focusing attention on the counterproductive aspects of reliance on complex technology, and the dangers of sacrificing quantity to quality in weapons deployments. By insisting on incorporation of the maximal technical capability available in new weapons—particularly tactical aircraft and tanks—U.S. force structure has developed to the point that it has a small number of weapons, but those weapons are sometimes so sophisticated that they spend much of their time being repaired instead of standing ready for combat. Moreover, past experience and recent exercises have suggested that in many likely combat scenarios the most sophisticated aircraft subsystems could not be brought to bear, and numbers (rather than individual capability) would dominate the battle.[26]

The solution suggested by some is, if not Luddite, at least reactionary: emphasis on simpler technology to reduce procurement costs (allowing more weapons to be deployed) and to reduce maintenance loads (allowing greater readiness). The defenders of the status quo point out that this course—for example, abandoning the state-of-the-art F-15—would deprive the U.S. fighter force of nightfighting and all-weather capability, while enemy "armies move forward under darkness and bad weather."[27] Moreover, the Soviets have not only greater numbers but now equivalent quality as well in many of the systems that U.S. weapons would have to engage.[28] Finally, some of the critics have based parts of their case on analytical sleight-of-hand. For

---

26. See for example James Fallows, *National Defense* (New York: Vintage, 1981), Chapter 3, and Michael I. Handel, "Numbers Do Count: The Question of Quality versus Quantity," *Journal of Strategic Studies*, Vol. 4, No. 3 (September 1981), pp. 225–260.
27. Brigadier General Robert Rosenberg, quoted in Edgar Ulsamer, "We Can't Afford to Lose the Technological Edge," *Air Force*, February 1982, p. 92.
28. Handel's critique emphasizes this point.

example, one prominent gadfly persisted in presenting briefings which contrasted the readiness rates of brand-new M-1 tanks and F-15 fighters with older systems, to demonstrate the fragility of the new systems; he also emphasized the alleged superiority of the lower-cost F-16 to F-14, -15, and -18 by presenting a graph of their respective acceleration capability. A more rigorous presentation would emphasize that readiness rates are always lower at the beginning of a new weapon's deployment than after it has been broken in,[29] and that acceleration is not necessarily the most crucial index of aircraft capability.

Even if the critics were correct in the assertion that in practice less sophisticated systems are as effective as the most advanced, they overlook a crucial barrier to substituting large numbers of cheap aircraft or tanks for expensive ones. James Fallows, for instance, presents data purporting to show that because an F-5 costs only one-fourth as much as an F-15 and can fly 2.5 sorties for each one by an F-15, the same dollar investment could produce an F-5 force that could put ten times as many planes in the air per day as an F-15 force.[30] This overlooks the elementary difference between unit flyaway cost and system life-cycle cost—especially the huge increase in manpower requirements attached to the larger F-5 force (not to mention the comparably greater fuel requirements). This is the principal reason that the Soviet Union faces less of an agonizing quality/quantity tradeoff than the United States. As former Under Secretary of Defense William Perry notes:

. . . the United States spends more than half of its defense budget on manpower while the Soviets—with twice the manpower—spend only a fourth of theirs on manpower. As a result, they can devote half of their budget to equipment procurement while we devote less than a quarter of ours to equipment. . . . even with equal defense budgets, the Soviets can—and do—*spend twice as much on equipment procurement* as the United States.[31]

Counter-critics such as Perry argue that technology is not synonymous with complexity (the real *bête noir*), and that exploitation of the right technological advantages, such as microelectronics (which have not all risen in cost the way other products have), is the best hope for offsetting Soviet advantages in manpower and numbers of weapons.[32] And Air Force leaders

---

29. For example see Leonard Famiglietti, "Ready-to-Go Rate Climbing as TAC Fine-Tunes Its F-15s," *Air Force Times*, March 8, 1982. p. 14.
30. Fallows, *National Defense*, pp. 42–43.
31. William Perry, "Fallows' Fallacies," *International Security*, Vol. 6, No. 4 (Spring 1982), p. 175 (emphasis in original).
32. Ibid., pp. 181–182.

attack the critics' glorification of simple systems with examples such as the destruction of the Thanh Hoa bridge in North Vietnam. During the 1960s 873 sorties were mounted against the target, with eleven planes lost, but the bridge did not go down. When bombing was renewed in 1972 eight planes with laser bombs knocked the bridge down in one mission with no losses. Moreover, the choice between simple and sophisticated systems is not dichotomous; the logical solution is a "high-low mix," combining both for a force structure of balanced capability and cost. Thus critics should remember that F-15s constitute only about 20 percent of the Air Force's complement of fighters.

These counter-criticisms naturally face problems too. Precision-guided munitions (PGMs) may be wonderful for attacking bridges, but their revolutionary implications across the board are more ambiguous. Anti-tank guided munitions, at least in the current generation such as TOW and Dragon, are likely to be far less effective under combat conditions—where the soldier launching the PGM must expose himself for an extended time to guide it to target, and where terrain and countermeasures may vitiate accuracy—than in laboratory tests.[33] (The alternative recommended by some "reformist" reactionaries—use of the old 106 mm recoilless rifle—is not appealing. Though it requires less exposure, it cannot engage tanks before they come within range to shoot back, as TOW can. The real solution is Hellfire, a "fire-and-forget" PGM now in development— in short, yet more advanced technology.) PGMs are also not unalloyed defensive weapons; they can be put to good use in offensive operations. What empirical evidence exists is mixed. The Egyptians used PGMs to decimate the 190th Israeli armored brigade on October 9, 1973. "The real instruction of the Middle East War," however, ". . . is not to be drawn from the early slaughter of a single unsupported, and incautious Israeli tank brigade. The true lessons may be extracted from the knowledge that, of the approximately 3,000 Arab and Israeli tanks destroyed or damaged . . . at least 80 percent were knocked out by other tanks."[34] And terrain and climate in the Sinai are more conducive to PGM accuracy than in Central Europe.

American planning has also not succeeded well in disciplining the pursuit of a high-low aircraft mix. The F-18, for example, was originally conceived

---

33. See Fallows, *National Defense*, pp. 22–24, and Michael Handel's forthcoming monograph on PGMs.
34. Staff Study, "The Military Balance," in Kenneth Rush et al., *Strengthening Deterrence: NATO and the Credibility of Western Defense in the 1980s* (Cambridge: Ballinger, for the Atlantic Council, n.d.), p. 129.

as a low-cost complement to the F-14 and F-15. In the course of development, however, the F-18's cost advantage disappeared (although its mission versatility grew). The systems analysts who attack such results, and are attacked by strategists as petty "bookkeepers," do well to hold planners' feet to the managerial fire.

Conclusion

This essay's insistence on the complexity of defense planning is perforce conservative in its implications. Both the intellectual power and policy weakness of reformist critiques lie in their simplicity and the clarity of their theoretical premises. Because the purpose of theory is to simplify, any theory's implications for policy can be made vulnerable by focusing on whatever complexities it does not encompass. Analysis has to treat critical variables and hold other factors constant, so any policy conclusion can be shaken by pointing out that some of the constants are really variables. This essay does this to critics, which is a bit unfair because it is always easier to debunk an intellectual position than to prescribe a more viable policy position. But it is no more unfair than what the most provocative critics have done to conventional wisdom.

Some degree of strategic innovation and technological reform are vital, but more as gyroscopic adjustments than as guides to fundamental redirection of policy. Because conventional wisdom does not offer a sufficient solution does not mean that it has less to offer than unconventional criticism. The overall size of U.S. forces (that is, their comparative smallness) is more the source of difficulties than is their structure or doctrine. The essential problems for U.S. strategy lie in immutable geography and only marginally tractable politics. Geography makes the U.S. homeland more secure than the USSR, but reverses the advantage where defense of allies and conflict in crucial third areas is concerned. Washington must inevitably sacrifice combat power to logistics more than Moscow, so combat force levels are limited by support force structure. Political, social, and economic constraints further inhibit overall force size by limiting military manpower, which reinforces the orientation to qualitative solutions by technological substitution. Better strategy *and* management could ameliorate these problems but not solve them. Reformist critics will do more to translate acute thought into feasible action if they pull in their horns, become less polemical, categorical, and confrontational, and slightly more forgiving of "business-as-usual" conventional wisdom.

The Operational Level of War

Edward N. Luttwak

It is a peculiarity of Anglo-Saxon military terminology that it knows of *tactics* (unit, branch, and mixed) and of *theater strategy* as well as of *grand strategy*, but includes no adequate term for the *operational* level of warfare—precisely the level that is most salient in the modern tradition of military thought in continental Europe. The gap has not gone unnoticed, and Basil Liddell-Hart for example attempted to give currency to the term "grand tactics" as a substitute (already by his day the specialized usage of the directly translated term "operational-functioning machine/unit," was too well established to be redeemed.)

The operational level of war, as opposed to the tactical and strategic levels, is or ought to be of greatest concern to the analyst. In theater strategy, political goals and constraints on one hand and available resources on the other determine projected outcomes. At a much lower level, tactics deal with specific techniques. In the operational dimension, by contrast, schemes of warfare such as blitzkrieg or defense in depth evolve or are exploited. Such schemes seek to attain the goals set by theater strategy through suitable combinations of tactics. It is not surprising that the major works of military literature tend to focus on the operational level, as evidenced by the writings of Clausewitz.

What makes this gap in Anglo-Saxon military terminology important for practical purposes is that the absence of the term referring to the operational level reflects an inadvertence towards the whole conception of war associated with it, and this in turn reflects a major eccentricity in the modern Anglo-Saxon experience of war. It is not merely that officers do not *speak* the word but rather that they do not *think* or practice war in operational terms, or do so only in vague or ephemeral ways. The causes of this state of affairs are to be found in the historic circumstances of Anglo-Saxon warfare during this century. In the First World War, American troops were only employed late, and then under French direction; their sphere of planning and action was essentially limited to the tactical level. As for the British, who did have to endure the full five years and more of that conflict, they mostly did not

I am greatly indebted to my partner, Steven L. Canby, for many key ideas developed in this essay.

Edward N. Luttwak is a co-founder and executive officer of C & L Associates, a consulting firm specializing in defense analysis. He has authored The Grand Strategy of the Roman Empire, *several works on modern military affairs, and more recently,* Strategy & Politics: Collected Essays.

International Security, Winter 1980/81 (Vol. 5, No. 3) 0162-2889/81/030061-19 $02.50/0
© 1981 by the President and Fellows of Harvard College and the Massachusetts Institute of Technology.

transcend their pre-1914 experience, characterized by battalion fights in the colonies.

It was precisely the failure of the British Army to extend its mental horizons that the "English" school of post-World War I military thinkers so greatly deplored, and which it set out to correct. The advocacy of large-unit armored warfare in depth by Fuller, Liddell Hart, etc. was aimed at expanding operations to transcend the tactical battlefield—and was not simply inspired by the need to find employment for the newly invented tank. In other words, their ideas were not tank *driven* but merely tank *using*. The motivating factor was not the attraction of the technology, but rather the powerful urge to escape the bloody stalemate of the tactical battlefields of World War I.

Nor did the radically different character of the World War II suffice to establish the operational level in the conduct, planning, and analysis of Anglo-Saxon warfare. To be sure, there were isolated examples of generalship at the operational level, and indeed very fine examples, but they, and all that they implied, never became organic to the national tradition of warfare. Instead such operational approaches remained the trade secrets and personal attributes of men such as Douglas MacArthur, Patton, and the British General O'Connor, victor of the first North African campaign.

Otherwise, in World War II as in Korea and of necessity in Vietnam, American ground warfare was conducted almost exclusively at the tactical level, and then at the level of theater strategy above that, with almost no operational dimension in between. Thus the theater strategy of 1944 in France (as earlier in Italy) was characterized by the broad-front advance of units which engaged in tactical combat *seriatim*. Above the purely tactical level, the important decisions were primarily of a logistic character. The overall supply dictated the rate of advance, while its distribution would set the vectors of the advancing front. And these were of course the key decisions at the level of theater strategy. Soon after the end of World War II it became fashionable to criticize the broad-front theater strategy pursued after D-Day. But such criticisms overlooked the central fact that the American comparative advantage was in sheer material resources while U.S. (and British) middle-echelon staff and command skills were of a low order. The overly personalized criticism of Eisenhower's strategy that characterized this literature certainly did not result in the popularization of any "operational" concepts of war.

In Korea once again, the predominant pattern of warfare was set by a front-wide advance theater strategy, which practically left no scope for anything more ambitious than tactical actions. The brilliant exception was of course the Inchon landing, but characteristically this experience was assimilated as the virtuoso performance of Douglas MacArthur, instead of being recognized as a particular manifestation of a general phenomenon, i.e., the concerted use of tactical means to achieve operational-level results that are much more than the sum of the (tactical) parts.

Since the Korean War, as before it, American ground forces have continued to absorb new generations of weapons, their mobility in and between theaters has continued to improve, logistic systems have been computerized and much attention has been devoted to the management of resources at all levels. Nevertheless the entire organism continues to function only at the lowest and the highest military levels, while the operational level in between remains undeveloped. This is not due to any lack of military knowledge as such. Rather, it reflects the limitations of an attrition style of war, where there is an exaggerated dependence on firepower as such to the detriment of maneuver and flexibility. In the extreme case of pure attrition, there are only techniques and tactics, and there is no action at all at the operational level. All that remains are routinized techniques of reconnaissance, movement, resupply, etc. to bring firepower-producing forces within range of the most conveniently targetable aggregations of enemy forces and supporting structures. Each set of targets is then to be destroyed by the cumulative effect of firepower, victory being achieved when the proportion destroyed suffices to induce retreat or surrender, or, theoretically, when the full inventory of enemy forces is destroyed.

It is understood of course that in deliberately seeking to engage the largest aggregations of enemy forces, their reciprocal attrition will also have to be absorbed, so that there can be no victory in this style of war without an overall superiority in net attritive capacity. But aside from that, attrition-style warfare has the great attractions of predictability and functional simplicity, since efficiency is identical to effectiveness, and since the whole is (if no more) no less than the sum of the parts. Hence the optimization of *all* military activities in peace as in war, whether research and development, procurement, manpower-acquisition, training, staff work, or command can all be pursued in a systematic fashion—the goal being of course to improve the techniques (target acquisition, force-movement, re-supply, etc.) whose combined effect determines the overall efficiency of attritive action. Thus in seeking to enhance overall capabilities, each resource increment can be unfailingly allocated into the right sub-activity, merely by establishing which of them yields the highest marginal return: manpower or equipment, numbers or quality, fire-control or ammunition enhancements, and so on. Under a pure attrition style, all the functions of war and war preparation are therefore governed by a logic analogous to that of microeconomics, and the conduct of warfare at all levels is analogous to the management of a profit-maximizing industrial enterprise. This in turn renders possible the overall management of defense by the use of marginalist analytical techniques, with uncertainties being confined to technical unknowns. Only structural obstacles (e.g. self-serving bureaucracies, or local political pressures) remain to interfere with the pursuit of efficiency.

Thus in the whole complex of war preparation and action, uncertainties are confined to a few irreducibles. Otherwise everything can be routinized on the basis of efficiency-maximizing managerial procedures with the lowly exception of the command of men in direct contact with the enemy, in which non-managerial methods of combat leadership remain necessary.

The other main phenomenon of war, which stands in counterpoint to attrition along the spectrum that makes up the overall style of war of nations and armed services is *relational-maneuver*. In the case of relational-maneuver the goal of incapacitating enemy forces or structures—and indeed the whole enemy entity—is pursued in a radically different way. Instead of cumulative destruction, the desired process is systemic disruption—where the "system" may be the whole array of armed forces, some fraction thereof, or indeed technical systems pure and simple.

In general terms, attrition requires that strength be applied against strength. The enemy too must be strong when and where he comes under attack, since a concentration of targets is required to ensure efficiency in the application of effort. By contrast, the starting point of relational-maneuver is precisely the *avoidance* of the enemy's strength, to be followed by the application of some selective strength against a known dimension (physical or psychological) of enemy weakness. While attrition is a quasi-physical process so that fixed proportionalities will govern the relationship between the effort expended and the results achieved, relational-maneuver by contrast does not guarantee any level of results (being capable of failing totally). But neither is it constrained by any proportional ceiling between the effort made and the maximal results that may be achieved. It is because of this non-proportionality that relational-maneuver methods are compulsory for the side weaker in resources, which simply cannot prevail by attrition. But if relational-maneuver methods offer the possibility of much higher payoffs than those of attrition they do so at a correspondingly higher risk of failure.

And relational-maneuver solutions are apt to fail catastrophically—unlike attrition solutions which normally fail "gracefully," that is to say gradually.

The vulnerability of relational-maneuver methods to catastrophic failure reflects their dependence on the *precise* application of effort against correctly identified points of weakness. This in turn requires a close understanding of the inner workings of the "system" that is to be disrupted, whether the "system" is, say, a missile, in which case the knowledge needed has an exact technical character, or an entire army, where an understanding of its command ethos and operational propensities will be necessary. Somewhat loosely, one may characterize attrition methods as resource-based and relational-maneuver methods as knowledge-dependent. Both the high potential payoff of the latter, and also their vulnerability to catastrophic failure, derive from this same quality.

Since in any real-life warfare, both pure attrition and pure relational-maneuver are very rare phenomena, what matters is the content of each phenomenon in the overall action, whether that is as narrow as a single tactical episode, or as broad as national style of warfare or some war preparation activity, such as the development of weapons.

Both attrition and relational-maneuver are still perhaps most familiar in the form of ground warfare. Certainly the most vivid comparison is provided by the contrasting images of the trench battles of World War I on the one hand—symmetrical brute force engagements not far removed from pure attrition—and the great encirclement battles of the 1939–1942 Blitzkrieg period on the other, warfare characterized by low-casualty, high-risk actions. Or to show equal contrast in one national army, in one war and in a single theater of operations, the theater-scale disruptive maneuver of MacArthur's Inchon landing may be compared with the cumulative firepower engagements of General Ridgeway's offensives.

It is to be recognized, however, that both attrition and relational-maneuver are universal phenomena, which pervade all aspects and all forms of war and war preparation. This can be illustrated by a number of direct comparisons, a sample of which are shown in table 1.

Both attrition and relational-maneuver will be present in all real-life contexts, such that different national (or service) styles of warfare will be distinguished by the proportion of each mode in the overall spectrum, rather than by the theoretical alternatives in pure form.

Having thus suggested the universality of the phenomenon, one may focus on the attrition/maneuver spectrum in ground warfare without fear that

Table 1
Attrition vs. Relational-Maneuver

	Attrition	**Relational-Maneuver**
Methods of Target Planning in Strategic Nuclear Warfare	Incapacitate enemy society by destroying high percentage of all industry and all population by the least variable of kill effects (e.g., blast rather than weather-dependent heat).	Incapacitate enemy political-military system by destroying political and military command centers and organizational headquarters; destroy selected critical war-fighting and recovery facilities (e.g., industrial bottlenecks *viz.* straight floor-space). Rely on fine-tuned kill effects.
Deployments of Ground Forces at the Theater Level	Deploy standard-format general-purpose forces to match total computed enemy capabilities. Freely rotate command, staff, and formations between different theaters.	Deploy theater-specialized formations configured especially to exploit the weaknesses of the particular enemy forces in each theater on a long-term basis, with in-theater promotion.
Methods of War Preparation, Research and Development Goals	Develop "best possible" systems to maximize all-round capabilities; hence develop systems *ab initio* to minimize design constraints. Hence long time-lags between generations, and broad changes needed in supporting maintenance structures upon introduction. Thus, only *major* advances can justify development efforts; hence the state of the art must be advanced. Because of long time lags between design and introduction, there will be only a coincidental correspondence between the systems so acquired and the specific configuration of combat needs upon deployment. Engineering priorities lead to revolutionary innovation, from time to time. Final design determined by limits of engineering feasibility and costs.	Examine in detail the relevant enemy forces and weapons. Identify specific limitations and weaknesses. Develop or modify equipment to obtain fine-tuning of capabilities against those forces and weapons. Modify and develop incrementally to maintain a "good fit" as enemy forces also evolve. Since new items are introduced at short intervals, accept design constraints to ensure compatibility (inter-equipment and also with supporting structures). No need to force advances on the state of the art. Create a continuum between in-theater modifications and the central development process.

relational-maneuver will be confused with mere movement, or indeed that attrition itself will be understood only in its narrowest tactical form of a straight exchange of firepower.

One may usefully begin to give concrete definition to the concepts here defined by way of two examples, one well-worn and the other somewhat less familiar, one offensive in strategic orientation and the other defensive, but both examples of *operational* schemes of warfare with a low attrition content: the deep-penetration armor-driven offensive of the classic German Blitzkrieg, and the contemporary Finnish defense-in-depth for Lappland.

The Blitzkrieg Example

The classic German Blitzkrieg of 1939–1942 was an operational scheme designed to exploit the potential of armored fighting vehicles, motor transport and tactical airpower against front-wide linear defenses. Three phases of the overall actions can be distinguished: the initial breakthrough, the penetrations, and the "exploitation."

In the breakthrough stage, axes of passage were opened through the (linear) defenses of the enemy by fairly conventional frontal attacks (and the Germans did so in World War II largely with foot infantry and horse-drawn artillery), but these attacks were focused on enemy forces holding selected, and narrow, segments of the front. The "relational" element of this stage was visible only at the theater level, insofar as soft points could freely be selected for attack (since the immediate areas behind the breakthrough points were of no particular significance in themselves).

The tactical battles fought at the front were not an end in themselves but merely a pre-condition for the next phase. Hence, neither the planning effort nor high value forces were at all focused on this stage. So long as the mobile columns spearheaded by the (scarce) tank forces could gain entry into the depth behind the front, it hardly mattered what happened in the frontal area itself. This in turn allowed the command to choose the break-in points opportunistically, thus already achieving an advantage over a defender whose command remained focused on the tactical battles at the front. The eventual reward of successful defense against any one breakthrough attempt would be encirclement and capture once the next phase was executed anyway, through some other breakthrough points.

In the penetration phase, the goal of each mobile column was to advance as fast as possible, eventually to intersect at nodal points deep behind the front, there to cut off the corresponding sections of the frontal defenses.

In a tactical view, the long thin columns of vehicles penetrating through hostile territory were very weak, seemingly highly vulnerable to attacks on their flanks. Tactically, the columns were of course all flank and no "front." But in an operational view, the mobile columns of penetration were very strong, because their whole orientation and their method of warfare gave them a great advantage in tempo and reaction time. Most important, the columns were able to maintain a ceaseless forward movement since they could proceed opportunistically, moving down whatever roads offered least resistance. By contrast, such forces of the defense more capable of organized movement would have to find and intercept the invasion columns, and would thus need to go in specific directions along particular routes, failing in their mission if delayed by the frictions of war or by enemy flank-guard forces that cut across their path.

This strictly mechanical advantage was usually dominated by a command advantage. While the invasion forces did not need detailed instructions—being sufficiently guided by General Mission Orders and by tactical opportunism along the axes of advance—the action of the mobile forces of the defense depended on a command adequately informed of the shape of the unfolding battle. But this was a thing most difficult to achieve; the advance of the invasion columns would in itself generate much more "noise" than signals. Typically, the victims of the Blitzkrieg were left only with the choice of paralysis or potential gross error in "reading" the battle. Flooded with reports of enemy sightings across the entire width of the front and in considerable depth as well, the defending commanders either chose to wait for "the dust to settle" (i.e., paralysis) or else they sent off their mobile forces in chase of the sightings that seemed most credible and whose direction seemed most dangerous. In a situation characterized by the multiplicity of signals thrown out by the high tempo of armor-driven invasion columns, the chances of sorting out the data from the confusion were small indeed.

Moreover, the offense had the advantage of moving vertically across a front organized horizontally, and its advance would therefore cut lines of communication (LOCs), occupy successive nodal points in the road network, and not infrequently overrun command centers, thus further immobilizing the defenders.

These three factors in combination resulted in a net advantage for the offense in the intelligence decision-action cycle, the decisive factor in all forms of *reciprocal* maneuver.[1] So long as the invasion columns kept up a high tempo of operations, their apparent tactical vulnerability was dominated by their operational advantage since the defender's intercepting and blocking actions would always be one step behind.

A closer look at the process reveals that it was deception that provided security for the main thrusts of penetration, which were hidden in the multiplicity of movements generated by flank-guard columns, side-rails, and "abandoned spurs" in the opportunistic flow of the advance. Actually, deception was inherent to the mode of operations. A successful resistance at any one roadblock would be reported as a victory by the defense and indeed it was, but only at the *tactical* level. Operationally, resistance was made irrelevant, as the invasion columns ultimately by-passed such points.

In the "exploitation" phase, effects purely physical were compounded (and usually dominated) by the psychological effects of the penetrations, and the resulting envelopments. The bulk of the defending forces still holding the front in between the narrow axes of penetration would begin to receive reports of LOCs cut, rear headquarters fallen and famous towns to their rear overrun. At the command level, this precipitated attempts to carry out remedial actions still within the initial conceptual framework of the defense, i.e. attempts to execute "orderly withdrawals" in order to reconstitute a linear front beyond the maximum depth of enemy penetration. But that line of frontal reconstitution receded ever deeper as the invasion columns continued on their way. "Orderly withdrawal" soon acquired the character of a rearward race (with the abandonment of heavy weapons etc.). Since in 1939–1942 large, infantry-heavy forces were trying to race against small armor-mobile forces, the defense, Polish, French, or Russian, could not win the race. This in turn demoralized the commanders, since even "correct" action was soon shown to be futile. And of course among the troops the abandonment of frontal defenses still intact and often entirely unattacked, news of well-known places behind the front already fallen to the enemy, and finally the actual mechanics of the rearward race (including logistic insufficiency) easily had catastrophic morale effects—not uncommonly leading to the outright disintegration of units.[2]

---

1. Parade ground infantry drill (right-turn/left-turn) preserves in symbolic form what was once a crucial attainment in the maneuver of foot forces.
2. In the German Blitzkrieg of 1939–1942, the particular form of the employment of the *Luftwaffe* had its own powerful morale effects. Since the air-to-ground potential was used selectively in great concentration (*viz.* diffuse interdiction efforts) troops witnessing the intensive dive bombing of scattered points would form a grossly inflated conception of the power of the *Luftwaffe*.

The exploitation phase culminated in double envelopments with a final stage of annihilation—when the foot infantry, now advancing across the abandoned frontage, finally came to grips with the fragmented forces of the defense trapped within the encirclements.

Since the attrition content of the entire action was low (and indeed almost entirely limited to the breakthrough phase) the decisive level was the *operational*. The power of the Blitzkrieg was not conditioned by the weight of resources employed, and not at all by the firepower of the forces involved; it derived rather from the method of command, from the all-mobile organization of some formations, and from the training, all of which endowed the offense with a systematic advantage in the observation-decision-action cycle. Had the Germans encountered a defender itself superior in the tempo of operations, the tactical weakness of their advancing columns would then have become an operational weakness also, with fatal consequences since: 1) the defending forces on either side of the breakthrough sectors could have "flowed" sideways to close off breakthroughs faster than the enemy could act to keep them open; and 2) the mobile forces of the defense could have intercepted or actually ambushed the invasion columns, thus capitalizing on the inherent tactical weakness of forces which are all flank and no front.[3]

THE ELEMENTS OF THE BLITZKRIEG STYLE

Though the following analysis is confined to the operational level,[4] it suffices to illustrate the essential principles involved in the relational-maneuver method of warfare that distinguishes the Blitzkrieg:

THE MAIN STRENGTH OF THE ENEMY IS AVOIDED AS MUCH AS POSSIBLE. In the breakthrough phase, avoidance is manifest at the theater level in the fact that only a small fraction of the total frontage is attacked in serious fashion, to break open gaps through which the penetration columns can pass. Hence the overall numerical relationship between the total force of the offense

---

3. That is indeed what happened in the Golan Heights during the 1973 war from the fourth day of the war, when the Israelis were able to outmaneuver the powerful but slower Syrian tank columns and—in more spectacular fashion—were later able to ambush the second Iraqi division sent into combat.

4. The two most important tactics involved in the Blitzkrieg operational method were: at the breakthrough stage, wedging and "rolling out," where concentric attacks by infantry-artillery forces open the way for shallow penetrations by more agile infantry which then widens the initial passage by attacks on the flanks; and, in the penetration phase, the use of light-armor and motorized (including motorcycle) elements as "precursors," to trigger ambushes and to "develop" islands of resistance, so that the tank units can directly by-pass them without delay.

employed in the breakthrough attempt, and the total defending force holding the full frontage, is irrelevant to the outcome. Avoidance is manifest at the operational level in the fact that recognized "strategic" locations are not attacked, the selected points of attempted breakthrough being rather those which happen to be least well-defended (with the proviso that subsequent deep penetrations should be possible from those points). Avoidance is manifest at the tactical level, in the use of "rolling out" tactics to minimize frontal engagements as much as possible. In the penetration phase on the other hand, the salient form of avoidance is tactical: cross-country movement and all the flexibility of opportunism in the detailed routing are exploited to avoid islands of resistance, which are to be by-passed rather than reduced or even encircled.

DECEPTION IS OF CENTRAL IMPORTANCE AT EVERY PHASE. The breakthrough phase presumes successful deception. While the wedging and "rolling out" attacks are launched against selected narrow segments of the frontage, the bulk of the defensive forces along the unattacked frontage must be prevented from moving towards the intended breakthrough axes by feints and demonstrations all along the front, to mask the real foci of attack. Alternatively, where multiple breakthroughs are attempted, deception can be retroactive insofar as costly persistence is avoided, and whichever breakthroughs are successful are then exploited. Either way, success absolutely requires that the defending command remain in a state of uncertainty. This cannot be achieved by mere secrecy since the maximum period of immunity (even assuming perfect security) could not then extend beyond the outbreak of hostilities. In practice, this elevates the deception plan to full equality with the battle plan; certainly deception planning cannot remain a mere afterthought.

In the penetration phase, deception is inherent in the mode of operation. Unless the advancing columns of penetration move with sufficient speed and directional unpredictability to be masked by confusion, they must be highly vulnerable to attacks on their flanks. While it must be assumed that the progressive advance of the invasion columns will be reported, such "signals" will be masked by the "noise" of the multiplicity of sightings mentioned above. If the signal-to-noise ratio is high, and the defenders can therefore develop a more or less coherent picture of the situation (and do not lose their nerve) then the thin columns of penetration will be as vulnerable operationally as they are tactically.

In the exploitation phase, deception is embodied in the process whereby the columns of penetration cut off and encircle enemy forces that can be much larger than themselves; by then the enemy must be reduced to an incoherent mass (cf. the 1941 battles of encirclement in the Ukraine). The most complete achievement of *systemic disruption* is manifest in the final round-up stage of such battles of encirclement, when the ratio of prisoners of war to captors may be very high indeed. By that stage conventional Order of Battle comparisons between the two sides have lost all meaning. It is obvious that such successes cannot be achieved against an undeceived enemy. Even at a fairly late stage of disintegration, the victim forces could regroup in improvised fashion to defeat the encirclement if they had certain knowledge of a highly favorable force ratio.

THE INTANGIBLES DOMINATE. Momentum dominates other priorities (e.g. firepower capacity and lethality). Even in the breakthrough stage, the "rolling out" must quickly follow the "wedging," for otherwise the forces engaged in the latter become vulnerable to flank attacks. In fact, the breakthrough as a whole must be accomplished rapidly, because otherwise the defense will have the opportunity to redeploy its forces to secure the segments of the frontage under attack—or at least to hold the shoulders firmly. The columns of penetration in turn must pass through as soon as their way is open in order to begin their disruptive process before the defense can react. In fact, the whole operation obviously rests on the ceaseless maintenance of momentum. Organizationally, this implies a very restricted deployment of heavier/slower elements and especially artillery. Even with self-propelled artillery, the need to keep the supply tail light and fast moving will restrict the amount that can usefully be deployed. Tactically, the imperative of momentum will downgrade the importance of accuracy (for lethality) in such firepower as is employed. With the artillery, it is suppressive rather than physically destructive firepower that is wanted. And the same applies to the small-arms firepower of the infantry, the troops being trained for suppressive fire with automatic weapons, rather than for the slow-paced delivery of aimed shots. Technically, this in turn results in a requirement for combat vehicles from which infantry can fire on the move.

It is in the exploitation phase that the importance of force-ratios as such declines to its lowest point, while the importance of sheer momentum is supreme. Accordingly, a progressive thinning down of the advancing columns is preferable to the more deliberate pace that full sustainability across the geographic depth would require. It is not uncommon for the battle to end with the victors depleted and exhausted, their strength reduced to very little at the culminating moment, and in the climactic place of the battle, i.e., where the encirclement pincers close. At that time, in that place, the forces of the offense are quite likely to amount to a congerie of improvised battle groups and assorted sub-units that happen to have reached that far. The implied renunciation of full-force sustainability and formation integrity stands in sharp contrast to the principles of war upheld by attrition-oriented armies (cf. "unity of command" in the U.S. Army).

It is clear that the three operational principles here discussed (avoidance, deception, and the dominance of the intangible momentum) are all interrelated, and indeed their connection is the true essence of all offensive operational methods of warfare that have a high relational-maneuver content. First, the ability to apply "localized or specialized" strengths against the enemy's array of forces implies reciprocally that the enemy's own strength is successfully avoided. That in turn can only be done by deception, since it is only a barrier of ignorance that can prevent the enemy from coming to grips with the attacking forces. Deception in turn can only be sustained if the whole operation has a momentum that exceeds the speed of the intelligence-decision-action cycle of the defending forces. Any one deception scheme must be highly perishable, so that the barrier of ignorance can only be preserved if rapid-paced operations generate deceptive impulses faster than they are exposed as such. It is because of this interrelationship that the decisive level of warfare in the relational-maneuver manner is the operational, that being the lowest level at which avoidance, deception, and the dominance of momentum can be brought together within an integrated scheme of warfare.

The Finnish Example

The Blitzkrieg was offensive strategically, as well as during most tactical phases. It was dependent on the use of armor (even if not at all on any superiority in armor capabilities as such). And of course it was an historical episode repeatable only in special circumstances (e.g. the Sinai fighting of 1967). The Finnish operational method for the defense of the Lappland is by contrast strategically defensive, and tactically defensive also in most respects. It is based on the assumption that no armor at all will be available to the defense. Finally, it is a contemporary scheme theoretically reproducible in a wide variety of circumstances, subject only to availability of expendable space. These dramatic contrasts make the parallelism of operational principles between the Finnish method and the Blitzkrieg all the more persuasive evidence of their universality.

AVOIDANCE OF THE ENEMY'S MAIN STRENGTH
At the level of national strategy, this principle is manifest in the whole conduct of Finnish external policy. Soviet power is deflected by a conciliatory foreign policy. But to set limits on the degree of obedience that Moscow can exact, Finnish policy exploits the "Nordic Balance" in which Soviet pressure on Finland is inhibited by the expectation that it would evoke an increased level of NATO activity in Norway, and a proportionate adjustment in the Swedish alignment towards NATO. It follows at the level of theater strategy that the Finnish contribution to the Nordic Balance by the defense of the invasion corridors to Norway and Sweden is more important than the defense of the major Finnish population centers in the southern part of the country. Hence the most reliably powerful of Soviet capabilities, i.e., to invade the well-roaded south and to bomb Finnish cities, are virtually unopposed. It is the Nordic equilibrium that would deny to the Soviet Union the full strategic advantage of an invasion. Even with Finland conquered, Sweden's adherence to NATO would weaken the overall Baltic position of the Soviet Union. On the other hand, Finnish compliance with Soviet foreign policy desiderata pre-empts intimidation based on the capability of destroying Finnish cities. This then leaves Finnish theater strategy with a task that is much more manageable than either a defense of the South against invasion, or of the cities against air attack—that is resistance against an invasion across the largely uninhabited and mostly roadless Lappland. Even there, the task is not really to *deny* passage to Soviet forces but merely to *delay* them up to a point, and weaken them as much as possible, in order to enhance correspondingly the defensive potential of the Norwegian and Swedish forces in the North.

At the operational level, avoidance is manifest in the form of deployment of the defense, and in its mode of action. Far from trying to set up anti-invasion barriers near the border to intercept Soviet invasion columns as soon as they cross, no firm barriers are to be set up at all on the invasion routes leading to Norway and Sweden. Instead, Finnish forces are to operate on either side of the invasion routes, to attack advancing Soviet columns on their flanks after side-stepping their frontal thrusts. Since the Finns can have neither effective air cover from their small air force, nor ground-based anti-aircraft defenses of great value, their protection against air attack must come from dispersal and camouflage. Dispersed Finnish forces arrayed in depth from the Soviet border across the full width of the country are to attack Soviet columns by a variety of hit and run methods, including a multiplicity of raids mounted from whatever cover is available, ambushes where practical, non-persistent mortar and artillery fires, and so on.

At the tactical level, avoidance is manifest in the fact that the tank and mechanized elements of Soviet invasion columns will not be the main target of Finnish attacks. The major efforts of the defenders will instead be concentrated against supply trucks, artillery trains, and support units—all of which can be attacked effectively without need of ATGMs, or other high-grade anti-armor weapons. In this way, even if Soviet tank and mechanized elements can reach the Norwegian and/or Swedish borders intact, they will do so with their combat-support elements weakened and their supply columns depleted.

DECEPTION

At the operational level, deception is inherent in the structure of the Finnish forces to be deployed in the North. Large and highly visible formations of brigade and divisional size will only be deployed on the southern fringe of the trans-Lappland invasion routes, ostensibly to provide a local defense for the small towns in the area, and chiefly Rovaniemi. The main effort on the other hand, will be mounted by far less visible company sized and smaller units detached from the larger formations, and also by *Sissi* raiding teams (trained by the Frontier Guards) which may operate beyond the Soviet border. The more visible formations of the Finnish deployment will not therefore seem threatening or indeed relevant to the Soviet forces, for which any operation mounted southwards from the invasion routes would be a diversion of effort without strategic meaning.

At the tactical level also, deception will be a necessary part of each combat action. Since Soviet invasion columns will routinely provide flank guards for the "soft" elements following in the van of each armored/mechanized contingent, each Finnish tactical action must be based on two separate elements: a diversionary move, to distract the relevant flank-guard elements, and the attack proper. In a company-sized action for example, one platoon might open fire from a safe distance on the soft elements of a Soviet invasion column to attract the attention of the corresponding flank-guard forces. As soon as the latter move towards the scene, the diversionary platoon will retreat to evade their counterattack while the rest of the Finnish force attacks the now unguarded "soft" elements. Finnish forces will then break off the engagement as soon as possible, to seek safety in dispersal and any cover before regrouping to launch the next action. Similarly, the Finns cannot just mount ambushes against the invasion columns, for any ambush astride the main invasion routes would quickly be defeated by the intervention of Soviet armed helicopter elements and/or artillery fires along with direct attacks. Ambushing actions therefore require that lesser Soviet contingents (and chiefly flank-guard units) be lured into prepared killing grounds by some prior attack against the main columns, followed by a deliberate, enticing retreat. In a battalion-level action for example, a Finnish company may attack the soft elements of a Soviet invasion column, wait until flank-guard detachments arrive on the scene and then retreat from the invasion axis, allowing the Soviet detachments to pursue it until the place of ambush is reached, where the rest of the battalion intervenes.

DOMINANCE OF THE INTANGIBLES

At the level of theater strategy, the Finnish purpose is to weaken as much as possible the Soviet invasion forces without, however, engaging in costly battles against an enemy so vastly superior in heavy weapons. Hence the imperative of elusiveness. This, incidentally, explains the Finns' lack of interest in the acquisition of modern armor (which the Soviet Union offers to Finland at very reasonable prices) or much modern artillery (Tampella itself produces an excellent 155mm gun-howitzer—mainly for export), or even anti-tank missiles. Only less visible and fully portable weapons (small arms, rocket launchers and light mortars) are compatible with the principle of elusiveness that runs through the theater strategy, the operational method and the tactics. (Even TOW, the principal U.S. anti-tank weapon, presumes motor or helicopter transport; it is not truly man-portable.) Thus the solitary Finnish armored brigade (equipped with Soviet tanks and BRT-50 and BTR-60 combat carriers) is not the nucleus of an armored force eventually to be acquired, nor the tool of a quixotic intent to fight armor with armor, but rather a *training* unit that mimics the potential adversary's war-fighting behavior, used very much in the manner of the USAF's "aggressor" squadrons.

At the tactical level, the small but important *Sissi* elements would fight as outright guerillas with a special emphasis on offensive demolitions while the rest of the Finnish forces would fight as light infantry, using strike/withdraw routines with a heavy emphasis on the tactical use of expedient minefields, to the extent that mines remain available.

Conclusion

So very different in all other respects, the two examples here reviewed share one fundamental thing in common. In both cases, the genesis of the military ideas involved was a recognition that material weakness would ensure the defeat of any symmetrical application of forces. In the German case, the front-piercing Blitzkrieg was the alternative to the *materialschlacht* on elongated fronts that Germany could not win, if only because blockade would progressively erode the industrial strength of a Germany poorly endowed with raw materials. In the Finnish case, the gross imbalance in military power is such that Finnish forces can only provide a limited war-fighting capacity, in a limited part of the national territory, even when the methods used entail a degree of avoidance which approaches that of outright guerilla warfare. (In normal guerilla conflict, however, war protracted in time substitutes for depth, whereas in the Finnish case the operational dimension is still geographic depth.)

A sense of material superiority by contrast inspires quite other military ideas and allows other priorities to surface. In the American case historically the goal has been to accelerate the evolution of any conflict with maximal mobilization of the economy for the fastest possible build-up of forces on the one hand, and on the other, the deployment of the largest forces sustainable against the largest concentrations of enemy forces possible, to maximize the overall rate of attrition. A broad-front advance theater strategy directly followed from this, if only because the broader the advance, the greater is the usable transport capacity on the ground. Therefore the larger the force that is deployable, the greater its attritive capacity. At the operational level—a level not at all important in this style of warfare—little more was needed than to coordinate the tactical actions which in turn were simple in nature, consisting mainly of frontal attacks.

The principles of avoidance and deception have not been absent in this style of warfare historically, but they were largely confined to the level of theater strategy. For example, the selection of Normandy for the opening of a second front was of course a most notable example of avoidance and deception. But the selection of Northwest France itself contradicted the principle of avoidance—which would have favored other places offering greater outflanking opportunities, e.g. southern France or, better still, the Balkans. At the operational and tactical levels on the other hand, avoidance and deception have been little used, since they stand in direct conflict with the imperative of maximizing the application of force upon the enemy's array. The aim was not to obtain high payoffs at low cost, but rather to obtain *reliable* payoffs on the largest possible scale.

The principle of momentum was manifest only at the highest level of all, the level of grand strategy, whence came insistent pressures for quick results. It was certainly incompatible with broad-front advance theater strategies, which of necessity result in a gradual progression, rather than in rapid penetrations. Nor was momentum compatible with operational methods that amounted to little more than the alignment of tactical actions—or with the tactics. A pattern of schematically predictable frontal attacks would naturally result in gradual step-by-step sequence of forward movement, sustained attack, regroupment, resupply and reinforcement, and then more forward movement, and so on. At both the operational and tactical levels, the goal of maximizing attritive results stands in direct contradiction with the maintenance of momentum; if the integrity of formations must be preserved to maximize the efficiency of firepower production, the speed of the action cannot exceed the rate of forward movement which the artillery and its ammunition supply can sustain. By contrast, in rapid-paced actions, opportunistic routing is *de rigueur* and the breakdown of formations into *ad hoc* battle groups is virtually routine, so that a progressive decline in the volume of sustainable firepower must be accepted. This is a natural consequence of rapid penetrations in depth, if only because "soft" supply vehicles cannot follow in large numbers until enemy resistance ends.

Of late, as a result of the experiences of Korea and Vietnam, a "short-war" imperative has emerged as far as third world involvements are concerned, on the presumption that the contemporary American political system cannot sustain prolonged conflict. To the extent that the short-war imperative is accepted, a serious problem emerges, for it conflicts with a military style that precludes the very methods that can produce quick results. In this regard, the American military mindset, still firmly rooted in attrition methods, is *not* congruent with what has become an accepted political imperative. Nevertheless, far from inspiring any structural change, the poor fit between the political imperatives and the military style of preference has not even been recognized.

Worse, it also appears that the American military mindset is not congruent with the European military balance either. In the Central European theater of NATO, U.S. ground forces are still deployed to implement pure attrition tactics which presume a net material superiority (or more precisely, a net superiority in firepower production). The expected enemy, however, is in fact superior in firepower capacity overall, and would most likely achieve even greater superiorities at the actual points of contact, where its column thrusts would collide with the elongated NATO frontage. Current tactics must virtually guarantee defeat against a materially superior enemy, since strength is to be applied against strength in a direct attritive exchange.

Given the defensive orientation imposed by the grand strategy of the NATO alliance, only some relational-maneuver operational method based on the principles of avoidance (to side-step the major Soviet thrusts), deception (to mask the defenses), elusiveness (in small scale counterattacks) and momentum (on the counterstroke) would offer some hope of victory, although with considerable risks. On the other hand, it is also true that the politically-imposed theater strategy of Forward Defense precludes the adoption of the only operational methods that would offer some opportunity to prevail over a materially more powerful enemy.

Maneuver, Mobile Defense, and the NATO Central Front

John J. Mearsheimer

In response to the Reagan Administration's plan to increase defense spending significantly, a highly visible group of critics has emerged which argues that spending greater amounts of money is not the answer to American problems. According to these critics, the shortcomings in America's defense posture are largely the consequence of overly sophisticated weaponry and flawed doctrine.[1] The most prominent example of this latter deficiency is NATO's strategy of forward defense, which is designed to engage the attacking Warsaw Pact forces in large-scale battles of attrition along the inter-German border. The critics maintain that this strategy will lead to ruin and that therefore NATO should adopt a fundamentally different approach—a maneuver-oriented defense.[2] Since this argument has received widespread public attention while attracting

John J. Mearsheimer is a research associate at Harvard University's Center for International Affairs. He is currently completing a book on conventional deterrence.

I would like to thank Mary Mearsheimer and Barry Posen for their most helpful comments.

1. Two of the most prominent examples of this viewpoint are: James Fallows, *National Defense* (New York: Random House, 1981); and Franklin C. Spinney, "Defense Facts of Life" (unpublished paper), December 5, 1980.
2. See Steven L. Canby, "Mutual Force Reductions: A Military Perspective," *International Security*, Vol. 2, No. 3 (Winter 1978), pp. 122–135; Steven L. Canby, "NATO: Reassessing the Conventional Wisdoms," *Survival*, XIX, No. 4 (July/August 1977), pp. 164–168; Fallows, *National Defense*, pp. 19–34; William S. Lind, "Military Doctrine, Force Structure, and the Defense Decision-Making Process," *Air University Review*, XXX, No. 4 (May–June 1979), pp. 21–27; William S. Lind, "Some Doctrinal Questions for the United States Army," *Military Review*, LVII, No. 3 (March 1977), pp. 54–65; Edward N. Luttwak, "The Operational Level of War," *International Security*, Vol. 5, No. 3 (Winter 1980/81), pp. 61–79; and Edward N. Luttwak, "The American Style of Warfare and the Military Balance," *Survival*, XXI, No. 2 (March/April 1979), pp. 57–60. Also see questions submitted by Senator Gary Hart in U.S. Congress, Senate Armed Services Committee, *Hearings on DOD Authorization for Appropriations for FY 1979, Part 2*, 95th Cong., 2nd Sess. (Washington D.C.: GPO, 1978), pp. 1572–1575; and in U.S. Congress, Senate Armed Services Committee, *Hearings on the DOD Authorization for Appropriations for FY 1980, Part 1*, 96th Cong., 1st Sess. (Washington D.C.: GPO, 1979), pp. 676–678. For an interesting discussion about the members of this school, see Morton Kondracke, "Defense Without Mirrors," *The New Republic*, January 24, 1981, pp. 11–13.

International Security, Winter 1981/82 (Vol. 6, No. 3) 0162-2889/82/030104-19 $02.50/0
© 1982 by the President and Fellows of Harvard College and of the Massachusetts Institute of Technology.

very little critical treatment, it is appropriate to examine the case for a maneuver-oriented defense.[3]

Proponents of maneuver argue that there are two types or methods of warfare between which a defender can choose: attrition and maneuver. Attrition warfare emphasizes directly engaging the main body of the attacker's forces and relying on firepower to wear down the opponent in a series of slugging matches. "The object of military action is physical destruction of the enemy."[4] Maneuver warfare, on the other hand, calls for the defender to avoid bloody battles and instead to maneuver his forces so that they can strike at the attacker's Achilles' heel. Much emphasis is also placed on presenting the attacker with "a series of rapid and unexpected moves" which will "break the spirit and will of the enemy high command" and "destroy the enemy's mental cohesion."[5] Not surprisingly, the advocates of a maneuver-oriented defense have an undisguised contempt for the attrition warfare that they identify with the American military. To make matters worse, however, NATO has adopted "the American style of warfare." This is reflected in NATO's attrition-oriented strategy of forward defense.

In essence, forward defense means that NATO will meet and attempt to thwart a Pact attack at the inter-German border. The aim is to prevent the Pact from penetrating into West Germany by stopping an offensive before it makes any headway. Appropriately, NATO has deployed the majority of its forces in linear fashion along the 800-km Central Front, where they expect to meet the attacking Pact forces from prepared positions. NATO's principal objective will be to wear down the Pact's forces by engaging them in attrition warfare. U.S. Army doctrine makes this point clearly: "The purpose of defensive operations is to kill enough men and vehicles to convince the enemy that his attack is too costly and he must break it off."[6]

Although the emphasis is certainly on attrition, NATO commanders recognize that they must utilize the mobility inherent in their mechanized forces to shift them about the battlefield to reinforce threatened positions and to

---

3. For a recent attempt to debate the merits of a maneuver-oriented defense, see the "Symposium" in *Armed Forces and Society*, Vol. 7, No. 1 (Fall 1980), pp. 70–87.
4. Lind, "Military Doctrine," p. 22.
5. Lind, "Military Doctrine," p. 23.
6. *FM 71-100, Armored and Mechanized Division Operations* (Washington D.C.: Dept. of the Army, September 29, 1978), p. 5-1. This emphasis on attrition is also reflected in the U.S. Army's capstone field manual, *FM 100-5, Operations* (Washington D.C.: Dept. of the Army, July 1, 1976), chapters 1–3, 5; and in the equivalent German field manual, *HDv 100/100, Command and Control* (Bonn: Ministry of Defense, September 1973), chapter 27.

deliver counterattacks.[7] It is widely acknowledged that it will be necessary to maneuver the forward-deployed forces to insure that NATO's defense is elastic and not brittle. However, this is a limited form of mobility. NATO forces can move about within the specific corps sectors to which they are assigned (NATO's front is divided into eight corps sectors), and it is also possible to "bump" forces from one corps sector into an adjacent one. Nevertheless, there is no doubt that NATO's forces do not have *strategic* mobility.[8] By and large, they are restricted to fighting in specific areas of the NATO front. In short, there is simply not a great deal of flexibility built into NATO's deployment pattern.[9]

The proponents of a maneuver-oriented defense object to NATO's strategy basically for two reasons. First, they maintain that the Pact, by concentrating overwhelming force at specific points, can easily pierce NATO's linear-shaped defense. Once this is accomplished, these analysts claim that NATO is doomed, since it does not have adequate reserves for dealing with a large-scale breakthrough.[10] Second, the maneuver proponents reject NATO's emphasis on attrition warfare. They maintain that for an outnumbered defender like NATO, engaging in a war of attrition is not feasible. In such a slugging match, victory will go to the side with superior resources—which they believe would be the Pact. Most importantly, they reject NATO's attrition-oriented strategy because they feel that there is an alternative which promises the outnumbered defender victory at a low cost: maneuver-oriented defense.

---

7. For example, FM 71–100 (p. 5-2) states: "As the enemy attack moves into the defended area, it encounters fires of increased intensity delivered from the front and *especially the flanks*. The defender *constantly shifts forces* to take maximum advantage of the terrain and put himself in a favorable posture to attack [emphasis mine]." Also see General Bernard Rogers' (former U.S. Army Chief of Staff and present commander of NATO) comments in *Hearings for FY 1980*, pp. 676–678. This emphasis on using tactical mobility (see fn. 8) to support a forward defense is also clearly reflected in the German field manual *HDv 100/100* (see chapter 27). Also see fn. 52 and the attendant text.

8. Although it is difficult to draw a clear distinction between tactical and strategic mobility, it is important to define these terms carefully. Strategic mobility obtains when one has the capability to move a significant number of forces to virtually all parts of the theater of battle to engage the attacking forces. A force with strategic mobility has a very great radius of movement within the theater of battle. Tactical mobility, on the other hand, is the ability to move forces to a limited number of parts of the theater of battle.

9. However, it is very important to note that NATO does have some reserves located in its rear. They will be used to reinforce those forward-deployed forces which have to thwart the Pact's main attacks. Especially important is the fact that NATO is presently making arrangements to deploy an American corps (3 divisions) as a reserve in the northern half of West Germany. Heretofore, there have been no American forces and few reserve units in this region.

10. This pessimism is most clearly reflected in Lind, "Doctrinal Questions," pp. 56, 63. Also see Canby, "Mutual Force Reductions," pp. 124–125.

At first glance, the case for a maneuver-oriented defense is very appealing: there is no need to spend large sums of money to strengthen NATO's forces; and there is the promise of a stunning, yet bloodless battlefield success. A close examination of the prescribed maneuver-oriented defense, however, reveals a fundamentally flawed idea. At best, it is a vague prescription so lacking in substance that its impact on future policy will be negligible. At worst, it is a formula for disaster.

A major problem with the case for a maneuver-oriented defense is that it has not been outlined in sufficient detail. The proposed strategy is defined in vague generalities, thus making it difficult to determine how it works. As noted, its proponents argue that NATO must maneuver its forces about the battlefield so as to present the Soviets with "rapid and unexpected moves" that will "destroy [their] . . . mental cohesion" and "break [their] . . . spirit and will." [11] This sounds appealing, but what do these rapid and unexpected moves look like? *How* are they going to lead to the collapse of the attacking forces? Given the unwieldy nature of modern armies and the attendant command and control problems, one cannot help but wonder how the defender is going to be able to move his forces so rapidly and intelligently that the result will be the unravelling of the attacking forces. Instead of providing a detailed explanation of how the Soviet war machine will be rendered helpless, the maneuver advocates offer explanations such as this:

While it [maneuver warfare] is often characterized by strikes into the enemy's flank and rear, tactics are never a formula; they vary almost infinitely to take advantage of the weaknesses of the specific opponent in the specific time and place. [12]

The maneuver advocates are somewhat more specific when they mention that the attacking forces have an Achilles' heel that should be sought out and targeted. In essence, this means striking against the exposed flanks of the attacking forces and meeting those second-echelon forces that will be following behind the main armored spearheads. [13] Even here, however, the discussion is ambiguous. All the critically important questions are left unanswered. For example, how are NATO's forces to be deployed before the attack? Where exactly is the offense's Achilles' heel and how is NATO going to reach it? Moreover, why should the Pact leave itself open to such a

---

11. Lind, "Military Doctrine," p. 22.
12. William S. Lind, Letter, *Army*, Vol. 31, No. 3 (March 1981), p. 4.
13. See Luttwak, "American Style," p. 58.

devastating blow? And finally, what chain of events is going to lead to the collapse of the Pact offensive? The maneuver proponents have very definite views on what a Pact offensive will look like. Likewise, they should be able to provide a detailed explanation of precisely how NATO is going to stymie it.

The need for greater specificity is reinforced by the fact that there are no historical examples of a maneuver-oriented defense that has defeated an armored offensive. The maneuver advocates claim that in the Second World War, the German Army, which is invariably portrayed as maneuver-oriented, abandoned the strategy after 1941—just as the Soviets were beginning to assume the offensive.[14] Nevertheless, one maneuver advocate goes so far as to argue that "Germany could have beaten the Soviet Union had the maneuver doctrine not been abandoned after 1941."[15] Again, it would be helpful to know exactly how such a feat could have been accomplished.[16]

In contrast to this lack of specificity on the part of the proponents of maneuver warfare, the "other side" in this debate has advanced a comprehensive strategy for meeting a Soviet attack; that strategy is one of forward defense. In effect, they have moved beyond the simple maneuver-attrition dichotomy and operationalized attrition warfare. The maneuver advocates have yet to do this, which explains in large part why so much criticism has been aimed at NATO's forward defense strategy and so little at the case for a maneuver-oriented defense. It is impossible to argue against maneuver as an abstract concept, just as it is very difficult to be against a strategy which calls for inflicting a decisive defeat on an opponent without having to engage in bloody battles. Before such an argument can be taken seriously, it must be taken out of the realm of the abstract and placed squarely in the NATO context. It is necessary to explain exactly how this maneuver-oriented defense works.

Maneuver and Mobile Defense

Although the maneuver advocates have not clearly stipulated what NATO's defensive strategy should look like, it is possible to ascertain from their

---

14. Lind, "Doctrinal Questions," pp. 59–60; and Lind, "Military Doctrine," p. 23.
15. Lind, "Doctrinal Questions," p. 60.
16. For a direct challenge to this claim, see Colonel J. R. Alford, *Mobile Defense: The Pervasive Myth* (London: Dept. of War Studies, King's College, 1977), pp. 104–145.

general arguments that what they are prescribing is a mobile defense.[17] They call for the abandonment of forward defense, by definition an attrition-oriented strategy.[18] Theirs is not a case for forward defense with increased emphasis on maneuver; they are arguing for a fundamental shift in strategy. This fact, coupled with the emphasis on maneuvering forces about the battlefield, can only mean a mobile defense.[19]

Unlike a forward defense, a mobile defense calls for placing a small number of forces along the inter-German border, while locating the brunt of the defending forces in one or more powerful operational reserves. The defender literally ushers the attacking forces into his rear,[20] where he seeks to defeat them by maneuvering his main forces to where they can deliver a devastating blow against the attacker's Achilles' heel. In effect, this means striking at the attacker's lengthening flanks (which will undoubtedly be protected by second-echelon forces) and severing the lines of communication which connect the armored spearheads with their bases. This is certainly a very offensive-minded defensive strategy.[21] With a mobile defense, the danger that the Pact

---

17. Others who have examined their arguments have reached the same conclusion. See Phillip A. Karber's contribution to the "Symposium" in *Armed Forces and Society,* pp. 70–75; and Major Richard H. Sinnreich, "Tactical Doctrine or Dogma?" *Army,* Vol. 29, No. 9 (September 1979), p. 17. Also see Colonel Wayne A. Downing, "U.S. Army Operations Doctrine," *Military Review,* LXI, No. 1 (January 1981), pp. 64–73. It is clear from Downing, who argues for a maneuver-oriented defense, that this strategy is synonymous with a mobile defense. Downing, unlike the other maneuver advocates, outlines his strategic ideas in sufficient detail.
18. Responding to Phillip Karber's charge that Edward Luttwak's ideas on maneuver require the abandonment of NATO's forward defense strategy, Steven Canby denied this. Canby writes, "Luttwak has not argued against the NATO strategy of forward defense" (Canby in "Symposium," p. 84). However, Luttwak himself has written that "the politically-imposed theater strategy of forward defense precludes the adoption of the only operational methods [maneuver] that would offer some opportunity to prevail over a materially more powerful enemy" (Luttwak, "Operational Level," p. 79). Of course, Luttwak is the more reliable source concerning his own ideas. This confusion is a manifestation of the vagueness which characterizes the arguments of the maneuver advocates. One final point is in order concerning this confusion. Canby clearly implies in his defense of Luttwak that forward defense is compatible with his and Luttwak's ideas of maneuver. However, Canby has written elsewhere: "Operationally NATO has made *the cardinal error* of disposing its forces in cordon fashion, the 'layer-cake' in NATO jargon. This distribution of forces . . . is useful for symbolic effect . . . but as a posture for conventional warfare, *it is a prescription for defeat-in-detail* by armored forces penetrating in depth [emphasis mine]" (Canby, "Mutual Force Reductions," pp. 124–125).
19. I can think of no other recognized defensive strategy that has much in common with the maneuver-oriented defense.
20. Luttwak writes, "A manoeuvre alternative . . . might deploy all-armoured and highly agile strike forces which would side-step the oncoming thrust of Soviet armour columns . . ." Luttwak, "American Style," p. 58.
21. There is some evidence that the advocates of a mobile defense are really in favor of having NATO develop its own offensive capability. At least one has explicitly stated his preference for

will break into NATO's rear and meet with little opposition disappears. Equally important, NATO is no longer relegated to fighting a war of attrition. By adroitly maneuvering its forces to strike at the attacker's most vulnerable points, NATO can score what Liddell Hart referred to as a "bloodless victory."

Although the mobile defense may appear at first glance to be an attractive strategy, it is not a viable option for NATO. When carefully examined in the abstract, it is evident that a mobile defense has serious shortcomings; and when analyzed in the NATO context, it is clear that its adoption would lead to disaster.

Mobile Defense in Theory

A mobile defense is a terribly risky strategy.[22] The reason is simple: the defender's task is exacting and there is virtually no margin for error. Consider how a mobile defense is conducted. First, the defender must slow the attacker's main forces with a *small* portion of his own force, commonly referred to as the "fixing force," making sure that the attacker does not penetrate too deeply into the defender's rear. Simultaneously, the defender must locate the offense's vulnerable points and then deliver the decisive blow against them before the attacking forces land a knock-out blow. If the fixing force is overrun, if the defender has problems finding the attacker's Achilles' heel, or if the defender is slow in delivering this counterstroke, then the offense will undoubtedly triumph. A *blitzkrieg* depends for success on the deep strategic penetration, which leads to a complete paralysis of the defense.[23] The attacking forces, after making the initial breakthrough, attempt to drive straight into the depths of the defense, cutting lines of communication and overrunning key nodal points in the defender's communications network as they proceed. This pattern is clearly reflected in the German *blitzkrieg* against France (May 1940) and the Israeli *blitzkrieg* against Egypt (June 1967). By allowing the attacking forces into his rear, the defender is actually allowing the attacker to complete part of his task. The defender is wagering, however, that despite allowing the offense this initial advantage, he can still knock him

---

striking into East Germany in the case of a Pact attack. See Edward Luttwak's comments in "Can the U.S. Defend Itself?" *Time*, April 3, 1978, p. 21. As will be subsequently discussed, any military force that can effect a mobile defense surely has significant offensive capability.
22. For a superb examination of the concept of a mobile defense, see Alford, *Mobile Defense.*
23. See B. H. Liddell Hart, *Memoirs, I* (London: Cassell, 1967), pp. 64–65; *HDv 100/100*, chapters 30–31; and Luttwak, "Operational Level," pp. 67–73.

out before the attacker gets so deep that the defense collapses. Such a strategy leaves no room for second chances.[24] The risks involved with a mobile defense are recognized by at least one of the maneuver advocates, who candidly states that his proposed strategy "is not by any means a fully analyzed idea, and it is, of course, at the *extreme* end of the risk/payoff spectrum."[25]

With a mobile defense, it is imperative to have exceptional command and control so that the defending forces can be maneuvered about on what promises to be a very fluid battlefield. This raises an important issue which bears on the previous discussion. As noted, the armored spearheads in a *blitzkrieg* concentrate on driving directly into the defender's rear, maneuvering around enemy strongpoints when necessary, but otherwise racing straight ahead.[26] The mobile defender, on the other hand, will have to rely on maneuver in its classic sense, since he will have to move his main forces into a position where they can strike at the weak points along the attacker's flanks. Although the attacking forces face a formidable task, the defender's task is even more demanding. Even with superb command and control, the sheer size of modern combat units greatly limits one's flexibility to move them from point to point.[27] Maneuvering large units on the battlefield is a

---

24. It should be noted that in those exceptional cases where a defender has great amounts of territory to trade for time, as well as a substantial number of reserves, then he may very well be afforded a second chance. This is what happened to the Soviets in World War II. However, as will be discussed, NATO has little strategic depth.

25. Luttwak, "American Style," p. 87 (emphasis mine). In a different article, Luttwak emphasizes "the vulnerability of relational-maneuver methods to catastrophic failure" (Luttwak, "Operational Level," p. 65).

26. Prior to the mid-19th century, armies were small enough in size that maneuver was a very important element in warfare. Much emphasis was placed on encircling an opponent's army by striking at his exposed flanks. This was possible, not only because armies were small enough so that they could be moved about quite easily, but also because these armies had exposed flanks. With the advent of the mass army, and the increases in firepower available to those armies, not only was flexibility greatly reduced, but armies rarely had exposed flanks. Thus, it was pointless to talk about encircling armies which were stretched to cover extremely broad fronts. In place of the classic concept of maneuver, army leaders began searching for ways to penetrate the opponent's front. For a discussion of this distinction between maneuver and penetration, see Wilhelm Balck's classic *Development of Tactics—World War*, trans. Harry Bell (Fort Leavenworth, Kansas: The General Service Schools Press, 1922); and Hermann Foertsch, *The Art of Modern Warfare* (New York: Oskar Piest, 1940). The German Army's "Infiltration Tactics," which were used in their March 1918 offensive on the Western Front (see Balck, pp. 260–293), as well as the *blitzkrieg* (see sources cited in fn. 23), emphasize penetration and not maneuver in the classic sense.

27. For example, consider the difficulty Patton had pulling his battle-hardened Third Army out of the Allied front in December 1944, turning it 90 degrees, and then moving north to attack the flanks of the German forces which had just penetrated the Allied front in the Ardennes Forest. See H. Essame, *Patton: A Study In Command* (New York: Scribner's, 1974), pp. 224–233.

formidable undertaking, especially when compared with the attacker's task of simply racing forward, avoiding enemy strongpoints. In light of this asymmetry, it is likely that the attacker, not the defender, will deliver the knockout blow.[28]

There is another asymmetry which increases the risk of employing a mobile defense. A mobile defense requires excellent intelligence, since the defender must be able to locate the offense's weak points quickly.[29] Conversely, it is essential that the attacker's intelligence be deficient so that he will not be able to determine where the defender will deliver his counterstroke. It is highly unlikely that such a disparity in capabilities will obtain in a war between the Warsaw Pact and NATO.

The matter of risk aside, a mobile defense does not favor an outnumbered defender. In fact, the opposite is true. As a rule of thumb, defense analysts agree that an attacker would need somewhat more than a 3 to 1 force advantage at the point of main attack to overwhelm the defense, where the defender is fighting from fixed or prepared positions.[30] In such a circumstance, an outnumbered defender is capable of stopping an offensive. For the defender, the balance is least favorable when he cannot fight from protected positions, but must instead engage the attacking forces on an open battlefield. Such duels, which are usually referred to as "meeting engagements" or "encounter battles," are, in effect, the clashing of two offensive forces. In such cases, the defender enjoys none of the advantages that accrue to him when he fights from prepared positions. Thus, an outnumbered defender is likely to find himself in serious trouble in an encounter battle.

It is hardly surprising that the Soviets much prefer encounter battles to engaging NATO forces located in protected positions.[31] By moving from a forward defense to a mobile defense, the defender would be abandoning a strategy which emphasizes fighting from prepared positions for one which favors encounter battles. Accordingly, with a mobile defense, the defender

---

28. The defender's task is even more complicated if the attacker employs more than one main axis of advance (as the Soviets are expected to do). In such a case, the defender must employ an appropriate number of operational reserves. Since it is imperative that each operational reserve successfully thwart the attacking forces in its area of responsibility, the risks associated with such a defensive strategy are very great. For an excellent discussion of this matter, see Alford, *Mobile Defense*, pp. 11–14.
29. See Luttwak's trenchant comments on this matter in "Operational Level," p. 65.
30. See General William E. DePuy, "Technology and Tactics in Defense of Europe," *Army*, Vol. 29, No. 4 (April 1979), pp. 14–23. Also see *FM 100–5*, p. 3-4.
31. See Christopher Donnelly, "The Soviet Ground Forces," in *The Soviet War Machine*, edited by Ray Bonds (New York: Chartwell, 1976), pp. 166–171.

would need at least as many, if not more forces than the attacker. The manpower demands of a forward defense, on the other hand, would be much less since the defender would be fighting from prepared positions.

Of course, advocates of a mobile defense would argue that the main forces of the offense and the defense will not engage each other. Instead, the mobile defender will use a small fixing force to slow the attacker's main body of forces while the defender's powerful operational reserve strikes against the attacker's vulnerable flanks, bringing him to his knees. As noted, this is a very difficult and risky operation which only a first-rate army could carry out.[32] Moreover, it assumes that the offense will accommodate the defense— a dubious assumption.

The attacker, as he drives into the depths of the defense, will be very conscious of the fact that his lengthening flanks are vulnerable to a counter-stroke. He will undoubtedly seek to protect the flanks of his expanding salient. For a number of reasons, the attacker should be able to develop relatively strong defensive positions along his flanks. First, the Soviet Army, because it is almost completely mechanized, will be able to move second-echelon forces into the salient rapidly so that they can take up defensive positions along the exposed flanks.[33] Second, the proliferation of precision-guided munitions (PGM) should greatly facilitate the attacker's task of protecting those flanks. Finally, by studying the terrain beforehand and properly utilizing available intelligence during the battle, the attacker should be able to determine where the defender's counterstroke is likely to be delivered and to make the necessary preparations to thwart it. In effect, the attacker would be in a position to meet the defender's counterstroke from protected positions—thus standing the conventional wisdom, that the defender enjoys a 3 to 1 advantage, on its head.[34]

---

32. In his examination of German defensive strategy on the Eastern Front in World War II, Alford can only find one example of where the Germans actually attempted to employ a mobile defense. That was in a battle to the west of Leningrad in February 1944. The German effort failed, mainly because the Soviets overran the fixing force. See Alford, *Mobile Defense*, pp. 23, 121–123.

33. For example, the Germans made extensive preparations in 1940 to move second-echelon forces into their expanding salient for the purpose of protecting their exposed flanks. See Franz Halder, "Operational Basis for the First Phase of the French Campaign in 1940 (MS # P-151)" in *World War II German Military Studies*, edited by Donald S. Detwiler (New York: Garland, 1979), XII, pp. 18–19. The Soviet Army would be in a better position to accomplish this task than were the Germans in 1940—simply because Soviet second-echelon forces, unlike the equivalent German forces, are fully mechanized.

34. Taking this a step further, the defender's fixing force, since it is merely attempting to slow the main body of attacking forces, must, by definition, be involved in a very mobile form of

There is another major problem with a mobile defense. It is an unsatisfactory strategy for dealing with an attacker whose military objective is limited to capturing a slice of the defender's territory. What if the attacking forces, after penetrating into the defender's rear, simply stop and transition to a defensive posture before the defender delivers his main attack? The defender would then have to launch an attack against this offensive force, now occupying defensive positions. In effect, the original roles of the defender and the attacker would be reversed—hardly a desirable situation.

Mobile Defense and NATO

A fundamental question that has been begging for an answer throughout this discussion is: how well suited are NATO's forces for conducting a mobile defense? It is clear that NATO is not capable of employing this demanding strategy for several reasons. First, the NATO force on the Central Front is comprised of armies from six countries (including the French, but not the Canadians). These armies do not speak a common language, they have all been trained differently, and they are of uneven quality. The command and control problems associated with maneuvering such a heterogeneous force on a battlefield would be legion. The *sine qua non* of a mobile defense is superb command and control; and NATO's variegated structure is a mighty impediment to good command and control. The language problem alone would present great difficulties. For example, very few officers in the American Army speak German, let alone French, Dutch, or Flemish. To rectify the problem of different training experiences, it would be necessary to have large-scale training exercises so that the various armies could learn to fight together as a cohesive unit. This, however, would be virtually impossible since there are not adequate training sites in West Germany for such large-scale operations.[35]

If one considers the particular armies, the German Army is the only one that might have the wherewithal to conduct a mobile defense. The Americans, the British, and the French (not to mention the Dutch and the Belgians)

---

warfare. Thus, one has a situation where the defender's outnumbered forces (the fixing force) do not have the benefit of fighting from fixed positions, while the attacker's outnumbered forces are situated in fixed positions along the flanks of the expanding salient. From the defender's perspective, this asymmetry is disturbing.

35. See Ulrich De Mazière, *Rational Deployment of Forces on the Central Front,* study prepared for the Western Economic Union, April 2, 1975, p. 29.

are simply not prepared at this time to engage in such a demanding type of warfare with any reasonable expectation of success, nor is this situation likely to change in the foreseeable future.[36] Nevertheless, any defense of NATO would have to assign a large role to these armies.[37] In short, not only is NATO an amalgamation of armies but it is an amalgamation of armies of varying quality. This makes it virtually impossible to adopt a mobile defense.

Second, the geography of West Germany is not suitable for a mobile defense. West Germany is a long and narrow country and, as such, has little strategic depth. The defender, should he attempt to trade space for time as called for with a mobile defense, would quickly find himself backed up against the Rhine and the West German border. NATO will not have much room in which to make adjustments to a Warsaw Pact offensive. NATO will have to deliver its counterstroke quickly and with great precision. Also, many of NATO's key lines of communication run in a north–south direction and are located near the inter-German border. Frankfurt, a critical nodal point in NATO's communications network, is located a mere 100 kilometers from the inter-German border.[38] If these lines of communication were severed, which would undoubtedly occur with a mobile defense, it is difficult to see how NATO could continue to maintain a coherent defense.

Third, the terrain in West Germany does not lend itself to a mobile defense. For the most part, West Germany is covered with a wide variety of obstacles; there are few open areas which are conducive to the large-scale maneuvering of armored forces.[39] This circumstance would hinder the defender because

---

36. Aside from the question of the quality of NATO's various armies, it should be noted that a number of units that would be expected to take part in a European conflict are not presently located in West Germany. Very importantly, these units would be at a serious disadvantage in conducting a mobile defense, simply because they would not be familiar with the terrain.

37. Luttwak argues that while NATO's "high-quality forces" must be used in the operational reserve, "lower-cost forces" can be employed as the fixing force (Luttwak, "American Style," p. 59). Presumably, he believes that this latter task is ideally suited for NATO's weaker units. However, such is not the case. Containing the attacking armored spearheads is a most difficult and important task (see fn. 32) and high–quality forces are required. It is unrealistic to think that "lower-cost forces" or second-rate troops, which would be significantly outnumbered, could accomplish the formidable job of conducting retrograde operations against the attacker's main forces.

38. Generally, the lines of communication in Germany run in a pattern that is similar to a figure 8. Frankfurt is located in the center of the 8 and is the critical link between the northern and southern circles.

39. The southern portion of West Germany, which is mountainous and covered with forests, is generally considered to be obstacle-ridden territory which would present an attacker with significant problems. Northern Germany, on the other hand, is often portrayed as ideal territory for an armored offensive. However, this is not the case. Although there are few mountains in

it restricts freedom of movement—which should be maximized when employing a mobile defense.[40] Regarding the attacker, he is faced with a limited number of defined axes of advance, most of which tend to channel forces as they move across Germany. It would be very difficult for the Soviets to move rapidly along these axes if NATO were to defend them. And since the most obstacle-ridden terrain in West Germany is along the inter-German border, it would be to NATO's advantage to meet an attack as far forward as possible. In short, NATO would be well-advised to meet the Pact's attacking forces head-on as they move along these axes, instead of allowing them to penetrate into Germany—where the terrain, for the most part, would not facilitate the defender's efforts to maneuver his forces into a position where they could deliver a decisive blow.

A close look at three of the most likely axes of attack highlights the importance of meeting the Soviets immediately after they cross into West Germany.[41] It is widely agreed that the Soviets will place a main axis across the North German Plain, which is covered, in large part, by the British corps sector. There is significant urban sprawl in this region, most of which is located between Hannover (in the middle of the sector) and the inter-German border.[42] Armored forces simply will not be able to move rapidly through this urbanized area if NATO defends it. NATO has a vested interest in forcing the Pact to fight costly battles as its forces attempt to traverse the North German Plain. (See figure 1.)

A second likely axis is the Göttingen Corridor, which extends from Göttingen, near the inter-German border, to the Ruhr. The eastern half of this corridor, extending from Paderborn to the border, is covered with obstacles

---

the north, there are numerous obstacles (rivers, bogs, urban sprawl, etc.). See Paul Bracken, "Urban Sprawl and NATO Defense," *Survival*, XVIII, No. 6 (November/December 1976), pp. 254–260; General James H. Polk, "The North German Plain Attack Scenario: Threat or Illusion?" *Strategic Review*, VIII, No. 3 (Summer 1980), pp. 60–66; and *FM 100–5*, pp. 14-15–14-27.

40. Obstacle-ridden terrain not only hinders the defender by restricting freedom of movement, it also limits the number of points in the attacker's flanks which the defender can strike. Thus, the attacker is better able to anticipate where the defender's counterstroke will be delivered.

41. Aside from these three possible avenues of attack, there are actually very few others (the axes which run through Hof and Coburg in southern Germany are the most likely alternatives). And certainly, none of the others are as attractive as the three considered here. The notion that the Soviets can pick any point along the Central Front, mass their forces, and then pierce NATO's front, is not a realistic one. For this reason, NATO forces, in the context of a forward defense, should be well-positioned and equipped with the necessary contingency plans for meeting a Soviet attack.

42. See Bracken, "Urban Sprawl," p. 256; Polk, "The North German Plain Attack Scenario," pp. 61–62; and *FM 100–5*, p. 14-17.

Figure 1: Most Likely Axes of Advance in a Warsaw Pact Attack Against NATO

that would channel the attacking forces and facilitate the defender's task of thwarting a deep strategic penetration. The territory to the west of Paderborn, on the other hand, is virtually obstacle-free and therefore ideal for maneuvering large armored forces.[43] Although this is excellent terrain for employing a mobile defense, it would make absolutely no sense to allow the attacking forces to pass through the more obstacle-ridden eastern half of the corridor and then engage them in a free-wheeling armored battle on the doorstep of the Ruhr. As the Germans argue in their principal field manual, "Surrendering terrain for no compelling reason goes against the essence of the defense."[44] NATO should meet the Soviets at the inter-German border and bleed them white as they attempt to move toward Paderborn.

Finally, there is the possibility of an attack from the Thuringian Bulge, through the Fulda Gap, aimed at Frankfurt. As noted, Frankfurt is of crucial importance for the defense of Germany; since it is located a mere 100 kilometers from the border, NATO cannot afford to risk employing a mobile defense in this sector. Instead, NATO will have to meet an attack on this axis as close to the border as possible so as to guarantee that Frankfurt is not overrun. This should not cause any significant problems, since the axis is rather well defined and lends itself to a forward defense.[45]

The Soviet Threat

When choosing the optimum defensive strategy for NATO, it is essential to consider how the Soviets plan to fight a conventional war. The Soviets emphasize that should a war start, they want to be in a position to win a quick and decisive victory. Appropriately, their forces are configured for a short war; and throughout their writings they emphasize the importance of using deep strategic penetrations to defeat NATO quickly.[46] As noted earlier,

---

43. This is one of the few such areas in West Germany.
44. *HDv 100/100*, p. 27-5.
45. Analyzing the merits and deficiencies of NATO's strategy of forward defense is outside the scope of this article. However, it should be noted that in light of the limited number of avenues of attack available to the Soviets, the obstacle-ridden nature of West Germany, and the fact that the most likely axes of attack are rather well defined, there is every reason to believe that a forward defense is well suited for NATO.
46. See Christopher N. Donnelly, "Tactical Problems Facing the Soviet Army: Recent Debates in the Soviet Military Press," *International Defense Review*, Vol. 11, No. 9 (1978), pp. 1405–1412; and Christopher N. Donnelly, "Soviet Tactics for Overcoming NATO Anti-Tank Defenses," *International Defense Review*, Vol. 12, No. 7 (1979), pp. 1099–1106. Concerning the organization of Soviet ground forces for a short war, see Donnelly, "The Soviet Ground Forces"; and John Hemsley, "The Soviet Ground Forces," in *Soviet Military Power and Performance*, edited by John Erickson and E. J. Feuchtwanger (Hamden, Conn.: Archon Books, 1979), pp. 66–68.

the Soviets hope to engage NATO's main forces in encounter battles, rather than having to dislodge them from prepared positions. They certainly do not want to repeat their experience on the Eastern Front in World War II, where they were engaged with the Germans in a lengthy war of attrition. Hence, the best way to deter the Soviets in a crisis is to convince them that a war in Europe will be a lengthy, costly struggle.

A mobile defense means that the conflict will be a wide open, free-wheeling one, which is precisely the kind of war the Soviets are likely to think that they can win. After all, the Soviets have prepared themselves for such an eventuality and, furthermore, it should be obvious to them that NATO would have major problems handling a mobile defense. It is hard to imagine the Soviets' accepting the assumption that NATO would be more adept than they at fighting on a fluid battlefield. Why accommodate the Soviets by fighting on their terms? Why not make them fight the kind of war that they find categorically distasteful and for which they are unprepared?[47] In other words, why not force the Soviets to engage in a war of attrition? This is precisely what a forward defense is designed to do.

The maneuver advocates have the same negative attitude towards a prospective war of attrition as do the Soviets. These Western analysts maintain that threatening to engage the Soviets in a protracted slugging match is an unacceptable defensive strategy. They argue that NATO has an alternative: by adopting a mobile defense, NATO can avoid a war of attrition and decisively defeat a Warsaw Pact offensive. They are wrong, however. Even if NATO were capable of employing a mobile defense to defeat a Pact offensive (a dubious assumption), that would not end the war. The Soviet Union has the capability to raise massive new armies, and it is nearly certain that those new armies would not fall prey to the mistakes that doomed their predecessors. As Heinz Guderian wrote about the Soviet Union's performance in World War II,

Our adversaries so far as they were accessible to our first onslaught, were beaten by our new methods. They did not hesitate to learn from their defeats and, supported by their recurring numerical and material superiority, they

---

47. In a recent article, two respected experts on the Soviet military argue that the Soviets place "a disproportionately high value on *any* measure taken which enables the attacker *to avoid the need to fight through prepared defensive positions* [emphasis in original]." See Peter W. Vigor and Christopher N. Donnelly, "The Manchurian Campaign and Modern Strategy," *Comparative Strategy*, Vol. 2, No. 2 (1980), p. 169. Also see Phillip A. Karber, "The Soviet Anti-Tank Debate," *Survival*, XVIII, No. 3 (May/June 1976), pp. 105–111.

then turned our own combat methods against us with the same result as in World War I.[48]

It is virtually impossible to defeat the Soviets decisively in a land war in Europe. NATO simply cannot escape a war of attrition with the Soviets, unless the Pact wins a quick and decisive victory. Successful execution of a mobile defense would only result in a short-term victory that would quickly be forgotten as the war turned into a long and costly struggle.

Mobile Defense and Crisis Stability

A mobile defense not only fails to provide an alternative to a war of attrition; it also presents a potentially unstable situation. If NATO's forces were capable of conducting a mobile defense, those same forces would surely have a significant offensive capability. As noted, a mobile defense is actually a very offensive-minded defensive strategy. Its principal ingredient is the counterstroke, which is an offensive tactic. An army that could satisfy the demands of a mobile defense would be well suited for conducting offensive operations.

If NATO had a realistic offensive capability, it would not be unreasonable to assume that in a crisis, serious consideration would be given to striking first. Thus, a highly unstable situation would obtain, since both the Pact and NATO would be considering offensive operations. Moreover, since each side would undoubtedly be aware of the other's offensive capabilities, there would be great pressure on both sides to launch a preemptive strike. Currently, there is virtually no chance that NATO would launch an offensive, since NATO is capable only of defensive operations. It is the Pact that must be deterred, and the best way to achieve that end is to convince its military leaders that an offensive would lead to a lengthy war of attrition. A forward defense provides the best means for insuring this outcome. A mobile defense, on the other hand, would lead to a situation where both the Warsaw Pact and NATO would be contemplating military action.[49]

---

48. Heinz Guderian, "Unification or Coordination: The Armed Forces Problem (MS # T–113)," in *World War II German Military Studies,* VI, p. 11. Also see B. H. Liddell Hart, *The German Generals Talk* (New York: William Morrow, 1948), chapter 16.

49. As noted earlier, the German Army (which is widely recognized as the finest army in Europe—the Soviets' included) is the only army in NATO that might be capable of effecting a mobile defense. Thus, if NATO were to pursue this strategy, the responsibilities as well as the size of the German Army would have to be increased. For a mobile defense to have any chance

Conclusion

This discussion has focused on the purely military aspects of mobile defense. It is very important to note, however, that even if this strategy were feasible and desirable from a military viewpoint, it would be politically unacceptable to the West Germans. They have continually emphasized that "there can be no alternative to forward defense . . . any conceptual model of defense involving the surrender of territory is unacceptable."[50] The Germans are not going to change their minds on this matter. For understandable reasons, they have no interest in turning their country into a giant battlefield.[51] Thus, any attempt to pressure the Germans into accepting a mobile defense is bound to cause very serious trouble within the alliance. Given existing tensions among the Allies, that would be a most unwelcome development—the more so since this strategy is a blueprint for disaster on the battlefield. The inviolability of the German commitment to forward defense raises an important issue. The maneuver advocates argue that attrition warfare is characteristic of the American military. The implication is that the Americans have adopted a deficient strategy, which they then foisted on their allies. There is no evidence, however, that the American way of defending against a Soviet attack is different in any meaningful way from the German way or the Dutch way.[52] More importantly, there is no evidence that the Germans,

---

of succeeding, the German Army would have to assume a greater share of the defense burden. Therefore, a mobile defense would not only result in a NATO with real offensive capability, but one which was largely dominated by Germany—a development with very significant political consequences.

50. *White Paper 1979: The Security of the Federal Republic of Germany and the Development of the Federal Armed Forces* (Bonn: Federal Minister of Defense, September 4, 1979), p. 126. To appreciate fully the importance that the Germans place on holding as much of their territory as possible, one only has to review the controversy surrounding the leaking of the minutes of the National Security Council meeting where the Carter Administration's Presidential Review Memorandum No. 10 (PRM-10) was discussed. See Rowland Evans and Robert Novak, "Conceding Defeat in Europe," *Washington Post*, August 4, 1977, Sec. A, p. 19; Edward Walsh, "'Pullback' Policy in Europe is Denied," *Washington Post*, August 4, 1977, Sec. A, p. 12; and Secretary of Defense Harold Brown's testimony in U.S. Congress, Senate Subcommittee on Manpower and Personnel of the Armed Services Committee, *Hearing on NATO Posture and Initiatives*, 95th Cong., 1st Sess. (Washington D.C.: GPO, August 3, 1977). Undoubtedly, one of the reasons that the maneuver advocates have not clearly outlined their strategy is that they recognize that if they did so, the Germans would reject their arguments.

51. One of the main conclusions of Alford's excellent study is that nations rarely employ a mobile defense for political as well as military reasons. See Alford, *Mobile Defense*, p. 279.

52. This is evident from a comparison of the chapters on defense in the capstone field manuals of the German and American Armies (*HDv 100/100* and *FM 100-5*, respectively). Also see fns. 6 and 7.

or any of the Allies, are dissatisfied with the present strategy of forward defense. On the contrary, it is the Germans who vigilantly watch their alliance partners to insure that they remain duly committed to forward defense. Ironically, it is a handful of Americans who are calling for abandoning forward defense.

Instead of heeding this bad advice, NATO should concentrate on improving its capability to implement a strategy of forward defense. In this regard, every effort should be made to insure that NATO has adequate reserves for reinforcing potential trouble spots along the forward line. More specifically, it is imperative that the plan to locate an American corps in reserve in the northern part of Germany be completed. Furthermore, it is essential to insure that the Belgians, the Dutch, and the British continue to appropriate monies to support forces capable of protecting their respective corps sectors. Finally, NATO must insure that its component armies recognize the importance of tactical mobility. It will be necessary to maneuver NATO's forward-deployed forces about the battlefield to deliver counterattacks and to reinforce threatened units. Although a forward defense is somewhat rigid by design, NATO must seek to maximize flexibility. In the end, there is no reason why NATO, employing a forward defense, should not be able to thwart a Soviet offensive. Certainly, a forward defense holds more promise of accomplishing this than a mobile defense.

Conventional Deterrence and Conventional Retaliation in Europe

Samuel P. Huntington

For a quarter century the slow but continuing trend in NATO strategy—and in thinking about NATO strategy—has been from emphasis on nuclear deterrence to emphasis on conventional deterrence. When it became clear that the famous Lisbon force goals of 1952, embodied in MC 14/1, had no hope of realization, NATO strategy appropriately stressed the deterrent role of nuclear weapons, in terms of both massive retaliation by U.S. strategic forces and the early use of tactical nuclear weapons in Western Europe. This strategy was codified in MC 14/2 in 1957. Shortly thereafter, however, the development of Soviet strategic nuclear capabilities and, more particularly, the massive deployment by the Soviets of theater nuclear weapons raised serious questions as to the desirability of NATO's relying overwhelmingly on early use of nuclear weapons to deter Soviet attack. In the following years, the emphasis shifted to the need for stronger conventional forces capable of mounting a forward defense of Germany for a period of time and to a strategy of flexible response, in which, if deterrence failed and if conventional defenses did not hold, NATO would have the options of resorting to tactical, theater, and eventually strategic nuclear weapons. In 1967 this strategy became official NATO policy in MC 14/3.

The past several years have seen increasing support for shifting the deterrent emphasis even further in the conventional direction. This perceived

This paper, prepared for a conference at the U.S. Army War College, Strategic Studies Institute, Carlisle Barracks, Pennsylvania, July 29–30, 1983, will be published in William O. Staudenmaier and Keith Dunn, eds., *Strategy in Transition: Defense and Deterrence in the 1980s*. It elaborates in more refined and detailed form arguments which I originally set forth in "The Renewal of Strategy," in Huntington, ed., *The Strategic Imperative: New Policies for American Security* (Cambridge, Mass.: Ballinger, 1982), pp. 21–32, and in "Broadening the Strategic Focus," in *Defense and Consensus: The Domestic Aspects of Western Security, Part III*, Adelphi Paper No. 184 (London: International Institute for Strategic Studies, 1983), pp. 27–32. In a few spots in this essay I have shamelessly plagiarized these earlier writings. I am grateful to Richard K. Betts and Eliot Cohen for their helpful critical comments.

Samuel P. Huntington is the Eaton Professor of the Science of Government and Director of the Center for International Affairs, Harvard University.

International Security, Winter 1983/84 (Vol. 8, No. 3) 0162-2889/84/030032-25 $02.50/0

need derives, of course, from the facts of strategic parity between the U.S. and the Soviet Union, Soviet achievement of substantial predominance in theater nuclear forces, and a continued and, in some respects, enhanced Soviet superiority in conventional forces. In these circumstances, in the event of a successful Soviet conventional advance into Western Europe, how credible would be the threat of a nuclear response? In the face of Soviet superiority at that level, why would NATO resort to theater nuclear weapons, with all the destruction to both sides that would entail? Even more significantly, why would the United States use or even threaten to use its strategic nuclear forces, if that would ensure massive Soviet retaliation against North America? The concerns which DeGaulle articulated (even if he may not have believed them) in the early 1960s had by the early 1980s come to be first believed and then articulated by a broad spectrum of statesmen and strategists. The standard reassurances of the validity of the American nuclear guarantee, as Henry Kissinger put it in 1979, "cannot be true" and "it is absurd to base the strategy of the West on the credibility of the threat of mutual suicide."[1] Even McGeorge Bundy, who immediately countered Kissinger's statement with an argument for the continued efficacy of nuclear deterrence in Europe, dramatically abandoned that position three years later.[2]

Current NATO strategy also has little support among Western publics. In 1981 in the four major Western European countries, for instance, overwhelming majorities (66 percent in Germany, 71 percent in Britain, 76 percent in France, 81 percent in Italy) favored either no NATO use of nuclear weapons "under any circumstances" or NATO use only if the Soviet Union "uses them first in attacking Western Europe." In all four countries only small minorities (12 percent in Italy, 17 percent in France and Germany, 19 percent in Britain) supported existing NATO strategy that "NATO should use nuclear weapons

---

1. Henry A. Kissinger, "The Future of NATO," in Kenneth A. Myers, ed., *NATO: The Next Thirty Years* (Boulder, Colo.: Westview Press, 1980), p. 7.

2. McGeorge Bundy, "Strategic Deterrence Thirty Years Later—What Has Changed?", in *The Future of Strategic Deterrence, Part I*, Adelphi Paper No. 160 (London: International Institute for Strategic Studies, 1980), pp. 10–11: ". . . the strategic protection of Europe is as strong or as weak as the American strategic guarantee. . . . the effectiveness of this American guarantee is likely to be just as great in the future as in the past." Cf. McGeorge Bundy, George F. Kennan, Robert S. McNamara, and Gerard Smith, "Nuclear Weapons and the Atlantic Alliance," *Foreign Affairs*, Vol. 60, No. 4 (Spring 1982), pp. 754, 765: U.S. "willingness to be the first . . . to use nuclear weapons to defend against aggression in Europe . . . needs reexamination now. Both its cost to the coherence of the Alliance and its threat to the safety of the world are rising while its deterrent credibility declines. . . . [T]he present unbalanced reliance on nuclear weapons, if long continued, might produce [some deeply destabilizing] political change."

to defend itself if a Soviet attack by conventional forces threatened to overwhelm NATO forces."[3] Somewhat similarly, in the United States, public opinion generally opposed a "no first use" declaration but also by an overwhelming margin (62 percent) answered "no" to the question as to whether the United States "would *ever* be justified in using nuclear weapons first during a war against another country."[4] In democratic societies, expert opinion and public opinion often differ on nuclear weapons issues. In the West today, however, they agree in rejecting reliance on the use of nuclear weapons to respond to conventional attack. In its current formulation, flexible response is seen as inadequate by the strategists, unsupportable by the public, and, one must assume, increasingly incredible by the Soviets.

The conclusion almost universally drawn from this perceived deteriorating credibility of the nuclear deterrent to Soviet conventional attack in Western Europe is the need to strengthen NATO conventional forces. The desirability of doing this is broadly supported by conservative, liberal, and, in Europe, socialist politicians. It has been endorsed in one form or another by a wide variety of military experts and strategists, including General Bernard Rogers, Professor Michael Howard, Senator Sam Nunn, the Union of Concerned Scientists study group, the No First Use "Gang of Four," the American Academy of Arts and Sciences European Security Study, informed Social Democratic Party (SPD) analysts, the Reagan Administration, and, so far as one can gather, those Democratic presidential aspirants who have addressed the issue.[5] The conventional wisdom is, in short, that stronger conventional forces are needed to enhance conventional deterrence and thus compensate for the declining effectiveness of nuclear deterrence.

---

3. Leo P. Crespi, "West European Perceptions of the U.S.," Paper presented at the International Society of Political Psychology convention, June 1982, Table 4, quoted in Bruce Russett and Donald R. Deluca, "Theater Nuclear Forces: Public Opinion in Western Europe," *Political Science Quarterly*, Vol. 98 (Summer 1983), p. 194.
4. CBS/*New York Times* poll, May 1982, cited in "Opinion Roundup," *Public Opinion*, Vol. 5 (August–September 1982), p. 38.
5. General Bernard W. Rogers, "Greater Flexibility for NATO's Flexible Response," *Strategic Review*, Vol. 11 (Spring 1983), pp. 11–19; Michael Howard, "Reassurance and Deterrence: Western Defense in the 1980s," *Foreign Affairs*, Vol. 61, No. 3 (Winter 1982–83), pp. 309–343; Senator Sam Nunn, "NATO: Can the Alliance Be Saved?", Report to the Committee on the Armed Services, United States Senate, 97th Congress, 2d Session, May 13, 1982; *The Washington Post*, February 2, 1983, p. 10; *Strengthening Conventional Deterrence in Europe: Proposals for the 1980s*, Report of the European Security Study (New York: St. Martin's Press, 1983); Bundy et al., "Nuclear Weapons and the Atlantic Alliance," pp. 753–768; Eckhard Lübkemeier, "Problems, Prerequisites, and Prospects of Conventionalizing NATO's Strategy," Unpublished paper, Bonn, Friedrich-Ebert-Stiftung, February 1983; English version, July 1983, pp. 3 and *passim*.

The Requirements of Conventional Deterrence

The conventional wisdom suffers from two significant weaknesses.

First, NATO countries are unlikely to commit the resources necessary to achieve the required strengthening of NATO defenses. Ever since the Lisbon conference, various efforts have been made to bolster NATO's conventional capabilities so as to decrease reliance on nuclear retaliation. Except for a brief period in the mid-1960s, these efforts have not been notably successful. After a quarter of a century, deterrence by conventional forces remains appealing, but it also remains an unreality. For understandable reasons, European governments and publics have been unwilling to appropriate the funds and make the sacrifices that would be required to make it effective. This pattern continues. In 1978 the Alliance committed itself to the Long Term Defense Program requiring 3 percent annual increases in defense spending by its member countries. Apart from the United States, however, the members of NATO have, with occasional exceptions, generally failed to meet that goal. General Rogers now argues that an effective conventional defense for NATO can be achieved if its members increase their military spending by 4 percent annually. The European Security Study comes to a similar conclusion. But if NATO countries have failed to achieve a sustained 3 percent increase, how realistic is it to talk of 4 percent increases? The attitudes of European publics and governments do not seem to be more favorable to voting larger defense budgets than they have been in the past, and economic conditions for such increases are at present far less propitious. This does not mean that no increases in NATO conventional defense capability will occur. Clearly they will. The budget increases are likely, however, to be no more than 2.0–2.5 percent, and hence they will not achieve the levels thought necessary by those who see increased conventional capability as the solution to the problem of deterrence. Thus, while nuclear deterrence of a Soviet conventional attack on Western Europe suffers from a lack of credibility, conventional deterrence of such an attack suffers from a lack of capability.

The second problem with the strengthening-conventional-forces approach is more serious. It concerns not inadequate resources but erroneous, if generally unarticulated, assumptions. It would still be present in some form even if NATO defense spending did increase by 4 percent a year. It is much more salient if that goal is not achieved. It involves the requirements of deterrence.

Military forces can contribute to deterrence in three ways. First, they may deter simply by being in place and thus increasing the uncertainties and potential costs to an aggressor, even though they could not mount an effective defense. Allied forces in Berlin have performed this role for years, and the argument for being able to move airborne forces and Marines rapidly to the Persian Gulf, in the event of a Soviet invasion of Iran, rests on a similar premise. Simply the presence of American forces in Khuzistan might deter the Soviets from moving in on the oil fields. Second, military forces can deter by raising the possibility of a successful defense and hence forcing the aggressor to risk defeat in his effort or to pay additional costs for success. This has been the traditional deterrent role assigned to NATO forces in Germany. Third, military forces can deter by threatening retaliation against assets highly valued by the potential aggressor. This, of course, has been the classic role of strategic nuclear forces. Unlike deterrence by presence or deterrence by defense, however, this form of deterrence is not effective simply because the requisite military capabilities exist; it requires a conscious choice by the defender to retaliate; and hence the aggressor has to calculate not only the defender's capabilities to implement a retaliatory threat but also the credibility of that threat.

One of the striking characteristics of the new conventional wisdom is the extent to which stronger conventional defenses are identified with a stronger conventional deterrent. If only NATO can enhance its military defenses, Soviet aggression will be deterred: this assumption is implicit in most of the arguments for stronger NATO forces and it is at the heart of the report by the European Security Study. That report, indeed, treats conventional defense and conventional deterrence as virtually interchangeable concepts. The title of the report is "Strengthening Conventional Deterrence in Europe"; the central sections of the report deal with "The Specific Requirements for Effective NATO Conventional Defense" and "The Means for Enhancing NATO's Conventional Defensive Capability"; throughout it is assumed that improved conventional defenses mean improved conventional deterrence.

To a limited degree, this assumption is, of course, justified. The stronger NATO forces are, the greater the investment the Soviets would have to make to achieve a given set of goals in Western Europe. Yet the easy identification of deterrence with defense flies in the face of logic and in the face of long-standing traditions in strategic thought. One of the landmark works on this subject (still valuable after twenty years), *Deterrence and Defense* by Glenn Snyder, is. indeed, based on the opposition between defense and deterrence and the extent to which strategies and forces appropriate to serve one goal may not be suited to achievement of the other. In addition, deterrence itself, that is, the effort to influence enemy intentions, may be pursued through both "denial capabilities—typically, conventional ground, sea, and tactical air forces" and "punishment capabilities—typically, strategic nuclear power for either massive or limited retaliation."[6] In the years since Snyder, strategists have generally tended to make the same identification. In the process, concern with the distinction between nuclear and conventional capabilities has tended to obscure the equally important distinction between defensive and retaliatory capabilities. In current NATO planning, nuclear and conventional capabilities can both be used for defensive purposes; only nuclear capabilities can be used for retaliatory purposes. Eliminating or drastically downgrading nuclear forces means eliminating or drastically downgrading the retaliatory component that has always been present in NATO strategy. Those who argue for conventional defense are, in effect, arguing for deterrence without retaliation. This is a fundamental change in NATO strategy, at least as significant in terms of deterrence as the shift from nuclear to conventional forces. For as both logic and experience make clear, a purely denial strategy inherently is a much weaker deterrent than one which combines both denial and retaliation.

For a prospective attacker, the major difference between denial and retaliation concerns the certainty and controllability of the costs he may incur. If faced simply with a denial deterrent, he can estimate how much effort he will have to make and what his probable losses will be in order to defeat the enemy forces and achieve his objective. He can then balance these costs against the gains he will achieve. He may choose zero costs and zero gains; he may decide to limit his gains to what can be achieved by a given level of costs; he may decide to incur whatever costs are necessary to achieve the gains he desires. The choice is his. If, however, he is confronted with a retaliatory deterrent, he may well be able to secure the gains he wants with relatively little effort, but he does not know the total costs he will have to pay, and those costs are in large measure beyond his control. The Soviet general staff can give the Politburo reasonably accurate estimates as to what forces it will require and what losses it will probably suffer to defeat NATO forces in Germany and extend Soviet control to the Rhine. For years, however, it could not predict with any assurance whether U.S. nuclear retaliation to such a move would be directed to battlefield targets, military targets in

---

6. Glenn H. Snyder, *Deterrence and Defense: Toward a Theory of National Security* (Princeton, N.J.: Princeton University Press, 1961), pp. 4, 14–16.

Eastern Europe and/or the Soviet Union, or industrial and population centers in the Soviet Union. Precisely this uncertainty and absence of control made the threat of retaliation a strong deterrent. If these problems of uncertainty and uncontrollability are eliminated or greatly reduced, the effectiveness of the deterrent is seriously weakened.

The difficulties of relying on deterrence by defensive means have long been emphasized in the strategic field. No defense system—antiaircraft, ABM, or civil defense—deployable now or in the foreseeable future could prevent some nuclear weapons from reaching their targets and causing unprecedented destruction. Hence deterrence of an attack must depend upon the ability to retaliate after absorbing the attack. Much the same is true at the conventional level. In the past, conventional deterrence has usually meant deterrence-by-denial, and the frequency of wars in history suggests that this conventional-denial deterrence was not often effective. Nor has it been effective in the modern era. In a careful survey, John Mearsheimer identified twelve major instances of conventional deterrence between 1938 and 1979. In two of these cases, deterrence worked; in ten, deterrence failed.[7] This 83.3 percent failure rate for deterrence by conventional defense after 1938 contrasts rather markedly with the zero failure rate for deterrence by nuclear retaliation for a quarter century after 1945.

An initial offensive by a strong and determined attacker, particularly if accompanied by surprise, inevitably will score some gains. As Saadia Amiel summed up the lessons of the 1973 Arab–Israeli war and the implications of precision guided munitions (PGMs): "without very clear offensive options, a merely passive or responsive defensive strategy, which is based on firepower and fighting on friendly territory, cannot withstand an offensive strategy of an aggressor who possesses a relatively large, well-prepared standing offensive military force."[8] This is certainly the case in central Europe. Given NATO's current conventional defenses and any likely improvements in them, a Soviet conventional offensive in Europe is, inevitably, going to be at least a partial success. The Soviets may not reach the Pyrenees, or the English Channel, or even the Rhine. They may or may not occupy Frankfurt, Hamburg, or Munich. Inevitably they will, however, score some gains. They may

---

7. John J. Mearsheimer, *Conventional Deterrence* (Ithaca, N.Y.: Cornell University Press, 1983), pp. 19–20. Mearsheimer identifies six additional possible cases of conventional deterrence, in five of which deterrence failed.
8. Saadia Amiel, "Deterrence by Conventional Forces," *Survival*, Vol. 20 (March–April 1978), p. 59.

pay a substantial price in losses of men and equipment, but they will still occupy West German territory and conquer West German population and industry. That is a certainty produced by geography and any realistically conceivable balance of conventional forces in central Europe. Given the nature of existing forces and strategies, these gains could well be substantial, but that is not necessary for the argument.

Assume that the Soviet offensive does grind to a halt after Soviet forces have occupied a greater or a lesser portion of West Germany. What then? In theory, the Allies should bring in their reinforcements from North America and put together a counteroffensive to drive the Soviets back. This would, however, be an extraordinarily difficult military and logistical undertaking. Inevitably the pressures would be on all parties to attempt to negotiate a cease-fire and a resolution of the conflict. With their armies ensconced in Hesse, Lower Saxony, and Bavaria and the differing interests of the Allies manifesting themselves, the Soviets would clearly have the upper hand in such negotiations. It takes little imagination to think of the types of appeals the Soviets would make to West German authorities and political groups to accept some degree of demilitarization or neutralization in order to secure Soviet withdrawal and to avoid the replay of World War II in their country.

A Soviet invasion of West Germany that ended with the neutralization and/or demilitarization of all or part of that country would be a tremendous success from the Soviet point of view. It would decisively alter the balance of power in Europe and in the world. Its costs, in terms of losses of men and equipment, would have to be very substantial to outweigh these political, military, and diplomatic gains. In 1939 and in 1941, once they had devised means to neutralize possible Allied retaliation by bomber attacks on cities, Hitler and the Japanese launched their offensives into Poland and southeast Asia expecting, not entirely unreasonably, that their democratic opponents would lack the staying power to deprive them of their initial territorial conquests.[9] In the absence of a credible retaliatory threat against valued

---

9. For analyses in depth of the failure of pre-World War II deterrence, see Mearsheimer, *Conventional Deterrence*, esp. chapters 3, 4, and Scott D. Sagan, "Deterrence and Decision: An Historical Critique of Modern Deterrence Theory" (Ph.D. dissertation, Harvard University, 1983), chapters 4–7. The bomber introduced the possibility of more effective deterrence by retaliation and compelled aggressors to take countermeasures. Both Hitler and the Japanese were deeply worried about retaliatory air attacks on their cities. Hitler guarded against this by mutual deterrence through an informal understanding with the Allies that neither side would target population; Japan guarded against it by a disarming first strike. Neither Axis power was deterred by Allied defensive measures, including the Maginot Line.

Soviet assets, the Allies would be tempting fate to assume that the Soviets would not be tempted to make a comparable move into Western Europe sometime in the next decade or two.

In sum, a substantial increase in NATO conventional forces is unfeasible politically. Even if it could be achieved, it would not compensate for the decline in the credibility of nuclear retaliation as a deterrent. To be effective, deterrence has to move beyond the possibility of defense and include the probability of retaliation. Conventional deterrence requires not just an increase in conventional forces; it also requires a reconstitution of conventional strategy.

The Role of Conventional Retaliation

The new element required in NATO strategy is conventional retaliation. NATO has four possible means of deterring Soviet aggression: defense with conventional or nuclear forces and retaliation by conventional or nuclear forces. Under MC 14/3, NATO relied on a sequence of three responses, conventional defense, nuclear defense, nuclear retaliation (Figure 1). The decreasing credibility of NATO use of nuclear weapons, however, has loosened the connections between these responses (indicated by the dotted lines in Figure 2). As a result, both nuclear and retaliatory deterrence are weakened. The problem is to restore the latter without resorting to the former. The need, in short, is to add some form of conventional retaliation to NATO strategy (Figure 3). That retaliatory component can best take the form of provision for, in the case of a Soviet attack, a prompt conventional retaliatory offensive into Eastern Europe.

For the threat of retaliation to be an effective deterrent it must (a) be directed against a target that is highly valued by the potential aggressor and (b) have a high degree of probability it will be implemented. It is reasonable to assume that the Soviet elite values, next to the security of the Soviet Union itself, the security of its satellite regimes in Eastern Europe. If the threat of nuclear attacks against the Soviet Union has lost its credibility, the next most effective threat NATO can pose surely is the possibility of a conventional retaliatory offensive directed against the Soviet empire in Eastern Europe. In addition, as Snyder observed, the credibility of the threat of retaliation to "a large-scale Soviet ground attack on Western Europe depends on convincing the enemy that we would gain more by carrying out this threat than we

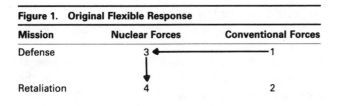

Figure 1. Original Flexible Response

Mission	Nuclear Forces	Conventional Forces
Defense	3	1
Retaliation	4	2

Figure 2. Deteriorated Flexible Response

Mission	Nuclear Forces	Conventional Forces
Defense	3	1
Retaliation	4	2

Figure 3. Reconstituted Flexible Response

Mission	Nuclear Forces	Conventional Forces
Defense	3	1
Retaliation	4	2

would lose."[10] Precisely because this condition is no longer met, the threat of nuclear retaliation has lost its credibility. No such problem arises, however, by the threat of a conventional retaliatory offensive into Eastern Europe.

Almost every other form of retaliation against conventional attack involves escalation, either vertical, as in NATO doctrine, or, conceivably, horizontal. A conventional offensive into Eastern Europe, in contrast, is retaliation in kind, at the same level and in the same theater as the initial attack. It thus has unimpeachable credibility. Just as the Soviets have to believe that the United States would retaliate in kind against a strategic attack on American cities or a theater nuclear attack on Western Europe, they would also have to believe that the United States and its allies would retaliate in kind against a conventional attack on West Germany. Deterrence without retaliation is weak; retaliation through escalation is risky. Conventional retaliation strengthens the one without risking the other.

10. Snyder, *Defense and Deterrence*, p. 79.

Strategy should exploit enemy weaknesses. A deterrent strategy that included provision for conventional retaliation would do this in two ways. First, it would capitalize on the uncertainties and fears that the Soviets have concerning the reliability of their Eastern European allies, and the uncertainties and fears that the governments of those countries have concerning the reliability of their own peoples. It would put at potential risk the system of controls over Eastern Europe that the Soviets have developed over thirty years and which they consider critical to their own security. The deterrent impact of the threat of conventional retaliation would be further enhanced by prior Allied assurances to Eastern European governments that their countries would not be invaded if they abstained from the conflict and did not cooperate in the Soviet attack on the West. At the very least, such an invitation would create uneasiness, uncertainty, and divisiveness within satellite governments, and hence arouse concerns among the Soviets as to their reliability. In practice, the Allied offensive would have to be accompanied with carefully composed political-psychological warfare appeals to the peoples of Eastern Europe stressing that the Allies were not fighting them but the Soviets and urging them to cooperate with the advancing forces and to rally to the liberation of their countries from Soviet military occupation and political control. A conventional retaliatory strategy is based on the assumption that the West German reserves, territorial army, and populace will put up a more unified, comprehensive, and determined resistance to occupation by Soviet armies than the East German, Czech, Polish, and Hungarian forces and populations will to liberation from Soviet armies. (If this assumption is unwarranted, the foundations of not only a conventional retaliatory strategy but also of NATO would be in question.) Politically speaking, the Soviet Union has more to lose from Allied armies invading Eastern Europe than NATO has to lose from Soviet armies invading Western Europe. The Soviet Union should, consequently, give higher priority to preventing an Allied offensive into Eastern Europe than to pushing a Soviet offensive into Western Europe.

If the satellites did fight, the extent of their participation in a war, it is generally recognized, would depend on the scope and speed of Soviet success in the conflict. So long as the Soviets are moving westward, they are more likely to have complacent and cooperative allies. If, however, they are stalemated or turned back, disaffection is likely to appear within the Warsaw Pact. A prompt Allied offensive into Eastern Europe would stimulate that disaffection at the very start of the conflict. Neither the Soviets nor, more importantly, the satellite governments could view with equanimity West German tanks on the road to Leipzig and Berlin and American divisions heading for Prague and Cracow. From the viewpoint of deterrence, such a prospect would tremendously enhance the undesirability of war for the governments of these satellite countries. Those governments, which provide more than one-third of the Warsaw Pact combat forces on the central front, would lose more than anyone else in such a war and hence would become a puissant lobby urging their Soviet partner not to initiate war.

A conventional offensive into Eastern Europe would thus threaten the Soviets where they are politically weak. It would also be aimed at Soviet military weakness. Both Western observers and Soviet military leaders agree that Soviet officers and NCOs are much better at implementing a carefully detailed plan of attack than they are at adjusting to rapidly changing circumstances. A conventional offensive into Eastern Europe would confront the Soviets with just exactly the situation their doctrine and strategy attempt to avoid: one in which they do not have control of developments and in which they face a high probability of uncertainty and surprise. It would put a premium on flexibility and adaptability, qualities in which the Soviets recognize themselves to be deficient. One knowledgeable observer has even argued that, "If the Soviet Union were poised to launch an offensive, and were preempted in this by a NATO spoiling attack, there is little doubt that, in their own eyes, the Soviets reckon that *they* stand a good chance of collapse."[11]

A prompt Allied offensive into Eastern Europe would also greatly increase the probability of a protracted war. Soviet planning, however, is in large part directed toward a short-war scenario in which the Soviets score a breakthrough, occupy a substantial portion of West Germany, and then negotiate a cease-fire from a position of strength. With a retaliatory strategy, Soviet armies might be in West Germany but Allied armies would also be in East Europe, and driving them out would require more time for mobilization and organization of a counteroffensive.

The basic point, moreover, is deterrence. The prospects for the sustained success of the Allied offensive into Eastern Europe do not have to be 100

---

11. Christopher N. Donnelly, "Soviet Operational Concepts in the 1980s," in European Security Study, *Strengthening Conventional Deterrence*, p. 135. See also the report of the Steering Group of this study, p. 18, and Joshua M. Epstein, "Soviet Confidence and Conventional Deterrence in Europe," Unpublished paper, Harvard University, Center for International Affairs, 1982.

percent. They simply have to be sufficiently better than zero and to raise sufficient unpleasant uncertainties to increase significantly the potential costs and risks to the Soviets of starting a war.

Current NATO strategy already contemplates the possibility of a counter-offensive. It would occur after the enemy's offensive forces have penetrated NATO territory and then been slowed or brought to a halt and NATO forces have been reinforced. A counteroffensive follows sequentially after the enemy's offensive and is directed to retrieving the initiative and recovering occupied territory.[12] A retaliatory offensive, in contrast, occurs simultaneously with the enemy's offensive. Its primary purpose is not to strike the enemy where he has furthest advanced, as is usually the case with a counteroffensive; rather it is to attack him in an entirely different sector. It thus would have a very different impact on Soviet force planning. The threat of a counteroffensive will lead the Soviets to make their offensive drive as strong as possible in order to advance as far as they can and do as much damage as they can to NATO's defensive forces and thus to postpone or blunt NATO's counteroffensive possibilities. The threat of a retaliatory offensive, on the other hand, will lead the Soviets to worry about their defensive capabilities and hence to deploy their forces more evenly across the entire front. A counteroffensive threat, in short, will lead the Soviets to strengthen their offense; a retaliatory offensive threat will lead them to weaken it.

NATO adoption of a conventional retaliatory option would thus pose a new problem to the Soviets. The Soviet military forces in Europe are now almost entirely offensively oriented. Soviet doctrine places overwhelming emphasis on the importance of the offensive and, in particular, on the need for both speed and surprise so as to achieve Soviet objectives before NATO reinforcements arrive and NATO decides to use nuclear weapons. At present the Soviets are free to develop their plans and forces for a lightning and overpowering offensive into Western Europe without having to worry about any defensive needs, other than air defense. The Soviets, as Richard Burt has observed, "have designed and trained a force to attack, not to defend. Whatever their ultimate plans, the Soviets have deployed their forces to seize territory, not to hold it."[13] They have been able to do this, however, only

---

12. See, for example, Richard B. Remnek, "A Possible Fallback Counteroffensive Option in a European War," Unpublished paper, Airpower Research Institute, Air University, Maxwell Air Force Base, Alabama, 1983.

13. Richard Burt, "The Alliance at a Crossroad," Address, Friedrich-Ebert-Stiftung, Bonn, December 2, 1981. Seè also European Security Study, *Strengthening Conventional Deterrence*, p. 55.

because NATO has permitted them to do so. NATO strategy has given the Soviet offensive a free ride. If, however, the Soviets also had to consider the possibility of a prompt NATO conventional offensive, they would either have to reallocate forces from offensive to defensive missions or to devote still more scarce resources to military purposes to meet this need.

The purpose of a conventional retaliatory option is to deter Soviet attack on Western Europe. The capability to exercise that option, however, could also contribute to the deterrence of Soviet aggressive moves in other parts of the world. At present the Soviets know that they could advance in force into the Persian Gulf area without having to worry about the security of their flank in central Europe. Their position is, in this respect, similar to that of Hitler in the 1930s. Although France had various commitments to Poland and the Little Entente, which presupposed, as DeGaulle argued, an offensively oriented army, it could not in fact pose any deterrent threat against Hitler's moving eastward because it had adopted a purely defensive strategy, symbolized by the Maginot Line. French military strategy left Hitler free to do what he wanted in Eastern Europe. In similar fashion, NATO forces do not now pose even a theoretical restraint on Soviet moves elsewhere. If, however, NATO were prepared to launch a military offensive into Eastern Europe, the Soviets would have to assure themselves as to the adequacy of their defenses there and as to the loyalty of their allies before they could take the offensive against Iran, Pakistan, China, Japan, or any other neighboring state.[14]

The point is sometimes made that NATO is a defensive alliance and that a defensive alliance requires a defensive strategy. This argument has no basis in logic or history. NATO is a defensive alliance politically, which means that its purpose is to protect its members against Soviet attack through deterrence if possible and through defense if necessary. There is, however, no reason why a politically defensive alliance cannot have a militarily offensive strategy. Such a strategy may, indeed, be essential to securing the deterrent purposes of the alliance. For two decades NATO did in fact pursue its purposes primarily through the threat of launching a strategic nuclear offensive against the Soviet Union. If a nuclear offensive is compatible with the defensive purposes of the Alliance, certainly a conventional offensive should be also. Given long-standing NATO reliance on the possible first use

---

14. For elaboration of this point, see Huntington, "Renewal of Strategy," in Huntington, ed., *Strategic Imperative*, pp. 24–29.

of tactical nuclear weapons and, if necessary, strategic retaliation against the Soviet Union itself, it would be rather anomalous for its members to find something unduly abhorrent about a conventional offensive into Eastern Europe. On moral and political grounds, surely it is far more desirable to deter by threatening to liberate Eastern Europeans than by threatening to incinerate Russians.

The Military Feasibility of Conventional Retaliation

At this point, the reader may well be saying to himself: "Your argument is all wonderful in theory, *but* (a) as you've pointed out, NATO is not meeting its own already-established conventional buildup goals, and (b) the strategy you advocate would require a buildup far larger than anything NATO has contemplated. Conventional retaliation just is not practical." The question is: What are the military requirements of a conventional retaliatory offensive?

The answer is not as great as one might think.

First, it is necessary to clear away the popular cliché that the offensive requires a three-to-one overall superiority. If this were the case, NATO's problems would be over. Under no circumstances, given the current balance and probable rates of mobilization on each side, could the Warsaw Pact achieve an overall three-to-one superiority over NATO. Most scenarios do not deviate much from Fischer's 1976 estimate that Pact superiority in men in combat units would peak at about 2:1 two weeks after Pact mobilization began, assuming NATO mobilization lagged one week.[15] Unfortunately, however, 3:1 overall superiority is not what is required to attack. It is instead what may be required at the exact point of attack. Achieving that superiority is the product not of overall superiority in numbers but rather of superiority in mobility, concentration of forces, deception, and surprise.

Second, while the Soviets clearly do have a significant conventional superiority in Europe in numerical terms, that superiority is not enough, in itself, to give them a decisive advantage. In 1981, Pact superiority in divisional manpower was roughly 1.36:1, but in terms of overall manpower there was almost equality, with a ratio of 1.09:1. The Pact had many more tanks than NATO, but NATO was better off in attack aircraft. In terms of armored

---

15. Robert Lucas Fischer, *Defending the Central Front: The Balance of Forces*, Adelphi Paper No. 127 (London: International Institute for Strategic Studies, 1976), pp. 24–25.

division equivalents (ADEs), perhaps the single most useful measure, the ratio was 1.2:1. Overall the Pact wins the numerical bean count, but it does not have an advantage which would guarantee victory in war.[16] If a high probability currently exists of the Soviets' achieving substantial success in a central European war, that stems as much from their strategy as from their numbers. They are planning to concentrate their forces and use them offensively in the most militarily effective manner possible, while NATO has, for a variety of understandable reasons, been committed to a defensive strategy which almost ensures military defeat.

Third, a force which is inferior in overall strength can still pursue an offensive strategy. History is full of successful examples. The German offensive into France in 1940 and the North Vietnamese offensive in 1975 are two such cases. As U.S. Army FM 100-5 points out, other examples are the Third Army's attack through France in 1944, the U.S. offensive in Korea in 1951, and the Israeli Sinai campaign of 1967. In these cases, as in Grant's Vicksburg campaign (cited at length in FM 100-5 as a model offensive), the attackers succeeded "by massing unexpectedly where they could achieve a brief local superiority and by preserving their initial advantage through relentless exploitation."[17]

Obviously, stronger forces are more desirable than weaker ones. Implementing a strategy that includes conventional retaliation, however, requires more changes in the NATO military mind-set than it does in NATO military forces. For thirty years NATO has thought about conventional warfare exclusively in defensive terms. It has assumed that all the ground war and the bulk of the war generally would be fought in West Germany. It has pursued a strategy of forward defense, entirely defensible and necessary in terms of German interests, that leaves NATO forces strung out along the entire eastern border of the Federal Republic and hence highly vulnerable to an overpowering Soviet concentration of offensive forces. It has, moreover, done this without being able, also for understandable political reasons, to construct major fortifications that could slow down and greatly complicate a Soviet

---

16. For two excellent analyses emphasizing the uncertainties on the Central Front, see John J. Mearsheimer, "Why the Soviets Can't Win Quickly in Central Europe," *International Security*, Vol. 7, No. 1 (Summer 1982), pp. 5–39, and Anthony H. Cordesman, "The NATO Central Front and the Balance of Uncertainty," *Armed Forces Journal International*, Vol. 120 (July 1983), pp. 18–58.
17. U.S. Army, *FM 100-5 Operations* (20 August 1982), p. 8-5.

attack. NATO developed, as *The Economist* put it, "a Maginot-line mentality without the Maginot line."[18]

Fortunately there are signs that this mentality may be changing. SHAPE is developing plans for the deep interdiction of Warsaw Pact second-echelon forces. The aim is to locate Pact follow-on forces through improved intelligence and to attack them with long-range conventional means before they reach the battle zone, while at the same time NATO forces are holding the forward defense line against Pact first-echelon forces. It is, as General Rogers said, a way of adding "depth to the battlefield by extending the area of NATO's operations into the *enemy's* rear area."[19] A conventional retaliatory offensive as proposed here is compatible with and would supplement this emphasis on deep interdiction. It would involve NATO operations into the enemy's rear at the operational rather than simply the tactical level. It would employ not just conventional PGMs and missiles but the full range of conventional combined arms, and it would also serve to disrupt enemy logistics and reinforcements. Similarly, a retaliatory offensive is highly compatible with U.S. Army AirLand Battle doctrine, with its emphasis on the initiative, deep attack, and maneuver: "*Initiative*, the ability to set the terms of the battle by action, *is the greatest advantage in war*. . . . The offense is the decisive form of war, the commander's only means of attaining a positive goal or of completely destroying the enemy force."[20] There are at least some signs that German military thinking may be moving in a similar direction.[21]

A strategy with an offensive component would better capitalize on the current capabilities of NATO forces in Europe than does a purely defensive strategy. By and large, these forces are heavy forces; two-thirds of the Allied divisions in Germany are armor divisions; most of the rest are mechanized infantry. It is often said, of course, that these forces will enable NATO to have a mobile defense and to launch counteroffensives. That is true, and the

---

18. "Thrust counter-thrust," *The Economist*, May 9, 1981, p. 15: "Nato . . . should plan an armoured counter-thrust towards the Warsaw pact's rear areas from the part of the front that is not under communist attack. The knowledge that such a counter-offensive was part of Nato's strategy would, at the very least, complicate the Soviet plan of attack. It could even prevent the attack from happening. The Warsaw pact should not have the luxury of thinking that attack is its monopoly."
19. Rogers, "Greater Flexibility for NATO's Flexible Response," p. 17.
20. U.S. Army, *FM 100-5*, pp. 7-2, 8-1.
21. See K.-Peter Stratmann, "Prospective Tasks and Capabilities Required for NATO's Conventional Forces," in European Security Study, *Strengthening Conventional Deterrence*, p. 163.

same qualities also make them suited for a retaliatory offense. It is a misuse of expensive resources to consign these heavy forces primarily to a defensive role. In addition, NATO's forward defense strategy has always caused problems with respect to how Allied forces in the various sectors could reinforce each other. If the Soviets, for instance, launch their principal attack across the North German plain, what role could the substantial American and German forces in southern Germany play in bringing that advance to a halt? To move those forces laterally, that is parallel to the front, would be a logistical nightmare and could leave Bavaria open to a secondary Soviet attack. Not to move those forces northward, on the other hand, would greatly facilitate the Soviets' overwhelming the NATO forces in the north. The most efficient use of any substantial Allied forces not close to the Soviet attack corridors is to carry the war to the enemy.

The solution to NATO's deterrence problem is not to be found in any particular technological or doctrinal gimmick. It requires a diversified effort including more resources, qualitative improvements, and strategic innovations. Preparing for a retaliatory offensive will not do it alone, but it cannot be done without preparing for a retaliatory offensive.

In practical terms, what might a retaliatory offensive look like?

If the threat of such an offensive is to serve its deterrent purpose, the Soviets must have good reason to believe that an offensive is possible and little knowledge as to exactly where and when it might occur. NATO military planning for such an offensive would have to encompass a variety of alternative scenarios and possible options reflecting:

a. Warsaw Pact deployments and axes of advance;
b. NATO force capabilities and deployments;
c. East European politics, which might dictate withholding or limiting NATO offensive actions.

It is clearly not possible to spell out in this paper detailed plans for a NATO offensive. Many different possibilities exist. To give some idea as to what could be involved, however, it might be desirable briefly to elaborate what is undoubtedly the most obvious scenario for both Soviet and NATO planners. Because it is the most obvious scenario, it could also be one which is unlikely to be realized in practice.

Three of the most probable Soviet invasion routes are across the North German plain to Hannover and then northward towards Bremen and Hamburg, through the Göttingen corridor towards the Ruhr, and through the

**POSSIBLE SOVIET OFFENSIVES AND
NATO RETALIATORY OFFENSIVES**

Fulda Gap towards Frankfurt. These attacks would be led by the powerful Third Shock Army (which includes 4 tank divisions and one motorized rifle [MR] division) in the center of the front and the 2nd Guards Tank Army (1 tank and 2 MR divisions) to the north.[22] They would engage the Dutch, German, British, and Belgian forces in NORTHAG and the III German and V American Corps in CENTAG. In these circumstances, the most appropriate retaliatory offensive would be by the VII American and II German Corps plus the 12th Panzer Division from the III German Corps. These are among the strongest and best equipped Allied forces in Central Europe; their Leopard II and Abrams tanks would provide the heart of the offensive thrust.

The offensive could well consist of two prongs. The major thrust would be through the Hof corridor towards Jena and Leipzig. Its primary axis of advance would not be west-east but rather south-north, and hence the problem of river barriers would be minimized. The Soviet forces immediately on the scene include the three motorized rifle divisions and one tank division of the 8th Guards Army, headquartered in Weimar. Such an offensive would threaten the most direct Soviet supply routes supporting their forces in the Fulda Gap. The second prong would be launched in a more easterly direction towards Karlovy Vary and Teplice in Czechoslovakia. The immediate Soviet resistance would come from a single division deployed north of Pilsen. If this advance reached the Elbe, it could then either swing north towards Dresden or south towards Prague. The second prong would also help protect the southern and eastern flanks of the main prong.

The Allied forces engaged in these offensive moves would be superior in manpower, tanks, and ADEs to the Soviet forces immediately deployed against them. To the north and east of the 8th Guards Army, however, is the 1st Guards Tank Army. It is roughly comparable to the 3rd Shock Army and clearly is designed to make a major contribution to the Soviet offensive into West Germany. If it joined that offensive, however, the Soviets would have to face the possibility of the Allies' overrunning their other forces in the south. If they used the 1st Guards Tank Army to blunt the Allied offensive, they would risk not achieving their breakthrough in the north. The

---

22. Information on the deployments and strengths of Soviet and Allied forces comes from: Fischer, *Defending the Central Front*; Cordesman, "The NATO Central Front," pp. 18ff.; and John Erickson, *Soviet–Warsaw Pact Force Levels* (Washington: United States Strategic Institute, Report 76-2, 1976). For simplicity's sake, the discussion here is couched purely in terms of deployed forces, without reference to the reinforcements possible on both sides. In addition, the data used are meant to be illustrative, not necessarily definitively accurate.

purpose of a retaliatory offensive is to confront them with precisely that sort of dilemma.

Allied military dispositions should supplement political and diplomatic measures in helping to minimize the enthusiasm of satellite forces for the Soviet cause. The Allied offensive should be directed at Soviet forces. The thrust into East Germany should be primarily by German forces and that into Czechoslovakia exclusively by American ones. At present the deployment of Allied forces in Bavaria is not the most satisfactory from this point of view, although it would not necessarily prevent Allied forces from being used in this manner. The movement of Allied divisions into East Germany and Czechoslovakia could also be supplemented by the infiltration by sea and air into Poland and Hungary of specially trained Special Forces units to encourage disaffection and resistance in those countries.

For many years NATO strategists have bemoaned the deployment of Allied forces in Germany, a legacy of the occupation, which left U.S. forces in the south, some distance from the highly probable Soviet axis of advance across the North German Plain. This deployment is, however, made to order for a retaliatory offensive. It places U.S. forces as well as German forces in a favorable location for a move into the heart of East Germany which would be highly threatening to Soviet lines of communication (LOCs). In addition, the French forces in southern Germany constitute a reserve which could reinforce Allied forces in the Frankfurt area or respond to any Soviet counteroffensive against Germany, e.g., through Austria.

How successful would be a retaliatory offensive such as this? That clearly would depend, among other things, on:

—the size, character, and leadership of the NATO forces committed to the offensive;
—the strength and readiness of the opposing Warsaw Pact forces;
—the degree of surprise NATO achieved; and
—the extent to which non-Soviet Warsaw Pact forces fought vigorously alongside their Soviet allies.

Just how these factors would play out is impossible to predict in advance. At one extreme, it is conceivable although unlikely that NATO forces could sweep north towards the Baltic and join up with amphibious forces in a giant pincer movement cutting East Germany in half and isolating Soviet forces to the west. At the other extreme, they might penetrate only a few kilometers into East Germany and Czechoslovakia. The point is that neither side could know for sure in advance, and that uncertainty is precisely what is required to reinforce deterrence. The Soviets would only know that, if they went to war under these circumstances, they would be putting at risk far more of great value than they would be at present.

Some changes in NATO forces are desirable to enhance the feasibility of a conventional offensive. These would not necessarily involve expansion in force levels. They would, however, require:

a. redeployment of German forces in II Corps to positions closer to the inter-German border and compensating movement of some U.S. forces to positions on the Czech border;

b. major improvements, already called for in NATO plans, in stockpiles of fuel, ammunition, spare parts, equipment, and other supplies necessary to sustain an offensive movement; and

c. emphasis in weapons procurement on those items most relevant to offensive needs, e.g., attack aircraft, attack helicopters, long-range PGMs.

In addition to these actions, it would also be highly desirable to strengthen NATO defensive capabilities through the construction of fortifications and improvement in West German reserves and territorial forces. At present NATO follows a forward defense strategy but lacks forward fortifications. The principal reason for this has been the reluctance of the West German government to create a major fortified line that would give concrete embodiment to a permanent division of Germany. If, however, NATO strategy included provision for the invasion and liberation of at least portions of East Germany, a fortified line along the inter-German border would no longer have the symbolism that the Bonn government fears. The construction of such a line would, of course, make it possible to release additional Allied forces to offensive missions. The same result will also be achieved to the extent that territorial army units play a larger role in area defense.[23]

The special requirements for a conventional offensive capability will obviously compete with other claims on the modest and only slowly growing

---

23. See, for example, the supportive but contrasting views of Steven L. Canby, "Territorial Defense in Central Europe," *Armed Forces and Society,* Vol. 7 (Fall 1980), pp. 51–67, and Waldo L. Freeman, Jr., *NATO Central Region Forward Defense: Correcting the Strategy/Force Mismatch* (Washington, D.C.: National Defense University Research Directorate, National Security Affairs Issue Paper Series 81-3, 1981).

NATO resources. The central criterion for allocating resources among these competing claims, however, should be the extent to which they contribute to deterrence. Improvements in NATO defensive capabilities strengthen deterrence, but only marginally so. At the most they simply require the Soviets to invest comparable additional resources in their forces so as to maintain the same probability of success. Enhancement of NATO offensive capabilities, on the other hand, confronts the Soviets with an entirely new danger in terms of Allied penetration into and disruption of their Eastern European empire. It thus forces them to set this risk off against the advantages of attacking NATO and to mobilize or to divert resources from other sources if they are to meet that threat. A given increase in NATO offensive capabilities, in short, will produce a considerably higher return in terms of deterrence than the same investment in defensive capabilities. As a result, this addition to NATO strategy will also lower the total new resources NATO needs to invest to achieve effective deterrence. It could make conventional deterrence not only more credible but also cheaper than it would otherwise be.

The Politics of Conventional Retaliation

If conventional retaliation is strategically desirable and militarily feasible, the final question is whether it is politically possible. Will the Alliance agree to this amendment to the long-standing strategic doctrines set forth in MC 14/3?

Some may say that this proposal involves a fundamental change in NATO strategy for which it will be difficult if not impossible to mobilize support within the Alliance. In fact, however, incorporation of a conventional retaliatory offensive into NATO's strategy would, in many respects, be less a change in strategy than an effort to prevent a change in strategy. As it is, flexible response is inexorably becoming a dead letter. NATO strategy is changing fundamentally from a multi-pronged flexible response to a single-prong conventional defense. The addition of a conventional retaliatory option would, as the figures on p. 41 indicate, simply restore some element of flexibility to a strategy that is rapidly becoming inflexible. It would pose new uncertainties for the Soviet Union. It would adapt flexible response to the conditions of the 1980s. In similar fashion, a retaliatory offensive is not incompatible with the idea of forward defense. The latter is a necessary and appropriate response to German concern that as little of their country as possible become the locus of battle and subject to Soviet occupation. A retaliatory offensive would move at least some of the battle from West Germany to East Germany and Czechoslovakia. It is thus not a substitute for a strategy of flexible response and forward defense, broadly conceived, but rather a fleshing out of that strategy in changed circumstances. It would, in effect, make flexible response more flexible and forward defense more forward.

Adoption of a conventional retaliatory option would reinvigorate flexible response through conscious choice. Inevitably, the political feasibility of making such a conscious choice is a function of time and circumstance. In democratic societies, no new policy suggestion is immediately feasible. Every new proposal has to go through a process of discussion, consideration, analysis, amendment, and often initial rejection before it becomes reality. This is true in military policy as well as domestic policy, and it is doubly true in *alliance* military policy. The changes in NATO strategy in the mid-1950s and in the mid-1960s each required about five years to be implemented. There is no reason to think that the time required for change in the mid-1980s will be much different, nor to think that such change will not occur.

A broad consensus already exists on the need to enhance conventional deterrence. The political support of NATO governments and peoples for moving in this direction will in due course emerge, as is true of any new policy, from consideration of the unpalatability of the alternatives. In this instance, there are, broadly speaking, two such alternatives. One is to acquiesce in a greatly weakened deterrent, as the credibility of a U.S. nuclear response declines. This is, in terms of short-range politics, unquestionably the easiest way out, but it is one which also will have its political costs in terms of both heightened Soviet influence over alliance members and heightened political tensions among alliance members. The other alternative to effective conventional deterrence is to recreate a credible nuclear deterrent. Nuclear deterrence of a conventional attack is most credible—and, indeed, may *only* be credible—when the national existence of the deterring state is at risk. No one doubts that an Israeli government would use nuclear weapons to prevent Arab armies from overrunning Tel Aviv. A similar rationale furnishes the explicit justification for the French nuclear force and the implicit justification for the British one. Nuclear deterrence could be restored in central Europe if an independent, invulnerable, modest-sized German nuclear force were brought into being. The Soviets would have to believe that such a force would be used in the event of a Soviet attack on the Federal Republic. The political problems involved in the creation of such a force, however, dwarf those that arise from adoption of a conventional retaliation strategy.[24]

The strategic environment in the United States is increasingly favorable towards conventional retaliation becoming a NATO option. The other key locus of decision-making is the Federal Republic. One would think that German leaders would endorse a military strategy that, in comparison to the alternatives, promised to produce stronger deterrence at lower cost, to reduce the probability that nuclear weapons would be used in the territory of the Federal Republic, and to shift at least some of the fighting, if war did occur, from the Federal Republic to East Germany and Czechoslovakia. It is hard to see why it might be good politics in West Germany to oppose such a move. If, after the normal debate necessary for policy innovation in any democratic country, the West German government was unwilling to support such a change, the United States would clearly have to reconsider its commitment of forces to a strategy and posture that is doomed to be found wanting. "For deterrence to be credible," as General Rogers has said, "it requires capabilities adequate for successful defense and effective retaliation."[25] Effective retaliation means credible retaliation, and, in today's world, credible retaliation means conventional retaliation. That is the inescapable logic that will drive NATO's strategic choices in this decade.

---

24. For further discussion of this option, see Huntington, "Broadening the Strategic Focus."
25. Rogers, "Greater Flexibility for NATO's Flexible Response," p. 15.

Constraints on America's Conduct of Small Wars

Eliot A. Cohen

$\mathbf{I}$t is the characteristic military dilemma of a world power that it finds itself forced to prepare for two entirely different kinds of wars, large-scale conflicts on the continent of Europe, on the one hand, and lesser battles on its periphery or on other continents, on the other. This difficulty perplexed British statesmen throughout the latter nineteenth and early twentieth centuries; it is now the problem of the United States, Britain's heir as the foremost global power. This article examines the constraints on America's ability to prepare for, wage, and win small wars.

It is often argued that American statesmen will find themselves constrained from using force in the future by public and Congressional repugnance over a repetition of the Vietnam experience. There is some truth in this. What follows, however, will suggest that institutional constraints and to a lesser extent foreign pressures, rather than the vagaries of public opinion, will inhibit American leaders from commencing such wars, and from prosecuting them successfully.

We begin by addressing three questions: What precisely do we mean by the term "small war"? Why is there reason to think that such wars are inevitable? How do the requirements of preparing for such wars differ from the normal military measures of a Great Power?

The Small War Problem

At the end of the last century, British strategists defined small wars as conflicts waged against the forces of the lesser powers, to include indigenous guerrilla-type movements.[1] Today, we would include in our definition wars

---

The author is grateful to Robert Blackwill, David Cohen, Judith Cohen, Aaron Friedberg, Samuel Huntington, William Kristol, Arie Ofri, Stephen Rosen, Andrew Ross, Scott Sagan, and Stephen Walt for their comments on earlier drafts of this article.

Eliot A. Cohen is Assistant Professor of Government and Allston Burr Senior Tutor in Quincy House at Harvard University.

---

1. Definition derived in part from Cyril Falls, *A Hundred Years of War* (New York: Collier, 1953); C.E. Callwell, *Small Wars* (London: HMSO, 1906), pp. 21–24.

International Security, Fall 1984 (Vol. 9, No. 2) 0162-2889/84/020151-31 $02.50/1

waged against the proxy forces of other Great Powers. For the British, this type of conflict—"wars of the second or third magnitude"—characterized by "relative unimportance, long duration, or unfavorable climatic conditions" posed the greatest challenge to their military system.[2] They tailored their military establishment and system of high command to cope with this problem, even at the expense of their capacity to intervene in European warfare.

I will use the term "small war" rather than "limited war" here for a number of reasons. First, I thereby exclude the consideration of limited nuclear warfare, which provided the subject matter for many of the first American treatises on limited war in the 1950s (for example, Henry Kissinger's *Nuclear Weapons and Foreign Policy*). Although the possibility (a remote one) of controlled nuclear exchanges between the superpowers exists and should be studied, it must be considered separately from the much more likely contingencies of conventional warfare. Limited nuclear war involves consideration of means (theater and strategic nuclear weapons and advanced command and control technology), ends (above all, avoidance of escalation to cataclysmic levels of destruction), and political conditions (acute anxiety and extremely brief periods of time available for choice) quite different from those of conventional small war.

The term "limited war" also includes the possibility of direct conventional engagement between the superpowers when such conflicts remain regionally contained. In public at least, soldiers and statesmen argue that programs and policies to prepare for conventional war on a less than total scale have as their primary purpose deterrence or containment of Soviet conventional aggression. This has been most noticeably true in the case of the Persian Gulf: policymakers have justified the creation of the Rapid Deployment Force, since its inception, as a measure to counter Soviet conventional threats to the region.[3]

For a variety of political reasons, soldiers and statesmen find it easiest to justify force procurement aimed at deterring, or at least containing, Soviet aggression. The Soviet Union poses the greatest overall threat to American interests and forces, particularly in an age when its capability to project power overseas has grown enormously. On the other hand, the history of the past three decades suggests that armed conflict between the United States

---

2. Frederick Sleigh Roberts, *Facts and Fallacies* (London: John Murray, 1911), pp. 151–152.
3. See Harold Brown, *Annual Report of the Secretary of Defense, Fiscal Year 1982* (Washington: U.S. Government Printing Office, 1981), pp. 81–83.

and the Soviet Union is the *least* likely contingency America faces. In every postwar crisis which involved potential direct military conflict between the two superpowers—in Iran, Berlin, Korea, Cuba, Vietnam, and the Middle East—both sides have exercised great restraint, hoping to avert all-out war by avoiding the slightest direct hostilities. American troops have actually *fought* only Soviet clients or allies and, occasionally, autonomous but no less hostile powers.

The rules for limited engagement with the Soviets differ from those with lesser powers. In the former case, preemptive deployment of troops to serve as a tripwire may either signal resolve or force on the opponent the onus of unwelcome escalation. In such situations (as during the Cuban missile crisis or as might happen in the Persian Gulf), the successful application of force—military victory—is far less important than the use of military force as a means of communication. In most cases, the highest political leadership will exercise extremely tight control over deployments and actions, even at the expense of militarily sound procedure. A case in point is the shrinkage of the American naval quarantine of Cuba in 1962 to allow the Soviets more time to back down.

The term "low-intensity conflict" has come into vogue more recently to define wars waged against Third World opponents.[4] This too is inaccurate however. From the point of view of the average company commander in Vietnam, there was nothing low in intensity about the conflict, and the heavy casualty rates of the war's peak period compare with those of some World War II battles. Moreover, in the future (particularly in the Persian Gulf), we may expect to see American forces committed against indigenous forces equipped with a variety of modern weapons, from high-performance aircraft to modern main battle tanks. The term "low-intensity warfare" suggests conflicts which can be handled by a few thousand specialists: the reality is that such wars may require the services of tens or even hundreds of thousands of combat and support troops. Thus, where the term "limited war" is too all-inclusive to be useful, the term "low-intensity warfare" excessively narrows the scope of our concern.

The question of terminology is an important one, for the proper term forces us to confront the messy military and political realities small wars embody and the military and political costs they exact. The likelihood of

---

4. See Sam C. Sarkesian and William L. Scully, eds., *U.S. Policy and Low Intensity Conflict* (New Brunswick: Transaction Books, 1981).

direct U.S.–Soviet conflict is low, but military bureaucracies suffer few political costs in publicly planning to meet such contingencies; such scenarios are, moreover, organizationally congenial to institutions still gripped by the model of World War II. Hence, the public strategic debate has an air of unreality about it. Government officials, experts of various kinds, and politicians talk about the least likely war, and the armed forces prepare for it. When the small war problem does arise, statesmen express the vain hope that such conflicts can be referred to small, specially designed agencies and forces.

Inevitably, the United States will fight small wars, and hence ought to allocate a large proportion of its military resources to preparing to cope with them. More importantly, it must prepare its institutions to fight such wars. Postwar history (Vietnam, Korea, and lesser conflicts such as the Lebanese intervention in 1958, the Dominican Republic affair in 1965, and the Grenada invasion/rescue of 1983) reveals that these are the kinds of wars Americans have fought for over a generation. To be sure, the advent of the Nixon Doctrine has lessened the chances that American troops will find themselves committed to combat before every effort has been made to train and equip local forces. Nonetheless, by treaty and informal agreement the United States has committed itself to the defense of a number of states, all of which could very easily find themselves subject to attack by stronger Third World states: the most prominent examples include South Korea, Thailand, Saudi Arabia, Oman, Sudan, and Honduras. In many cases, American troops are already deployed in these states, either for training or simply as a symbol of American intentions. Nor does the American public, by and large, disapprove of these commitments.

America's need to prepare for small wars flows directly from its role in the postwar world as the preeminent maritime power and the leader of the Western bloc of nations. Such a position requires (as, under similar circumstances, it did of Great Britain) a readiness and a capability to fight small wars to maintain its world position and the global balance of power outside the continent of Europe. The creation of the Rapid Deployment Force (now Central Command) in the late 1970s highlighted one of several major overseas interests of the United States, namely, American interest in the secure and continuous flow of oil to the industrial economies of Western Europe and Japan. In most cases, the United States is the only Western power capable of promptly and substantially reinforcing a Third World state under attack or of sustaining a substantial military commitment should that become necessary. Even the two most important ex-colonial powers, Britain and France, find themselves at least partially dependent on American logistic support for their operations overseas, as the French counterintervention in Zaire in 1978 and the Falklands War of 1982 demonstrated.

During the past decade, American military commitments abroad have, if anything, expanded beyond their 1950 limits. The Carter Doctrine extended American military commitments to the Persian Gulf; turmoil in Central America and the growth of Soviet forces in Cuba have recently forced renewed military attention to that region; the activities of Libya threaten the stability of a number of North African countries, including Chad and Sudan; Libyan airplanes have actually engaged American naval aircraft in the Mediterranean. Even in southeast Asia the potential for a recommitment of American forces remains, as Thailand has come under pressure from a Vietnamese Communist state consolidating its hold on Indochina. In all of these cases, the potential exists for American use of force against hostile minor powers; in many cases, that potential is growing. Three examples of small wars one would imagine the United States fighting in the next decade are: a war to preserve the independence of Honduras, Costa Rica, and Panama; a war to prevent Iranian disruption of Western and Japanese oil supplies; a war to preserve the independence of Thailand.

None of the above should be construed as an argument that small war is anything but a sad necessity; certainly, it is not a foreign policy instrument of choice. Nonetheless, unless one is prepared to advocate a modified form of isolationism—a repudiation of foreign policy commitments outside Europe and Japan, for example—one must confront the need for a small war capability. Small wars present, therefore, a unique military challenge and an inevitable one. Our larger questions remain: What constraints will delay or prevent future American small wars? How will these constraints affect American conduct of such wars once the government embarks on them?

Public Opinion as a Constraint

We can distinguish three types of political constraints on the waging of small wars, all of which were intensified by the war in Vietnam. The first of these is public opinion, i.e., public revulsion against any kind of military commitment which could involve American troops in a war such as that which took 50,000 American lives in the jungles of Southeast Asia. It is axiomatic in American politics that the American people want "no more Vietnams"; thus, it is assumed, popular opinion will severely limit the willingness of the American people to support a similar kind of war. Although it is conceivable that an American administration could engage in war despite the vehement disapproval of the American public, few politicians would care to do so, realizing as they must the likely consequences for their chances of future success and reputation.

How would the American public react to a small war in the future? The answer is by no means as simple as the "Vietnam syndrome" argument would suggest. For one thing, it is important to realize the complexity of American public opinion *vis-à-vis* the Vietnam War and its remarkable similarity to that in the Korean War.[5] In both cases, the war received a high degree of initial support, declining steadily but surprisingly slowly as American casualties increased and the prospects of success dimmed. Indeed, in retrospect, it is remarkable that it was not until after three years of combat—in the case of Vietnam, until 1968—that a majority of the American public finally turned against the war.

The experience of the Grenada operation of October 1983 would seem to confirm this: elite disapproval and media skepticism did not prevent the operation from being an extremely popular one. To be sure, the invasion went smoothly and ended very quickly. It took place virtually next door to the United States, had as its avowed purpose the rescue of American citizens (who later appeared grateful for the effort), and received the fervent support of a half dozen small local democracies. If any military operation should have been popular, in fact, it was the invasion (or liberation) of Grenada. The willingness of the American public to tolerate a much more ambiguous, much more distant, and far bloodier military presence in Lebanon was more significant.

Most studies of popular opinion in small wars rely heavily on public opinion polls, which is understandable. Nonetheless, in order to assess the political consequences of public opinion—in other words, its effects on real policy decisions—one must look beyond the polls. Indeed, only if we do so can we understand why Vietnam seemed to contemporary observers to have generated far more antiwar sentiment than Korea, even though both wars exhibit a similar public opinion profile. The political reality of vociferous opposition in the streets played the dominant role in influencing political

---

5. This is a theme of John E. Mueller, *War, Presidents, and Public Opinion* (New York: John Wiley and Sons, 1973). See in particular pp. 23–66.

leaders, although political leaders were aware of and concerned by the larger slippage in public support revealed in the polls.

The depth of anti-Vietnam sentiment stemmed in part from the length of the war, as John Mueller points out in his comparative study of public opinion in Korea and Vietnam. The antiwar movement, however, drew its strength primarily from the existence of a large, vocal, and politically active group of middle and upper-middle class draft-aged youth. As the coordinator of the Vietnam Moratorium Committee between 1969 and 1970 put it:

[A] fundamental reason for the failure [*sic*] of the antiwar movement was overdependence on upper-middle-class draftable young men. This is a notion I resisted for a long time.[6]

The Korean War draft was much more popular than its Vietnam successor for a number of reasons. Among these was the legitimacy of conscription following World War II (proposals for more radical forms of military service such as Universal Military Training were extremely popular in the polls). The universality of the Korean War draft (over three-quarters of the eligible cohort served in the military) helped contain popular disenchantment with the war. During Vietnam, by way of contrast, the Selective Service draft inducted less than 50 percent of the eligible young men. Whereas in Korea military service was correctly perceived as a virtually inevitable responsibility, by the time of Vietnam it was a burden to be avoided by adroit manipulation of the draft deferment and exemption rules.[7] Paradoxically, a system of selection which offered a good chance of escaping military service fostered more opposition than an all-inclusive draft. More importantly, the initial stages of the Korean War were fought by reservists, most of them World War II veterans recalled for over a year of service. There could be no question thereafter of a twenty-year-old's draft call seeming unusually harsh or unreasonable: rather, he was being asked to make a sacrifice already made in greater degree by older men. Of course, the nature and timing of the war—its beginning with a clear-cut act of aggression and its occurrence at the very opening of the Cold War—made it more acceptable than might otherwise have been the case.

---

6. Anthony Lake, ed., *The Vietnam Legacy* (New York: New York University Press, 1976), p. 124. See also Peter Osnos's similar observations on pp. 69, 112. In addition, see Michael Charlton and Anthony Moncrieff, *Many Reasons Why* (New York: Hill and Wang, 1978), pp. 162–165. For another view from a college student at the time, see Steven Kelman, *Push Comes to Shove* (Boston: Houghton Mifflin, 1970), pp. 117–120.
7. On the Vietnam era draft, see Lawrence M. Baskir and William A. Strauss, *Chance and Circumstance* (New York: Alfred A. Knopf, 1978).

In addition, the nature of antiwar sentiment in the American public varied greatly. As John P. Roche has put it, working class opposition to the Vietnam War could be summed up by a phrase that recurred in letters to the President: "end the —ing war and shoot the —ing draft dodgers."[8] As policymakers knew, much of centrist antiwar sentiment stemmed from a frustrated desire to finish the war victoriously and reasonably quickly. The major reason given in *The Pentagon Papers* for President Johnson's unwillingness to mobilize the reserves to fight the Vietnam War was administration fear that a massive call-up would create pressure to *expand* the war, perhaps to include the use of nuclear weapons.

All of this is not to say that the Vietnam War had no effect on American public support for the use of force overseas: the forbearance shown by the public in 1965–1967 might not reappear in the late 1980s. Opposition to conscription and to military commitments abroad rose after Vietnam, and remains high to this day. A 1975 survey found that a majority of the public would favor U.S. military involvement in a foreign country, including the use of troops, only to defend Canada against invasion. By a narrow margin (41 percent to 39), they opposed the use of troops to defend Western Europe. The same poll, however, conducted again only three years later found a majority willing to fight for Europe; in 1980, majorities were willing to send troops to fight in Europe, the Persian Gulf, Japan, and Pakistan.[9] As the mass (though not necessarily the elite) public reaction to the Iranian hostage crisis of 1980 and the Grenada operation of 1983 (as well as the defense expansion of 1978–1983) indicated, opinion returned to its pre-Vietnam position in favor of a large peacetime military establishment and willingness to use force abroad. Nor has the Vietnam experience created a generational

---

8. There are numerous studies of public opinion and the Vietnam War. See *inter alia* Hazel Erskine, "The Polls: Is War a Mistake?," *Public Opinion Quarterly*, Vol. 34 (Spring 1970), pp. 134–150; Mueller, *War, Presidents, and Public Opinion*, especially pp. 148–152; Allen H. Barton, "The Columbia Crisis: Campus, Vietnam, and the Ghetto," *Public Opinion Quarterly*, Vol. 32 (Fall 1968), pp. 333–351; Ole R. Holsti and James N. Rosenau, "Vietnam, Consensus, and the Belief Systems of American Leaders," Paper delivered at the 1977 Hendicks Symposium on American Politics and World Order, University of Nebraska, October 6–7, 1977.

9. Compare John E. Rielly, ed., *American Public Opinion and U.S. Foreign Policy, 1975* (Chicago: Chicago Council on Foreign Relations, 1975), p. 18, with a similar table three years later (*American Public Opinion and U.S. Foreign Policy, 1978*, p. 26). Even more bellicosity is revealed in Bruce Russett and Donald R. DeLuca, "'Don't Tread On Me': Public Opinion and Foreign Policy in the Eighties," *Political Science Quarterly*, Vol. 96, No. 3 (Fall 1981), pp. 381–400. The table on p. 387 reveals an across-the-board increase in willingness to fight, i.e., an increase not simply attached to one country or region.

cleavage of major proportions, younger people taking "dovish" and their elders more "hawkish" positions, as some observers had expected it would.[10]

A final lesson can be derived from a study of British public opinion during the Falklands War of 1982. The British fought that war for the sake of some desolate islands that the British Foreign Office had long hoped to cede unobtrusively to Argentina. After the fact, all commentators agreed that it was an enormously popular war, one which enhanced the reputation and stature of the Prime Minister, Margaret Thatcher, who waged it. Yet when the naval task force was initially dispatched to the Falklands (with the approval of 60 percent of the public), less than half the population (44 percent in mid-April) thought the retaking of the Falklands worth a single British serviceman's death. And yet, six weeks later, after heavy fighting by sea and land, 62 percent of the population approved the war despite the human costs. Those who felt the retaking of the Falklands *not* worth loss of life totaled 49 percent of those polled in early April. By the end of May, they made up only 34 percent of the population.[11] This confirms earlier findings from Korea and Vietnam that public support for a war—even a war in a previously unfamiliar or marginal region of the world—increases once troops actually engage in fighting.[12]

All this is not to imply that popular support for small wars is automatic or wholehearted. An important factor in the case of the Falklands was the fact that the islands were British property, not a foreign country. At a deeper level, we find the phenomenon described by Tocqueville in his analysis of democracies at war:

No kind of greatness is more pleasing to the imagination of a democratic people than military greatness which is brilliant and sudden, won without hard work, by risking nothing but one's life.[13]

Small wars (the Falklands might prove an exception) offer few such prospects: they require long and patient efforts and offer little of the dramatic advances and victories which can characterize conventional warfare. Nonetheless, it is more surprising and important that democratic peoples have supported mi-

---

10. Ole R. Holsti and James N. Rosenau, "Does Where You Stand Depend on When You Were Born? The Impact of Generation on Post-Vietnam Foreign Policy Beliefs," *Public Opinion Quarterly*, Vol. 44, No. 1 (Spring 1980), pp. 1–22.
11. See *The Economist*, May 29, 1982.
12. A point made by Mueller in *War, Presidents, and Public Opinion*, p. 53.
13. Alexis de Tocqueville, *Democracy in America*, trans. George Lawrence (New York: Anchor Books, 1969), pp. 657–658.

nor conflicts waged in remote corners of the world and for obscure purposes for years at a time than that they have eventually turned against those wars. Support for Presidential authority, the instinct which leads citizens to rally around the flag in a time of crisis, and above all a sense of national pride (such as that displayed following the Grenada invasion in 1983) will ensure sufficient initial support to allow a President to initiate a small war. Thereafter, support must depend on such variables as the seeming ability to win the war, the justification for it, the President's skill at evoking popular support, and the nature of the burdens (particularly military service) it imposes. The point is not that the Vietnam syndrome does not exist: it does, and will exercise a restraint on American Presidents for some time. However, the effects of a public opinion shaped by the Vietnam War may be less than were originally expected, or at least more predictable.

A President has the power to start a war. The arguments we have examined here suggest that in the opening stages, at least, he will get popular support as well; difficulties will only mount as the war drags on.

International Politics as a Constraint

Undoubtedly, the most important change in world politics since 1946 has been the passing of the old colonial order and the associated transformation of the European role in world politics. Most of the small wars of the early postwar period—the Indochina war, the Algerian insurrection, the Malayan insurgency, and the war in Aden—were outgrowths of the decolonization of Africa and Asia. During this period, American policymakers found themselves torn: on the one hand, they were allied to European states which were willing and able to project force overseas and, on the other, they recognized the inevitability, and believed in the desirability, of the collapse of European hegemony outside Europe. The Suez crisis of 1956 revealed this contradiction with exceptional vividness.

By the end of the Vietnam period, the ambivalence had been resolved by external events, and, for the first time in their postwar history, the Americans found themselves uncomfortably isolated in both their willingness and their ability to use force overseas.[14] Where other states had contributed substantial

---

14. See Alfred Grosser, *The Western Alliance*, trans. Michael Shaw (New York: Vintage Books, 1982), pp. 237–243, for the European reaction to Vietnam.

or symbolic contingents of troops to fight under American command in Korea, Vietnam called forth only mistrust from allies who either feared a misdirection of American resources or simply thought the war an improper and unjust one. Where the problem in the 1950s had been to persuade the Europeans to reduce their military commitments overseas, the difficulty in the 1970s and 1980s was to get them to make appropriate efforts for their own defense and the projection of force overseas. The failure of President Carter's drive for a sustained 3 percent real growth in NATO defense budgets is a case in point.

There were some exceptions to this trend, of course. The Falklands War of 1982 revealed the willingness of the British to engage in military action in defense of their own interests, although the very narrowness of their margin of victory (indeed, the mere fact of the Argentine *coup de main*) revealed how greatly British power had shrunk since the late 1950s. The French continued to maintain a military sphere of influence in North Africa, although following the election of a Socialist President in the mid-1980s they exercised increasing restraint over their troop deployments there. Three European states contributed forces to aid the Lebanese government in 1983. More characteristic, however, was European reaction to the American creation of a Rapid Deployment Force in the late 1970s, and their often and publicly expressed mistrust of its utility as an instrument of policy. Equally striking was the uniformly hostile reaction of America's allies to the invasion of Grenada in 1983.

The character of the likely opponents in a small war, and more importantly the backers of those opponents, has changed as well. China has temporarily disappeared as a source of either military or even substantial ideological threat. Instead, the Soviet Union has emerged as the most likely backer of those states and movements America is likely to fight, and we have also seen the emergence of autonomous but no less anti-Western Third World states—Iran being the most notable example. Additionally, where analysts in the 1960s saw the threat as primarily one of subversion through the mechanism of "wars of national liberation," the 1980s witnessed the use of a mixture of unconventional and conventional means, particularly (but not exclusively) in Africa. This pattern first appeared during the Indochina War: in 1965, American troops engaged a Vietnamese enemy predominantly organized and equipped for guerrilla warfare; in 1972, it helped fight a much more conventionally organized force; and in 1975, its hapless South Vietnamese ally succumbed to a thoroughly conventional invasion, spearheaded by armored columns. These forces were sustained by a Soviet logistical and naval apparatus far greater than that of the 1950s and 1960s, and one comparable (if yet inferior) to that deployed by the United States. Throughout the 1970s and beyond, the Soviet Union displayed repeatedly (in Syria, Ethiopia, and other states) a capacity to transport vast quantities of arms to client states, and to provide proxy troops (Cubans primarily, but East Germans and others as well) to use them. Third World states demonstrated an increasing ability to acquire and use (in some cases, to manufacture) fairly sophisticated modern weaponry. The Iraqi use of indigenously manufactured poison gas in 1984 against Iran offers but one indication of the range of military options open to many Third World states.

The number of potential adversaries (most though not all of them Soviet clients or allies) has increased to include such geographically and culturally diverse states as Vietnam, Syria, Iran, Libya, Cuba, and Nicaragua. Whereas the small wars of the 1950s and the early 1960s were fought primarily against insurgent movements, by the late 1970s and early 1980s the prospect emerged of wars conducted against regional powers such as those listed above. The current crises in Chad, Lebanon, and Central America pose peculiar problems precisely because of their mixed quality and because, in most cases, war would entail a substantial conventional conflict with a regional medium power, coupled with a prolonged campaign of counterinsurgency. Moreover, for the first time since Korea, the increased conventional power of Third World states raises the possibility that, at least in the initial stages of a war, substantial American forces could meet defeat in the field. This possibility never really existed in Vietnam, where North Vietnamese efforts to duplicate the battle of Dienbienphu suffered a gory defeat in the face of overwhelming American firepower. The enormous increase in the quality and quantity of arms in the hands of Third World nations, coupled with increased organizational competence in the handling of such weapons, renders many local conventional balances far more even than before.

A further complicating factor is the role played by regional actors. In Central America, for example, the Contadora group of states (led by Venezuela and Mexico) can exercise influence quite independent of the United States. More importantly, perhaps, a desire to maintain a favorable attitude on the part of these states towards the United States is likely to constrain American Presidents from committing troops overseas. As late as the 1960s, Presidents could commit troops to operations in Latin America with only minimal attention to the wishes and opinions of the Latin American states.[15] This is no longer the case.

The political sensitivities of the regional powers (Egypt and Saudi Arabia, for example) and their real independence will constrain American ability to deploy substantial forces overseas. This trend has been particularly noticeable in the successful efforts of host nations to limit the flexibility of American military bases located in their countries. The European allies' uncooperative attitude towards American military movements during the October 1973 Middle East crisis is indicative of a more general trend.

In short, America is likely to fight its next small war with few and suspicious allies and against well-equipped enemies, some of them supported massively by the Soviet Union or its clients. War diplomacy played a minor role in Korea and Vietnam, but in the next conflict statesmen will have to act from the very beginning to neutralize opponents, woo neutrals, and reassure friends. This task is not an impossible one, as Britain's remarkable diplomatic successes (particularly in Europe) during the Falklands War indicated. It is, nonetheless, a major departure from the foreign policy independence with which American Presidents have been accustomed to operate.

Congress as a Constraint

From the point of view of each post-Vietnam administration, the most important inhibition on America's small war capabilities has been Congress, which, ever since the late Vietnam period, has attempted to erode Presidential authority to engage American troops in battle without its approval. In particular, after Congress passed the War Powers Act of 1973 over Presidential veto, it seemed to many observers that Presidential war-making power was on the ebb.[16]

We usually assume that greater Congressional involvement in war-making means greater restraint, although cases have occurred in the past (such as

---

15. See Abraham F. Lowenthal, *The Dominican Intervention* (Cambridge: Harvard University Press, 1972).

16. On the history and meaning of the War Powers Resolution, see: Cecil V. Crabb and Pat M. Holt, *Invitation To Struggle: Congress, the President, and Foreign Policy* (Washington: Congressional Quarterly Press, 1980); Pat M. Holt, *The War Powers Resolution: The Role of Congress in U.S. Armed Intervention* (Washington: American Enterprise Institute, 1978); Edward Keynes, *Undeclared War: Twilight Zone of Constitutional Power* (University Park: Pennsylvania State University Press, 1982); W. Taylor Reveley, *War Powers of the President and Congress* (Charlottesville: University Press of Virginia, 1981).

the Spanish–American War and possibly World War I) in which Congress displayed more interest in going to war than did the President. Nonetheless, the character of the modern Congress and the language of the War Powers Act itself make it likely that Congress will act as a restraining rather than a propelling force on a President bent on making war. The critical provision of the War Powers Act is Section 5(b), which requires that any American troops sent into combat be withdrawn after sixty days (or ninety, if the President declares that to be necessary) unless Congress has authorized the continuance of the commitment.

President Nixon found this paragraph particularly vexing, and said so in his veto of the measure.[17] The other provisions of the War Powers Act—the requirement for prompt reporting to Congress of imminent engagement in hostilities, and Congressional authority to require the withdrawal of troops—added no new powers to Congress and merely confirmed the existence of old ones. In any event, through its control of federal expenditure and military organization, Congress can effectively bring to a halt any military adventure or deployment it cares to. The novelty in Section 5(b) was the automatic brake it imposed on Presidentially inspired military adventures: simply by virtue of inaction, Congress could (in theory) cause a small war to cease.

This, the most potent instrument of the War Powers Act, has recently been called into question by the Supreme Court's striking down of the legislative veto as unconstitutional. Congress therefore must turn to the financial and legislative instruments it has used in the past (for example, the Cooper–Church Amendment of 1970, which prohibited the funding of American operations in Cambodia). The difficulty here is that *positive* Congressional action will always be inhibited in a crisis by the Presidency's inherent advantages—its superior sources of information, its ability to appeal to popular opinion, and above all the fact that it is a unitary actor and Congress a composite of 535 actors. The easy passage of the Tonkin Gulf Resolution in 1964 testified to that imbalance; six long years of warfare passed before Congress summoned up the will to repeal it. More recently, Congress endorsed a Presidential decision to deploy vulnerable American land forces in Lebanon for eighteen months, and to support them with air and naval firepower for that time, despite considerable public and official misgivings over their presence and a hideous loss of life in an attack on the Marine

---

17. Reveley, *War Powers of the President and Congress*, p. 295.

compound in October 1983. The Marines were subsequently withdrawn well before the year-and-a-half deadline, but more because of the fact that they lacked a useful mission to perform than because of Congressional pressure.

The most important aspect of the War Powers Act lies not in the restrictions it actually imposes on a President, but in its function as a starting point for any debate about military involvement overseas. Whether or not they invoke it, Congressmen and Senators opposing a particular operation can use the War Powers Act to raise the issue of Presidential war-making, and thereby lead the debate beyond a discussion of the merits of any individual military commitment. The mere date of the War Powers Act—almost always included in television newscasts mentioning it—facilitates a comparison of any military involvement overseas with Vietnam, no matter how feeble the true resemblance.

There can be no doubt that Congress (now fortified by a vastly expanded staff and research agencies) can and will exercise its ability to complicate Presidential war-making. Moreover, it is reasonable to think that Presidents will want to assure themselves of Congressional support before embarking on any military adventures, and in any event they will find themselves forced (in part by the War Powers Act) to report periodically to Congress on the progress of such operations. Perhaps most important, future Presidents will bear in mind the effects Vietnam had on two Presidencies, and therefore act cautiously.

Institutional Inadequacy as a Constraint

The most substantial constraints on America's ability to conduct small wars result from the resistance of the American defense establishment to the very notion of engaging in such conflicts, and from the unsuitability of that establishment for fighting such wars. One may, as we have noted, debate the merits of any particular military involvement overseas: it is difficult to argue, however, that the United States should not have the capability to enter one.

Before analyzing the American defense establishment's attitudes and capabilities, let us first consider the peculiar military requirements of small war. To understand the peculiar problems of small war, we must understand the differences between it and large war, that is, conventional conflicts such as World War II. Large war, in the current context, means war waged primarily for the domination of Europe, fought side by side with the West

European allies. It means war conducted in developed lands, supported by the infrastructure of modern—and above all, friendly—nation-states. It means war prosecuted with full national economic, psychological, and military mobilization, and fought primarily on familiar kinds of terrain, i.e., the urban and cultivated lands of Central Europe, and in familiar climate.

Small wars, by way of contrast, are often fought in remote corners of the world, devoid of logistical infrastructure, and subject to extreme climatic conditions (the Korean and Falklands Wars are good examples of this). Such wars occur suddenly, without much advance warning. No American statesman would have predicted in 1949 that American troops would soon wage a mountain war in Korea. In 1981, no British statesman would have predicted that Britain would shortly fling the best part of its navy and seven or eight thousand of its best soldiers at bogs and hills of the Falkland Islands. Great Powers usually fight such wars with little or no mobilization (including psychological mobilization on the home front). So far, at least, these have been primarily light infantry wars, fought in mountains or jungles by foot soldiers, although light mechanized forces have also been important in deciding their outcome. The foreign policy context of such wars is also peculiar: where Great Powers wage total war side by side with major allies who must occasionally be appeased or succored, they usually fight small wars on the side of a weak client, with minimal or no help from allies, who may find the cause unattractive or the costs disproportionate.

From the point of view of the Great Power that fights them, small wars are usually wars for a limited political objective, although from the point of view of the minor power this is rarely the case. Even in the Falklands War, the two states had very different stakes in the outcome. On the British side was hurt pride; on the Argentine side, the very essence of national assertion. This disproportion appeared even more clearly in the Vietnam War. By way of contrast, total wars are struggles for survival: there is an equivalent level of commitment and hence of resolve. Because a Great Power will often find itself unwilling to make a full commitment to victory in small war, its opponent will often attempt to drag the war out, in the hope that its enemy will simply lose patience and give up.[18]

These two kinds of wars require very different kinds of military forces and systems of military command, for it is not the case that an army suited for

---

18. See Andrew J.R. Mack, "Why Big Nations Lose Small Wars: The Politics of Asymmetric Conflict," in Klaus Knorr, ed., *Power, Strategy, and Security: A World Politics Reader* (Princeton: Princeton University Press, 1983), pp. 126–151.

European war can handle all other contingencies with aplomb. This is a particularly important point, often obscured by the habit of defense analysts in speaking of America's "one-and-a-half-war" force posture: small war is not a "half" a war, but rather a completely different kind of conflict.[19] It takes its peculiar coloration from the geopolitical circumstances which call it forth, and hence requires special means for its conduct.

In order to wage small war successfully, a military establishment must meet its requirements in five respects: *expectations* (*vis-à-vis* the foreign and domestic political context of such conflicts), *doctrine, manpower, equipment,* and *organization.*[20] In all respects (though some more than others), the American defense establishment—civilian as well as military—is deficient. In some cases, what is lacking is an understanding of the problem; in others, the ability to implement the solutions.

EXPECTATIONS. The American armed forces' understanding of the domestic political context of small wars has been shaped, and in fact distorted, by the experience of Vietnam. The emotional reaction of the professional officer corps towards its experience in Indochina was one of frustration and shock: frustration, at the American military's seeming inability to crush an opponent inferior in strength and mobility; shock, at the psychological gap that suddenly opened up between American society and the armed forces.[21] Accustomed since World War II to a large measure of popularity and respect, the

---

19. A point made by Stephen P. Rosen in "Vietnam and the American Theory of Limited War," *International Security,* Vol. 7, No. 2 (Fall 1982), pp. 83–113.
20. For the British approach to the problem, see first and foremost the official manual on the subject, Callwell, *Small Wars,* cited above. The literature on this subject is vast, including memoirs (e.g., those of Lord Roberts, cited above) and detailed histories (e.g., Philip Mason's *The Men Who Ruled India*) as well as treatises. Some particularly interesting books are Jay Luvaas, *The Education of an Army: British Military Thought 1815–1940* (Chicago: University of Chicago Press, 1964), and Ian Hamilton, *Compulsory Service* (London: John Murray, 1910). Richard Burdon Haldane, *Army Reform and Other Addresses* (London: T. Fisher Unwin, 1907), gives the views of Britain's great Secretary of State for War. Charles à Court Repington, *Imperial Defense* (London: John Murray, 1906), is also valuable, as is Charles W. Gwynn, *Imperial Policing* (London: Macmillan, 1934). More modern writers include Richard Clutterbuck, Frank Kitson, and Sir Robert Thompson on the insurgency in Malaya. For a good brief summary of the problem, see Major General Sir Edmund Ironside, "Land Warfare (II)," in George Aston, ed., *The Study of War for Statesmen and Citizens* (1927; Port Washington: Kennikat, 1973), pp. 140–147. For the lessons of a recent small war, see Henry Fairlie, "What the Falklands Teaches Us," *The New Republic,* July 12, 1982, pp. 8–12.
21. One gets a good sense of this from Ward Just, *Military Men* (New York: Alfred A. Knopf, 1970). See General Frederick Weyand, "Vietnam Myths and American Realities," *Armor,* September–October 1976, and General Edward Meyer's remarks in Richard Halloran, "U.S. Army Chief Opposes Sending Combat Forces to Aid El Salvador," *The New York Times,* June 10, 1983, p. 1.

armed services found themselves during the Vietnam era the target of criticism and occasional abuse.

Professional officers returning from Vietnam—including the junior and middle-level officers who now run the armed forces—were seared by the experience of public repudiation by large segments of society, including the intellectual elite. Not only (many felt) was appreciation for the heroism and technical competence of the American military lacking; but officers also found themselves pilloried as mass murderers, incompetents, or both.

In reaction to this brutally unfair treatment, the military leadership has determined never again to fight a war without public backing of the fullest kind, a public backing more appropriate to the conditions of world war than small war. One reporter writes of the

deep belief that political leaders in the Vietnam era failed to define their political goals and, instead, gave military commanders shifting objectives. The officers contend they were prevented from winning because strategy and tactics were restrained. They are vehement in asserting that they were left to twist alone in the wind without public support back home.[22]

This craving for popular support, which has translated itself into a profound reluctance to use force and which apparently led the Joint Chiefs of Staff to oppose (initially) even the successful Grenada operation, is at once understandable and unacceptable for a country that must fight small wars. It extends beyond the natural conservatism of military leaders, who are trained to consider the worst possibilities and to plan accordingly.[23] Such military pessimism is probably desirable and in any case inevitable: what is *not* inevitable is the insistence on massive public support for any use of force.

Small wars are, by definition, wars fought under limitations. In order to fight them successfully, a country must limit the resources—material and psychological—it devotes to them. To do otherwise would be to indulge in a disproportionate use of a country's power resources, and to expose itself to premature exhaustion. Small wars are frequently long wars, which require skill and patience to conduct rather than (as in the case of European warfare) the sudden and massive use of power. Even a cursory examination of British

---

22. Richard Halloran, "For Military Leaders, The Shadow of Vietnam," *The New York Times*, March 20, 1984, p. B10. It is instructive that in Secretary of State Alexander Haig's memoirs of the first years of the Reagan Administration, the only two references to the Joint Chiefs of Staff refer (albeit sympathetically) to their opposition to any limited use of force abroad for precisely this reason, i.e., a fear of domestic political isolation.

23. See Harry G. Summers, "Critics Say Pentagon is Dovish: Limited War is Back in Vogue," *The Los Angeles Times*, May 6, 1984, Section IV, p. 2.

history reveals that (with the possible exception of the Boer War) the British government waged war without conjuring up popular efforts on the scale of those summoned forth by the world wars. For that matter, America's three-year-long conflict in the Philippines at the turn of the century was a success despite vocal and persistent dissent (much of it directed at the military per se) back home.

The sad fact is that, with regard to small wars as well as other matters, American civil-military relations are in a state of profound but hidden crisis. Even as portions of the elite (the "military reform" group, for example, but substantial numbers of both liberals and conservatives) have lost operational confidence in the military, the military has developed an acute mistrust of its civilian masters. The military leadership in particular has developed a set of requirements for public support unlikely to be met save in the context of a European war; it has convinced itself that it fought the Vietnam War with "a hand tied behind its back," although the amount of human and material resources poured into the war belies that notion.[24]

Nor is there any evidence that the United States has improved its understanding of how its weaker allies, on whose side a small war might be waged, think and how they should be handled. The curious combination of a reluctance to interfere in "internal politics," so noticeable in the American handling of South Vietnam, with a military desire to operate autonomously again runs counter to the requirements of small war. It is a frequent condition of such conflict that one must build or re-build an allied army, purging a corrupt officer corps while designing organizational structures suitable to both the society and its military predicament. The Indian army and the Arab Legion (the precursor of the modern Jordanian army) stand out as sterling examples of such patiently constructed forces. The American experience—which has a long tradition going back to Stilwell's feuds with Chiang Kai Shek—suggests that American proficiency at imparting technical skills is matched only by American insensitivity to local conditions. The most recent example of this is the apparent failure of U.S. Army trainers (or, more likely, their superiors) to understand the impact of Lebanese politics on the Lebanese army, which disintegrated suddenly in early 1984.[25]

---

24. See Richard Halloran, "For New Commanders, A Key Word is Caution," *The New York Times*, November 16, 1983, p. A22. For an example of the public criticism, some fair, some not, of the operational effectiveness of the military, see Arthur T. Hadley, "America's Broken War Machine," *The New Republic*, May 7, 1984, pp. 18–25.
25. See "The Collapse of Lebanon's Army: U.S. Said to Ignore Factionalism," *The New York Times*, March 11, 1984, p. 1. On the general problem involved here, see Stephen P. Rosen,

Small war almost always involves political interference in the affairs of the country in which it is waged: it is in the very nature of such wars that the military problems are difficult to distinguish from the political ones. The skills of manipulation which successful coalition warfare in such circumstances requires are not only scarce, but in some measure anathema to the American military. The desire of the American military to handle only purely "military" problems is, again, understandable in light of its Vietnam experience, but unrealistic nonetheless.

DOCTRINE. Colonel Harry G. Summers has argued in his fascinating study of the Vietnam War, *On Strategy*, that the model for modern limited war should be that of the Korean conflict. Such, however, was not the assessment of the American high command, which has determined never again to plunge into such a long, low-level war. What this means in practice is that if the military *is* forced to engage in a small war, those who oppose it in the first place will then argue for the largest use of resources to bring it to a close. As Roger Hilsman has pointed out, it was precisely the so-called "Never Again Club" after the Korean War that advocated the most extreme—the most inappropriate and thoughtless—prosecution of the Vietnam War once it had begun.[26]

The American style of war as it evolved in the world wars calls for a vigorous strategic and tactical offensive under conditions of full domestic mobilization, making use of the full array of military assets that the United States can bring to bear. It is a style unsuited, however, to the exigencies of small wars, which often require a strategic defensive and which must be fought under a host of political constraints. Throughout the Vietnam War, the U.S. Army thought primarily in traditional terms, using resources aggressively on a scale appropriate to total war, but unsuited and indeed counterproductive in the context of the war they were fighting (for example, the vast expenditure of artillery and air-delivered munitions for the purposes of "harassment and interdiction"). In the words of one internal critic, there

---

"Brown Soldiers, White Officers: Foreign Military Advisers and Third World Armies," *The Washington Quarterly*, Vol. 5, No. 2 (Spring 1982), pp. 117–130. On the specific problems of the United States Army in El Salvador, see Edward N. Luttwak, "Notes on Low-Intensity Warfare," *Parameters*, Vol. 13, No. 4 (December 1983), pp. 11–18.

26. Roger Hilsman, *To Move A Nation: The Politics of Foreign Policy in the Administration of John F. Kennedy* (New York: Doubleday, 1967), pp. 129, 534. See also his penetrating comments on American inability to adjust to small war, pp. 112–113, 435–444. See also Harry G. Summers, *On Strategy: A Critical Analysis of the Vietnam War* (Novato, Calif.: Presidio, 1982).

is "no evidence of institutional learning in the services" as regards this kind of war, no understanding of the differences between the constraints of small war and America's current "offensive, give-them-everything-you've-got military doctrine."[27] The new AirLand Battle doctrine enshrined in the Army's operational manual, Field Manual 100-5, embodies notions and procedures clearly aimed at European warfare alone, despite lip service to the idea that American forces must prepare to fight virtually anywhere. It is a doctrine which celebrates the kind of offensive aggressiveness so characteristic of the American military style.

Even at a tactical level, American offense-mindedness is occasionally at odds with local realities. The Kissinger Commission Report on Central America makes the following observation:

U.S. tactical doctrine abjures static defense and teaches constant patrolling. But this requires the provision of expensive equipment such as helicopters. In their absence, the Salvadoran military abandon their static defenses for intensive foot patrolling, only to find the strategic objective they had been guarding destroyed in their absence.[28]

In the absence of a serious small war doctrine (there is no treatise comparable to the British army's early twentieth-century manual on the subject by General C.E. Callwell), the American defense establishment, civilian as well as military, has turned to a concept borrowed from nuclear strategy, deterrence. Rather than planning to fight small wars, the defense establishment from the Secretary of Defense on down hopes to intimidate potential opponents and therefore obviate the need for actual fighting. Thus, when Secretary of the Army John O. Marsh Jr. described to Congress the Army's new Light Division, he said, "It is expected that such a force, quickly inserted in the first days of a crisis, could defuse the crisis, thereby precluding the deployment of a much larger force later."[29] The general commanding the Rapid Deployment Force told an audience of sympathetic military men and defense officials, "I do not want you to think that we are an intervention force—because our job is deterrence."[30]

---

27. James A. Bowden, "The RDJTF and Doctrine," *Military Review*, Vol. 62, No. 11 (November 1982), p. 62.
28. *The Report of the President's National Bipartisan Commission on Central America* (New York: Macmillan, 1984), p. 115.
29. Eric C. Ludvigsen, "Elite Light Divisions Among Major Focuses in '85 Army Budget," *Army*, Vol. 34, No. 4 (April 1984), p. 35.
30. Robert C. Kingston, "From RDF to Centcom: New Challenges?," *Journal of the Royal United Services Institute*, Vol. 129, No. 1 (March 1984), p. 17.

The failure to grapple with the difficult task of providing a doctrine for the employment of forces in small war is an old one. A British author writing on the subject in the early 1960s noted that where Britain at the time had "combat forces" for use in the Third World, the United States had "deterrent forces."[31] In the absence of serious doctrine—the kind of doctrine that can only be created by men who expect to fight, not simply deter—one can only expect improvisations like the Grenada operation, in which a tiny island was divided between the Army and the Air Force on one hand, and the Navy and the Marine Corps on the other. To be sure, Grenada was a victory, although that was inevitable given the correlation of forces. It is by no means clear that in the future similar deployments overseas will be equally successful, or even nearly so.[32]

MANPOWER. One reason for the success of British small wars has been Britain's development of a military manpower system uniquely suited to such conflicts. In the early nineteenth century, British statesmen created the quasi-tribal regimental system, in which enlisted men and officers (all volunteers) served together for long periods of time, alternating between duty overseas and duty at home. It was a system that provided an emotional substitute for the sense of public approbation on which the American military relies: it sustained the fighting spirit of soldiers stationed for years in the remote and alien locations where British power was needed.[33] The United States Army has attempted to create an American regimental system with some success, although such efforts continue to meet the resistance of officers who find such a system administratively inefficient and potentially detrimental to individual careers.

31. Anthony Verrier, "Strategically Mobile Forces—U.S. Theory and British Practice," *Journal of the Royal United Services Institute,* Number 624 (November 1961), pp. 479–485.
32. It is instructive to consider the American intervention in Lebanon in 1958 in this regard. One semi-official study suggests that had that intervention been opposed, disaster could well have resulted from the lack of a common approach to the operation. By implication, the difficulties remain. Roger J. Spiller, "'Not War But Like War': The American Intervention in Lebanon," *Leavenworth Papers,* Number 3 (Fort Leavenworth: U.S. Army Command and General Staff College Combat Studies Institute, 1981).
33. On the regimental system, particularly as it relates to small war, see John Keegan, "Regimental Ideology," in Geoffrey Best and Andrew Wheatcroft, eds., *War, Economy, and the Military Mind* (London: Croom Helm, 1976), pp. 3–17; G.F.R. Henderson, *The Science of War* (London: Longmans Green, 1913), pp. 365–434. For a recent assessment, see Jeremy J.J. Phipps, "Unit Cohesion: A Prerequisite for Combat Effectiveness," *National Security Affairs Issue Paper,* Number 82-3 (Washington: National Defense University, 1982).

The renewal of the regimental system in the United States, plus efforts at unit as opposed to individual rotation policies, enhances American abilities to conduct small wars. The reliance on a standby draft in the event of any sizable conflict and, even more importantly, the Army's dependence upon reservists are as detrimental, however, as the reforms mentioned above are useful. A major reason for the success of British small wars has been Britain's near-exclusive reliance on volunteer professional soldiers rather than draftees or reservists. Not only are such soldiers more adept at the difficult kinds of operations mandated by small war: their use also involves fewer domestic political complications, since it does not raise the issue of sending unwilling men to fight obscure and protracted wars.

The American armed forces today, volunteer though they may be, could not conduct any major operation (save a brief defense of Europe) without a reserve mobilization. Many Army units require reserve forces for up to a third of their front-line combat strength, and the Army as a whole relies heavily on reserve tactical support forces. Even the Rapid Deployment Force depends for about one-third of its manpower and most of its combat support on the National Guard and Reserves. Moreover, it is important to realize that a mobilization would inevitably require, in the interests of equity, a resumption of conscription. As the hue and cry over the 1961 mobilization of reservists demonstrated, it is far harder to uproot civilians with jobs and families to support than to draft eighteen-year-olds: to do the one without the other would be virtually unthinkable. Thus, the so-called All Volunteer Force is merely a peacetime construct, unsustainable in any but the most minor of military conflicts. The leaders of the military do not necessarily object to this, however, because they see dependence upon reserve mobilization and conscription as guarantees of the public support for war discussed above. In reality, however, dependence on reserves is only a formidable brake on the government's ability to conduct small wars *successfully*. It is inevitable that most army reserve units would perform their missions less well, and at far greater cost in casualties (some resulting from sheer physical stress) than the active duty units might.[34] Small wars frequently entail fast deployments to extreme climates (e.g., the Persian Gulf), and it is absurd to think that reservists can be as physically hardened to such challenges as their

---

34. See Philip Gold, "What the Reserves Can—and Can't—Do," *The Public Interest*, No. 75 (Spring 1984), pp. 47–61.

active duty counterparts, or that they can be equally practiced in their individual and group skills.

A small war may require both a swift intervention and a long period of consolidation. This pattern—a sudden beginning and a protracted sequel—occurred even in the 1983 Grenada operation, a petty conflict to be sure, but an instructive one. Instead of the invasion force remaining only a few weeks, as the White House first announced, the force remained two months, not merely to mop up resistance, but to stabilize a nation suddenly deprived of all orderly administration. (Indeed, if one considers the presence of several hundred military police, who are in fact combat troops, the follow-up lasted well over six months.) Since most small wars consist of high-intensity conventional phases (e.g., Korea in 1950–1951, and Vietnam in 1965–1966) and low-intensity insurgency operations, the manpower system must be suited to both.

Draftees, however, are not well suited to the protracted counterinsurgency phase of a small war, for both narrow military and broader political reasons. For the sake of equity, a draft-based army will minimize the length of tours in the theater of war, thereby obstructing unit cohesion and the development of familiarity with the environment. Politically, the use of draftees presents domestic difficulties in maintaining public support for a war, and indeed in maintaining the morale of the army in the field. Small wonder, then, that both the British and the French, with one or two notable exceptions, fought both the high and low intensity phases of their small wars with volunteer professional soldiers. Similarly, America's successful campaigns in the Philippines in 1899–1902 and in the Caribbean and Central America during the first third of this century made use only of volunteer professional armed forces.

EQUIPMENT. Small war often requires unique types of equipment and technology, types that may have no utility in large or all-out warfare. This was true even in the nineteenth century: the heliograph and light mountain pack howitzer are only two examples of technological innovations which met the peculiar requirements of small war but had no larger applications.[35] As military establishments have become increasingly specialized, this is even more true than before.

---

35. See V.G. Kiernan, _From Conquest to Collapse: European Empires From 1815 to 1960_ (New York: Pantheon, 1982), pp. 123–128.

The United States armed forces have begun to acquire some of the specialized equipment they will need for warfare in the extreme climates where they can expect to fight—mobile water purification plants, for example, and hospital ships to treat casualties. In other respects, however, virtually no headway has been made, for example, in the Army's attempt to procure a light tank, which would be easily transportable by air.[36] Despite the oft-declared need for vastly increased airlift and sealift to transport American forces to non-European theaters of war, spending on such needs has remained low. In 1983, the United States Air Force had precisely as many C-5A heavy transport aircraft (the mainstay for airlifting "outsized" cargo such as tanks and helicopters over long distances) as it did in 1976; it had only thirty more short-range transports (the aging C-130 Hercules) than it did seven years earlier (294 vs. 262). A bias towards pre-positioning of equipment detracts from the flexibility of American forces, as well as presenting attractive targets for preemptive attacks, although some compensating advantages also exist.[37]

In some cases, service rivalries prevent the acquisition of suitable small war equipment. A case in point is "ARAPAHO," a relatively cheap set of prefabricated modules that can be used to convert a merchant vessel into a mini-aircraft carrier. On the basis of their experience in the Falklands (where improvised helicopter and Very Short Take-Off and Landing aircraft landing pads were of great use), the Royal Navy has demonstrated an interest in procuring ARAPAHO. The U.S. Army is interested in ARAPAHO as a means of suddenly improvising support vessels in off-shore operations, but the United States Navy has little interest in the program.[38]

ORGANIZATION. On the face of it, the United States has available a large force suited to the waging of small wars. In addition to the Marine Corps (which, until the postwar period, traditionally fought such conflicts), numbering three divisions plus combat support, the United States has an airborne and an airmobile division, a light infantry division (the 9th Division, also

---

36. For a discussion of the long-standing utility of light tanks in certain kinds of mountain warfare, see D.A.L. Mackenzie, "Operations in the Lower Khaisora Valley, Waziristan, in 1937," *Journal of the Royal United Services Institute*, Number 528 (November 1937), pp. 805–822.
37. On these and other RDF-related issues, see Congressional Budget Office, "Rapid Deployment Forces: Policy and Budgetary Implications" (Washington: CBO, 1983). See also Richard Halloran, "Poised for the Persian Gulf," *The New York Times Magazine*, April 1, 1984, p. 38 ff.
38. Millard Barger, "USN Abandons Arapaho; British Employ It; US Army Considers It," *Armed Forces Journal International*, April 1984, pp. 22, 27.

known as the High Technology Test Bed), two (soon to be three) Ranger battalions, several Special Forces Groups (soon to be expanded and placed under a separate command), and other infantry units currently dedicated to Third World missions (the 2nd Infantry Division in Korea and the 25th Division in Hawaii), plus, in the future, two more light divisions, the 7th (currently an understrength unit in California) and a new one to be created in 1985.

On paper, this force would seem both substantial and diverse enough to meet any contingency. Yet much of this strength is deceptive, not only because of the deficiencies alluded to above, but because of organizational difficulties. The Marine Corps, for example, is spread over the globe, and must prepare for its traditional mission of amphibious warfare (which it holds exclusively) in such diverse locales as Southeast Asia, the northern flank of NATO (Norway and Denmark), and the Mediterranean. It is primarily an infantry force and hence lacks the mechanized punch to cope with serious armored forces. The 82nd Airborne and 101st Airmobile Divisions are not merely small war forces, but part of America's overall strategic reserve, and hence have multiple missions, including European ones. Similarly, the 2nd Division is stationed in and the 25th Division is committed to the reinforcement of South Korea; and the 24th Mechanized Division, the Army's most powerful contribution to the Rapid Deployment Force, is committed to European tasks as well. The 9th Division is, and for one or two years will remain, in the throes of continual reequipment and innovation because of its role as the test division for future light divisions.

The incredibly varied locales of small wars require specially trained and acclimatized troops. The United States lacks the specialized units—mountain and jungle divisions, for example—trained in such unique environments and suited to operations in them. Since the very first years of World War II, the U.S. Army has resolutely opposed the creation of specially adapted divisions, in contrast to the practice of other countries.

These problems are compounded by the anomalous setup of the avowed small war force of the United States, the Rapid Deployment Force. The RDF consists of forces from the four major services, none of which, however, comes under the peacetime control of Central Command, which would control their use in a war in the Persian Gulf. No command or other exercises can provide the intimate cooperation and mutual understanding necessary for rapid deployment missions: thus, the separation between peacetime and wartime command is a serious deficiency. In addition, the limitation of

Central Command to the Persian Gulf precludes sustained work on joint deployments in other areas. The problems of cooperation became manifest in the Grenada operation, in the course of which a tiny island was divided in half, the Air Force and the Army in the south, the Navy and the Marine Corps in the north. In matters ranging from communications to coordination of attacks, failures of service cooperation were revealed. Similar chain-of-command and coordination difficulties appeared in the deployment of American Marines to Lebanon in 1983, and may have been partly responsible for the disastrous lack of security at the Marine compound in Beirut.[39]

At a higher level, there is no evidence that lessons have been learned from either Vietnam or the Falklands concerning the higher organization of government for small war. The need for the unity of command under central civilian control (as in Malaya, where one official controlled both military and civic operations) has been ignored. Similarly, no provisions have been made to centralize a war's strategic and diplomatic coordination in the hands of a full-time civil servant or political appointee, a practice often urged in Vietnam but never implemented there, but a practice which the British adopted and which contributed to their military and diplomatic victory in the Falklands.[40]

Conclusions

Of all the constraints on the conduct of small wars by the American government, the most important is the institutional one, and in particular the difficulties created by the unsuitability of the American national security apparatus to conduct small wars. The other factors constraining the conduct of small wars—public opinion, foreign pressures, and Congressional struggles for control over war powers—will vary with the particular crisis and the way it is handled. The reluctance of the armed services to prepare suitably for such wars and the inability of the United States' higher command to conduct such wars with the finesse they require are deeper, more permanent, and more dangerous problems.

---

39. See Samuel P. Huntington, "Defense Organization and Military Strategy," *The Public Interest*, No. 75 (Spring 1984), pp. 20–46, especially pp. 41–45.
40. See Robert W. Komer, *Bureaucracy Does Its Thing: Institutional Constraints on U.S.–G.V.N. Performance in Vietnam*, R-967-ARPA 1972 (Santa Monica: Rand, 1973), pp. 75–105; and Summers, *On Strategy*, pp. 141–150. The work of Sir Michael Palliser's small coordinating committee of senior civil servants and military men was particularly important (communications with senior British officials).

The institutional deficiencies of the United States defense establishment regarding small wars result from a number of causes: the ineptitude of some civilian and military leaders, Congressional micro-management of various procurement and organizational policies, and the understandable psychological trauma of the American officer corps consequent upon the Vietnam War. It would be neither just nor profitable to condemn one group or the other: rather, it would be desirable to begin thinking about means of redressing American weaknesses in this area.

The first and most important measure is a search for a sound theoretical understanding of the problems and perplexities of small wars, because unlike the British, Americans cannot assume the existence of institutions adapted to this challenge. However, it is not simply the case that more study is required. Rather, what is needed is a willingness to publicly acknowledge the implications of what we already know. The American defense establishment must cure itself of an obsession with European warfare, and the officer corps must be weaned from its understandable but pernicious belief in the need for public support of the kind it had during World War II. Additionally, American force structure, including emphasis on airlift, percentage of forces dedicated to European missions, and organization for rapid deployment, must reflect the realities of where American forces are likely to fight.

Two options have been advanced as possible solutions to the small war dilemma: one, that small war missions be devolved upon the Marine Corps; the other, that American strategists contrive to make such wars as short as possible.[41] There is something to be said for each policy, but neither separately nor together can these solve the problem. Service rivalries preclude the exclusive assignment of such an important mission to the Marines, and, as we have noted above, the Marines are already thinly stretched and are not equipped to handle certain contingencies (for example, those requiring mechanized or airborne forces). There is room for improved utilization of the Marine Corps, however, most importantly by relieving it of responsibility for the *conduct* of all amphibious operations. During World War II, after all, the

---

41. The former seems to me to be implicit in the position of Colonel Summers's book on Vietnam; the latter is put forward by Samuel P. Huntington in his edited work, *The Strategic Imperative: New Policies for American Security* (Cambridge: Ballinger, 1982), p. 49. On the Marine contribution to the Rapid Deployment Force, see David A. Quinlan, "The Role of the Marine Corps in Rapid Deployment Forces," *National Security Essay*, Number 83-3 (Washington: National Defense University, 1983).

Army conducted more amphibious operations than did the Marine Corps. In the future, the Marine Corps could continue to prepare the *doctrine* for such operations, while it concentrated more closely on small war missions outside Europe.[42]

Although speed is of the essence in all military operations, it may be particularly important in small wars—hence the importance of substantial airlift capabilities, even though air transport is a highly uneconomic means of moving men and materiel. Nonetheless, it is in the nature of small wars that they frequently require sustained commitments of forces to stabilize a country following an initial victory. Hence, the attractive notion of a violent but brief conflict is chimerical. Even in the Falklands, where a victory seemed fairly swift and complete, the war led the British armed forces to deploy several thousand troops plus air and naval forces in a region hitherto guarded by a cutter and fewer than a hundred marines. To take but one example, it is hard to envision a war fought to protect small Persian Gulf states against Iran which would not involve prolonged deployments of American armed forces overseas. As we have noted above, it is in the nature of small wars that they alternate between high- and low-intensity phases.

The United States cannot fashion a small war capability from an instrument prepared mainly for all-out war in Europe, a replay of World War II except with more advanced technology and conducted against the Soviets rather than the Germans. The lessons of the Grenada micro-war are instructive, for in it admittedly conservative military planners underestimated both the intensity and the duration of the operation. Initially, planners committed some 4,000 paratroops, Marines, and Rangers in two waves: within a few days 5,000 paratroops were flown in to replace the initial 2,000-man assault force. Invasion forces peaked at over 7,000 men, or nearly twice the force originally envisioned. As I have pointed out above, the invasion entailed a far longer commitment than that originally envisioned. A further lesson from the Grenada operation concerns its unfortuitous timing. Even as American troops fought in the Caribbean, others began to recover from a far bloodier debacle in Lebanon; indeed, the Marines who fought in Grenada were on their way to replace the Marine contingent there. Small wars do not necessarily occur

---

42. Such was the Marine Corps role in World War II. See Jeter A. Isely and Philip A. Crowl, *The U.S. Marines and Amphibious War: Its Theory, and Its Practice in the Pacific* (Princeton: Princeton University Press, 1951), especially pp. 3–71, 580–590.

one at a time. Indeed, they are as or more likely to occur simultaneously, and hence no single small war "fire brigade" can hope to cover all contingencies.

A public and institutional acknowledgment of the small war problem is but the first step in dealing with it. An intellectual comprehension of the demands of small war does not necessarily translate itself into implementation of the policies required to wage it successfully, a point on which Robert Komer's study of the Vietnam era bureaucracy is eloquent.[43] One necessary step is surely the procurement of the proper kinds of equipment to deal with small war. More importantly, the United States should consider reorganizing its forces to cope with it. Here, the manpower problems alluded to above become particularly sharp. If, as has been argued above, a small war expeditionary force should consist exclusively of professional or at least volunteer active-duty soldiers, the force structure of the Army in particular will need to be changed. One possibility might be the creation of, in effect, two armies: a self-contained professional expeditionary force consisting of seven or eight specialized divisions (plus the Marines), and a Europe-oriented draft-based army. By executive declaration or law, it could be established that no draftees could be dispatched overseas, except to Europe, without a Congressional declaration of war. Even in such a case, it might be necessary to reduce U.S. standing forces in Europe somewhat while increasing U.S. commitment to European reinforcement late in a conflict.

There is ample precedent for this kind of institutional arrangement in the case of France, the only Great Power to have sustained both European and overseas commitments for well over a century. From the late nineteenth century until the present, with the exception of the Algerian war, French law and policy have prohibited the use of conscripts overseas. Partly as a result of this wise policy, France sustains even today effective forces in such contested countries as Chad and Djibouti, as well as a substantial Europe-oriented conventional force.

The two most probable loci for American small wars are in the Persian Gulf and Central America, yet paradoxically Central Command and Southern Command have the fewest forces assigned to their peacetime control for training and operations. Certainly, both Commands should have adequate forces under their peacetime control for at least the first stages of any fore-

---

43. Komer, *Bureaucracy Does Its Thing.*

seeable small war. This would further help reduce the mismatch between the types of forces the United States has and the locations where it is likely to use them.

American participation in small wars remains an inevitable concomitant of America's world role. Civilians and soldiers cannot avoid the problem by simply refusing to believe that they will again send soldiers into obscure corners of the world to fight for limited political objectives against a hostile non-European power. If they are sincere in this disbelief, they must accept the consequences for American foreign policy. Such a disbelief put into practice would mean a unilateral American rejection of its status as a world power, a status held to with enormous benefit for this country and others since 1945.

The choice, then, is between being ready to fight well when it is necessary to fight and fighting badly. The costs in the latter case include the loss of American and foreign lives and failures in American foreign and security policy. The best way to reduce the likelihood of small wars is to be well prepared for them, but it is a delusion to think that they are escapable through conventional deterrence, any more than they were in the late 1950s through a policy of massive nuclear retaliation. The first task, therefore, is to acknowledge the problem and study it. At the moment, however, one must concur regretfully with the judgment of Lieutenant General Wallace H. Nutting, former commander of U.S. forces in Central and Latin America, who recently said of small war, "As a nation we don't understand it and as a government we are not prepared to deal with it."[44]

---

44. Quoted in *Newsweek*, June 6, 1983, p. 24.

Soviet Vulnerabilities in Iran and the RDF Deterrent

Joshua M. Epstein

It is difficult to imagine a region at once so vital economically and so volatile politically as the Persian Gulf today. To its economic importance, the Arab oil embargo of 1973 was, for many, the first rude awakening. Since then, a stormy sequence of events has underlined its political instability. The Iranian revolution, the fall of the Shah, and the bitter ordeal of the hostages were, for many Americans, a shocking demonstration of that fact; the seizure of the Great Mosque at Mecca and the Iraq–Iran War, part of its grim and continuing confirmation.

Concurrent with these stark realizations, the West saw Soviet foreign policy enter a particularly adventurist phase, one in which regional instabilities—in Angola, in Ethiopia, and in South Yemen—were made targets of military opportunity. The possibility that a crumbling order in the Gulf would present the Soviets with even more attractive opportunities was lost on a very few.

And when the Soviets invaded Afghanistan, the West's worst fears suddenly seemed ominously at hand. Jolted by the alarming convergence of events, former President Carter threw down the gauntlet, warning in his 1980 State of the Union Address that "an attempt by any outside force to gain control of the Persian Gulf region—will be repelled by any means necessary, including military force." [1]

Today, few would deny the claim of former CIA Director, Admiral Stansfield Turner that ". . . the most demanding need for military force in the region would be to oppose a direct thrust by the Soviets into Iran." [2] Indeed, this contingency, under the Carter Doctrine has served as a principal basis for planning of the Rapid Deployment Joint Task Force (RDF).

While the author bears sole responsibility for all views expressed here, he is grateful to William W. Kaufmann, Barry Posen, Steven Miller, and Ted Greenwood for their suggestions.

Joshua Epstein is a Research Fellow at Harvard's Center for Science and International Affairs, and a consultant to the Rand Corporation.

---

1. U.S., Congress, Senate, Committee on Foreign Relations, "U.S. Security Interests and Policies in Southwest Asia," Hearings Before the Subcommittee on Near Eastern and South Asian Affairs, Ninety-Sixth Congress, second session, February–March 1980, p. 350.
2. Admiral Stansfield Turner (USN–Ret.), "Toward a New Defense Strategy," *New York Times Magazine*, May 10, 1981, p. 16.

International Security, Fall 1981 (Vol. 6, No. 2) 0162-2889/81/020126-33 $02.50/0

Given the exceedingly grave consequences that would attend its successful execution, and the uncertainty surrounding Soviet intentions in the region, it is a contingency which no responsible analyst can ignore. And, of the numerous Persian Gulf contingencies of interest, a Soviet drive for the oil of Khuzestan is the threat to be examined here.

The prevailing view of American deterrent capabilities is frighteningly pessimistic. In peacetime, there are twenty-four Soviet divisions in the region, while the RDF's ground complement is assumed to number around four divisions.[3] The Soviets enjoy proximity. They share a border with Iran while the bulk of the U.S. force is thousands of miles away. It is widely assumed in addition that simultaneous contingencies pose far more serious problems for the United States than they do for the Soviets.

As a consequence, there is a general consensus that without using nuclear weapons, the United States would stand little chance of handling an all-out invasion of Iran, and that in no event can there be a feasible defense without a dramatic expansion of American basing in the region.

Columnist Jack Anderson reports Government testimony to the effect that "the Rapid Deployment Force would be no more than a 'trip wire' against the Soviets. The contingency plan calls for a nuclear strike to stop the Soviets from annihilating the force."[4] Defense Secretary Weinberger himself has warned that "the U.S., at present, is incapable of stopping an assault on Western oil supplies,"[5] while prominent analysts have gone so far as to say that Iran "may be inherently indefensible."[6]

The military situation, however, has not received the close examination that it deserves. In divisions, the Soviets outweigh the RDF, and the larger force is the closer to Iran; those are undeniable facts. But the conclusions drawn from them are unwarranted.

If planned and postured according to the strategy proposed in this essay, the RDF can present an imposing deterrent to Soviet aggression. Further-

---

3. James Wooten, *Rapid Deployment Forces, Issue Brief Number IB80027* (Washington, D.C.: The Library of Congress Congressional Research Service, 1980), p. 4 and Sir John Hackett, "Protecting Oil Supplies: The Military Requirements," Paper presented to the International Institute For Strategic Studies, Twenty-Second Annual Conference, Stresa, Italy, September 1980, pp. 9–10.
4. Jack Anderson, "Frightening Facts on the Persian Gulf," *The Washington Post*, February 3, 1981, p. 18.
5. Robert S. Dudney, "The Defense Gap that Worries the President," *U.S. News and World Report*, February 16, 1981.
6. Jeffrey Record, "Disneyland Planning for Persian Gulf Oil Defense," *The Washington Star*, Friday, March 20, 1981, p. 17.

more, under such a strategy, tactical nuclear employment would be not only unnecessary, but ill-advised. Contrary to the prevailing view, moreover, the constraint of simultaneous contingencies weighs at least as heavily upon the Soviets as it does on the United States.

The essential features of that strategy are the abandonment of forward defense and the exploitation of warning time. But first, two issues must be addressed: the Soviet overland threat to Iran and the prospects for Soviet airlifted assaults. Each must be appreciated if Soviet tactics combining them are to be assessed.

The Soviet Overland Threat

As a consequence of the terrain (see map), this may be divided into three successive phases:

Phase I: The advance through northern Iran, over the mountains south to the Tehran line.

One might postulate the seizure of Qazvin and/or Tehran as Phase I goals. These might then be seen as the main bases of operation for

Phase II: The advance south through central Iran for a build-up at Dezful (or some other appropriate area at the southern base of the Zagros Mountains).

Phase III: The final thrust south to drive the RDF out of Khuzestan, securing Soviet control of Iran's principal oil and shipping facilities.

This plan closely resembles that set forth in the *Soviet Command Study of Iran* (1941).[7] There, the Soviet General Staff wrote,

After the capture of Tehran and Qazvin, an advance in a straight line on to Hamadan and on to the Persian Gulf along the Southern leg of the Trans-Iranian railroad will be possible. Here is where the entire supply of weapons and munitions for Iran [read the RDF] will probably be concentrated. This line leads most directly to the center of Iran's oil industry.[8]

The objective, given this not entirely hypothetical plan, is to delay and wear down the Soviets' southern advance in such a way that an adequate coun-

---

7. *Soviet Command Study of Iran (Moscow 1941): Draft Translation and Brief Analysis*, Gerold Guensberg (trans.) (Arlington, Virginia: SRI International, January 1980).
8. *Soviet Command Study*, p. 160.

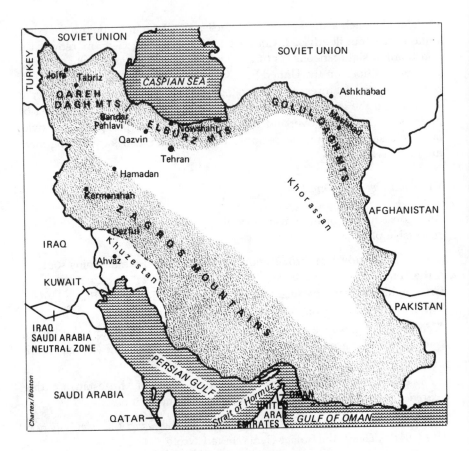

terpose can be inserted for the Battle of Khuzestan, as it were. Accordingly, the RDF strategy proposed here falls into three phases corresponding to those of the threat itself.

Phase I: Delay the advance into northern Iran while constructing a defense perimeter in Khuzestan.

Phase II: Delay and attrit the advance over the Zagros Mountains while building up for the ground war in Khuzestan.

Phase III: Battle of Khuzestan. (This would be a combined arms conflict including ground, air, and naval forces.)

The goal of this strategy is to deter aggression by the credible threat that its object—the oil—will be denied. Whether or not the RDF is adequate to that deterrent mission is the basic question to be addressed here.

Let us examine each of these phases in turn. It will become evident that the defensive plan exploits many of the vulnerabilities stressed in the Soviets' own *Command Study*.

PHASE I: DELAYING ACTION IN THE NORTH

There are three axes from the Soviet Union into Iran by land: from the Caspian Sea directly, and across the Soviet borders to the East and West of the Caspian. All three axes suffer a number of common problems. First, there is a very limited transportation system along each axis: there are roughly a dozen surface arteries from the Soviet Union to Tehran.[9] Moreover, each (rail or road) must pass over formidable mountain ranges, notably the Qareh Dagh in the northwest, the Elburz south of the Caspian, and the Golul Dagh in the northeast. Third, each artery is punctuated by so-called "choke points." These are points at which a) destruction or blockage of the artery is feasible; b) bypassing the resultant obstacle is not feasible; and where c) clearing the blockage or restoring the route is time-consuming. The Soviets were, and doubtless are, very well aware of the vulnerability this represents, and especially, as the *Command Study* emphasized, of each route's vulnerability to air interdiction. Consider their commentary on the road (of which there remains essentially one) from Ashkhabad, in the northeast, to Mashhad. In reference to the Dash Arasy gorge, through which that road must pass, the Soviets wrote,

At km-25 the gorge narrows at some places down to 3 to 4 meters. The walls of rock on both sides reach heights of 200 to 300 m. The gorge can be easily destroyed which would seriously impede traffic.

---

9. This, and all subsequent statements concerning the number, length, or condition of surface arteries in the various sectors of Iran are derived primarily from *Map of Iran*, Central Intelligence Agency, 1977 and *Road Map of Iran*, Sahab Geographic and Drafting Institute (Tehran, Iran, 1977). A careful attempt has been made to compare the Soviets' 1941 discussion to the current transportation system. The match remains very close in the sectors of interest. While certain arteries have doubtless been upgraded for commercial use, this need not entail any reduction in vulnerability to military attack. Lightweight construction materials, for example, may be efficient from the point of view of economic growth while representing no enhancement in hardness or reduction in susceptibility to structural attacks. Moreover, even where arteries have been upgraded in the latter respect since 1941, so have air-to-ground munitions grown in effectiveness. In the view of experts interviewed by the author, the net effect of these developments has not been to reduce the vulnerability of the Iranian transportation system significantly. Indeed, some feel that it is more vulnerable (to modern ordnance) than it was in 1941.

In general, the Soviets stressed that

The road—along its entire stretch—is easily attackable from the air. Mountain sides and the narrow width of the plain (15–20 km) provide cover and allow divebomber attacks with ease.[10]

In each of the successive mountain chains of the northern Khorassan, the Soviets enumerated "narrow gorges which can be easily blocked."[11] Roads are very scarce and vulnerable, as they were in 1941. For these reasons, it is difficult not to concur in the Soviets' own view that the mountain range of the northeast

constitutes a mighty frontier protection which makes very difficult an invasion from the north into the Khorassan interior.[12]

Looking westward to the Caspian approaches, the Soviets wrote of the Elburz mountains that

they simplify considerably the defense of the important central areas of Iran against an enemy who has landed along the southern shores of the Caspian Sea.[13]

Why? Because, of the roughly five roads over the Elburz to Tehran or Qazvin, all must cross bridges over precipitous faults thousands of meters in the mountains, or must pass through narrow gorges.[14] So concerned were the Soviets that the few available arteries would be closed off, that they took an inventory of all draught animals (horses, donkeys, mules, and camels) in Iran, anticipating that air interdiction might force them to advance over the pack animal tracks that lace this craggy terrain.[15]

There is one railroad from the Caspian to Tehran, the trans-Iranian railroad. It is the only railroad from Tehran south to Dezful. It traverses the above terrain first in the Elburz and again south in the Zagros Mountains. Of the passage over the Elburz, the Soviets wrote that the line "can be easily

---

10. *Soviet Command Study*, pp. 218–219, and 220.
11. *Ibid.*
12. *Ibid.*, pp. 20–21.
13. *Ibid.*, p. 164.
14. From the coastal city of Now Shahr, south of the main port of Pahlavi, for example, the meticulous Soviet planners noted that "the more deeply the path penetrates the gorge (up to km. 20) the more difficult becomes the traffic. A dynamiting of the rocks or the destruction of the road or the bridges would greatly slow down the movement of troops. . . . Bypassing the road in the event of destruction is nearly impossible. The traffic can be resumed only after the road has been repaired." *Ibid.*, p. 176.
15. *Ibid.*, p. 100.

attacked from the air."[16] Even in the lowlands near Tehran, they cautioned that "the entire section is observable from the air and it can be easily attacked."[17]

Finally, in the northwest, the Iranian Azerbaidjan, the same vulnerabilities prevail. There is a single road from Jolfa (just across the Soviet border in Iran) to the first main city, Tabriz. Of that crucial artery, the detailed *Command Study* records:

At km 22 from Dshulfa [Jolfa] begins the Daradis gorge which is 7 km long. The advance of troops through this small and narrow pass can be most difficult. The movement of troops can be made even more difficult if the enemy employs roadblocks or attacks from the air.[18]

Again, bypass is virtually infeasible. The shoulders of the gorge are walls of boulder. Detonations creating rockslides would severely hamper troop movement, and could be cleared only with extensive military engineering efforts.

NUCLEAR VS. CONVENTIONAL WEAPONS. The first phase of the defensive plan is to delay the advance of Soviet units by choking off this transportation system. This mission could be accomplished with nuclear weapons or with conventional forces.

As to the feasibility of nuclear interdiction, a study conducted for the Office of the Assistant Secretary of Defense for Program Analysis and Evaluation (PA&E) concluded that "ADM [Atomic Demolition Munitions] alone could quickly seal all avenues of approach into Iran."[19]

It is far from clear, however, that nuclear employment is necessary, despite claims to the contrary.[20] Those claims generally fail to draw a critical distinction. They begin by noting that the RDF is, among other things, designed to *protect* the West's "oil lifeline"; this is located in *southern* Iran. In the same breath, however, recourse to nuclear weapons is deemed necessary, for lack

---

16. *Ibid.*, p. 201.
17. *Ibid.*
18. *Ibid.*, p. 127.
19. Captain Henry Leonard and Mr. Jeffrey Scott, *Methodology For Estimating Movement Rates of Ground Forces in Mountainous Terrain With and Without Defensive Obstacles: First Draft* (Washington: Study for the Office of Assistant Secretary of Defense, Program Analysis and Evaluation, October 12, 1979), p. 3.8.
20. While at *The New York Times*, now Director of the State Department's Bureau of Politico-Military Affairs Richard Burt related that:
"A Defense Department report on the military situation in the Persian Gulf region has concluded that American forces could not stop a Soviet thrust into northern Iran and that the

of other means, to *blunt* a Soviet violation of *northern* Iran. The prevailing assumption that the use of nuclear weapons is necessary therefore rests critically upon the premise that a forward defense of the northern Iranian border is required to prevent Soviet control of Khuzestan's oil riches. But why should it be? The oil lies roughly a thousand kilometers and two formidable mountain chains south of the "inviolable" border.

If, by a series of conventional delaying operations, enough time can be bought to permit the emplacement of an adequate American defense force there, Soviet control of Khuzestan could be denied. In the final analysis, the RDF's problem is time. To be sure, nuclear weapons would buy more time, and more quickly, for a Western build-up in the south than would conventional munitions. But if *enough* time can be bought conventionally, that, for a host of reasons, is surely the approach to be preferred.[21] And it *is* a feasible approach.

United States should therefore consider using 'tactical' nuclear weapons in any conflict there." Richard Burt, "Study Says a Soviet Move in Iran Might Require U.S. Atom Arms," *The New York Times*, February 2, 1980, p. 1.
Columnist Jack Anderson reported in *The Washington Post* that
"President Carter established the far-flung, multi-service Rapid Deployment Force to protect our oil lifeline. Yet top military hands warn that it . . . could never be a match for the Soviet juggernaut across the Iranian border." Jack Anderson, "Frightening Facts on the Persian Gulf."
21. In addition to being adequate to the deterrent goal, denial, conventional operations would avoid those externalities which could attend nuclear employment. Assume for the moment that in the face of American nuclear use the Soviets did not respond in kind, but for example, simply "threw in the towel" and withdrew their surviving troops. The entire world would be watching. The event would have provided it a graphic example of the military utility of nuclear weapons and could thus be a positive stimulant to nuclear proliferation. The United States would be hard pressed, having successfully relied upon them, to argue their superfluity to, for example, the Saudis, Pakistanis, South Koreans, even the Iranians themselves.
In the latter regard, it might be noted that collateral nuclear damage to Iran and the untoward consequences for its northern populations could eventuate in such bitter and enduring enmity toward the United States and its Allies as to produce economic consequences indistinguishable in their gravity from those the employment was intended to avert.
As for Europe, such a demonstration of U.S. willingness to use nuclear weapons in a forward defense could reinforce whatever preemptive inclinations the Soviets may harbor toward NATO's vulnerable land-based theater nuclear weapons; "the Americans used them first to buy mobilization time in Iran and they'd use them first to buy mobilization time in central Europe." The implications of this altogether natural train of thought for "Euro-strategic crisis stability" should be obvious.
All of these perfectly plausible and very unfortunate consequences—for Western energy, for proliferation, and for European security—could attend the "best case" in which the Soviets fail to respond in kind. And there is always the grave risk of Soviet escalation itself, a risk which is certainly associated with any use of nuclear weapons. If, in closing roads, ground bursts were

The first step is to delay the Soviets' advance through northern Iran.

To do this, the major units with forces available to the RDF are impressive, and include the following:

Army
  82d Airborne Division
  101st Airborne Division (Air Assault)
  24th Infantry Division (Mechanized)
  194th Armored Brigade
  6th Combat Brigade (Air Cavalry)
  Various Ranger and Special Forces units
Air Force
  27th Tactical Fighter Wing (F-111)
  49th Tactical Fighter Wing (F-15)
  347th Tactical Fighter Wing (F-4)
  354th Tactical Fighter Wing (A-10)
  366th Tactical Fighter Wing (F-111)
  552nd Airborne Warning and Control Wing (E-3A)
  150th Tactical Fighter Group, Air National Guard (A-7)

---

the *modus operandi,* then, depending upon the prevailing winds, the Soviet Union (which "enjoys" proximity) could be subjected to substantial fallout.

While seeking to avoid unnecessary risks of escalation by one's adversary, it is equally important to avoid imposing escalatory pressures upon oneself. Casualties are, of course, to be minimized on humane grounds. But they should be minimized for this less immediate reason as well. As one's casualties mount, so may the pressure to prosecute the war to an extent, or in a manner, not called for by its original, limited objectives. That is, if the human "sunk costs" quickly come to outstrip the original objectives, since the former cannot be reclaimed, the latter may be raised to ensure that death was not in vain. Ill-considered expansions of war goals, and an ever-increasing commitment of troops may follow.

While the risk of Soviet escalation is associated with a nuclear defense, these considerations would counsel against airborne and in favor of air power as the conventional instrument in Phase I; first, because transport of airborne (dropped) troops into the northern mountains of Iran would be quite vulnerable to Soviet-based fighters. Even assuming that a sufficiently large contingent of airborne troops could be securely delivered, are they to be recovered or left to "fend for themselves"? To pick them up would require the use of vulnerable helicopters or fixed-wing aircraft, while to resupply them for a sustained defense would be equally demanding. To lose them and/or the forces engaged in either their recovery or resupply, could be escalatory.

The classic method of dealing with the vulnerability of airdropped forces would, of course, be to press an advance north, expanding one's perimeter until the airborne forces were within it. Aside from being totally inconsistent with all of America's expressed aims in Iran, this tactic—essentially an occupation—would subject the U.S. to all those vulnerabilities upon whose exploitation its strategy should be based.

For all of these reasons, then, conventional air forces seem the most intelligent instruments in the first delay phase.

188th Tactical Fighter Group, Air National Guard (A-7)
Reconnaissance squadrons
Tactical airlift squadrons
Conventional Strategic Projection Force
Various other units

Navy

3 Aircraft carrier battle groups
1 Surface action group
5 Squadrons of antisubmarine warfare patrol aircraft
6 Amphibious ships
7 Near-term prepositioning ships (NTPS)

Marine Corps

Marine amphibious force (division + wing)
7th Marine Amphibious Brigade (NTPS MAB)[22]

While the regional basing currently available is inadequate to accommodate so large an air arm, that does not warrant fatalism regarding the first delay phase. Its limited goal, recall, is to bound the Soviets' rate of advance sufficiently to ensure enough time to mount an adequate combined arms defense in Khuzestan. As will become evident, if the interdiction campaign were to ensure a month in transit from the Soviets' bases to the point at which the second delay phase is conducted (in the southern Zagros), that should be adequate (as always, on the assumption that warning time is exploited).

The on-road distances involved are all on the order of 1000 kilometers at least. To ask that the RDF's air operation yield a month in transit is therefore merely to require that it limit the Soviets' overall (repair plus movement) rate to no more than roughly 33⅓ km/day. But that, history records, would be a remarkable pace. It would exceed that achieved by Hitler's armies in their blitz of Flanders in 1940 (31 km/day) and in Operation Barbarossa the following year (29 km/day). The Normandy Breakout of 1944 saw a rate of 28 km/day, while 13 km/day was logged by the North Koreans in their offensive of 1950. The Israeli's victories on the West Bank and the Golan in 1967 were achieved under advance rates of 27 and 18 km/day respectively.[23] Notwithstanding the myriad differences between each of the above and the Soviet

---

22. *Fact Sheet*, Public Affairs Office, HQ Rapid Deployment Joint Task Force, April 1981, pp. 2–3.
23. Colonel T. N. Dupuy, *Numbers, Predictions and War*, (Indianapolis: The Bobbs–Merrill Company, Inc., 1979), p. 16.

advance as posited here, 33⅓ km/day is a very spirited clip. And in none of these historical cases was the cited rate sustained over so great a distance as that facing a Soviet "drive for oil."

In short, the Soviets would be operating in truly forbidding terrain, over northern Iran's limited and vulnerable transportation system—a system so constricted that at its narrowest points, the mere disabling of lead elements would bring whole columns to a standstill; it is a network dotted with severe choke points. Under such conditions, to hold the Soviets down to one of the highest advance rates in history must be seen as a modest goal. And although more ambitious goals may fall within its grasp should the RDF's regional basing expand, current resources should be capable of holding a Soviet advance to that rate or lower. Indeed, an array of options present themselves.

The less stringent is one's demand for time urgency, the less demanding the interdiction operation becomes. And there is no compelling military reason, if the United States exploits warning time, either to strike every lucrative choke point in a single day or to conduct the operation solely with tactical air. In one of the most innovative moves of recent years, twenty-eight B-52Hs (in North Dakota) "have been organized into a quick-response outfit called the Strategic Projection Force, or *Spif*."[24] Designed specifically for conventional bombing operations in the Gulf region, *Spif*'s "war plans call for the bombers to strike at night at low level." As of this writing, *Spif* planners report that "training for Persian Gulf missions has reached the point that a full-dress exercise will be conducted soon."

While feasible from the continental United States, such conventional B-52 operations could also be staged from bases in Guam, Australia, Clark Field in the Philippines and elsewhere. Diego Garcia will shortly be capable of accommodating the B-52s. It can be hoped, as SAC Commander General Ellis notes, that

sending B-52s to the trouble spot in the first hours of a crisis might be enough to freeze the Soviet military. Bombs might not have to be dropped at all, as long as the will and ability to do so were demonstrated . . .[25]

If deterrence fails, however, the RDF could initially create the northernmost tier of choke points, working south only as reconnaissance dictates, relying primarily on the bombers, and phasing in air from the Khuzestan perimeter

---

24. George C. Wilson, "'Anytime Anywhere:' A New Conventional Role for B-52 Bombers," *The Washington Post*, March 31, 1981, p. 6.
25. *Ibid.*

as it becomes available. This "tiered interdiction" could effectively deny Soviet engineering units any opportunity to restore routes before the main columns arrive. Aircraft from the two carriers now on station in the region could, from the Gulf of Oman, be used to provide escort for the bombers or, if they were aerially refuelled, to conduct a portion of the interdiction operation. The carriers' classical mission, however, would be to provide tactical air cover (power projection) for the Marine beachhead in Khuzestan, cover which could be augmented by offshore support (if necessary) from smaller surface combatants inside the Persian Gulf. As the Marine perimeter expands and establishes its air defense, the carriers can be withdrawn while, from within the perimeter, Air Force and/or Marine aircraft take over the continuing air interdiction campaign from the bombers. The latter could then be withheld as an intra-war deterrent or could strike targets in central Iran, Afghanistan, or elsewhere. With the establishment of a perimeter air defense, carrier air, arrayed from the Gulf of Oman to the Arabian Sea, could be flexibly employed in a variety of ways, including fleet defense, power projection, and Sea Line of Communication (SLOC) protection. With warning, the RDF's third carrier could supplement aerial refuelling and air defense of the two on-station carriers, used in any of the above capacities.

This particular scheme is not the only one possible. The range of tactical combinations and employment schedules is wide. It is one of many alternatives to carrier operations, however brief, inside the Persian Gulf. Although further regional basing—particularly Turkish, Omani, or Saudi— would simplify it, the RDF's northern interdiction campaign is feasible and, while limited in scope, it would form an effective spearhead to an imposing deterrent posture.

PHASE II: DELAYING ACTION IN THE ZAGROS
Phase II is conducted in the Zagros Mountains from within the southern perimeter by highly mobile (heliborne) special forces. The tactics are similar to those used by the Finns in the Soviet–Finnish Winter War, in which ambush and "hit and run" tactics figured prominently. Termed *"motti"* tactics, their employment by the vastly outnumbered defenders thoroughly frustrated the Soviets' continuing attempts to penetrate the waist of Finland.

The Soviets' overland passage through the Zagros would be as difficult as in the north; there are again very few arteries. In every case, choke points abound, and they may be selected to maximize defensive opportunity. Of the countless gorges through the parallel chains which are the Zagros, the

Soviets wrote, ". . . with the use of obstacles or roadblocks, these can be turned into excellent defensive positions."[26]

The RDF would have two objectives in Phase II: delay and attrition. Both can be made quite severe with surprising economy. Regarding attrition, the above-mentioned study for PA&E concludes that,

The mission of light forces in the delay phase should be to inflict losses on the invader without becoming decisively engaged. . . . Airmobile infantry forces employed in small-unit (company or even platoon) ambushes can seriously harass heavier enemy forces for very short periods without risking severe losses or entrapment. . . . Our forces could choose the time and place of the ambush, and enjoy, briefly, the advantage of surprise.[27]

Indeed,

gaming of a five-minute engagement between a U.S. light infantry company and the point of a Soviet mechanized column . . . indicates that the U.S. unit would incur minor losses while practically wiping out the opposing force.[28]

Finally, and consistent with the Soviets' own observations:

The use of a small expedient obstacle such as a point minefield would make the engagement even more lopsided, as it would provide the ambush force with stationary targets from the onset of the fighting . . . Ideally, the ambush force would be positioned only a short time before the enemy column came into range. It would be withdrawn immediately after the ambush. Given adequate helicopter transportation and ammunition, a light infantry company could conduct three or four such ambushes per day for a period of time. . . . A battalion of 3 companies could impose practically constant attrition and harassment on enemy columns . . .[29]

It is difficult to say precisely how severe the attrition exacted by these measures would be. There seems little doubt, however, that it could significantly reduce the force that the RDF would face in Khuzestan, and the same campaign affords the United States still more time to expand its force there.

In addition to the delay imposed by the Phase I air interdiction campaign, one can use the study's "planning guideline of two days' delay per engineer platoon day of effort"[30] to gauge the extent of further delay imposed upon

---

26. *Soviet Command Study*, p. 190.
27. Leonard and Scott, *Methodology For Estimating Movement Rates*, p. 4.1.
28. *Ibid.*
29. *Ibid.*, p. 4.3.
30. *Ibid.*, p. 4.5. This planning factor is given in connection with Zagros operations specifically.

Soviet troops in the Zagros. Bearing in mind that a platoon is one eighty-first ($1/81$) of a division,[31] the economies available are quickly evident.

There are literally two roads over the Zagros directly onto Dezful. The trans-Iranian railroad is a third avenue, assuming it has survived the air campaign in the north. The two roads which descend on Dezful from Kermanshah bring the total to roughly five arteries. From the above planning factor, it follows that a force of six platoons could, with two weeks of effort, close each of those approaches for thirty-four days.[32]

Time is the name of this game. And under reasonable assumptions, the Phase I air interdiction operation should have ensured thirty days of mobilization and deployment time for the battle of Khuzestan, while these Phase II *motti*-like tactics should raise the Soviets' time in transit (movement plus repair time) to Dezful by roughly another month. As far as the Soviet overland advance is concerned, then, sixty days does not seem overly optimistic as an estimate of the time the Soviets would require to emerge at the base of the Zagros. Is that all the time the RDF would have for mobilization and deployment for the final pitched battle in Khuzestan? It seems unlikely that it is. The RDF would have warning time as well. The question is, how much?

SOVIET READINESS, U.S. WARNING, AND DECISION TIME. The 1968 invasion of Czechoslovakia was preceded by a three-month build-up of which Western intelligence was aware. The invasion of Afghanistan was also preceded by three months of warning.[33] Should the Soviets invade Poland, that move will, in retrospect, have been preceded by at least three months of warning.

Of the roughly 24 divisions stationed in peacetime in the Southern Military Districts of the Soviet Union (North Caucasus, Transcaucasus, and Turkestan), none are accounted as Category I.[34] Indeed, over eighty percent are rated as Category III divisions.[35] To ready these forces for combat, the Soviets

---

31. A standard U.S. division structure is: 3 platoons/company; 3 companies/battalion; 3 battalions/brigade; 3 brigades/division.

32. Needless to say, the planning factor is a linear approximation of a more complicated relationship. However, even if it overestimates the effectiveness of such tactics by a significant margin, the effort involved in imposing the same delay would remain very modest. Some of the demolition responsibilities could also be assumed by tactical air.

33. See Jiri Valenta, "From Prague to Kabul: The Soviet Style of Invasion," *International Security*, Volume 5, Number 2 (Fall 1980).

34. *The Military Balance 1980–81* (London: The International Institute for Strategic Studies, 1980), p. 10–11. Soviet divisions have three degrees of combat readiness: Category I, between three-quarters and full strength, with complete equipment; Category II, between half and three-quarters strength, complete with fighting vehicles; Category III, about one-quarter strength, possibly complete with fighting vehicles (some obsolescent).

35. Henry Stanhope, "New Threat—or Old Fears?" in Derek Leebaert (ed.) *European Security: Prospects for the 1980s* (Lexington, MA: Lexington Books, 1979), p. 49.

would have to call up manpower and train or refresh much of it. Petroleum, oil, lubricants, spares, water, ammunition, and other supplies would have to be marshalled and loaded. The shipment of combat equipment into the area would be required while backlogged maintenance and, in some cases, final assembly of equipment would be performed. If the current mobilization for Poland is any indication, a great many trucks would be impressed from diverse quarters.

All of this activity takes time, and much of it would be visible to the West. Recent reports do indicate that, since the invasion of Afghanistan, the readiness of these forces has increased somewhat.[36] There is no indication, however, that Category I levels have been widely attained, while even those would credit the Soviets with as little as seventy-five percent of their full wartime manpower.

The standard category ranking of forces is, moreover, a static indicator. The "readiness" of forces depends on the missions facing them. One should not think of forces as "ready," but as "ready *for*" something; something specific.

In Czechoslovakia, resistance was essentially passive while in Afghanistan it, while tenacious, has lacked the sophisticated air force or the ground firepower that today's Soviet planner must anticipate in Iran. Thus, while granting some increase in "static readiness," if you will, to the Soviet units of interest, one must also assume that the Soviet planner recognizes the vast difference between the resistance of the Czechs and Afghans and that for which his forces must be "ready" in Iran. For all of these reasons, it is perfectly plausible that warning time would stay in the neighborhood of the usual three months. But let us be conservative and assume only one month of warning. The entire mobilization and deployment (M&D) time available to the main ground force of the RDF would thus appear to be 90 days.

Warning Time	1 month
Phase I Delay (air)	1 month
Phase II Delay (special forces)	1 month
Total M & D Time	**3 months**

It must be stressed that warning time, in this military sense, and decision time among political figures are radically different entities. A great deal can

36. William W. Kaufmann, "Defense Policy," in Joseph A. Pechman (ed.), *Setting National Priorities: Agenda for the 1980s* (Washington D.C.: The Brookings Institution, 1980), p. 305.

be done with warning time: to broadcast one's cognizance of developments, to enhance the credibility of one's deterrent commitments, as well as to ready one's forces.[37] The availability of warning time, however, does not ensure that it will be used. Among the most important peacetime goals for the United States is to ensure that it *is* used, through procedural agreements with U.S. intelligence services and forces, and through diplomatic understandings with countries in the region. Time bought with warning is cheaper than time bought with force. Indeed, if it is utilized in the communication of one's military readiness and political determination, warning time may, by deterrence, avoid the conflict. If war *should* come, however, the Soviets would have little basis for confidence.

PHASE III: THE BATTLE OF KHUZESTAN

There are three basic issues concerning the ground balance. First, how many divisions could the Soviets support south of the Zagros? Second, in the time available (total M & D time), what is a conservative estimate of the U.S. build-up in Khuzestan? And finally, what confidence could the Soviets have of defeating that force in battle?

As to the second question, a range of estimates has appeared regarding the size of the RDF that could be brought to bear in sixty days. There is a well-founded consensus, however, that in addition to a Marine contingent of three brigades, three divisions and their initial support increments could be deployed to Khuzestan in roughly that time.[38] Since ninety, rather than sixty days of mobilization and deployment time would likely be available to all but the very spearhead of the force, the four division figure may even be conservative. A force considerably larger than this might be brought to bear if equipment and stocks were pre-positioned at, for example, Australian facilities, Clark Field, and Subic Bay in addition to Diego Garcia, particularly if warning time were exploited in a pre-arranged commitment of allied commercial shipping to the RDF's sea line of communication. This valuable

---

37. For example, load cargo, fuel-up for the lift, pre-deploy certain materiel, increase reconnaissance densities, move further Marine units into position, marshal allied commercial shipping, stand down and perform backlogged maintenance, and increase NATO alerts.
38. See for example, Sir John Hackett, "Protecting Oil Supplies," p. 14, and *U.S. Airlift Forces: Enhancement Alternatives for NATO and Non-NATO Contingencies* (Washington: The Congressional Budget Office, April 1979), pp. 23, 55. Relevant force weights, airlift planning factors, and computational methods are provided in that study and in *U.S. Projection Forces: Requirements, Scenarios, and Options* (Washington D.C.: The Congressional Budget Office, April 1978).

contribution would be a clear signal of allied involvement without being a commitment of allied troops to combat.

SIMULTANEOUS CONTINGENCIES. It is true that, at present, the 4-division figure assumes use of the full fleet of 77 C-5As,[39] the only U.S. aircraft capable of lifting outsized cargo. This represents a compromise in the U.S. ability to reinforce other theaters simultaneously. Maturation of the RDF's near- and long-term maritime pre-positioning programs, however, will relieve the outsized constraint, while oversized and bulk cargo capacities will rise with the C-141 "stretch" and aerial refuelling programs. Procurement of SL-7 fast sealift ships would further loosen these logistical constraints. Eight alone would allow the movement of "a mechanized infantry division from the East Coast to the Persian Gulf in about three weeks."[40] Commitment of U.S., Japanese, and European commercial air and shipping to logistical support would add a further measure of confidence to the sustainability of combat operations.

Since a Soviet attack on Iran would raise the specter of nuclear war, the Strategic Air Command would probably rank high in the pecking order for tanker support. While this is not a crippling constraint, either through procurement of additional long-range tankers, or by other measures, it is one that must be addressed.

Finally, third parties, such as North Korea, could take a superpower conflict in Iran as the occasion to settle vendettas of their own. Were such contingencies to coincide with wars in Central Europe and Iran, current U.S. strategic mobility and *active duty* forces might be stretched far too thin for comfort. That problem, however, is not irremediable.[41]

The United States faces challenges in the area of simultaneity. But those facing the Soviets are no less severe. The only Soviet aircraft with an outsized capability is the Antonov-22, of which there are reported to be but 75.[42] And, in reference to a statement by Defense Secretary Weinberger, the *New York*

---

39. Jeffrey Record, *The Rapid Deployment Force and U.S. Military Intervention in the Persian Gulf* (Cambridge, MA: Institute for Foreign Policy Analysis, 1981), p. 50.
40. RDJTF Fact Sheet, p. 7.
41. For a detailed discussion of U.S. corrective options, and their relative merits and costs, see William W. Kaufmann, "The Defense Budget," in Joseph Pechman (ed.), *Setting National Priorities, The 1982 Budget* (Washington D.C.: The Brookings Institution, 1981).
42. Robert P. Berman, *Soviet Airpower in Transition* (Washington D.C.: The Brookings Institution, 1978), p. 35. Berman notes that "about two-thirds of their fleet of seventy-five is in operation at any one time."

Times has reported that, "The airlift capacity of the Soviet Union was said to be unable to cope with two large operations at one time."[43]

Thus, while the lift to Iran would initially tie up the U.S. C-5A fleet, any comparable lift on the Soviets' part would similarly strain their outsized airlift capacity. (The vulnerability of Soviet airlift is discussed below). Moreover, with China, NATO, the Poles and Afghanistan, Iran would be, not their third, but rather, the Soviets' *fifth* contingency—one which could severely hamper their capability elsewhere.

The force with which a four-division RDF would have to contend, over a thousand kilometers south of the Soviet border, depends upon other factors which have not been widely appreciated. While the peacetime deployment of twenty-four divisions in the southern Soviet Union has been publicized, the pertinent questions have not been raised. Over what duration of conflict could the Soviets *support* a field force of a given size? To provide a force with the consumables required to sustain combat at the distances facing the Soviets is a major logistical challenge, and one they have never faced before. Indeed, they have addressed far less challenging logistical problems with something less than virtuosity.

For example, in the invasion of Czechoslovakia, the Soviets met little resistance.

No bridges were destroyed, no road blocks erected, and no minefields were planted in the invaders' path. Under such conditions, there was no reason to expect anything other than a brilliant performance by the Soviet Army.

Yet,

Short of organic transport, the armored and mechanized divisions were left without basic supplies on the third day of occupation. Under actual combat conditions, they would have lacked many essential items after the first 24 hours.[44]

Although the Soviets appear to have expanded their organic transport somewhat, logistics remains among the weakest links in the Soviet military machine.

At daily consumption rates (of ammunition, spare parts, petroleum, oil, and lubricants) consistent with a high offensive lethality (discussed below),

---

43. Richard Halloran, "U.S. Is Weighing Aid to China If Soviet Acts Against Poles," *The New York Times,* April 5, 1981, p. 6.
44. Leo Heiman, "Soviet Invasion Weaknesses," *Military Review,* August 1969, p. 39 and p. 43.

it is implausible that the Soviets could sustain a combat force of more than about seven divisions in Khuzestan without degrading their European, Far Eastern, or Afghanistan capabilities. Beyond that level, the requirement in logistics trucks alone grows at so disproportionate a rate that to sustain the full 24-division[45] "threat" could dictate a draw-down (from other theaters) on the order of 55 Category I divisions' worth of trucks.[46] This would exceed the supply available from the sum of Soviet forces deployed opposite China (46 divisions) and in Afghanistan (6 divisions), even if those forces were all Category I. And since they are not all Category I, a 24-division force in Khuzestan would, in fact, denude an even greater number of divisions.

The calculation underlying these assertions, moreover, is quite conservative. It assumes *no* attrition of Soviet trucks and that *none* suffer mechanical breakdown. It leaves out of account *all* limitations on road capacity, a factor which alone could limit the Soviet force to the same low level. In calculating the Soviets' combat tonnage requirement, such necessities as food and water were excluded, again to be conservative.

Giving the Soviets the benefit of some rather serious doubts, then, and assuming that a seven-division combat force could be supported for a Battle of Khuzestan, what confidence would that force have of defeating an RDF of four divisions?

LETHALITY, DEFENSIVE ADVANTAGE, AND THE GROUND BATTLE IN KHUZESTAN. Although the RDF would not be grossly outnumbered, history in fact records innumerable cases in which even the vastly outnumbered defender staves off aggression. The defense, for example, may enjoy the advantage of operation from prepared, or even fortified, positions while an attacker must come out into the open to advance, exposing himself to fire.

If he is not to increase his vulnerability further by halting, the attacker must locate the more concealed target and fire on it while in motion; but

---

45. The 24 divisions facing Iran are those of the Southern Soviet Military Districts (Northern Caucasus, Transcaucasus, and Turkestan). For conservatism's sake, let us add the six divisions of the Central Military Districts (Urals and Volga). From this theater total, subtract again six, the force now in Afghanistan. The remaining 24 divisions is then the theater pool with which we are concerned. All other forces are either deployed to the Sino–Soviet border, to Eastern Europe or to the latter's reinforcement in the Military Districts of the European USSR. Requirements beyond those organic to the theater pool of 24 divisions must therefore be seen as draw-downs from these other contingencies, and thus as representing sacrifices in the Soviets' capacity to undertake them simultaneously. *The Military Balance, 1980–1981*, pp. 10–11.

46. These calculations are presented in Joshua M. Epstein, *The Soviet Threat to Iran and the Deterrent Adequacy of U.S. Rapid Deployment Forces*, (Paper presented to the Oil and Security Roundtable, July 23–24, 1981, Harvard University).

motion generally reduces accuracy. In this case, moreover, the defender (the RDF) is agreed to retain a significant technological edge in the areas of target acquisition, battlefield reconnaissance, and its processing.

Where these defensive advantages apply, military experience has handed down the general planning factor that a defender should be able to hold the front essentially stable so long as the attacker enjoys no more than a 2 to 1 advantage in lethality.[47] More conservative planning factors (1.5 to 1) and less conservative ones (3 to 1) are available, as are more or less demanding tactics than holding the front stationary. But, even under the most conservative tactics and planning factors, an RDF of four divisions should be expected to fare rather well.

Such judgments, of course, are based on some measure of relative lethality, a difficult entity to gauge. By the crudest of indices, the division count, the 4-division RDF balances the Soviet 7-division threat, at the above-cited Army planning factor of 2 to 1. However, the more refined is one's measure of lethality, the more powerful grows the RDF in relation to the Soviets. For example, under the Army's WEI/WUV scoring, a U.S. armored division on the defensive is rated as being 50 percent stronger than a Soviet tank division on the offensive; a Soviet tank division, that is, represents 0.67 U.S. Armored Division Equivalents (ADEs).[48] At relative lethalities in this range, the 7-division Soviet force is the equivalent of 4.69 U.S. divisions of the same class; the lethality ratio falls thus to $4.69/4 = 1.17$, well within the more conservative planning factor of 1.5 to 1. But, the WEI/WUV scoring considers only the assets of the division and, in leaving support and non-divisional (corps) assets out of account, attributes disproportionate weight to the Soviet divi-

---

47. U.S. Army Field Manual FM 105-5, *Maneuver Control* (Department of the Army, 1967), p. 212.
48. In the WEI/WUV system, the U.S. armored division is assigned the value of 1.0. In relation to the U.S. armored division, the lethality of any other force may be gauged by a weighted aggregation of the strength of its component units. By a combination of test range data and military operational judgment, the components are assigned weapon effectiveness indices (WEIs). These are then added up to obtain the weighted unit values (WUVs), expressed in U.S. Armored Division Equivalents. The procedure differs from the older firepower scoring in "working down," as it were, from the U.S. armored division rather than "working up" to a firepower score in M-16 rifle equivalents. The WEI/WUV system also incorporates accuracy and other factors not embodied in the firepower scoring. Remarkably enough, the systems do not differ notably in their estimates of the relative lethality of U.S. and Soviet units. Given their comparable valuations, since it embodies factors, such as accuracy, in which the U.S. is generally agreed to enjoy an edge, the WEI/WUV system may be considered the more conservative of the two. The methodology is fully elaborated in *Final Report: Weapon Effectiveness Indices/Weighted Unit Values: Volume I, Executive Summary,* Prepared by The War Gaming Directorate, U.S. Army Concepts Analysis Agency (Study Report CAA–ST–73–18) Bethesda, Maryland, April 1974.

sion's front end, or "teeth," as it were. Not only should the United States be able to position *corps* assets in the region, but the second delay phase has, as one of its primary functions, the attrition of precisely those teeth which weigh so heavily on the WEI/WUV scale. In addition, at these distances from the Soviet Union, the RDF would have a clear advantage in close air support, another factor not embraced by the 1.17 ratio derived above. When all these factors are considered, parity, the most conservative planning factor of all, seems altogether plausible.

DYNAMIC FACTORS AND THE BATTLE OF KHUZESTAN. Division counts and these more refined measures—indeed all static indicators—ignore a host of factors which may prove decisive in war. For this reason, over-reliance on such approaches is ill-advised. Morale, mobility, logistics, and coordination—factors not reflected in such static measures—have often tipped the balance. Granted. But where, in any of these less tangible and perhaps decisive areas, would the Soviets enjoy a relative advantage?

The least tangible, morale, is by far the most difficult to assess. But, descriptions of the Allied resupply of Russia through the Persian Corridor may suggest the type of fatigue these routes would exact.

Mile after mile of washboard roads took toll on men as well as vehicles. As an anonymous military scribe put it, vibration "shook the trucks to pieces . . . and pounded the men's kidneys to jelly."[49]

Though an open question, such physical stress, when compounded by the trauma of surprise ambush day and night in the Zagros, would hardly seem to contribute to the élan of Soviet troops.

Even were such punishment to galvanize the steely invaders, the Soviets would not enjoy the advantage of mobility, canalized as their descent would be, into a very few corridors onto Dezful. The RDF would not be so chan-neled, operating from the relatively open lowlands south of the Zagros. Moreover, insofar as Soviet training consists in refining the advance in broad echelons, that training and that tactic are wholly inappropriate to this terrain.

As for relative sustainability, in Khuzestan it is the RDF which could avail itself of a shorter and more secure line of communication certainly for the first few weeks, after which time the RDF's reliance on long-distance sea-lift

---

49. T. H. Vail Motter, *The Persian Corridor and Aid to Russia*, (Washington D.C.: Office of The Chief of Military History, Department of The Army, 1952), p. 327. More historical information on aid to Russia through the Persian Gulf may be found in Richard M. Leighton and Robert W. Coakley, *Global Logistics and Strategy 1940–1943* (Washington D.C.: Office of the Chief of Military History, Department of The Army, 1955).

would grow. And, while there is debate concerning the interdiction which that sea line of communication might suffer, it is hard to see it as being any *more* vulnerable than Soviet lines, strung out as they would be over hundreds of miles of vulnerable terrain. Nor, as we shall see, would the Soviets be likely to enjoy any advantage in the aerial resupply of forces.

More important, perhaps, than questions of morale, mobility, training, or sustainability is that of coordination. In particular, even the quite acceptable WEI/WUV estimate of a 1.17 to 1 lethality ratio was predicated on the assumption that all of the Soviet divisions emerge from the Zagros *at the same time* and instantaneously constitute themselves as a seven-division fighting force. If they come through two divisions or three divisions at a time, they can be taken on piecemeal and, by such measures as those above, would be grossly outweighed by the RDF. Indeed, at anything less than a simultaneous arrival, the Soviet forces would be unlikely to achieve parity with the RDF.

The coordination problem was not lost on the thorough Soviet planners, who wrote,

As a result of the mountainous terrain structure and because of the few roads, the combat engagements will be carried out mostly with mixed units which, at times, must operate completely independently. For this reason, the coordination of individual separate columns . . . is of exceptional importance.[50]

To recognize the problem is one thing. To solve it is another. And there is no neat way for the Soviets to circumvent it. Concentration (reducing the number of advance axes) in the interest of simultaneous arrival merely raises the value of each choke point while reducing their number, thus simplifying the RDF's delaying operations. On the other hand, dispersion (raising the number of advance axes), while forcing the United States to spread its resources over a greater (but still very small) number of choke points, exacerbates the coordination problem, possibly reducing the land threat with which the RDF would ultimately contend in Khuzestan. Neither alternative should be especially attractive to the Soviets.

The above points are summarized in Table 1.

While the more refined WEI/WUV ratio falls well within the conservative defensive criterion of 1.5 to 1, elimination of the WEI/WUV's pro-Soviet bias, and inclusion of close air and other factors would reduce the actual ratio to

50. *Soviet Command Study*, pp. 240–241.

Table 1. Relative Capabilities: Battle of Khuzestan

Measure	Soviets	RDF	Lethality Ratio
Divisions	7	4	1.75
U.S. Division Equivalents	4.69	4	1.17
Other Factors			**Effect on Ratio**
Morale	?	?	?
WEI/WUV Bias	−	+	reduces
Close Air Support	−	+	reduces
Battlefield Mobility	−	+	reduces
Coordination	−	+	reduces

still less than the quite acceptable 1.17. Indeed, without virtually perfect coordination, the Soviets would be unlikely to achieve more than parity with the RDF.

A DRIVE FROM AFGHANISTAN? It might be added that an overland drive from Afghanistan, which would be extremely difficult in its own right, would merely exacerbate the coordination problem if attempted as the eastern axis of a grand envelopment. The distances to Khuzestan from Afghanistan are considerably greater than those from the Soviet Union. This alone would make a simultaneous arrival difficult. In addition, there are no surfaced roads directly across the intervening desert of the Khorassan. There, the Soviets tell us,

During summer the temperature is so high that the inhabitants of the cities withdraw to the so-called "Sirisamin" (cellar) and along the caravan routes, the caravans usually do not continue travel during the day.[51]

Water sources are confined to a few oases. In addition to sending up clouds of dust to advertise its position, a summer blitz across this terrain would ensure a very high mechanical breakdown rate. Roads south of the desert either terminate in the difficult Zagros or traverse them. On the other hand, the "end run" above the Khorassan (which reduces to a single road along the base of the Golul Dagh Mountains.) would force a crossing of the Zagros from the north, over the same limited and vulnerable system of roads already glutted by the advance from the Soviet Union. To pull any significant

---

51. *Ibid.*, p. 42.

force from Afghanistan would require a reinforcement of Soviet efforts there, thus entailing a draw-down from other theaters.

While summer is surely the worst time in the Khorassan, winter finds the mountain passes of northern Iran snowed in. In the spring thaw, lowlands, particularly those of the Caspian basin, are transformed into a swampy morass, precluding off-road traffic.[52] Finally, fall, though probably the best season in general, is the rainy season in the northwest, opposite which the bulk of Soviet forces are deployed. During that time, the main rivers of the Azerbaidjan become unfordable torrents, making indispensible what few bridges exist. In any season, an attempt to coordinate the simultaneous advance of forces along all of these axes would be, in short, a logistician's nightmare.

For all these reasons and by any measure—static or dynamic—a pure overland advance would be exceedingly risky for the Soviets. Thus, one may expect them to consider airlifted assault. Airlift, however, would face vulnerabilities which are just as severe.

Airlifted Assault

The Soviets have developed a considerable airlifted power projection capability, as demonstrated in the October War, Angola, Ethiopia, and Afghanistan. However, none of these lifts was opposed by anything even remotely resembling the kind of airpower the Soviets would face in Iran. Their problem is not one of lift capability *per se*; rather it is fighter escort for the lift. Without the protection provided by that escort, the Soviets' chances for an airborne insertion and aerial resupply of forces would be slim. If the United States exploited warning, the Soviets' prospects would be very slight indeed.

Recognizing the importance of fighter escort, it is important to note that, despite strides since Khrushchev's ouster, the Soviets remain outclassed in the air-to-air combat arena.

In addition to the technological edge,[53] U.S. pilot skill exceeds that of the Soviets. Soviet pilot training is far more routine and is far less realistic than

---

52. In fact, the main port of Pahlavi is situated in an area called the "Gilan," meaning "swampy, muddy place." *Ibid.*, p. 161.
53. While the very sophistication of U.S. systems has created serious problems in areas of support, notably those of sortie generation and sustainability, it is far from clear that the Soviets have avoided the same problems. There is every reason to believe, in fact, that while Soviet air systems are by some measures, simpler than those of the United States, the Soviet ground

American.[54] Furthermore, the U.S. pilot flies roughly twice as much as his Soviet counterpart.[55] American non-flying hours are spent, in part, on very sophisticated simulators, of which the Soviets are reported to possess nothing comparable. Finally, U.S. training has built on a great deal of combat experience gained since World War II, in Korea and in Vietnam, far more than the Soviets. Given these advantages—more realistic training, and more of it, in addition to the benefits of far more combat experience—it is difficult to imagine the United States enjoying anything less than a significant margin in pilot skill, the importance of which cannot be overemphasized. Essentially alone, it accounted for the exchange ratios of 12.5 to 1 recorded in Indochina (F-4 *vs.* MiG-21). And when combined with a technological advantage, it goes a long way toward explaining the extraordinarily high exchange rates logged by the Israelis in 1967 and 1973 (20 to 1 and 40 to 1 respectively).[56] Thus, even if this conflict presented a classical air-to-air combat situation, the Soviets would have little basis for confidence that they would enjoy air superiority. That being the case, under the highly *non*-classical conditions of Iran, the RDF would enjoy a number of pronounced advantages.

For one, the exchange ratios of the Korean and Vietnam conflicts, as well as the remarkable Israeli ratios, were kills of *fighters* by other fighters. In opposing a Soviet airlift, however, U.S. pilots would be attempting to shoot down Soviet *transports*—very sluggish, easily acquired, and highly vulnerable

---

support (maintenance, logistics) system is so much less efficient than the American that, in the net, the Soviets find their advanced systems to be no more supportable than the U.S. finds its own to be. In turn, it can be argued that, due to the inefficiency of their ground support environment, the Soviets face equally severe problems in sortie generation and sustainability. Joshua M. Epstein, *Political Impediments to Military Effectiveness: The Case of Soviet Frontal Aviation* (doctoral dissertation, MIT, 1980).

54. The Soviet military literature is full of high-ranking commentary attesting both to the routinized character of Soviet pilot training and to its adverse effect on flexibility. Characteristic examples are: Pavlov, General–Lieutenant G., "Inexhaustible Reserve," *Krasnaya Zvezda*, August 4, 1976 (April 1977); Konstantinov, General–Colonel Anatoliy Ustinovich, "Thorough Knowledge of Affairs," *Krasnaya Zvezda*, March 13, 1977 (June 1977); or Babayev, General–Colonel Aleksandr Ivanovich, "Flight and the Combat Maneuver," *Krasnaya Kvezeda*, December 23, 1976 (April 1977). For these and all subsequent Russian citations, the parenthesized date is for the English language version appearing in *Soviet Press Selected Translations*, Directorate of Soviet Affairs, Air Force Intelligence Service.

55. Robert P. Berman, *Soviet Air Power in Transition*, p. 57.

56. All of these data are given in Steven J. Rosen, "What a Fifth Arab–Israeli War Might Look Like," *International Security*, Volume 2, Number 4 (Spring 1978), p. 160. See, in general, Peter de Leon, *The Peacetime Evaluation of the Pilot Skill Factor in Air-to-Air Combat R–2070–Pr* (Santa Monica, CA: The Rand Corporation, January 1977).

targets. The situation then is highly preferential to the defense. Khuzestan, moreover, is simply out of range of virtually all Soviet tactical fighters, based either in Afghanistan or the Soviet Union.[57] The direct airlift to Khuzestan, for these reasons, would be vulnerable in the extreme.

Much of central Iran is also out of range for all but late model Soviet fighters (whose adaptibility to the local basing system must be considered an open question).

Even where central Iran is within range of those aircraft, it may be well out of range of Soviet ground control.[58] Under Soviet ground-controlled intercept (GCI), target acquisition, vectoring, and other critical intercept instructions are transmitted from stations on the ground. If not actually out of range of Soviet-based GCI, then fighter operations in much of central Iran and all of southern Iran could be at ranges where the GCI link is highly susceptible to jamming by, for example, carrier-based EA-6B (4 per carrier) electronic warfare aircraft. However rigidly the Soviet pilot is trained to fight under ground control, he is virtually untrained to fight without it.[59]

The problem, from the Soviets' perspective, is how to get the GCI south of the northern mountains. Overland, as we've seen, would not be promising and would certainly be slow. So, if the GCI is to be established with any dispatch, it must be airlifted in. In order to airlift it in however, fighter escort would be essential. But the escort cannot be run effectively until the GCI is in place! There is the rub.

Even if airlanded in central Iran, the GCI radars and other components would be highly vulnerable to low-altitude attack by U.S. aircraft, especially if, with forward-looking infra red (FLIR) technology, the strikes were conducted under cover of darkness. And, while Soviet airborne reconnaissance of low-level attack is progressing, it is generally agreed that, even in daylight,

---

57. The possibility of re-equipping the longer-range SU-24 advanced ground attack aircraft for air-to-air combat is unpromising. First, it is an open question whether rudimentary Afghan bases could accommodate the system. But more important is the fact that the SU-24 pilot, rigidly drilled in his ground attack mission, cannot easily be converted to a master of air-to-air combat, even if his aircraft could be so adapted. Similarly, air-to-air pilots are unlikely ever to have flown the SU-24 and would be ill-prepared to substitute for its usual operators.

58. Soviet problems in maintaining the integrity of the ground control data link as range increases are discussed in Colonel V. A. Uryzhnikov, "In a Complex Situation," *Krasnaya Zvezda*, January 7, 1977 (April 1977).

59. *Soviet Aerospace Handbook AF Pamphlet 200–21* (Washington D.C.: Department of the Air Force, May 1978), p. 45.

Soviet fighters do not possess a sophisticated look-down/shoot-down capability.[60] These factors support the assessment of General David Jones, Chairman of the Joint Chiefs of Staff, who in June of 1980,

told the Senate Armed Services Committee that "a few AWACS (Airborne Warning and Control Aircraft) and a few fighters could just devastate an airborne operation," if the Soviet Armed Forces sought to seize oil fields in the Persian Gulf region.[61]

Thus, while the Soviet overland invasion is highly vulnerable, the airlifted assault would not be any less so.

It is implicit in such assessments that warning time is exploited and that the decision to use force be taken. Otherwise, the West's significant advantages could erode and her promising defensive avenues could quickly close.

Carrier Vulnerability

In a Soviet invasion of Iran, the "worst case" scenario would posit the simultaneous initiation of airlifted and overland assaults, coordinated with a massed Soviet bomber attack on the carriers. In discussing that threat, certain points should be stressed.

First, the strategy proposed here has four basic elements: two delay phases against the overland threat, the interdiction of Soviet airlift, and a build-up and combined arms defense in Khuzestan. *This*, and not the carriers, *per se*, is what the Soviets must overcome to secure control of Khuzestan's oil. After all, even to sink the carriers would not, in and of itself, transport a single Russian to Khuzestan. Nor would it guarantee that the United States would be incapable of carrying out its own strategy. If the carriers can survive long enough to ensure that the four basic operations are executed, they will have performed their war mission.

Just as carrier interdiction is not, *per se*, the Soviets' war goal, so, carrier survival is not, *per se*, the RDF's goal; that is to deny Soviet control of Khuzestan. And if American interests in the area are vital, then the United States should be willing to run the risk that carriers will be lost. The carriers, after all, were bought to fight. And while their vulnerability can and should be minimized, in a fight, they may be destroyed.

---

60. *Ibid.*, p. 66.
61. John M. Collins, *U.S.–Soviet Military Balance, Concepts and Capabilities 1960–1980* (New York: McGraw-Hill, 1980), footnote, p. 394.

The carriers are at their most vulnerable only in the initial period, when the northern tier of Iranian choke points is being struck and the Marine perimeter in Khuzestan is being established. But even in that period, as noted above, the carriers can be employed in a way that avoids their passage into the Persian Gulf, leaves them substantial resources for air defense, and allows for their timely and rapid withdrawal to the Arabian Sea area. And while all is not lost even if the carriers are lost, there is no particular reason that they should be.[62]

THE SOVIET BOMBER THREAT. Of the two Soviet bomber forces, Long-Range Aviation (LRA) and Naval Aviation, the former is deployed solely to the European Soviet Union (2 Air Armies) and the Far East (1 Air Army).[63] A significant diversion of LRA's bomber resources would clearly represent a sacrifice in the Soviets' capacity to execute either the Sino–Soviet or NATO contingencies at the same time, not to mention those strategic nuclear missions for which LRA might be withheld. Particularly in the European theater, the presence of LRA and of Naval Aviation's Northern and Baltic Fleet bomber forces would be critical, if the Soviets are to credibly threaten the execution of their short-war doctrine, or the achievement of their vaunted preemption there.

Accordingly, unless we assume the Soviets are willing to free up forces otherwise earmarked to cope with those threats to Europe, our attention should first be directed to the Black Sea and Pacific Fleets of Naval Aviation. However, were the entire Pacific Fleet force reallocated to the Gulf, the Soviets would have sacrificed maritime strike operations in defense of critical facilities in the Vladivostok area. Similarly, a full redeployment of the Black Sea fleet would free U.S. forces in the Eastern Mediterranean from the threat of bomber attack. While these considerations could militate against such wholesale Soviet redeployments, even if they were attempted, one may doubt the basing capacity of the southern Soviet Union to accommodate them. Finally, the *total* Backfire inventory of Naval Aviation's *four* fleets is

---

62. Of course, should the carriers be destroyed by nuclear means, a U.S. nuclear response on the northern transportation system would still deny the Soviets their posited objective, as would the clearly more provocative nuclear response on division bases, rail lines, air fields, supply dumps, or other conventional military facilities in the southern USSR. For an insightful discussion of the latter action and its possible implications, see Thomas C. Schelling, *Arms and Influence* (New Haven, CT: Yale University Press, 1966), pp. 160–162.
63. *The Military Balance 1980–1981*, p. 9.

reported to be 70.[64] Thus, even on the questionable assumption that a size-able portion of *two* (Black Sea and Pacific) Fleet bomber forces were allocated to this mission, the number of Backfires involved could be even more limited.

As for warning of such an attack, the Soviets would need a certain amount of time to ready their forces. They might succeed in doing so under cover of deception. But if, as postulated, the bomber attack is to take place simulta-neously with the overland drive, it must wait until the Soviet ground forces are mobilized. And of that activity, the United States would have warning. It would certainly be odd for the Soviets to maximize surprise in the bomber attack by launching it a month before the ground forces were ready to exploit it. In short, the United States *would* have warning time in which to ready its resistance.

"LAYERED" CARRIER DEFENSES. Although there are uncertainties, when the above factors are taken into account, the bomber threat facing the carriers' multiple defensive "layers" does not seem unmanageable.

Assets for the so-called "outer air battle," in the words of the Chief of Naval Operations Admiral Hayward,

consist primarily of the E-2 B/C airborne early warning aircraft used to detect and track incoming aircraft and missiles, the F-14 variable-geometry fighter which is capable of launching and tracking as many as six AIM-54A long-range PHOENIX air intercept missiles, and the F-4 fighter aircraft capable of launching the AIM-7 SPARROW all-aspect air intercept missile.[65]

Secretary of the Navy Claytor has testified, moreover, that the F-14 "can go out and shoot down the Russian's Backfire out of range of its ability to launch a missile."[66]

Soviet bombers surviving that first layer, while remaining susceptible to further counterair (air-to-air) resistance and jamming, would pass into the second ring of carrier defenses. Again, the current debate presents an image of carriers operating alone. But the carrier, albeit a prima donna, is a social animal whose coterie of guided missile escorts is designed to provide it with a tough area defense.[67]

---

64. *Ibid.*, p. 11.
65. U.S., Congress, House, Committee on Appropriations, *Department of Defense Appropriations For 1980, Hearings before the Subcommittee on the Department of Defense*, Ninety-Sixth Congress, First Session, Part 2, p. 266.
66. *Ibid.*, p. 277.
67. *Ibid.*, p. 266.

Finally, the Soviet bombers would encounter the carrier battle group's so-called "self-defense." Here,

. . . we look at two types of "kills"—the "hard kill" in which we destroy the inbound missile and the "soft kill" in which we deceive the missile so that it misses the target.[68]

In addition, it should be borne in mind that the closer the Soviet bomber gets to the carriers, the thinner becomes its fighter escort. And, over a broad perimeter around the carriers, it would be likely to lack any fighter protection. Essentially the same very serious vulnerability would then prevail as in the case of Soviet airlift.

If the bomber survives to launch its missiles, and against the carrier battle group's layered defenses, the missiles are neither intercepted nor deceived, there still remains the question of accuracy. One may assume hit probabilities greater than fifty percent if one chooses, but it would be irresponsible not to raise those assumed on the RDF's side correspondingly. And to do so would allow the RDF's northern interdiction campaign (Phase I) to be conducted more quickly.

Finally, even a hit is not necessarily a kill. Carriers can be rather durable entities.

During training exercises in 1969, the nuclear carrier ENTERPRISE endured explosions of nine major caliber bombs (equivalent in explosive weight to 6 anti-ship cruise missiles) on the flight deck. All essential ship systems remained operable, effective damage control contained the effects of the fire, and the ship could have resumed flight operations within hours.[69]

While the remark applies to ship- and submarine-launched cruise missiles as well, the carrier's cruise missile defense is likewise one layered in depth, terminating in "rings of long- and medium-range surface to air missiles (SAM), close-in SAMs, and aircraft."[70] The F-14 is reported to have demonstrated a capacity to engage, again, six.[71] The tactical ASW system of the carrier task force is organized along the same principals and might be visualized as an inverted, underwater variation on its anti-air warfare rings.

These capabilities give the carrier battle group a more than fighting chance in the Gulf region; an area in which the limited Soviet surface fleet would

---

68. *Ibid.*
69. *Ibid.*, p. 268.
70. *Ibid.*, p. 282.
71. *Ibid.*, p. 264.

lack comparable defensive avenues and logistical support, i.e., underway replenishment. Indeed, Washington officials have stated that "even if they bring in the Minsk (V/STOL Carrier), it would be no contest." [72]

Destruction of the carriers would, *per se*, be a formidable task. Moreover, in order to frustrate the larger four-point RDF strategy proposed here, the Soviets would have to destroy them *very* fast. And, if the United States uses its warning time to ready the carriers' imposing defenses, then even focusing the bombers on their destruction, it is hard to imagine great Soviet confidence of success. And that allocation is questionable.

DIVERSION OF SOVIET BOMBERS. For the Soviets to focus the full bomber threat on the carriers would leave them virtually no resources with which to harass the Marine landing in Khuzestan. As noted above, the preponderance of Soviet *tactical* air effectively lacks either the range to attack the Khuzestan landing or the capacity to operate from the crude Afghan bases which might be within range. [73]

Diego Garcia, which the United States already controls, will shortly be capable of accommodating the B-52s. Given its importance as a maritime staging area generally, Diego Garcia would be yet another target to which the Soviets might be forced to divert bombers.

In short, the Soviets face a target system considerably more complicated than the two carriers. And this contributes to the carriers' already substantial survivability by forcing some dispersion of Soviet bomber resources.

If, during the warning time which should be available, a third carrier were brought on line, the RDF's interdiction and landing operations might be conducted even more rapidly. In that case, the Soviets would have a) yet more targets to destroy, b) an even denser air defense to overcome in doing so, and c) even less time in which to accomplish the task.

Conclusions

While facing a redundant, flexible, and in fact rather dispersed resistance, the Soviets possess only two viable modes of advance into Iran: airlifted and

---

72. "Soviet Naval Presence Doubles in Indian Ocean, Lacks Support," *Aviation Week and Space Technology*, April 6, 1981, p. 60.
73. If we are to assume that from Afghanistan, the BEAR can penetrate the F–14 net to attack U.S. carriers in the Persian Gulf or Gulf of Oman, then the B-52H should certainly be assumed capable of penetrating the MiG-21 (or MiG-23) net to attack Afghan bases. Spif's B-52H night-low altitude mission is specifically designed to exploit the weakness of Soviet look-down/shoot-down capabilities. George C. Wilson, ". . . New Conventional Role for B-52 Bombers," pp. 6–7.

overland. In exploiting the Soviets' numerous vulnerabilities, the RDF's essential missions are four: to delay, in two successive phases, the overland advance and to interdict Soviet airlift, while building up a combined arms defense in Khuzestan. If the Soviets' goal is control of Iran's oil, this strategy, rather than a forward defense is appropriate. And if warning time is exploited, U.S. forces should be able to execute the plan conventionally. In the pitched battle of Khuzestan, that is, the Soviet force which could be supported without penalizing their capacity to handle simultaneous contingencies would be unlikely to enjoy any meaningful superiority over an RDF assembled under the same strategic constraint. And if the deep problem of Soviet coordination were exploited, it is questionable whether the Soviet force would even achieve parity with that RDF.

The Europeans can contribute significantly to the defense of Western interests in the Gulf by maintaining Central Front forces in sufficient readiness that the Soviets are sternly reminded of their simultaneous contingencies.

To argue the feasibility of a conventional defense is not to deny that the RDF has substantial work ahead of it. It does, particularly in the areas of logistics, training, command and control, and in basic detailed planning for the employment of its forces, some of which must be tailored very precisely to the tactics contemplated here. However, while stressing that the RDF faces challenges, the current situation warrants neither the kind of pessimism that has been heaped upon it nor an ill-considered "drive for bases" which may flow from overassessments of the Soviet threat.

Militarily, the RDF is clearly better off with more regional basing than it is without it. And there is no reason for the United States to abandon its efforts to negotiate suitable arrangements in the event of crisis. In doing so, however, the United States can afford to bargain from a position of strength, eschewing entanglements with regimes less worthy of American political support than military relationships may suggest; regimes whose stability (as Iran should have taught) may be far more tenuous than Americans might wish to believe; regimes which, in the final analysis, may acquire political interests quite inimical to those of the United States and to those of its proven ally, Israel.

No one has found a way to predict with *certainty* the outcome of any given conflict. But the invasion of Iran would be an exceedingly *low confidence* affair for the Soviets—a fact which I believe they've known for roughly 40 years. Indeed, it can be argued that they now regard it as far less attractive even than their *Command Study* of 1941 portrayed it as being. While, to be sure, Soviet military capabilities have evolved very significantly since that time, so have those of the United States and, more importantly, so have the Soviets' military commitments and deterrent needs. Certainly to cover three contingencies simultaneously would strain the United States. But beyond China, NATO, the Poles, and Afghanistan, an invasion of Iran would be the Soviets' fifth contingency. And it is one which, as we've seen, could severely hamper their capability elsewhere.

The Soviets face the grave threat that the military cost of a move on Iran would vastly outweigh its potential benefits—indeed, the risk that all such benefits would be decisively denied. It can only be assumed, therefore, that the Soviets would prefer to secure their ends in the Gulf by other means, by coercive measures short of direct intervention. All of those measures find their underpinning, finally, in the appearance of crushing Soviet military power and in the perception that the Soviets are prepared to use it to get what they want, and are confident of doing so with success. The fundamental question, and it is a political one, is this: by overdrawing the direct Soviet threat to Iran—or to any country—do we not aid the Soviets in their diplomacy of coercion?

By presenting the United States as if it alone suffers simultaneous contingency problems, and by presenting the Soviets as if they enjoyed some clear superiority in the Gulf, we do. In the final analysis that is not "getting tough" with the Soviets.

One "gets tough" with an adversary by credibly threatening to exploit his military vulnerabilities, not by refusing to admit that any exist, as is the general practice among so-called "hard-liners." Such talk, however, is not "hard" on the Soviets. On the contrary, the rhetoric of an invincible Soviet threat, while alienating those whose cooperation we seek and/or exposing them to the coercion we fear, merely discredits the larger cause it purports to champion—management of the global competition and deterrence of war. These are feasible goals. In the case of the Gulf, forces exist which can and should be postured to communicate that fact. While they are not invincible, the Soviets are attentive. They will get the message.

Library of Congress Cataloging-in-Publication Data

Main entry under title:
Conventional forces and American defense policy.

"First published in International security"—
1. United States—Armed Forces—Addresses, essays, lectures. 2. United States—Military policy—Addresses, essays, lectures. 3. Warfare, Conventional—Addresses, essays, lectures. I. Miller, Steven E. II. International security.

UA23.C6724 1986   355'.0335'73   85-20992

ISBN 0-691-07700-2 (alk. paper)   ISBN 0-691-02246-1 (pbk.)